CIMA

OPERATIONAL

PAPER E1

ORGANISATIONAL MANAGEMENT

STUDY TEXT

Our text is designed to help you study **effectively** and **efficiently**.

In this edition we:

- **Highlight** the **most important elements** in the syllabus and the **key skills** you will need
- **Signpost** how each chapter links to the syllabus and the learning outcomes
- Use **overview and summary diagrams** to develop understanding of interrelations between topics
- **Provide** lots of **exam alerts** explaining how what you're learning may be tested
- **Include examples** and **questions** to help you apply what you've learnt
- **Emphasise key points** in **section summaries**
- **Test your knowledge** of what you've studied in **quick quizzes**
- **Examine your understanding** in our **practice question bank**

SUITABLE FOR EXAMS IN 2017

PUBLISHED NOVEMBER 2016

BPP
LEARNING MEDIA

Third edition 2016

ISBN 9781509706808
e-ISBN 9781509707249

British Library Cataloguing-in-Publication Data
A catalogue record for this book
is available from the British Library

Published by

BPP Learning Media Ltd
BPP House, Aldine Place
London W12 8AA

www.bpp.com/learningmedia

Printed in the United Kingdom by

Wheatons Exeter Ltd
Hennock Road
Marsh Barton
Exeter
EX2 8RP

Your learning materials, published by BPP
Learning Media Ltd, are printed on paper sourced
from sustainable, managed forests.

Contents

Review form

How our Study Text can help you pass

Streamlined studying	• We show you the best ways to study efficiently
	• Our Text has been designed to ensure you can easily and quickly navigate through it
	• The different features in our Text emphasise important knowledge and techniques
Exam expertise	• **Studying E1** on page xvi introduces the key themes of the syllabus and summarises how to pass
	• We highlight throughout our Text how topics may be tested and what you'll have to do in the exam
	• We help you see the complete picture of the syllabus, so that you can answer questions that range across the whole syllabus
	• Our Text covers the syllabus content – no more, no less
Regular review	• We frequently summarise the key knowledge you need
	• We test what you've learnt by providing questions and quizzes throughout our Text

Our other products

BPP Learning Media also offers these products for the Objective Test exams and the integrated case study (ICS) exams:

i-Pass	Providing computer-based testing in a variety of formats, ideal for self-assessment
Exam Practice Kit	Providing helpful guidance on how to pass the objective test and more question practice
Passcards	Summarising what you should know in visual, easy to remember, form
ICS Workbook	Providing help with exam skills and question practice for the integrated case study exam

You can purchase these products by visiting www.bpp.com/cimamaterials

Online Learning with BPP

BPP's online learning study modes provide flexibility and convenience, allowing you to study effectively, at a pace that suits you, where and when you choose.

Online Classroom live	Through live interactive online sessions it provides you with the traditional structure and support of classroom learning, but with the convenience of attending classes wherever you are
Online Classroom	Through pre-recorded online lectures it provides you with the classroom experience via the web with the tutor guidance and support you'd expect from a face to face classroom

You can find out more about these packages by visiting www.bpp.com/cima

Features in our Study Text

Chapter Overview Diagrams illustrate the connections between about to cover

 Section Introductions explain how the section fits into the chapter

 Key Terms are the core vocabulary you need to learn

KEY TERM

 Key Points are points that you have to know, ideas or calculations that will be the foundations of your answers

KEY POINT

 Exam Alerts show you how subjects are likely to be tested

 Exam Skills are the key skills you will need to demonstrate in the exam, linked to question requirements

 Formulae To Learn are formulae you must remember in the exam

LEARN

 Exam Formulae are formulae you will be given in the exam

EXAM

 Examples show how theory is put into practice

 Questions give you the practice you need to test your understanding of what you've learnt

 Case Studies link what you've learnt with the real-world business environment

CASE STUDY

 Links show how the syllabus overlaps with other parts of the qualification, including Knowledge Brought Forward that you need to remember from previous exams

 Website References link to material that will enhance your understanding of what you're studying

 Further Reading will give you a wider perspective on the subjects you're covering

 Section Summary Diagrams allow you to review each section

BPP
LEARNING MEDIA

Streamlined studying

What you should do	In order to
Read the Chapter and Section Introductions and look at the Chapter Overview Diagram	See why topics need to be studied and map your way through the chapter
Go quickly through the explanations	Gain the depth of knowledge and understanding that you'll need
Highlight the Key Points, Key Terms and Formulae To Learn	Make sure you know the basics that you can't do without in the exam
Focus on the Exam Skills and Exam Alerts	Know how you'll be tested and what you'll have to do
Work through the Examples and Case Studies	See how what you've learnt applies in practice
Prepare Answers to the Questions	See if you can apply what you've learnt in practice
Review the Chapter Summary Diagrams	Remind you of, and reinforce, what you've learnt
Answer the Quick Quiz	Find out if there are any gaps in your knowledge
Answer the Question(s) in the Practice Question Bank	Practise what you've learnt in depth

Should I take notes?

Brief notes may help you remember what you're learning. You should use the notes format that's most helpful to you (lists, diagrams, mindmaps).

Further help

BPP Learning Media's *Learning to Learn Accountancy* provides lots more helpful guidance on studying. It is designed to be used both at the outset of your CIMA studies and throughout the process of learning accountancy. It can help you **focus your studies on the subject and exam**, enabling you to **acquire knowledge**, **practise and revise efficiently and effectively**.

Syllabus and learning outcomes

Paper E1 Organisational Management

The syllabus comprises:

Topic and Study Weighting

		%
A	Introduction to organisations	25
B	Managing the finance function	15
C	Managing technology and information	15
D	Operations management	15
E	Marketing	15
F	Managing human resources	15

Learning outcomes On completion of their studies, student should be able to:		
Lead	**Component**	**Indicative syllabus content**
A Introduction to organisations (25%)		

1 Discuss the different types of structure that an organisation may adopt	(a) Discuss the different purposes of organisations	• Ownership:
		  – Private sector, public sector
		• Motive:
		  – For profit, non-profit
		• Mission and vision
		  – Shared values and beliefs
		• Creating value for stakeholders:
		  – Control and coordination of resources to achieve goals and outcomes
		  – Efficient production of goods and services
		  – Facilitating innovation

	(b) Explain the different structures organisations may adopt	• Organisational configuration (Mintzberg)
		  – Technical core
		  – Technical support
		  – Administrative support
		  – Top and middle management
		• Organisational configuration, contextual dimensions, the effect of:
		  – Technology
		  – Environment
		  – Culture
		• Structural dimensions, influence of:
		  – Size
		  – Formalisation
		  – Specialisation
		  – Organisation type eg sole-trader, partnership, company, multinational
		• Structural organisation:
		  – Functional
		  – Divisional
		  – Matrix
		  – Geographical

	(c) Explain the various forms and functional boundaries of the organisation including externalisation, shared service centres (SSC) and business process outsourcing (BPO)	• Closed and open systems • Vertical and horizontal structures • Outsourcing • Alliances • Virtual network structure

Learning outcomes On completion of their studies, student should be able to:		
Lead	**Component**	**Indicative syllabus content**
2 Discuss relationships between internal and external sources of governance, regulation and professional behaviour	(a) Discuss the purpose and principles of good corporate governance, the ethical responsibilities of the organisation and individuals, and ways of achieving corporate social responsibility	• Corporate governance, including expectations of stakeholders and the role of government • Creating an ethical organisation • Principles of corporate social responsibility (CSR) • Developing business government relations • The impact of regulation on the organisation • Role of institutions and governance in economic growth • Personal business ethics and the fundamental principles (Part A) of the CIMA Code of Ethics for Professional Accountants
B **Managing the finance function (15%)**		
1 Discuss the purpose of the finance function and its relationships with other parts of the organisation	(a) Demonstrate the contribution the finance function makes to the sustainable delivery of the organisation's strategies in a range of contexts	• Stewardship and control of physical and financial resources within the organisation • Interpreting and reporting the financial position of the organisation for external stakeholders (including statutory requirements) and internal management • Collating and providing information to enable efficient asset management and cost effective operation of the organisation • Comparing the current position with forecast/budget expectations and indicating where and how differences have occurred. Providing this in a timely and accurate manner • Assisting and interacting with other functions in providing solutions to variances

BPP LEARNING MEDIA

Learning outcomes On completion of their studies, student should be able to:		
Lead	**Component**	**Indicative syllabus content**
	(b) Analyse the components of the finance function (financial and management accounting, treasury, company secretarial and internal audit)	• Financial accounting – ensuring accurate asset values, efficient working capital management, statutory reporting • Management accounting – operational reporting (profit and loss) cost control, variance analysis. • Treasury management – sourcing finance, currency management, effective taxation administration • Company secretarial • Internal audit – ensuring compliance, fraud detection and avoidance

	(c) Discuss the potential for conflict within the role of the finance function	• Potential conflicts
		  – Interdependence/independence
		  – Short-term/long-term
		  – Capital/revenue

2 Explain how the finance function supports the organisation's strategies and operations	(a) Explain the activities fundamental to the role of the finance function (accounting operations, analysis, planning, decision making and control)	• Preparation of statutory reports • Preparation of plane, forecasts, budgets • Working capital reporting and control, inventories, receivables, payables, cash • Provision of analysis to support decisions • Performance reporting, budget/actuals • Cost reporting, product/process • Ensuring systems in place to provide timely and accurate control information

	(b) Explain the contemporary transformation of the finance function	• Reconfiguration:
		  – Bureaucratic to market oriented
		• Shared services:
		  – Outsourced market orientation
		• Business Process Re-engineering:
		  – Roles of process working
		• Relocation:
		  – Retained/near-shore/off-shore
		• Segregation of the finance function:
		  – Transactional/transformational activities
		• Business partners:
		  – Support involvement

Learning outcomes On completion of their studies, student should be able to:		
Lead	**Component**	**Indicative syllabus content**
C Managing technology and information (15%)		
1 Demonstrate the purpose of the technology and information function and its relationships with other parts of the organisation	(a) Demonstrate the value of information systems in organisations	• The role of information systems in organisations • Emerging information system trends in organisations. The networked enterprise, organisational benefits, customer relationship management systems
	(b) Demonstrate ways of organising and managing information systems in the context of the wider organisation	• Information technology – enabling transformation; the emergence of new, more virtual forms of organisation, technology infrastructure • Geographically dispersed (virtual) teams; role of information systems in virtual teams and challenges for virtual collaboration • Managing knowledge, enhancing internal and external relationships. • Ethical and social issues associated with information systems

2 Explain how information system support the organisation's strategies and operations	(a) Explain the technical components and options for information technology system design	• Evaluating costs and benefits of information systems
		• The internet, intranet, wireless technology, cloud technologies.
		• Privacy and security
		• Overview of systems architecture and data flows
		• Big Data information management:
		  – Large volumes of data
		  – Complexity and variety of data
		  – Velocity, real time data

	(b) Explain the role of emerging technologies eg Big Data, digitisation and their uses	• Enhancing decision making support using Big Data and analytics:
		  – Identifying business value
		  – Relating to customer requirements
		  – Developing organisational blueprint
		  – Building capabilities on business priorities
		  – Ensuring measurable outcomes.
		• Information system implementation as a change management process; avoiding problems of non-usage and resistance
		• System changeover methods (ie direct, parallel, pilot and phased)

BPP
LEARNING MEDIA

Learning outcomes On completion of their studies, student should be able to:		
Lead	**Component**	**Indicative syllabus content**
		• Information system outsourcing (different types of sourcing strategies; client-vendor relationships)
		• E-commerce, digital markets, social media, digital goods
		• Remote working, hot desking
		• Big Data and digitisation: – Addressing customer needs – Effective and speedy decisions
D Operations management (15%)		
1 Demonstrate the purpose of the operations function and its relationships with other parts of the organisation	(a) Demonstrate the contribution of operations management to the efficient production and delivery of fit-for-purpose goods and services	• Overview of operations strategy and its importance to the firm
	(b) Demonstrate how supply chains can be established and managed	• Procurement as a strategic process in supply chain management • Development of relationships with suppliers, including the use of supply portfolios • Supply chains in competitions with each other; role of supply network; demand networks as an evolution of supply chains • Design of products/services and processes and how this relates to operations and supply • The concept of CSR and sustainability in operations management
2 Apply tools and techniques of operations management	(a) Apply the tools and concepts of operations management to deliver sustainable performance	• Process design • Product and service design • Supply network design • Forecasting • Layout and flow • Process technology: – CNC, Robots, AGV, FMS, CIM – Decision support systems – Expert systems • Work study • Capacity planning and control, inventory control

Learning outcomes	On completion of their studies, student should be able to:	
Lead	**Component**	**Indicative syllabus content**

	(b) Explain how relationships within the supply chain can be managed	• Supply chain planning and control:
		  – Lean synchronisation
		  – Contractual/relational approaches
		  – Material requirement planning
		  – Quality planning and control
		  – Statistical process control
		  – Operational improvement, total quality management (TQM), Kaizen, Six Sigma, Lean thinking
		  – Reverse logistics

E Marketing (15%)		
1 Demonstrate the purpose of the marketing function and its relationships with other parts of the organisation.	(a) Apply the marketing concept and principles in a range of organisational contexts	• The marketing concept as a business philosophy • The marketing environment, including societal, economic, technological, political and legal factors affecting marketing (PESTEL) • The role of marketing in the business plan of the organisation • Marketing in public sector and not-for-profit organisations eg charities, non-governmental organisations, etc.

	(b) Apply the elements of the marketing mix	• The 7 Ps:
		  – Product
		  – Place
		  – Price
		  – Promotion
		  – Processes
		  – People
		  – Physical evidence
		• Theories of consumer behaviour (eg social interaction theory), as well as factors affecting buying decision, types of buying behaviour and stages in the buying process
		• Social marketing and CSR
		• Social media and its effect on the organisation

Learning outcomes	On completion of their studies, student should be able to:	
Lead	**Component**	**Indicative syllabus content**

2 Apply tools and techniques to formulate the organisation's marketing strategies, including the collection, analysis and application of Big Data	(a) Apply the main techniques of marketing	• Market research, including data gathering techniques and method of analysis
		• Segmentation and targeting of markets, and positioning of products within markets
		• How business to business (B2B) and business to government (B2G) marketing differs from business to consumer (B2C) marketing in its different forms:
		  – Consumer marketing
		  – Services marketing
		  – Direct marketing
		  – Interactive marketing
		  – E-marketing
		  – Internal marketing
		• Promotional tools and the promotion mix
		• The 'service extension' to the marketing mix
		• Devising and implementing a pricing strategy
		• Internal marketing as the process of training and motivating employees to support the firm's external marketing activities
		• Relationship marketing
		• Not-for-profit marketing
		• Experiential marketing
		• Postmodern marketing

	(b) Explain the role of emerging technologies and media in marketing	• Big Data analytics and its use in the marketing process:
		  – Predicting customer demand
		  – Improving the customer experience
		  – Monitoring multi-channel transactions
		  – Identifying customer preferences.
		• Marketing communications, including viral, guerrilla and other indirect forms of marketing
		• Distribution channels and methods for marketing campaigns, including digital marketing
		• Brand image and brand value
		• Product development and product/service life-cycles

Learning outcomes On completion of their studies, student should be able to:		
Lead	**Component**	**Indicative syllabus content**
		• The differences and similarities in the marketing of products, services and experiences • Product portfolios and the product mix • Marketing sustainability and ethics
F Managing human resources (15%)		
1 Demonstrate the purpose of the HR function and its relationships with other parts of the organisation	(a) Explain the contribution of HR to the sustainable delivery of the organisation's strategies	• The concept of HRM and its influence on organisational processes and performance • The psychological contract and its importance to retention • The relationship of the employee to other elements of the business • HR in different organisational forms, project based, virtual or networked firms and different organisational contexts
	(b) Apply the elements of the HR cycle	• Acquisition: – Odentify staffing requirement – Recruitment – Selection • Development: – Training – Evaluation – Progression • Maintenance: – Monetary and non-monetary benefits • Separation: – Voluntary and involuntary
2 Apply the tools and techniques of HRM	(a) Demonstrate the HR activities associated with developing employees	• Practices associated with recruiting and developing appropriate abilities including recruiting and selection of staff using different recruitment channels: – Interviews – Assessment centres, intelligence tests, aptitude tests – Competency frameworks • Issues relating to fair and legal employment practices (eg recruitment, dismissal, redundancy, and ways of managing these). • The distinction between training and development, and the tools available to develop and train staff

Learning outcomes On completion of their studies, student should be able to:		
Lead	**Component**	**Indicative syllabus content**
		• The design and implementation of induction programmes
		• Practices related to motivation including issues in the design of reward systems:
		– The roles of incentives
		– The utility of performance-related pay
		– Arrangements for knowledge workers
		– Flexible work arranges
	(b) demonstrate the role of the line manager in the implementation of HR practices	• The importance of appraisal, their conduct and their relationship to reward system
		• Practices related to the creation of opportunities for employees to contribute to the organisation including; job design, communications, involvement procedures and principles of negotiation
		• Problems in implementing HR plans appropriate to a team and ways to manage this
		• Preparation of an HR plan. Forecasting personnel requirements: retention, absence and leave, employee turnover
		• Ethical code and the interface with HR practice

Studying E1

1 What E1's about

E1 explores several discrete subjects which all affect how organisations operate. However, please note that exam questions may cover more than one of these subjects. You should therefore appreciate the various links between them.

1.1 Introduction to organisations

In Chapter 1 we introduce the **various types of form** that organisations may take, before turning our attention to the **mission and goals** that businesses may have. There are several different types of **structure** that organisations may use to build the business around and we conclude by considering situations where different organisations work together in **alliances**.

The main issues covered in Chapter 2 are **ethics**, **corporate governance** and **social responsibility**. These concepts will reappear several times throughout your studies, both in E1 the exam, and in the CIMA syllabus generally. We shall also cover the role of **Government** in trade and **market regulation**.

1.2 Managing the finance function

As accountants, CIMA members are primarily concerned with the operation of their business area – the finance function and that is the subject of Chapter 3. The **purpose** and **structure** of the **finance team** will be studied before our attention turns to more detailed matters. These include the various types of **information** relevant to the finance function, as well as the **various systems** that accountants will come across in their work. We conclude by looking at some **contemporary developments** in finance.

1.3 Managing technology and information

You are not expected to become an information systems (IS) expert, but the syllabus does require you to appreciate the **role IS plays in organisations**. This includes the various **types of system** and the role systems play in **transforming how organisations operate** and the **types of business** they do. These areas are all covered in Chapter 4.

Chapter 5 is primarily concerned with how organisations **implement new systems**. However, you should also understand the importance of organisations **aligning** their **information systems** with their **overall business strategy**.

1.4 Operations management

Operations are the main activities of an organisation. They are **'what it does'**, and it is the subject of Chapters 6, 7 and 8.

We begin by studying how operations develop around a **value chain** and how organisations join together to form **supply chains** and networks. **Quality** is an important issue for all businesses, whether in terms of products or services, and we shall see how quality can be **measured** and **managed** to ensure the customer is satisfied. We shall find out how organisations can **balance** their **inputs** (inventory) and **outputs** (products and services) with **changing demand levels**. Finally we will look at the different types of **processes** and **technology** that organisations may use to control their operations.

1.5 Marketing

Marketing is about **communicating** the organisation's **sales messages** to the customer. It forms a major part of its business strategy and is the subject of Chapters 9, 10 and 11. We shall firstly study the **marketing environment** and see how a **marketing strategy** and **plan** are put together. Following on from this, our study looks into how the **marketing message is communicated** to the customer and the important issue of **corporate branding**.

The syllabus also covers several smaller areas of marketing. These include **consumer behaviour**, marketing **not-for-profit organisations**, marketing an organisation's message to its employees (**internal marketing**) and how **corporate social responsibility** affects how an organisation markets its products and services. We shall cover all these areas in full as well.

1.6 Managing human resources

Many believe that an organisation's **employees** are its main asset and they should be **carefully managed** to get the best out of them. The E1 syllabus looks at all aspects of managing employees to **maximise their potential**. Motivation, remuneration, appraisals and various types of working arrangement are all important to this end and are covered in Chapters 12 and 13. We shall also look into what constitutes good **HR practice** and the importance of employees acting **ethically**.

2 What's required

2.1 Organisational management

The E1 exam covers a wide range of topics from **types of organisation** to **information technology**, **operations**, **marketing**, and **human resource management** as well as **ethics**, **corporate governance** and **social responsibility**. This means it is important to ensure that you have a good breadth of knowledge, rather than having highly detailed knowledge of only a few areas.

The E1 exam is based around **objective test questions**, such as the selection of one correct answer from a choice of four. These questions test your ability to make **quick decisions**. The other main type of question is the multiple choice question. When answering multiple choice questions the key is to try to **eliminate any obviously wrong answers first** before considering the others. Other question types might also be used.

3 How to pass

3.1 Study the whole syllabus

You need to be comfortable with **all areas of the syllabus**, as questions in the objective test exam will cover all syllabus areas. **Wider reading** will help you understand general business issues, which will be particularly useful in the integrated case study exam.

3.2 Lots of question practice

You can **develop application skills** by attempting questions in the Practice Question Bank. While these might not all be in the format that you will experience in your exam, doing them will enable you to answer the exam questions. Similarly, in the integrated case study exam you will have to answer questions that combine E1 syllabus areas with F1 and P1. By answering questions on E1 you will develop the technical knowledge and skills in order to answer those questions.

However, you should practise OT exam standard questions, which you will find in the BPP Exam Practice Kit.

4 Brought forward knowledge

The examiner may test knowledge or techniques you've learnt at lower levels. As E1 is the first exam of the Enterprise pillar, the main brought forward knowledge will be from **CIMA's Certificate Level**.

Before commencing your E1 studies you should carefully review the full Certificate Level Syllabus (available from www.cimaglobal.com) and ensure that you have full and complete knowledge of all topics.

5 The Integrated Case Study and links with F1 and P1

The integrated case study exam is based on the expectation that students are developing a pool of knowledge. When faced with a problem students can appropriately apply their knowledge from any syllabus. Students will avoid a historical problem of partitioning their knowledge and accessing, for example, their knowledge of IFRS only when faced with a set of financial statements.

- **Enterprise operational decisions** will **impact** upon financial and performance objectives, the financial reports, working capital, and the risks the organisation faces.

- **Financial and performance decisions** will likewise have an impact on enterprise operational decisions.

- At the same time **enterprise operations** will be **constrained** by the finance available and the level of risks the organisation is prepared to bear.

- **Financial operational decisions** will **impact** upon the **risks** the organisation bears and perhaps impose limitations on the plans the organisation can implement.

- **Costing techniques**, particularly in relation to manufacturing, environmental costing and costs of quality, will have an impact on the **choices available** for enterprise operational decisions.

6 What the examiner means

The table below has been prepared by CIMA to help you interpret the syllabus and learning outcomes and the meaning of questions.

You will see that there are 5 levels of Learning objective, ranging from Knowledge to Evaluation, reflecting the level of skill you will be expected to demonstrate. CIMA Certificate subjects only use levels 1 to 3, but in CIMA's Professional qualification the entire hierarchy will be used.

At the start of each chapter in your Study Text is a topic list relating the coverage in the chapter to the level of skill you may be called on to demonstrate in the exam.

Learning objectives	Verbs used	Definition
1 Knowledge What are you expected to know	• List • State • Define	• Make a list of • Express, fully or clearly, the details of/facts of • Give the exact meaning of
2 Comprehension What you are expected to understand	• Describe • Distinguish • Explain • Identify • Illustrate	• Communicate the key features of • Highlight the differences between • Make clear or intelligible/state the meaning or purpose of • Recognise, establish or select after consideration • Use an example to describe or explain something
3 Application How you are expected to apply your knowledge	• Apply • Calculate/ compute • Demonstrate • Prepare • Reconcile • Solve • Tabulate	• Put to practical use • Ascertain or reckon mathematically • Prove with certainty or to exhibit by practical means • Make or get ready for use • Make or prove consistent/compatible • Find an answer to • Arrange in a table
4 Analysis How you are expected to analyse the detail of what you have learned	• Analyse • Categorise • Compare and contrast • Construct • Discuss • Interpret • Prioritise • Produce	• Examine in detail the structure of • Place into a defined class or division • Show the similarities and/or differences between • Build up or compile • Examine in detail by argument • Translate into intelligible or familiar terms • Place in order of priority or sequence for action • Create or bring into existence
5 Evaluation How you are expected to use your learning to evaluate, make decisions or recommendations	• Advise • Evaluate • Recommend	• Counsel, inform or notify • Appraise or assess the value of • Propose a course of action

Competency Framework

CIMA has developed a competency framework detailing the skills, abilities and competencies that finance professionals need. The CIMA syllabus has been developed to match the competency mix as it develops over the three levels of the professional qualification. The importance of the various competencies at the operational level is shown below.

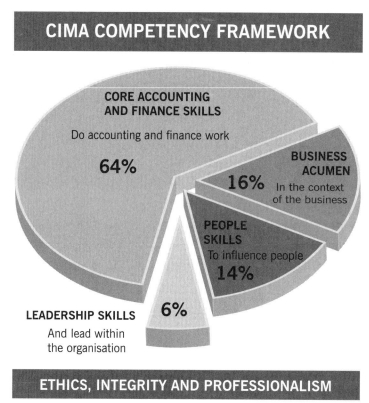

CIMA COMPETENCY FRAMEWORK

CORE ACCOUNTING AND FINANCE SKILLS
Do accounting and finance work
64%

BUSINESS ACUMEN
16% In the context of the business

PEOPLE SKILLS
To influence people
14%

LEADERSHIP SKILLS
And lead within the organisation
6%

ETHICS, INTEGRITY AND PROFESSIONALISM

Assessment

The CIMA assessment is a two-tier structure with objective tests for each subject and an integrated case study at each level.

Objective test

The objective tests are computer based and can be taken on demand. The student exam preparation on the CIMA website (www.cimaglobal.com) has additional information and tools to help you become familiar with the test style. Make sure you check back regularly as more information may be added.

Integrated case study

Candidates must pass or receive exemptions from the three objective tests at each level, before attempting the integrated case study exam for that level.

The integrated case studies are available four times a year.

The integrated case study exams combine the knowledge and learning from all the pillars. They will be set in the context of a preseen fictional organisation based on a real industry.

AN INTRODUCTION TO ORGANISATIONS

Part A

ORGANISATIONAL STRUCTURES

 We start our E1 studies by looking at the **types of business organisations** and their mission and objectives.

Once we have done that we shall consider the various forms and structures organisations may take. There are numerous choices that can be taken about form and structure and there are several factors that should be taken into account when making the decision or, more generally, about objectives and vision.

Finally, we consider **alliances** as alternative methods of doing business.

1

Topic list	Learning outcomes	Syllabus references	Ability required
1 Types of organisation	A1(a)	A1(i), A1(ii)	analysis
2 Vision, mission, goals and strategy	A1(a)	A1(iii), A1(iv)	analysis
3 Business goals and objectives	A1(a)	A1(iv)	analysis
4 Organisational structure	A1(b)	A1(v), A1(vi), A1(vii), A1(viii)	comprehension
5 Types of system	A1(c)	A1(ix), A1(x)	comprehension
6 Alliances	A1(c)	A1(xi), A1(xii), A1(xiii)	comprehension

Chapter Overview

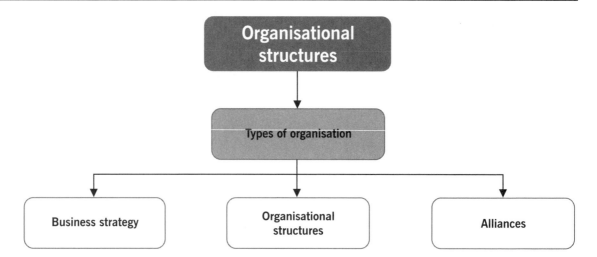

1 Types of organisation

Introduction

Economies contain **different types of organisation** and the economy itself can be divided into the **public** and **private sectors**.

In this section we consider the different types of organisation found in each sector.

1.1 Organisations

According to Buchanan and Huczynski an organisation is '… a **social arrangement** for the **controlled performance** of **collective goals**'.

This definition means that a **single person cannot be an organisation** because it would not be a social arrangement. There should be **systems** and **procedures** in place (such as budgets and sales targets) to **achieve goals** (for example, to treat sick patients, as in the case of a hospital).

The key benefit of an organisation is **synergy** – the achievement of more by the organisation as a whole than could otherwise be achieved by individual employees working on their own. Synergy is possible because in an organisation people have access to a wider range of **information** and **knowledge**, can share greater **resources** (such as time and money) and **specialise** in specific areas and skills which enables them to develop a greater level of skill and knowledge than they would be able to on their own.

1.1.1 Business sectors

The economy of a developed country can usually be divided into two sectors – **public** and **private**. Private sector organisations, also called businesses, are owned and operated by private individuals or institutions, while organisations in the public sector are usually owned by the State.

1.2 Private sector organisations

Private sector organisations are of two main types – those that **seek profit** for their owners and those that have **other objectives**. The latter are known as non profit making or not-for-profit organisations. However, the majority of organisations in the private sector are businesses which aim to make profits for their owners (shareholders).

1.2.1 Not-for-profit organisations

This terminology is a little misleading, in that 'not-for-profit' organisations often engage in profitable trade and they are not able to run consistently at a loss. The essence of their status is not that they seek to avoid generating a surplus of funds, but that the generation of wealth for their owners is **not the primary purpose** of their existence.

Such organisations still aim to operate as **efficiently** as possible, but their primary objective is to provide a service rather than to maximise profit. Not-for-profit organisations include charities and unincorporated clubs, societies and associations and government departments and services such as hospitals and schools.

Not-for-profit organisations use the surplus they generate to further their other objectives. Clubs and associations exist to provide some kind of benefit to their members. **Charities** and **voluntary organisations** generally exist to provide some kind of benefit to society at large.

Although not-for-profit organisations are not profit seekers, they still use economic factors of production to produce goods or services. Therefore they need to be **efficiently** managed so that their resources are used **effectively** to meet the objectives of the organisation while not making a financial loss.

1.2.2 Mutual organisations (co-operatives)

Mutual organisations (otherwise known as co-operatives) are a special type of not-for-profit organisation in the private sector. The essence of their nature is that they are commercial operations **owned by their customers** (members), rather than having capital and associated shareholders for whom they have to earn profit. This means that their customers benefit both from the **services** the mutuals provide to them and from the **trading surplus** they make by doing so.

It is also possible for the managers of mutuals to pursue **purposes other than maximising their trading surplus**. These can include a high level of charitable giving, the promotion of community interests and a high quality of service. Mutuals therefore resemble both not-for-profit organisations and profit-seeking companies but, as they don't produce profit for shareholders, strictly speaking they are not-for-profit organisations.

1.2.3 Profit-seeking organisations

In most countries the economy is driven by the profit-seeking part of the private sector. It is businesses that undertake the most enterprising aspects of economic activity. They provide the bulk of employment opportunities and tax revenue and create the growth needed to enhance economic welfare. Businesses are of two main types, distinguished by the extent to which the owners are liable for the debts of the undertaking.

(a)   An individual may set up business on their own account as a **sole trader** or in **partnership** with others. In either case, the law will not distinguish between the private assets and liabilities of the owners and those of the enterprise. The owners have **unlimited liability** for the debts of their businesses.

(b)   This degree of risk is unattractive to many potential investors so, to enable them to invest and therefore release more funds for wealth-producing enterprise, the legal systems of most countries provide for some form of **limited liability** enterprise. Such businesses are referred to as corporations or **companies**.

In the UK, there are two forms of **limited liability company**. They both limit the liability of investors to the nominal value of their shareholdings but they differ in the extent to which they are permitted to solicit investment from the general public.

KEY POINT

Private limited companies may not offer their securities to the public – **public limited companies** (plcs) may.

When the shares of plcs are regularly bought and sold on a stock exchange, they may be referred to as **quoted companies**, because the current price of their shares will be quoted in a journal of record.

Exam skills

Remember that not all public limited companies are quoted companies.

1.2.4 Multinational corporations

Some businesses may develop into **multinational corporations** (MNCs). These organisations have the capacity to produce in more than one country, by either owning or controlling a foreign subsidiary. They are often large, well-known organisations such as petrol companies, but they may also be small in size.

There is no **'typical' multinational**; some may operate in hundreds of countries, some in only a few. Many types of businesses may be multinational – from large-scale manufacturing operations to small-scale financial service companies. Finally, some may get the majority of their revenue from their foreign operations, whereas others may only do a fraction of their trade overseas.

Advantages of becoming multinational
Production should increase as products are sold more widely, and production costs may be lower in foreign countries. Therefore, a lower amount of costs can be spread over a greater amount of output.
Investment in new technology (also spread over higher output) can be made to take advantage of economies of scale and improve productivity.
Multinationals may attract a higher calibre of staff in terms of experience or ability.
Operations can be located to take advantage of low-cost materials, labour, transport and other operating costs. High-quality staff or government investment incentives may also be found.
The most appropriate business model can be used. For example, internalising costs of an overseas subsidiary might be better in one country, but contracting with a supplier to produce the goods might be better in another.
Distribution costs are lower if goods are produced locally and import duties and quotas can be avoided.

The **growth of MNCs** can be attributed to:

- Innovation in communications technology
- Improved transport and infrastructure
- Market homogenisation (eg the world's needs and wants have become increasingly similar)
- Political stability
- Increased merger activity

Due to these factors and especially **internet** improvements and **political changes** such as the opening of trading borders, some organisations, although they are still small, are actually 'born global' now.

MNCs have many opportunities because they are able to identify countries in which they can **maximise their competences** and make the most of the variances in the business environment.

Many UK-based **IT companies** are now retaining their sales divisions in the UK, but moving their system development activities to India where there is a large pool of newly qualified system development specialists who can be employed at a cheaper rate than in the UK.

MNCs also benefit from being able to **spread their risk** over many businesses in many countries. Companies such as **Procter & Gamble**, **PepsiCo**, **Philips** and **Nestlé**, for example, have large portfolios of businesses and brands which are located in many countries.

The **legal** and **tax differences** between countries in which they operate also mean that MNCs, through the process of internal transfer pricing, can reduce their overall tax burden and significantly increase profits.

Many **emerging nations** have made use of **MNCs** by attracting their investment through subsidies and low labour costs. We have already seen that (for some organisations) it no longer really matters where an organisation is based. This type of organisation has been the key to **export-led industrialisation**.

1.3 Public sector organisations

Public sector organisations used to be divided into **two main groups** – those that **provide public services** (such as hospitals, schools, the police and the armed forces) and **state-owned industries**. This distinction has become less clear over the last quarter-century as governments have privatised state-owned industries and sought to **reform the public sector** by involving private companies in the provision of public services. The objective has been to **curb waste** of public money and **improve efficiency** by importing the disciplined cost control found in the private sector.

In the UK, many providers of public services such as hospitals and schools, and formerly state-owned industries such as London Underground, are now involved in different forms of **public–private partnership**. In such partnerships, the private sector provides funds for public sector purposes such as education. For example, the Private Funding Initiative for schools seeks private partners to fund and manage school buildings in return for an agreed fee. Some services in the UK such as the National Health Service (NHS) are provided by self-governing trusts. These trusts sell their services to the NHS.

Public sector bodies are all, ultimately, **responsible to government** for their activities, and their purposes are defined in the laws that establish them. They have a range of aims and objectives but rarely will they set out to trade at a profit. Nevertheless, their managers will be expected to exercise **good stewardship** and **prevent waste of resources**. Public sector bodies' objectives will usually be defined in terms of the **provision of a service** that is deemed to be beneficial to society.

An important feature of **public sector bodies** is that they have little control over their income. This is because they depend on government for the funds they need to operate. The funds they receive will be influenced by a large number of factors, including current public opinion, government aspirations, the skill of their leaders in negotiation, the current state of the public finances overall and the current economic climate.

1.3.1 Non-governmental organisations (NGOs)

KEY POINT

Non-governmental organisations (NGOs) are defined by the World Bank as 'private organisations that pursue activities to relieve suffering, promote the interests of the poor, protect the environment, provide basic social services or undertake community development'. Many of the largest NGOs are charities such as Oxfam and the Red Cross.

Two key features of NGOs are:

- Generating a profit is not a primary goal, meaning they are not constrained by short-term financial objectives.

- They are not directly linked to governments or government departments.

There are two main types of NGO. The first type seeks to influence government policy through lobbying and generating public feeling in its favour – through marketing and public relations techniques. These are known as **campaigning NGOs**. The second type attempts to make a positive impact directly in the area it is interested in. This might be through specific projects or undertaking work to make a change. These are known as **operational NGOs**.

Many NGOs have developed relationships with **business organisations**, for example where they share a common goal. The benefits to each party of such an arrangement might include: the acquisition of skills and knowledge that it might not otherwise obtain, the creation value (through reduced duplication of effort and environmental impact), developing corporate social responsibility and improving their credibility in the eyes of their stakeholders.

Another type of NGO is the **quasi autonomous non-governmental organisation** (QUANGO). These share similar objectives to public sector organisations, but are actually private organisations independent of the Government, but to which the Government has devolved the authority for running public services. Examples of QUANGOs in the UK include ACAS (the independent employment relations mediator) and Ofsted (the school inspection body).

Section summary

The economy of a developed country can usually be divided into two sectors – **public** and **private**.

Private sector organisations are of two main types – those that **seek profit** for their owners and those that have **other objectives**.

Examples of **not-for-profit organisations** include **charities** and **voluntary or mutual organisations**.

Examples of **profit-making organisations** include **sole traders**, **partnerships** and **companies**.

Multinational companies have the capacity to produce in more than one country, usually with a centrally located head office.

Public sector organisations provide services to the general public such as **hospitals** and **schools**.

2 Vision, mission, goals and strategy

Introduction

Strategics are developed in order to achieve desired outcomes. These are inherent in the organisation's mission or defining purpose. Whether stated or not, the **mission** of a business always includes return to investors. Mission guides strategic decisions and provides values and a sense of direction.

A **company's vision**, often contained in a vision statement, is the organisation's view of where it sees itself going in the long term. It is a perspective on the **company's future**. This view may (but not necessarily) be derived from the business's mission and objectives, because these concepts concern the purpose of the organisation and its future strategy.

The Ashridge College model of mission **links business strategy to culture and ethics** by including four separate elements in an expanded definition of **mission**.

(a) **Purpose**. Why does the company exist? Who does it exist for?

    (i) To create wealth for shareholders, who take priority over all other stakeholders?

    (ii) To satisfy the needs of all stakeholders, including employees, for example?

    (iii) To reach some higher goal such as the advancement of society?

(b) **Values** are the beliefs and moral principles that underlie the organisation's culture.

(c) **Strategy** provides the commercial logic for the company (the **nature** of the organisation's business), and so addresses the following questions: 'What is our business? Or, what should it be? What are our elements of sustainable competitive advantage?'.

    When answering these questions, the mission should look at them from the **customer's perspective**. So, for example, a company which produces study materials for professional exams might say, 'We are in the business of producing high-quality books that help our readers pass their exams.' The competitive advantage will come from the quality of the books and the extent to which they help their readers pass their exams.

(d) **Policies and standards of behaviour** provide guidance on how the organisation's business should be conducted. For example, a service industry that wishes to be the best in its market must aim for standards of service, in all its operations, which are at least as good as those found in its competitors.

These **four elements will vary** from organisation to organisation. This is especially true when comparing **profit-making** businesses against **not-for-profit organisations** such as hospitals and charities. For example, a profit-making organisation may seek to maximise dividends to shareholders, but a charity may seek to maximise the amount of money it distributes to the needy.

2.1 The importance of mission for corporate strategy

There are several reasons why a business should give serious consideration to establishing a clear concept of its corporate mission.

(a) Values are acknowledged as integral elements of consumers' buying decisions; this is shown by the attention paid to them in advertising, brand building and market research. Customers ask not only 'What do you sell?' but also 'What do you stand for?'.

(b) Studies into organisational behaviour show that people are motivated by many things other than money; employees are likely to be both more productive and more satisfied with their work when they feel that what they are doing has significance beyond the mere pursuit of a living.

(c) Some writers believe there is an empirical relationship between strong corporate values and profitability.

2.2 Mission statements

KEY TERMS

A MISSION STATEMENT is a published statement, apparently of the entity's fundamental objective(s). This may or may not summarise the true mission of the entity. *(CIMA Official Terminology)*

A MISSION is an entity's 'fundamental objectives ... expressed in general terms'.

(CIMA Official Terminology)

In essence, a **mission statement** describes an organisation's basic purpose and what it is trying to achieve. There is no standard format, but the four elements in the Ashridge model of mission offer a good basis for writing a mission statement.

Mission statements are likely to have some of the following characteristics:

(a)   Stating the purpose of the organisation
(b)   Stating the business areas in which the organisation intends to operate
(c)   Providing a general statement of the organisation's culture
(d)   Acting as a guide to develop the direction of the entity's strategy and its goals/objectives

The authors of the Ashridge model make another important point. Mission statements contain only **statements** of purpose and strategy, but in order for an organisation to develop a 'sense of mission' that 'mission' must be exhibited in the performance standards and values of the organisation.

Lynch (in *Strategic Management*) has provided the following criteria by which to judge the effectiveness of a corporate mission statement:

(a)   Is it specific enough to impact on individuals' behaviour throughout the business?

(b)   Does it reflect the distinctive advantage of the organisation and recognise its strengths and weaknesses?

(c)   Is it realistic and attainable?

(d)   Is it flexible to the demands of a changing environment?

CASE STUDY

The following are the mission statements for some well-known companies:

Coca-Cola   –   'To refresh the world ... To inspire moments of optimism and happiness ... To create value and make a difference.'

Google   –   'To organise the world's information and make it universally accessible and useful.'

Starbucks   –   'Our mission: to inspire and nurture the human spirit – one person, one cup and one neighbourhood at a time.'

eBay   –   'To provide a global trading platform where practically anyone can trade practically anything.'

Microsoft   –   'To help people and businesses throughout the world realise their potential.'

Although a number of successful companies have mission statements, critics raise the following criticisms of mission statements:

(a)   They are often **public relations** exercises rather than an accurate portrayal of the organisation's actual values.

(b)   They can often be full of **generalisations** which are impossible to tie down to specific strategic implications and practical objectives.

(c)   They may be ignored by the people responsible for formulating or implementing strategy.

(d)   They become obsolete, as they fail to evolve over time to reflect changes in the organisation, or in its markets or the external environment.

However, there are no fixed rules about how long an organisation should keep the same mission statement. Therefore a company's mission statement could be periodically reviewed to ensure it still accurately reflects the company's position and its environment.

2.3 Mission and planning

The mission statement can play an important role in the strategic planning process.

(a) **Inspires and informs planning**. Plans should further the organisation's goals and be consistent with its values. In this way, the mission statement provides a focus for consistent strategic planning decisions.

(b) **Screening**. Mission acts as a yardstick by which plans are judged.

(c) Mission also affects the **implementation** of a planned strategy in terms of the ways in which an organisation carries out its business, and through the culture of the organisation. A mission statement can help to develop a corporate culture in an organisation by communicating the organisation's core values. A mission statement can also often help to establish an ethics framework.

CASE STUDY

The Co-operative Group in the UK, which includes the Co-operative foodstores, has explicit social objectives. In some cases it will retain stores which, although they are too small to be as profitable as a large supermarket, fulfil an important social role in the communities which host them. The Co-operative is run by its members rather than by shareholders, so instead of having to chase profits for its shareholders it can steer its business in a more socially responsible direction.

Section summary

Mission guides strategic decisions and provides value and direction.

Mission statements are formal documents that state an organisation's mission. They can play an important role in the strategic planning process, but have also been criticised for being overgeneralised, ignored in practice, static/obsolete, and little more than PR.

3 Business goals and objectives

Introduction

Goals and **objectives** derive from mission and support it. For a business, a primary corporate objective will be the return offered to shareholders; however, this is measured. There may be other primary objectives and there will certainly be supporting objectives for costs, innovation, markets, products and so on.

3.1 Goals, objectives and targets

An understanding of an organisation's mission is invaluable for setting and controlling the overall **functioning and progress** of the organisation.

However, mission statements themselves are open-ended and are not stated in quantifiable terms, such as profits and revenues. Equally, they are not time bound.

Therefore mission statements can only be seen as a general indicator of an organisation's strategy. In order to start implementing the strategy and managing performance, an organisation needs to develop some more specific and measurable objectives and targets.

Most people's work is defined in terms of specific and immediate **things to be achieved**. If these things are related in some way to the wider purpose of the organisation, this will help the organisation to function more effectively than if these tasks are not aligned to the organisation's overall purpose.

A good example is how organisations use their **available resources** to create value for shareholders and other company stakeholders. By designing **efficient** and **effective processes**, and making good use of **value chains** and **supply chains**, the maximum output can be generated for the least input. We shall look at processes, value chains and supply chains later in your studies.

Loosely speaking, these 'things to be achieved' are the goals, objectives and targets of the various departments, functions and individuals that make up the organisation.

In effective organisations, **goal congruence** will be achieved, such that these disparate goals, objectives and targets will be **consistent** with one another and will **operate together** to support progress with the mission.

It should be remembered that mission statements are high-level, open-ended statements about a firm's purpose or strategy and **strategic objectives** translate the mission into more **specific milestones and targets** for the business strategy to follow and achieve.

Controls are activities that are undertaken in order to help ensure the achievement of objectives and usually involve monitoring performance and corrective action if necessary.

Examples of controls include:

- **Plans** and **budgets**
- Sales and other **targets**
- Corporate **culture** and **policies**
- **Supervision** of staff
- **Self-control** and **discipline** of individuals

Co-ordination involves **organising business operations** and **managing resources** such as people, assets, finances and technology to enhance organisational **efficiency** and **effectiveness** to achieve objectives. We shall see later in this Study Text that efficiency means to make best use of resources and to minimise wastage. Technology can be used to increase efficiency and effectiveness by maximising the usage of assets.

3.1.1 A hierarchy of objectives

A simple model of the relationship between the various goals, objectives and targets is a **pyramid** analogous to the traditional organisational hierarchy. At the top is the **overall mission**; this is supported by a **small number of wide-ranging goals**, which may correspond to overall departmental or functional responsibilities. Each of these goals is supported in turn by **more detailed, subordinate goals** that correspond, perhaps, to the responsibilities of the senior managers in the function concerned. This pattern is continued downwards until we reach the work targets of individual members of the organisation.

As we work our way down this pyramid of goals we will find that they will typically become **more detailed** and will relate to **shorter time frames**. So, the mission might be very general and specify no timescale at all, but an individual worker is likely to have very specific things to achieve every day, or even every few minutes.

Note that this description is very basic and that the structure of objectives in a modern organisation may be much more complex than this, with the pursuit of some goals involving input from several functions. Also, some goals may be defined in very general terms, so as not to stifle innovation, co-operation and informal ways of doing things.

An important feature of any structure of goals is that there should be **goal congruence** – that is to say, goals that are related to one another should be **mutually supportive**. This is because goals and objectives drive actions, so if goals aren't congruent then the actions of one area of the business will end up conflicting with those of another area of the business.

Goals can be related in several ways:

- **Hierarchically**, as in the pyramid structure outlined above

- **Functionally**, as when colleagues collaborate on a project

- **Logistically**, as when resources must be shared or used in sequence

- In **wider organisational senses**, as when senior executives make decisions about their operational priorities

A good example of the last category is the tension between long- and short-term priorities in such matters as the need to contain costs but at the same time increasing productivity by investing in improved plant.

The words **goal**, **objective** and **target** are used somewhat imprecisely and, to some extent, interchangeably. The suggestions we make below about the usage of these words are only tentative and you should read as widely as you can in order to make your own mind up about how to employ them.

KEY TERMS

A GOAL is often a longer-term overall aspiration: Mintzberg defines **goals** as 'the intentions behind decisions or actions, the states of mind that drive individuals or collectives of individuals called organisations to do what they do'. Goals may be difficult to quantify and it may not be very helpful to attempt to do so. An example of a goal might be to raise productivity in a manufacturing department.

OBJECTIVES are often quite specific and well defined, though they can also embody comprehensive purposes.

TARGETS are generally expressed in concrete numerical terms and are therefore easily used to measure progress and performance.

3.1.2 Management by objectives

The contrast between objectives and mission statements can be highlighted by the fact that objectives should be 'SMART'.

Specific   **M**easurable   **A**chievable   **R**elevant   **T**ime-related

Relevant is sometimes replaced with **realistic**, but 'realistic' and 'achievable' could be seen as meaning similar things. An objective is relevant if it is appropriate to an organisation's mission.

There are other variants: **achievable** may be replaced with **attainable**, which has an almost identical meaning. Achievable is also sometimes replaced with '**agreed**', denoting that objectives should be agreed with those responsible for achieving them. However, note that whichever version you prefer, a SMART objective corresponds very closely with our description of the way the word **target** is commonly used.

(a)   **S**pecific: An objective must be a clear statement, and must be easy to understand. Whereas mission statements tend to be vague, objectives must be specific.

(b)   **M**easurable: Again, in contrast to mission statements, objectives must be measurable so that performance against the objectives can be assessed. Measuring performance against objectives is a key element of control in organisations.

(c)   **A**chievable: If the objectives set are not achievable, people will not bother trying to achieve them, so there is little point setting them.

(d)   **R**elevant: An objective is relevant if it is appropriate to an organisation's mission, and will help it fulfil that mission. (This reiterates the link between an organisation's mission and its objectives.)

(e)   **T**ime-related: Whereas mission statements tend to be open-ended, an organisation needs to define a specific time period in which objectives should be achieved. Again, this is very important for enabling management to judge whether or not the objective has been achieved. For example, if an organisation has an objective 'To increase sales revenue by 5%', how will managers know the time period over which this sales increase is expected? However, if the objective is 'To increase sales revenue by 5% per year' the time frame is clearly identified.

Functions of objectives

(a)   **Planning**: Objectives define what the plan is about.

(b)   **Responsibility**: Objectives define the responsibilities of managers and departments.

(c)   **Integration**: Objectives should support one another and be consistent; this integrates the efforts of different departments.

(d)   **Motivation**: The first step in motivation is knowing what is to be done. Objectives must be created for all areas of performance.

(e)   **Evaluation**: Performance is assessed against objectives and control exercised.

3.2 Primary and secondary objectives

Some objectives are more important than others. In the hierarchy of objectives, there is a **primary corporate objective** and other **secondary objectives** which should combine to ensure the achievement of the overall corporate objective.

For example, if a company sets itself an objective of growth in profits as its primary aim, it will then have to develop strategies by which this primary objective can be achieved. An objective must then be set for each individual strategy. Secondary objectives might then be concerned with sales growth, continual technological innovation, customer service, product quality, efficient resource management or reducing the company's reliance on debt capital.

Corporate objectives should relate to the business as a whole and can be both **financial** and **non-financial**:

- Profitability
- Market share
- Growth
- Cash flow
- Asset base

- Customer satisfaction
- The quality of the firm's products
- Human resources
- New product development
- Social responsibility

Equally, when setting corporate objectives, it is important that an organisation considers the needs of all of its **stakeholders**, to try to ensure that these are met wherever possible.

CASE STUDY

Jaguar Land Rover

In its 2011/12 Annual Report and Accounts, Jaguar Land Rover summarised its strategy and objectives:

'The company has a multifaceted strategy to position itself as a leading manufacturer of premium vehicles offering high-quality products tailored to specific markets. The company's success is tied to its investment in product development which drives the strategic focus on capital expenditure, R&D and product design.'

The focus on 'premium' and high quality is important here, because it shows how Jaguar Land Rover is looking to differentiate itself from the budget and mid-range vehicles. As if to reinforce this point, Jaguar Land Rover goes on to identify four objectives which it believes are the key steps it needs to take to achieve this strategy:

(1)   *Grow the business through new products and market expansion* – it aims to achieve this by diversifying the product range within existing segments (premium performance car and all-terrain vehicles) as well as greater product derivatives, for example the development of models that allow the company to compete in the small 'urban' off-road sector and the company car market. Expanding into new geographical locations would also assist the company in achieving this goal.

(2)   *Transform the business structure to deliver sustainable returns* – to mitigate the impact of cyclicality and provide a foundation for investment.

(3)   *Investment in product development and technology to maintain high quality* – to enhance its status as a leading manufacturer of premium passenger vehicles by investment in products, research and development (R&D), quality improvement and quality control.

(4)   *Products and environmental performance* – to invest in products and technologies that position its products ahead of expected stricter environmental regulations and ensure that it benefits from a shift in consumer awareness of the environmental impact of the vehicles they drive.

3.3 Subsidiary or secondary objectives

Whatever primary objective or objectives are set, **subsidiary objectives** will then be developed beneath them.

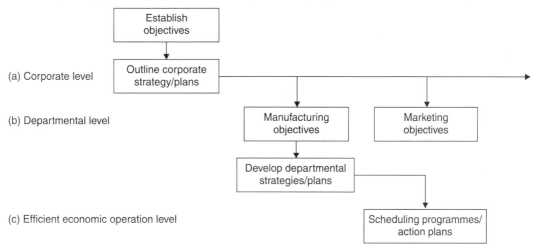

The overall objectives of the organisation will indicate different requirements for different functions. In this respect it is important to appreciate the structure of goals or objectives in an organisation:

Strategic (corporate) **objectives**:   Set the overall long-term objectives for the business as a whole

Tactical objectives: The 'middle tier' of objectives; designed to plan and control individual functions within the organisation. Tactical objectives are then implemented by setting operational objectives

Operational objectives: Day to day performance targets to ensure that the organisation's operations are carried out efficiency or effectively

3.3.1 Unit objectives

Unit objectives relate either to strategic business units or functions of the business.

(a)   Private sector objectives:

(i)   Increasing the number of customers by 10%

(ii)   Reducing the number of rejects by 50%

(iii)   Producing monthly reports more quickly, within five working days of the end of each month

(b)   Public sector objectives:

(i)   Responding more quickly to emergency calls

(ii)   Reducing the length of time a patient has to wait for an operation

3.3.2 Goals for markets and marketing

Goals for **markets** will involve the following types of decisions:

(a)   **Market leadership**: whether the organisation wants to be the market leader, or number two in the market, what rate of growth it desires and so on

(b)   **Coverage**: whether the product range needs to be expanded

(c)   **Positioning**: whether there should be an objective to shift position in the market – eg from producing low-cost for the mass market to higher-cost specialist products

(d)   **Expansion**: whether there should be an objective of broadening the product range or extending the organisation's markets

3.3.3 Goals for products and services

Labour productivity objectives are often quantified as targets to reduce unit costs and increase output per employee by a certain percentage each year.

Capital productivity is measured less often, but it can denote how efficiently a firm is using its equipment.

Quality objectives might be measured in low rejects (eg through quality targets set under 'Six Sigma' methodologies). In some environments, targets may be set for service delivery, such as speed in answering the telephone, customer satisfaction and service quality.

Goals for products include **technology**.

3.3.4 Goals for innovation

Innovation is the generation of new ideas of how to do business, or how to do current business better, and it is essentially a creative activity. Reducing costs and providing a basis for differentiation are two benefits of innovation.

The **creativity** needed to innovate can be achieved through a number of **organisational dimensions**:

- **Culture** – Creative cultures view failure as an important learning process to be expected. 'Learning organisations' don't view failure as something negative, but instead they learn from their mistakes.

- **People** – A team-based approach that creates a sense of ownership and encourages participation is important.

- **Leadership** – Vision and communication of ideas helps give direction.

- **Structure** – A flexible organisational structure encourages innovation. We shall look at flexible organisations later in your studies.

- **Communication** – An organisation that shares ideas can be more creative.

In the modern business environment, innovation efforts should be aimed at delivering the best possible customer experience. If customers like an organisation's innovations they may be more likely to give it their business.

The **process for setting innovation goals** might involve:

- Understanding customer needs
- Understanding the current customer experience
- Identifying gaps between customer needs and the current customer experience
- Identifying important issues that should be addressed by innovation

For example, if a business identifies that customers need a simple to use online shop and they are currently finding it difficult to use its online shop, the organisation should address this issue through innovation. The goal should be to ensure 'ease of use' for the website and innovations should be considered that help achieve this.

Section summary

Goals and **objectives** derive from and support the mission.

4 Organisational structure

4.1 Mintzberg's components of the organisation

Introduction

Mintzberg believes that **all** organisations can be analysed into five components, according to how they relate to the work of the organisation and how they prefer to co-ordinate.

Mintzberg's components of the organisation

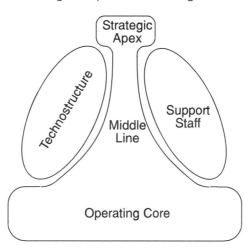

Component	Job	Preferred means of co-ordination
Top management (strategic apex)	Ensures the organisation follows its mission. Manages the organisation's relationship with the environment.	Direct supervision (especially in small businesses)
Technical (operating) core	People **directly** involved in the process of obtaining inputs, and converting them into outputs.	Mutual adjustment; standardisation of skills
Middle management (middle line)	Converts the desires of the strategic apex into the work done by the operating core.	Standardisation of outputs (results)
Technical support (technostructure)	• Analysers determine the best way of doing a job • Planners determine outputs (eg goods must achieve a specified level of quality) • Personnel analysts standardise skills (eg training programmes)	Standardisation of work processes or outputs
Administrative support (support staff)	Ancillary services such as public relations, legal counsel, the cafeteria. Support staff (such as IT staff) do not plan or standardise production. They function independently of the operating core.	Mutual adjustment

In most organisations, tasks and people are grouped together in some rational way: on the basis of specialisation, say, or shared technology or customer base. This is known as **departmentation**. Different patterns of departmentation are possible, and the pattern selected will depend on the individual circumstances of the organisation.

Six potential **organisational configurations** were identified by Mintzberg:

(a) **Simple structure**

In this structure the strategic apex is dominant. There is no formal structure and little planning. Control is exercised by direct supervision. A simple structure can be very effective in small, entrepreneurial organisations where flexibility is important, but they can be risky because they are heavily dependent on one person.

(b) **Machine bureaucracy**

In a machine bureaucracy, technostructure is dominant. Control is exercised through rules and procedures, and work is highly standardised. Machine bureaucracies are likely to have a hierarchical structure. This may be appropriate in a stable environment where the focus is on improving performance rather than solving problems.

(c) **Professional bureaucracy**

The operating core is dominant in a professional bureaucracy. Processes are too complex to be standardised, and so control is exercised via training, individuals' expertise and their professional ethos. Professional bureaucracies are common in professional firms and hospitals.

(d) **Divisionalised form**

In this structure the middle line is dominant. The organisation is too large or complex to be managed as one unit so is split into autonomous divisions. Control is exercised via performance measures such as profit. Each division may well be configured as a machine bureaucracy.

(e) **Adhocracy**

Support staff are dominant in an adhocracy, because they are the only group providing continuity. Innovation is critical and work tends to be project based. Teams with a mix of skills will form and disperse as required. There are few formal controls and work is complex and ambiguous. An example of an adhocracy could be a film production company.

(f) **Missionary organisations**

Missionary organisations have little structure or formal control but are held together by a shared set of values, reinforced in a strong culture. These beliefs are strong and there is a general aversion to compromising or changing them. They may be effective in simple or static business environments.

4.2 Functional departmentation

Introduction

Organisations can be **departmentalised** on a **functional** basis (with separate departments for production, marketing, finance etc), a **geographical** basis (by region or country), a **product** basis (eg worldwide divisions for product X, Y etc), a **brand** basis, or a **matrix** basis (eg someone selling product X in country A would report to both a product X manager and a country A manager). Organisation structures often feature a variety of these types, as **hybrid** structures.

Functional organisation involves grouping together people who do similar tasks. Primary functions in a manufacturing company might be production, sales, finance and general administration. Sub-departments of marketing might be market research, advertising, PR and so on.

Advantages include:

(a)   **Expertise is pooled** thanks to the division of work into specialist areas.

(b)   It **avoids duplication** (eg one management accounts department rather than several) and enables economies of scale.

(c)   It **facilitates** the recruitment, management and development of functional specialists.

(d)   It suits **centralised** businesses.

Disadvantages include:

(a)   It focuses on internal **processes** and **inputs**, rather than the **customer** and **outputs**, which are what ultimately drive a business. Inward-looking businesses are less able to adapt to changing demands.

(b)   **Communication problems** may arise between different functions, which each have their own jargon.

(c)   **Poor co-ordination**, especially if rooted in a tall organisation structure. Decisions by one function/department involving another might have to be referred upwards and dealt with at a higher level, thereby increasing the burdens on senior management.

(d)   Functional structures create **vertical barriers** to information and workflow. Management writer Peters suggests that customer service requires 'horizontal' flow between functions – rather than passing the customer from one functional department to another.

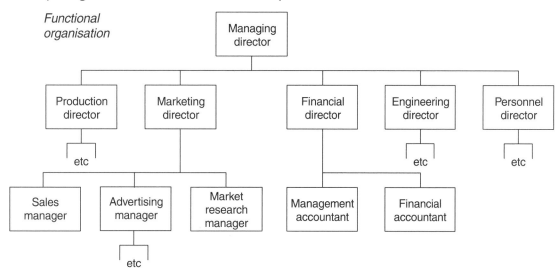

4.3 Geographical departmentation

Where the organisation is structured according to geographical area, some authority is retained at head office but day to day operations are handled on a **territorial** basis (eg Southern region, Western region). Many sales departments are organised territorially.

There are **advantages** to geographical departmentation:

(a)   There is **local decision making** at the point of contact between the organisation (eg a salesperson) and its customers, suppliers or other stakeholders.

(b)   It may be **cheaper** to establish area factories/offices than to service markets from one location (eg costs of transportation and travelling may be reduced).

But there are **disadvantages** too:

(a) **Duplication** and possible loss of economies of scale might arise. For example, a national organisation divided into ten regions might have a customer liaison department in each regional office. If the organisation did all customer liaison work from head office (centralised) it might need fewer managerial staff.

(b) **Inconsistency** in methods or standards may develop across different areas.

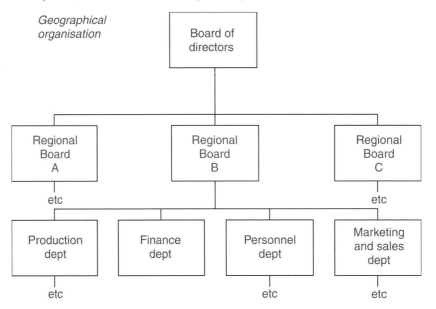

4.4 Product/brand departmentation

Some organisations group activities on the basis of **products** or product lines. Some functional departmentation remains (eg manufacturing, distribution, marketing and sales) but a divisional manager is given responsibility for the product or product line, with authority over personnel of different functions.

Advantages include:

(a) **Accountability**. Individual managers can be held accountable for the profitability of individual products.

(b) **Specialisation**. For example, some salespeople will be trained to sell a specific product in which they may develop technical expertise and thereby offer a better sales service to customers.

(c) **Co-ordination**. The different functional activities and efforts required to make and sell each product can be co-ordinated and integrated by the divisional/product manager.

Disadvantages include the following:

(a) It **increases the overhead costs** and managerial complexity of the organisation.

(b) Different product divisions may **fail to share resources** and customers.

A **brand** is the name (eg 'Persil') or design which identifies the products or services of a manufacturer or provider and distinguishes them from those of competitors. (Large organisations may produce a number of different brands of the same basic product, such as washing powder or toothpaste.) Branding brings the product to the attention of buyers and creates brand **recognition**, **differentiation** and **loyalty**: often customers do not realise that two 'rival' brands are in fact produced by the same manufacturer.

(a)   Because each brand is packaged, promoted and sold in a distinctive way, the need for specialisation may make brand departmentation effective. As with product departmentation, some functional departmentation remains but brand managers have responsibility for the brand's marketing and this can affect every function.

(b)   Brand departmentation has similar advantages/disadvantages to product departmentation.

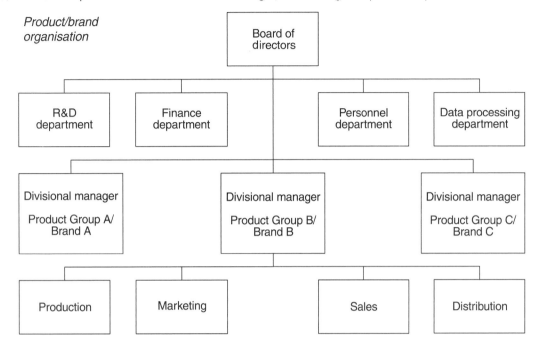

Product/brand organisation

4.5 Customer departmentation

An organisation may organise its activities on the basis of types of customer, or market segment.

(a)   Departmentation by customer is commonly associated with **sales departments** and selling effort, but it might also be used by a jobbing or contracting firm where a team of managers may be given the responsibility of liaising with major customers (eg discussing specifications and completion dates, quality of work, progress chasing).

(b)   Many businesses distinguish between **business customers** and **consumers**.

4.6 Divisionalisation

Introduction

In a **divisional structure** some activities are **decentralised** to business units or regions.

KEY TERM

DIVISIONALISATION is the division of a business into autonomous regions or product businesses, each with its own revenues, expenditures and capital asset purchase programmes, and therefore each with its own profit and loss responsibility.

Each division of the organisation might be:

*   A subsidiary company under the holding company
*   A profit centre or investment centre within a single company
*   A strategic business unit within the larger company, with its own objectives

Successful divisionalisation requires certain key conditions.

(a)   Each division must have **properly delegated authority**, and must be held properly accountable to head office (eg for profits earned).

(b)   Each unit must be **large enough** to support the quantity and quality of management it needs.

(c)   The unit must not rely on head office for excessive **management support**.

(d)   Each unit must have **potential for growth** in its own area of operations.

(e)   There should be **scope and challenge** in the job for the management of each unit.

(f)   If units deal with each other, it should be as an **'arm's length' transaction**.

The advantages and disadvantages of divisionalisation may be summarised as follows.

Advantages	Disadvantages
Focuses the attention of management below 'top level' on business performance.	In some businesses, it is impossible to identify completely independent products or markets for which separate divisions can be set up.
Reduces the likelihood of unprofitable products and activities being continued.	Divisionalisation is only possible at a fairly senior management level, because there is a limit to how much discretion can be used in the division of work. For example, every product needs a manufacturing function and a selling function.
Encourages a greater attention to efficiency, lower costs and higher profits.	There may be more resource problems. Many divisions get their resources from head office in competition with other divisions.
Gives more authority to junior managers, and so grooms them for more senior positions in the future (planned managerial succession).	
Reduces the number of levels of management. The top executives in each division should be able to report directly to the Chief Executive of the holding company.	

4.7 Hybrid structures

Organisation structures are rarely composed of only one type of organisation. 'Hybrid' structures may involve a mix of functional departmentation, ensuring specialised attention to key functions, with elements of (for example):

(a)   Product organisation, to suit the requirements of brand marketing or production technologies

(b)   Customer organisation, particularly in marketing departments, to service key accounts

(c)   Territorial organisation, particularly of sales and distribution departments, to service local requirements for marketing or distribution in dispersed regions or countries

4.8 The simple structure (or entrepreneurial structure)

The strategic apex exerts a pull to centralise, leading to the **simple structure**.

The **strategic apex** wishes to retain control over decision making, and so exercises what Mintzberg describes as a **pull to centralise**. Mintzberg believes that this leads to a **simple structure**.

Simple structure

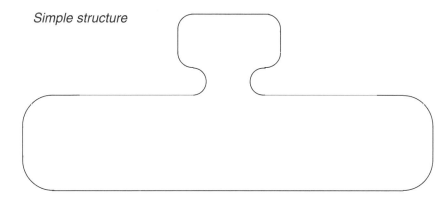

(a)   **The simple structure is characteristic of small, young organisations**. The strategic apex is a small group, or possibly one person, which exercises direct control over the people making up the operating core. There is little, if any, role for technical or support staff.

(b)   In small firms, a single entrepreneur or management team will dominate (as in the power culture). If it grows, the organisation might need more managerial skills than the apex can provide. Strategies might be made on the basis of the manager's hunches.

(c)   Centralisation is advantageous as it reflects management's full knowledge of the operating core and its processes. However, senior managers might intervene too much.

(d)   It is risky as it depends on the expertise of one person. Such an organisation might be prone to **succession crises**. This problem is often encountered in family businesses.

(e)   This structure can handle an environment that is relatively simple but fast moving, where standardisation cannot be used to co-ordinate activities.

(f)   **Co-ordination is achieved by direct supervision**, with few formal devices. It is thus flexible.

(g)   This structure has its own particular characteristics: wide span of control; no middle line and hence minimal hierarchy; and no technostructure, implying little formalisation or standardisation of behaviour.

4.9 Matrix and project organisation

Where hybrid organisation 'mixes' organisation types, **matrix** organisation actually **crosses** functional and product/customer/project organisation.

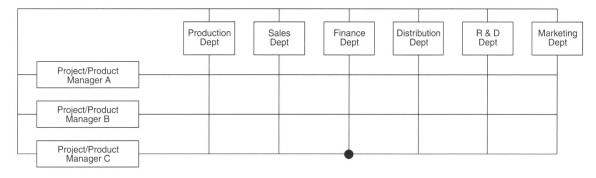

The employees represented by the dot in the above diagram, for example, are responsible to:

•   The finance manager for their work in accounting and finance for their functional department; and

•   The project manager C for their work on the project team: budgeting, management reporting and payroll relevant to the project, say.

Advantages of matrix organisation include:

(a) Greater **flexibility** of:

    (i) **People**. Employees develop an attitude geared to accepting change, and departmental monopolies are broken down.

    (ii) **Workflow and decision making**. Direct contact between staff encourages problem solving and big-picture thinking.

    (iii) **Tasks and structure**. The matrix structure may be readily amended, once projects are completed.

(b) **Interdisciplinary co-operation** and a mixing of skills and expertise, along with **improved communication** and **co-ordination**.

(c) **Motivation and employee development**: providing employees with greater participation in planning and control decisions.

(d) **Market awareness**: the organisation tends to become more customer/quality focused.

(e) **Horizontal workflow**: bureaucratic obstacles are removed, and department specialisms become less powerful.

There are **disadvantages**, however:

(a) **Dual authority** threatens a **conflict** between functional managers and product/project/area managers.

(b) An individual with two or more bosses may suffer stress from **conflicting demands** or **ambiguous roles**.

(c) **Cost**: product management posts are added, meetings have to be held, and so on.

(d) **Decision making is slower** due to the added complexity.

4.10 The new organisation

Some recent trends have emerged from the focus on **flexibility** as a key organisational value. There is a general trend to become **boundaryless** – this means to minimise or eliminate formality and chains of command to focus on speed and flexibility.

Key types of **boundaryless organisation** are: virtual, modular and hollow.

(a) **Virtual organisations**

    The organisation may consist of individuals, teams, companies or stakeholders. Members are geographically dispersed and the organisation usually only exists electronically on the internet, without any physical premises. For example, Amazon operates as a virtual store without incurring the cost of retail premises. We shall look at virtual organisations in more detail later in your studies.

(b) **Modular organisations**

    These organisations break the manufacturing process down into modules or components which are then either made by the business, or their production is outsourced. For example, a TV manufacturer may split production down into the screen, power supply, hardware, software and remote control. The organisation may manufacture each component or outsource their production and just assemble the finished product itself.

(c) **Hollow organisations**

    Hollow organisations split their activities into core and non-core. Core activities are strategically important and are kept in-house. Non-core activities are not strategically important and are outsourced.

Other types of new organisation include the following:

(a) **Flat structures**. The flattening of hierarchies does away with levels of organisation which lengthened lines of communication and decision making. Flat structures are more responsive because there is a more direct relationship between the organisation's strategic centre and the operational units serving the customer.

(b) **Horizontal structures'**. There is increased recognition that functional versatility (through multi-functional project teams and multiskilling, for example) is the key to flexibility.

(c) **Chunked and unglued structures**. So far, this has meant team working and decentralisation, or empowerment, creating smaller and more flexible units within the overall structure.

(d) **Output-focused structures**. The key to all the above trends is the focus on results, and on the customer, instead of internal processes and functions for their own sake.

(e) **Jobless structures**. The employee becomes not a jobholder but a seller of skills. This is a concrete expression of the concept of **employability**, which says that a person needs to have a portfolio of skills which are valuable on the open labour market; employees need to be mobile, moving between organisations.

4.11 The shamrock organisation

Largely driven by pressure to reduce personnel costs, there has been an increase in the use of part-time and temporary contracts of employment. These allow rapid downsizing in times of recession or slow growth and can save on the costs of benefits such as pensions, holiday pay and health insurance. The growth in the proportion of the workforce employed on such less-favourable contracts has attracted political attention but continues. It has produced the phenomenon of the **flexible firm** or, as Handy calls it, the **shamrock organisation**.

KEY TERM

Handy defines the SHAMROCK ORGANISATION as a 'core of essential executives and workers supported by outside contractors and part-time help'. This structure permits the buying-in of services as needed, with consequent reductions in overhead costs. It is also known as the FLEXIBLE FIRM.

Shamrock organisation

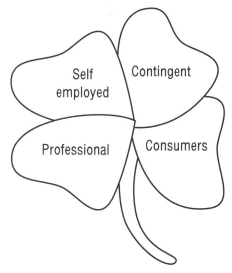

Professional core

The first leaf of the shamrock is the **professional core**. It consists of professionals, technicians and managers whose skills define the organisation's core competence. This core group defines what the company does and what business it is in. They are essential to the continuity and growth of the organisation. Their pay is tied to organisational performance and their relations will be more like those among the partners in a professional firm than those among superiors and subordinates in today's large corporation.

Self-employed professionals

The next leaf is made up of **self-employed professionals or technicians** or smaller specialised organisations that are hired on contract, on a project by project basis. They are paid in fees for results rather than in salary for time. They frequently **telecommute**. No benefits are paid by the core organisation, and the worker carries the risk of insecurity.

Contingent workforce

The third leaf comprises the **contingent workforce**, whose employment derives from the external demand for the organisation's products. There is no career track for these people and they perform routine jobs. They are usually temporary and part-time workers who will experience short periods of employment and long periods of unemployment. They are paid by the hour or day or week for the time they work.

Consumers

A fourth leaf of the shamrock may exist, consisting of **consumers** who do the work of the organisation. Examples are shoppers who bag their own groceries and purchasers of assemble it yourself furniture.

This type of organisation provides three kinds of flexibility:

(a) **Personnel costs** can respond to market conditions of supply and demand for different types of labour and to the employer's financial position.

(b) Overall **personnel numbers** can be changed as required.

(c) The **skills** available can be modified fairly rapidly and multiskilling can be encouraged.

4.12 Span of control

Introduction

Span of control or **'span of management'** refers to the number of subordinates responsible to a superior.

KEY TERM

The SPAN OF CONTROL refers to the number of subordinates immediately reporting to a superior official.

In other words, if a manager has five subordinates, the span of control is five.

A number of factors influence the span of control:

(a) A manager's **capabilities** limit the span of control: there are physical and mental limitations to any single manager's ability to control people and activities.

(b) The **nature of the manager's workload**

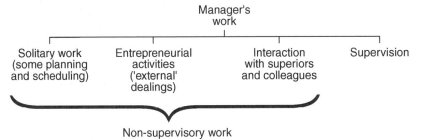

The more non-supervisory work in a manager's workload:

(i) The narrower the span of control
(ii) The greater the delegation of authority to subordinates

(c) The **geographical dispersion** of subordinates: dispersed teams require more effort to supervise.

(d) The **type of work** and **skills** of the **subordinates**: both repetitive work and highly skilled or motivated subordinates allow for a wider span of control. Simple work is easier to supervise, while with highly skilled or motivated subordinates the manager can place greater reliance on them to do their job and they therefore require less supervision.

4.13 Tall and flat organisations

Introduction

Recent trends have been towards **delayering** organisations of levels of management. In other words, **tall organisations** (with many management levels and narrow spans of control) are turning into **flat organisations** (with fewer management levels and wider spans of control) as a result of technological changes and the granting of more decision-making power to front-line employees.

The span of control concept has implications for the length of the **scalar chain**.

KEY TERMS

The SCALAR CHAIN is the chain of command from the most senior to the most junior.

A TALL ORGANISATION is one which, in relation to its size, has a large number of levels of management hierarchy. This implies a **narrow** span of control.

A FLAT ORGANISATION is one which, in relation to its size, has a small number of hierarchical levels. This implies a **wide** span of control.

Exam alert

The definitions of all the key terms above could easily be tested in a multiple choice question.

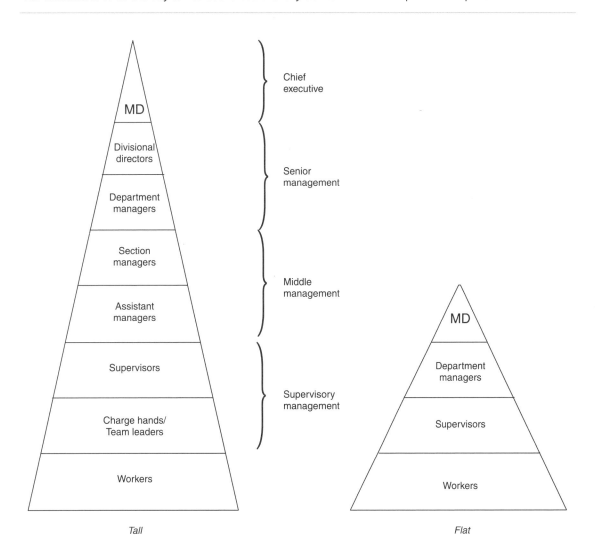

Tall   Flat

The advantages and disadvantages of these organisational forms can be summarised as follows.

Tall organisation

For	Against
Narrow control spans	Inhibits delegation
Small groups enable team members to participate in decisions	Rigid supervision can be imposed, blocking initiative
A large number of steps on the promotional ladders – assists management training and career planning	The same work passes through too many hands
	Increases administration and overhead costs
	Slow decision making and responses, as the strategic apex is further away

Flat organisation

For	Against
More opportunity for delegation	Requires that jobs **can** be delegated. Managers may only get a superficial idea of what goes on. If they are overworked they are more likely to be involved in crisis management
Relatively cheap	Sacrifices control
In theory, speeds up communication between strategic apex and operating core	Middle managers are often necessary to convert the grand vision of the strategic apex into operational terms

4.14 Delayering

KEY TERM

DELAYERING is the reduction of the number of management levels from bottom to top.

Many organisations are delayering. Middle line jobs are vanishing. Organisations are increasing the average span of control, reducing management levels and becoming flatter.

(a) **Information technology**. This reduces the need for middle managers to process information.

(b) **Empowerment**. Many organisations, especially service businesses, are keen to delegate authority down the line to the lowest possible level. Front-line workers in the operating core are allowed to take decisions, in order to increase responsiveness to customer demands. This perhaps removes the need for some middle management jobs.

(c) **Economy**. Delayering reduces managerial/supervisory costs.

(d) **Fashion**. Delayering is fashionable; if senior managers believe that tall structures are inherently inflexible, they might cut the number of management levels.

4.15 Choosing a structure

It should be remembered that no single model of organisation is suitable for all purposes. Robert Daft identified contextual and structural dimensions that influence organisational structure and design.

Contextual dimensions include:

(a) **Technology**

Technology allows workers to perform their duties from different geographical locations and collaborate with different groups of employees. Therefore, it supports geographical and matrix structures as well as virtualisation and remote working.

(b)   **Environment**

The industry that the organisation operates in will affect its structure. For example, managers will see how competitors are organised and, if successful, they may decide to adopt the same model. PEST factors (political, economic, social and technological factors) will all have an influence. We shall consider PESTEL in more detail later in your studies.

(c)   **Culture and formalisation**

The organisation's history and culture and the degree of formality present will affect the choice of corporate structure because any change may be resisted by employees.

In cultures where there is little formality and employees are granted a high degree of flexibility in their work, employees may find it difficult to change to a more formal structure because they will have less freedom. On the other hand, workers who are used to a high degree of formality and structure in their culture may find it difficult to adapt to being given flexibility because they are not used to acting autonomously and having greater responsibility.

Formalisation also relates to the extent to which policies and procedures are used within the organisation.

Structural dimensions include:

(a)   **Business size and type**

Organisational size and type will in many ways primarily determine structure. Geographical and divisional structures are mainly suited to very large businesses (such as large companies and multinationals) that can support them. Small organisations (such as sole traders, partnerships and small companies) do not have enough employees and departments to require being organised on a geographical or divisional scale.

On the other hand, functional and matrix structures may not be appropriate for large organisations because they can make lines of command and business processes more complicated, especially as many different business areas will be trying to work together.

(b)   **Specialisation**

Some organisations are highly specialised; in other words, they only perform a small number of processes. In highly specialised businesses, such as those producing bespoke software for local businesses, a more functional approach might be appropriate. There is no need for divisions or geographical structures because operations are very simple. A matrix structure might also be appropriate if staff work on a number of projects at once.

Local conditions and the **scale of operations** will also influence the organisational structure of companies. Very large and complex companies may be organised as a **heterarchy**. A heterarchy is a rather **organic structure** with significant local control.

(a)   **Some headquarters' functions are diffused geographically**. For example, R&D might be based in the UK, marketing based in the US. Or certain products might be made in one country and others elsewhere (motor manufacturers do not make every model of car at each factory). Some central functions might be split up – organisations may experiment with having several centres for R&D.

(b)   **Subsidiary managers have a strategic role for the corporation as a whole** (eg through bargaining and coalition forming).

(c)   **Co-ordination is achieved through corporate culture and shared values** rather than a formal hierarchy. Experienced employees might have worked in a number of different product divisions.

(d)   **Alliances** can be formed with other parts of the company and with other businesses, perhaps in joint ventures or consortia.

4.15.1 Assessing proposed structures

Goold and Campbell propose nine tests that may be used to assess proposed structures. The first four relate to the organisation's **objectives** and the **restraints** under which it operates.

(a) **Market advantage**: Where processes must be closely co-ordinated in order to achieve market advantage, they should be in the same structural element.

(b) **Parenting advantage**: The structure should support the parenting role played by the corporate centre. For example, a 'portfolio manager' would need only a small, low-cost corporate centre.

(c) **People test**: The structure must be suited to the skills and experience of the people that have to function within it. For example, skilled professionals used to a team working approach might be frustrated by a move to a functional hierarchy.

(d) **Feasibility test**: This test sweeps up all other constraints, such as those imposed by law, stakeholder opinion and resource availability.

The tests forming the second group are matters of **design principle**.

(a) **Specialised cultures**: Specialists should be able to collaborate closely.

(b) **Difficult links**: It is highly likely that some interdepartmental links will be subject to friction and strain. A good example would be the link between sales and production when there are frequent problems over quality and delivery. A sound structure will embody measures to strengthen communication and co-operation in such cases.

(c) **Redundant hierarchy**: The structure should be as flat as is reasonably attainable.

(d) **Accountability**: Effective control requires clear lines of accountability.

(e) **Flexibility**: The structure must allow for requirements to change in the future, so that unexpected opportunities can be seized, for example.

Section summary

There are several types of organisational structure, including functional, divisional, matrix and geographical.

Factors such as technology, environment, culture, organisational size, formalisation, specialisation and type will impact on organisational structure.

---

5 Types of system

Introduction

An **open** system has a relationship with its environment which has both prescribed and uncontrolled elements. A **closed** system is shut off from its environment and has no relationship with it.

5.1 Open systems and closed systems

One view of a business is that it is a system. In systems theory a distinction is made between open systems and closed systems.

KEY TERM

A CLOSED SYSTEM is a system which is isolated from its environment and independent of it. No environmental influences affect the behaviour of the system, nor does the system exert any influence on its environment.

Some scientific systems might be described as closed systems. An example of a closed system is a chemical reaction in a sealed, insulated container. Another is the operation of a thermostat. However, all **social** systems, including business organisations, have some interaction with their environment, and so cannot be closed systems.

KEY TERM

An OPEN SYSTEM is a system connected to and interacting with its environment. It takes in influences (or 'energy') from its environment and also influences this environment by its behaviour (it exports energy).

Open and closed systems can be described by a diagram as follows.

Closed system

Shut off from its environment

Open system

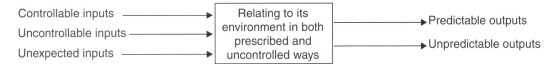

Controllable inputs	→	Relating to its environment in both prescribed and uncontrolled ways	→	Predictable outputs
Uncontrollable inputs	→		→	Unpredictable outputs
Unexpected inputs	→			

For example, a **business** is an open system where management decisions are influenced by or have an influence on suppliers, customers, competitors, society as a whole and the Government.

Employees are obviously influenced by what they do in their job, but as members of society at large they are also a part of the **environment**, just as their views and opinions expressed within the business are often a reflection of their opinions as members of society at large.

Every system has a boundary. An open system will have considerable cross-influences with its environment **across its boundary**, whereas a closed system's boundary would shut it off from its environment.

5.1.1 Semi-closed systems

Some writers also refer to semi-closed systems. A semi-closed system interfaces with the environment and reacts in a predictable, controlled way. This differs from an open system, as open systems interact with the environment in both a controlled and an uncontrolled way.

Semi-closed system

| Predictable inputs | → | PROCESS | → | Predictable outputs |

5.2 Feedback control and feedforward control systems

5.2.1 Feedback control systems

Feedback control systems describe the situation where part of system output is returned (fed back) as an input. An example is an accounting budgetary control system as the output (eg variance analysis) may result in changes to input and/or processes.

5.2.2 Feedforward control systems

Feedforward control systems involve the monitoring of the environment, the process and the output – and taking any corrective action on the basis of these factors.

This involves a predictive element as the corrective action is based on both current and future events.

5.3 Feedback control loops

The term 'feedback control loop' describes a situation where feedback is gathered and then used to influence future performance (ie exercise control) by adjusting input.

5.3.1 A single feedback loop

Single loop feedback follows a 'simple' path comparing actual results against expected results.

5.3.2 A double feedback loop

Double loop feedback involves making changes to the actual plans or systems as a result of changes in both internal and external conditions.

Single and double loop feedback

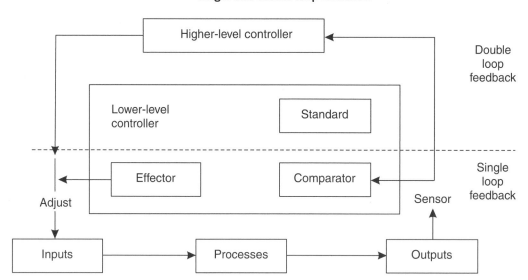

The diagram includes other elements of systems theory as explained in the table below.

Element	Description
Sensor	Measuring or recording device – may be an automated or manual checking process.
Comparator	Compares the actual result (obtained by the sensor) against the plan (or standard).
Effector	This is usually a manager or supervisor acting on the comparison by issuing new instructions relating to input.

If a higher-level controller is involved (ie double feedback loop) this would usually be senior management who revise plans, budgets and the control systems themselves.

5.4 Horizontal and vertical structures

Some organisations decide to **expand their boundaries** into the **external environment** by becoming horizontally or vertically integrated.

Horizontal integration makes use of an organisation's current capabilities by developing into activities that are competitive with or directly **complementary** to a company's present activities. An example would be a TV company that moved into film production.

Vertical integration occurs when a company expands backwards or forwards within its existing value network and therefore becomes its own supplier or distributor. For example, **backward integration** would occur if a milk processing business acquired its own dairy farms rather than buying raw milk from independent farmers. If a cloth manufacturer began to produce shirts instead of selling all its cloth to other shirt manufacturers, that would be **forward integration**.

Vertical integration has its greatest potential for success when **the final customer's needs are not being properly satisfied**. If there is potential for improving the satisfaction of the end-user by improving the links in the value network, then an integration strategy may succeed. Examples would be where there is a premium on speed, as in the marketing of fresh foodstuffs, or when complex technical features require great attention to quality procedures.

Note vertical integration could have significant benefits for **supply chain management**. We will look at supply chain management in more detail later in this Study Text.

Section summary

Organisations can be viewed as open or closed systems.

Horizontal and vertical integration are methods for businesses to expand.

6 Alliances

Introduction

A business may enter into various types of alliance with other businesses, creating business structures in the form of joint ventures, licences, strategic alliances, agency or a group structure.

There are various ways in which businesses (of whatever legal business structure: sole trader, partnership or company) can work together.

6.1 Joint venture

This involves **forming a separate business** in which the businesses take a financial stake (often as a shareholder) and management is provided as agreed.

Advantages of joint ventures

- Lower capital demands, and risk, than if the organisation enters the venture on its own
- Enables the business to gain access to restricted markets
- Provides the organisation with access to the skills that it would otherwise have no access to

Disadvantages of joint ventures

- Arguments over how the business should operate, the costs incurred, management style

- The special skills of the venture may be used against the organisation by its former joint venture partner if the relationship breaks down

6.2 Licences and franchises

Licensing is the granting of permission to another company to manufacture or sell a product, or to use a brand name. Licences are often restricted geographically by the licensor so they can control where the product is sold, and can prevent competition with their own products or those of other licensees.

Many soft and alcoholic drinks are manufactured under licence from the major drink brands in the country in which they are to be sold.

A common form of licensing agreement is the **franchise**. In a franchise, the franchisee pays the franchisor an initial sum as an investment which is followed by an annual fee and sometimes a share of the profits or royalties. In return, the franchisee is permitted to sell the franchisor's products or provide their services. The franchisor usually provides marketing and other advice and support and in return the franchisee is usually required to make a minimum order for goods from the franchisor.

The franchisee is also usually required to follow strict rules when doing business in order to protect the franchisor's brand; however, they are usually buying into a successful business model and so this is a price worth paying.

Fast food chains are a common example of the franchise model.

6.3 Strategic alliances

Strategic alliances are contractual agreements between parties and are similar to joint ventures, although normally no separate company is formed. Examples include national airlines that have created alliances to cross-book passengers.

There are **seven characteristics** of a well-arranged **strategic alliance**:

(1) **Synergy** – The organisations are stronger by working together.

(2) **Risk reduction** – The risks of the venture are shared and therefore each party reduces their risk.

(3) **Co-operation** – The organisations must want the venture to work.

(4) **Clarity** – Goals, milestones, results and methods must be communicated and clearly understood by all parties.

(5) **Positioning opportunity** – One of the parties should gain a market leadership position (such as gaining access to materials or markets, or selling new products that it otherwise would not be able to).

(6) **Complementary attributes** – The strengths and weaknesses of one party should complement those of the other party (for example, corporate cultures should be compatible).

(7) **Win–win** – The risks and rewards and share of the work should be fairly split between the parties.

The advantages and disadvantages are similar to those of joint ventures, although the agreement is looser and is easier to break and there is generally less commitment involved.

6.4 Agents

The use of agents can be effective as a distribution channel where local knowledge and contacts are important. The agent acts for the business in a certain geographical location. Agency agreements may be restricted to marketing and product support. The main issue for a business that uses agents is that it is cut off from direct contact with the customer.

6.5 Outsourcing, shared service centres and business process outsourcing

Outsourcing is the relocation of some part of an organisation's activities to another business, for example a customer service team being outsourced from Europe to Asia. However, outsourcing can also be to another company within the same country as well.

Shared service centres (SSCs) is the use of a single location (an SSE) to consolidate the organisation's transaction processing activities.

Business process outsourcing is the use of third-party organisations to perform some of the operations or responsibilities of a specific business function (or process), for example, where a soft drink manufacturer contracts out the production of its product to third parties in different countries.

We shall look at these concepts in more detail when we look at the finance function and outsourcing of information systems.

Section summary

Alliances are an alternative method for organisations to do business.

Chapter Summary

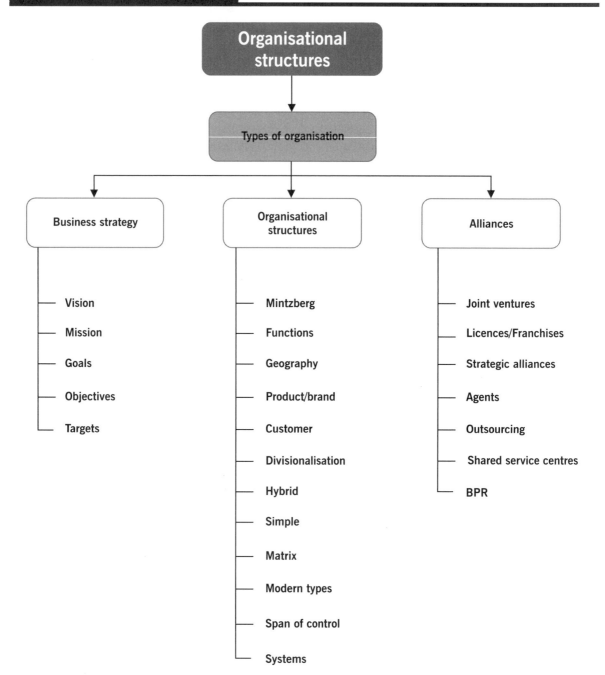

Quick Quiz

1   Which type of business is owned by its customers?

    A   Public company
    B   Private company
    C   Mutual company
    D   Multinational company

2   Which part of Mintzberg's organisation is described below?

    'The people directly involved in the process of obtaining inputs, and converting them into outputs.'

    A   Strategic apex
    B   Technostructure
    C   Operating core
    D   Middle line

3   What is 'span of control'?

    A   The number of departments in a division
    B   The number of subordinates responsible to a superior
    C   The number of products produced at a specific location
    D   The number of managers a worker reports to

4   A car manufacturer decides to produce metal that is used in its cars.

    This is an example of:

    A   Forward vertical integration
    B   Backwards vertical integration
    C   Forward horizontal integration
    D   Backwards horizontal integration

5   A franchise operation is an example of which of the following?

    A   A licensing arrangement
    B   A joint venture
    C   A strategic alliance
    D   An agency agreement

Answers to Quick Quiz

1   C   Mutuals are owned by their customers.

2   C   The description is that of the operating core.

3   B   Span of control refers to the number of subordinates responsible to a superior.

4   B   Producing materials used in a production process is an example of backwards vertical integration.

5   A   Franchising is an example of licensing.

Now try these questions from the Practice Question Bank	Number
	1, 2, 3, 4, 5

ETHICS, CORPORATE GOVERNANCE AND SOCIAL RESPONSIBILITY

In this chapter we consider the impact of three topical areas – **ethics**, **corporate governance** and **corporate social responsibility**. These are concepts that we will come back to several times throughout this Study Text.

Governments have a key role to play in the economy and development of a nation. The decisions they make and the policies they establish all have an effect on an organisation's business environment.

Government influence is usually associated with **economic policy** but, as we shall see, governments also affect a market through **regulation**.

Topic list	Learning outcomes	Syllabus references	Ability required
1 Government intervention in business	A2(a)	A2(iv)	analysis
2 Government and growth	A2(a)	A2(iv)	analysis
3 Institutions involved in global trade and growth	A2(a)	A2(vi)	analysis
4 Market regulation	A2(a)	A2(v)	analysis
5 Corporate governance	A2(a)	A2(i)	analysis
6 Ethical behaviour	A2(a)	A2(ii), A2(vii)	analysis
7 Corporate social responsibility (CSR)	A2(a)	A2(iii)	analysis

Chapter Overview

1 Government intervention in business

Introduction

In this chapter we consider how governments influence their economies and the competitive environment of organisations.

A country's **government** has a major role to play in the success or failure of its economy. We have already seen how it can influence a number of factors related to competitive advantage and foreign investment but these are only part of the story. Governments can **influence** a number of other areas:

- The macroeconomic environment
- Legal and market regulation
- Corporate governance and social responsibility

Section summary

Government influence over business extends to the **macroeconomic environment**, **legal** and **market regulations**, **corporate governance** and **social responsibility**.

2 Government and growth

Introduction

The **macroeconomic environment** is concerned with factors in the **overall economy**, for example interest rates and tax.

A government will usually have the following **objectives** for its **macroeconomic policy**:

- Economic growth
- Controlled inflation
- Employment

These objectives are affected by macroeconomic policy and, in particular, **fiscal and monetary policy**.

2.1 Growth, inflation and employment

Three key factors that indicate the strength of an economy are growth, inflation and employment.

2.1.1 Growth

Growth means the **expansion of the economy** and it is usually measured in percentage terms compared to previous years. It is the product of a number of factors, the main factor being **demand** in the economy. Demand from consumers and the Government for goods and services **stimulates business organisations** to increase production and sell more.

Growth can be measured using two figures: gross domestic product (GDP) and gross national product (GNP). **GDP** is the total value of a nation's income produced by economic activity from within its borders. **GNP** is a more complete figure than GDP because it also includes income earned overseas but deducts income earned domestically by overseas residents.

An effect of growth is that **employment levels rise** as more employees are required to produce the goods and services, and those employed should **enjoy increasing wages**. This means the cycle of demand is continued as consumer demand increases further. **'Real'** growth is net of the nation's inflation rate and therefore growth must exceed inflation for any benefits to be created.

Despite the positive aspects of growth, it is not without **issues**. If demand for goods cannot be met by what can be produced within the economy, then the amount of imported goods will rise to fill the gap, worsening the nation's **balance of trade**. Growth may also increase the **gap between the rich and the poor** if its effects are unevenly distributed across the population. The **environment** and the **poor may be exploited** by businesses taking advantage of commercial opportunities. For example, natural resources may be increasingly used up in the production of goods and low-paid workers may be forced to work harder as production levels rise. Finally, growth may occur in unwelcome areas, such as in the trade of illegal substances.

2.1.2 Inflation

Inflation is the **increase in prices over time** and, like growth, is measured in percentage terms compared to previous years. Governments seek low, stable inflation for a number of reasons:

(a)   Stable inflation creates certainty – the ideal condition for business investment.

(b)   Low inflation levels are fairer to those on low or fixed incomes. If incomes increase at a lower rate than the inflation rate then individuals will be worse off.

(c)   If the inflation rate is greater than interest rates then savers will be worse off as they see the value of their savings being eroded. Individuals are encouraged to spend rather than save.

(d)   Higher prices reduce the amount of money individuals have to spend and therefore spending within the economy falls. This may encourage savings to increase (the 'real balance' effect).

(e)   Inflation acts to distort the price mechanism as prices are driven increasingly by cost rather than true demand and supply factors.

(f)   In extreme cases, soaring inflation rates, where prices rise on a daily basis, can create civil unrest.

2.1.3 Employment

Although some degree of unemployment within an economy is **unavoidable** (as some people are unable to work and others will be between jobs), governments are keen to increase the overall level of employment for a number of reasons:

(a)   Large numbers of unemployed people can stifle economic growth because being on a low income means an individual can afford to spend less and therefore demand within the economy falls.

(b)   Welfare payments to those out of work have to be paid out of taxes collected from the working population. High levels of unemployment increase the welfare bill, resulting in pressure to increase taxes and cut back on other public services – both of which will harm economic growth.

(c)   A number of societal problems, such as crime, poor health and the breakdown of family units, are linked to unemployment.

2.2 Fiscal policy

KEY TERM

FISCAL POLICY refers to government policy on taxation and government spending.

Fiscal policy is based on the theories of British economist John Maynard Keynes. Keynesian economics is based around the theory that governments can influence macroeconomic productivity levels by increasing or decreasing tax levels and public spending.

The aim, generally, is to keep inflation relatively low (for example, in the UK, the Bank of England has set an annual inflation target of 2%) while maintaining high employment levels. This is a balancing act, as stimulating a stagnant economy to increase demand and employment may result in a decrease in the value of money – inflation.

2.2.1 Taxation

KEY TERMS

DIRECT TAXES are levied on earnings or profits, for example income tax for individuals and corporation tax for companies. Taxes may also be raised on unearned income such as dividends, or special one-off taxes may be brought in for particular purposes. Direct tax is often viewed as progressive (as higher earners tend to pay more tax), simple and easy to understand.

INDIRECT TAXES are levied on spending or expenditure – for example, value-added tax, specific sales taxes such as those imposed on tobacco and petrol, import duties and road tax. Governments favour indirect taxation as it is easy and cheap to collect. The tax is collected by sellers of goods and services and paid over to the Government. However, indirect taxes are often viewed by the public as regressive, unfair and difficult to understand.

A key decision that governments need to make in their fiscal policy is what **proportion of tax** should be paid by **individuals** rather than **businesses**.

By **mainly taxing individuals** the Government risks stopping the economy growing as people do not have enough disposable income to spend on goods and services; this will also reduce company profits and reduce the level of corporation tax collected.

If levels of **corporation tax** are too high then the country may become a less attractive place for foreign companies to set up business and they may relocate their operations to other countries with a more favourable tax regime. This may have an effect on the products and services available in the country as well as on growth and unemployment levels.

The second key decision that is required is what **proportion of tax** should come from **direct** and **indirect taxes**.

Indirect taxation is generally cheaper for the Government to administer as the cost of collecting and paying the tax is a burden on business organisations, but it will increase inflation since it increases the cost of goods and services. It is also generally more popular with the public than direct tax, as they feel that they have a choice of whether to incur it (by deciding whether or not to buy goods subject to the tax). It becomes unpopular where all goods and services are subject to indirect taxation and it is impossible to avoid.

Direct taxation is generally unpopular with the general population as they see that their income is reduced. This reduction in income helps to reduce inflation by reducing demand but it is expensive for the Government to administer and sometimes requires complex laws and regulations to be introduced.

2.3 Monetary policy

KEY TERM

MONETARY POLICY refers to government policy on the money supply, the monetary system, interest rates, and the availability of credit.

Monetary policy can be used as a means of achieving economic objectives for inflation, the balance of trade and economic growth. Most economists believe that an increase in the money supply will increase demand leading to increases in prices (inflation) and incomes.

2.3.1 Interest rates

The Government may change **interest rates** (the price of money) in an attempt to influence the level of expenditure in the economy and/or the rate of inflation.

A rise in interest rates increases the price of borrowing for both companies and individuals. If companies see the rise as relatively permanent, rates of return on investments will become less attractive and **investment plans may be curtailed**. Corporate profits will fall as a result of higher interest payments. Companies will reduce inventory levels as the cost of having money tied up in stocks rises.

Individuals should be expected to reduce or postpone consumption in order to reduce borrowings, and should become less willing to borrow for house purchases.

Although it is generally accepted that there is likely to be a connection between interest rates and investment (by companies) and consumer expenditure, the connection is **not a stable and predictable one**. Interest rate changes are only likely to affect the level of expenditure after a **considerable time lag**.

The table below explains some **impacts of a rise in interest rates**.

Impact	Comment
Spending falls	Higher interest rates increase the cost of credit. The higher interest rate makes it more attractive to hold money than to spend it.
Investment falls	The higher rate will increase the opportunity cost of investment (for example in new projects) and reduce the net present value of the investment. This will discourage organisations from investing.
	The increased interest rates will make borrowing more expensive.
Foreign funds are attracted into the country	Interest rates are the reward for capital, so a rise in interest rates will encourage overseas currency investors because of the increased rate of return relative to other countries.
Exchange rate rises	The inflow of foreign funds (above) increases the demand for the home currency and therefore strengthens the exchange rate making exports more expensive and imports cheaper.
Inflation rate falls	This is often the main goal of an interest rate rise. The reduction in spending and investment will reduce aggregate demand in the economy.
	The stronger exchange rate means imported goods will be cheaper.

An increase in interest rates will have a **deflationary** impact on the economy.

Note, however, the **potential conflicting objectives** which monetary policy faces. A change in interest rates will have effects on both the domestic economy and a country's international trade position (for example through exchange rate movements).

It may be the case that the interest rate movement required for the domestic economy **conflicts** with that required to achieve a balance on the external current account.

2.4 Corporate political activity

Corporate political activity is another aspect of business–government relations that has become increasingly important in recent years.

KEY POINT

Corporate political activity (CPA) refers to the involvement of companies in the political process with the aim of influencing policies towards their preferences. Common activities include lobbying and donating to political party campaigns.

Corporate political activities are generally used by companies to attempt to gain competitive advantage and can be classified into two types, **buffering** and **bridging**.

(a)   **Buffering** refers to proactive actions such as warning the Government about the impact of legislation while it's being considered, in an attempt to **influence** the content.

(b)   **Bridging** is more reactive and focuses more on ensuring the firm is aware of and meets required standards of behaviour, for example ensuring the company is aware of proposed new legislation and **complies** with it when it is passed.

Organisations may need to **deal with governments** and make their policy preferences known in a number of situations.

Examples include:

(a) **Multinational companies** (MNCs) from developed countries may negotiate terms for their investment in that country, for example finance, taxation and export agreements.

(b) **Multinationals** may **lobby governments** to **provide conditions** in the economy that benefit them, for example reducing restrictions or controls over labour such as working hours and minimum wages. The MNC may threaten to withdraw its investment if the Government fails to agree.

(c) **New industries** in **developing nations** may **seek protection** from their government, for example import restrictions.

(d) **Developing industries** may seek **government support** such as subsidies or tax breaks to help them compete in the global market.

There is a difference in **CPA** between businesses in **developed** and **developing nations**.

In **developed nations**, CPA is well organised, with large organisations nurturing close relationships with relevant government departments. Businesses often have special government liaison departments to foster their relationships. There are also organisations set up to **lobby** government on behalf of interested parties. Examples of lobby groups in the UK are Chambers of Commerce, the Confederation of British Industry, the Institute of Directors and the Federation of Small Businesses.

This contrasts with **developing nations** where relationships are not so subtly managed. Businesses are often more direct in approaching individual policy makers, government departments and politicians to put across their needs. In some instances, those with the power to make government policy may be subjected to bribery, corruption and threats.

Section summary

Fiscal policy refers to government policy on taxation and government spending.

Monetary policy refers to government policy on money supply, the monetary system, interest rates, exchange rates and the availability of credit. It can directly affect a nation's balance of trade.

Corporate political activity (CPA) refers to the involvement of companies in the political process with the aim of influencing policies towards their preferences.

3 Institutions involved in global trade and growth

A number of institutions are involved in developing and managing global trade and creation of growth. These include the **World Trade Organization** (WTO), the **G8**, the **International Monetary Fund** (IMF), the **World Bank, European Bank for Reconstruction and Development** (EBRD) and **central banks**.

3.1 The World Trade Organization (WTO)

The **WTO** was formed in 1995 as successor to the General Agreement on Tariffs and Trade (GATT) which was set up after World War II in 1948. It is an organisation that devotes itself to international trade in goods, services, traded inventions, creations and intellectual property.

The WTO has over 150 members and these represent 97% of international trade. The organisation seeks to **promote the free flow of trade** by removing obstacles to trade, and to make sure that individuals, companies and governments know what these rules are. The WTO:

- Administers trade agreements
- Is a forum for developing new trade agreements
- Settles trade disputes
- Reviews national trade policies
- Assists developing countries in trade policy issues (training/technical assistance)
- Co-operates with other international organisations

GATT is the WTO's main **guidelines on international trade** in goods. It is the result of negotiations between nations and is subject to updating and revision. For example, when the WTO was set up, GATT was extended to **intellectual property**, **services**, **dispute settlement** and other areas.

The WTO Agreements contain the principles of **liberalisation** of **free trade**. They include commitments by each country to lower customs tariffs and other trade barriers, and to open and keep open services markets. They also set procedures for settling disputes.

3.2 The G8

The **G8**, or **Group of Eight**, is a forum for eight of the main developed nations. Membership of the G8 comprises France, Germany, Italy, Canada, Russia, Japan, the UK and the US.

The forum, which has no official powers or resources, was originally established so that talks on **economics** and **trade** could take place; however, in recent years **politics** has also been discussed and agenda items have included global warming, AIDS and poverty. The group is seen to take a lead in world affairs and often sets a direction for the international community to follow.

The group meets at an **annual summit meeting**. The members rotate the presidency of the forum and responsibility for hosting the summit. Matters often discussed include:

- International trade generally
- Energy and pollution issues
- Developing nations
- Macroeconomic issues
- International crime

However, other issues that are often discussed include:

- Improved co-operation over trade and finance
- Strengthening the global economy
- Prevention and resolution of conflicts
- Promotion of peace and democracy

3.3 The International Monetary Fund (IMF)

The **IMF** was established at the Bretton Woods meeting in 1944 in the US. Its initial role, after the Second World War, was in the rebuilding of national economies. The IMF oversaw the international monetary system and took on the role of ensuring exchange rate stability and encouraging members to eliminate exchange restrictions that hinder trade. Since then, the IMF has played a major role in **world affairs**, for example in helping former communist nations transition into market economies.

In more recent times, the IMF has:

- Promoted financial co-operation
- Established stable exchange rates and easily convertible currencies
- Provided help and support for nations with trade deficits in order to help them overcome them
- Encouraged international liquidity

3.4 The World Bank

Like the IMF, the **World Bank** was founded at the Bretton Woods summit in 1944 and was initially known as the **International Bank for Reconstruction and Development** (IBRD). Its role was to help nations reconstruct their economies after the Second World War but once that was achieved it refocused its attention onto the developing world. The organisation (which is now known as the World Bank) is made up of five main bodies.

The **IBRD** provides loans to middle-income and creditworthy low-income countries. Funds are raised by the IBRD and provided to nations at a commercial (but low) rate of interest and on favourable terms.

The **International Development Association** provides interest-free (or low-rate) loans, called credits, and grants to the poorest countries. Funds are raised by subscription from donor countries and distributed to borrowing countries.

The **International Finance Corporation** provides loans, equity and technical assistance to stimulate private sector investment in developing countries.

The **Multilateral Investment Guarantee Agency** provides guarantees against losses caused by non-commercial risks to investors in developing countries.

The **International Centre for Settlement of Investment Disputes** provides international facilities for conciliation and arbitration of investment disputes.

3.5 The European Bank for Reconstruction and Development (EBRD)

The **EBRD** was established in 1991 as a response to the political and economic changes in Central and Eastern Europe. The role of the Bank was to support the development of market economies in the region following the widespread collapse of communist regimes. In more recent times, the EBRD has embraced a role as the world's only **transition bank**, and is helping nations around the world to move from state-controlled to market economies.

3.6 Central banks

A **central bank** is a bank which acts on behalf of the Government. The central bank for the UK is the Bank of England. The Bank of England (the Bank) is a nationalised corporation run by a Court of Directors, consisting of the Governor, Deputy Governor, and some Executive Directors and part-time Directors.

3.6.1 Functions of a central bank

Central banks have a **number of roles**, many of which **affect economic growth**.

(a) **Monetary stability**. The Bank's most important function is maintaining monetary stability in the economy. This includes **setting interest rates** at the level it considers appropriate in order to meet the Government's **inflation target**. Reducing interest rates may increase growth; increasing rates may reduce it due to the impact on the disposable income of individuals and businesses.

(b) The Bank also has a key role in maintaining the **stability of the financial system**. Some central banks **regulate the banking** sector.

(c) **Lender of last resort** when the banking system is short of money, the Bank will provide the money the banks need – at a suitable rate of interest.

(d) **Banker to the commercial banks**. Commercial banks keep a bank account with the Bank. This enables the cheque clearing system to operate. At the end of each day the net balances on each bank's accounts with all the other banks are settled through their clearing accounts at the central bank. The funds which banks hold with the central bank act as a liquid reserve for the commercial bank, and are controlled by the fractional reserve ratio.

(e) **Banker to the Central Government** and holds the 'public deposits'.

(f) **Central note-issuing authority** in the country – it is responsible for issuing bank notes.

(g) **Manages the National Debt** – ie it deals with long-term and short-term borrowing by the Central Government and the repayment of central government debt.

(h) **Holds the country's foreign currency reserves** and may use these to trade on the foreign exchange markets to **stabilise the exchange rate**.

(i) **Adviser** to the Government on **monetary policy**.

Section summary

A number of institutions are involved in developing and managing global trade and creation of growth. These include the **World Trade Organization** (WTO), the **G8**, the **International Monetary Fund** (IMF), the **World Bank**, the **European Bank for Reconstruction and Development** (EBRD) and **central banks**.

4 Market regulation

Introduction

Regulation can be defined as any form of state interference with the operation of the free market. **Efficient regulation** is where the total cost of the regulation is less than the benefit it provides to society. Regulation is **effective** if the function of business is not impeded and the end-product or service being controlled is safe and works as it should.

4.1 Regulation and competition policy

Regulation could involve regulating demand, supply, price, profit, quantity, quality, entry, exit, information, technology, or any other aspect of production and consumption in the market. The **power to regulate** is delegated by government to specific individuals and organisations, known as regulators.

In the UK, much regulation concerns **competition**. However, the Government also plays a part in regulating **externalities** (costs or benefits that arise from industry which are experienced by wider society rather than producers and consumers). The actions of **businesspeople** may also be controlled – for example to prevent insolvent companies trading and where market abuse, insider dealing and money laundering occur.

Regulation is said to be **efficient** if the total benefit it brings to society is greater than its cost. **Effective regulation** is where products or services are provided safely, while not restricting business functions.

4.1.1 The Competition Act 1998

In the UK, this Act sought to encourage competition by introducing the presumption that **anti-competitive arrangements** are against the public interest and so should be illegal. Competition is thought to be in the best interests of the consumer because the aim is to reduce prices, raise quality and encourage the efficient use of resources. The **Competition and Markets Authority** (CMA) has the power to investigate organisations suspected of breaching the Act. Fines of up to 10% of revenue may be imposed.

4.1.2 Industry regulators

Most countries have **specific industry regulators** to monitor the activities of private companies in 'essential' industries. For example, the UK has OFCOM to regulate the telecommunications market, while OFGEM regulates the gas industry.

The regulators aim to promote competition, for example by **imposing price caps** and **performance standards** or by **removing barriers** preventing new organisations from entering the market. Price caps will impact on organisational profitability and performance standards may create onerous obligations that must be met operationally.

4.2 The Competition and Markets Authority

The role of the Competition and Markets Authority is to promote competition, and to make markets work well for consumers, businesses and the economy. For example, it may investigate **proposed mergers**

where the assets involved exceed a certain value and recommend whether or not it should be allowed to proceed.

4.3 The Restrictive Practices Court

The UK **Restrictive Practices Court** (RPC) has jurisdiction to declare that certain agreements are contrary to the public interest and to restrain parties from enforcing them.

The RPC considers applications made by **the Director General of Fair Trading** in respect of agreements under which at least two parties are imposing restrictions on the price or supply of goods.

4.4 European Union competition policy

European Union competition policy is intended to ensure free and fair competition in the EU. The **Commission of the European Union** has authority under the Treaty of Rome (Articles 81 to 89) to prohibit price fixing and other uncompetitive arrangements, including limiting production and seeking to exclude competitors from a market.

The Commission also has authority to prevent national governments within the EU from offering subsidies or other **state aid** to organisations in their countries which will distort competition across the wider market.

4.5 Self-regulation

In many markets, the participants may decide to maintain a system of **voluntary self-regulation**, possibly in order to try to avert the imposition of government controls. Self-regulation often exists in the professions.

4.6 Costs of regulation

The **costs of regulation** include:

(a) **Enforcement costs**. Direct costs of enforcement include the setting up and running of the regulatory agencies. Indirect costs are those incurred by regulated organisations in conforming with the regulations relevant to them.

(b) **Regulatory capture**. This refers to the process by which the regulator becomes dominated and controlled by the regulated companies, such that it acts increasingly in the latter's interests, rather than in those of consumers. This is a phenomenon which has been observed in the US.

(c) **Unintended consequences of regulation**. Organisations will not react passively to regulatory constraints on their behaviour – instead they try to limit their effectiveness. In general, theory and observation suggest that if it's practical, businesses will move away from regulated activities towards those which are less constrained or completely unregulated.

4.7 Deregulation

Deregulation can be defined as the removal or weakening of any form of statutory (or voluntary) regulation of free market activity. Deregulation allows free market forces more scope to determine the outcome.

There was a shift in policy in the 1980s in the UK and in the US towards greater deregulation of markets, in the belief that this would **improve efficiency**.

A rational assessment of deregulation should weigh the potential benefits against the costs. If there will be a net gain to society, we can say that the deregulation should proceed. It would be simplistic to contend that all regulation is detrimental to the economy.

4.7.1 Advantages and disadvantages of deregulation

Deregulation measures are also known as **liberalisation**.

Those who favour deregulation quote **possible benefits** such as:

(a) **Increased incentive to find internal cost savings and efficiency.** Increased competition should lead to the most efficient organisations being the most successful.

(b) **Improved allocative efficiency.** Competition should result in prices closer to marginal cost and therefore result in overall production that is closer to the socially optimal output level.

In some industries, liberalisation could have certain **disadvantages**:

(a) **Loss of economies of scale.** If increased competition means that each organisation produces less output on a smaller scale, unit costs will be higher.

(b) **Lower quality or quantity of service.** The need to reduce costs may lead organisations to reduce quality or eliminate unprofitable but socially valuable services.

(c) **Need to protect competition.** It may be necessary to **implement** a regulatory regime to protect competition where inherent forces have a tendency to eliminate it.

Section summary

Regulation can be defined as any form of state interference with the operation of the free market.

In the UK there have been various pieces of **legislation** enacted to maintain competition in the marketplace and there are a number of industry regulators.

European Union competition policy is intended to ensure free and fair competition in the EU.

Deregulation can be defined as the removal or weakening of any form of statutory (or voluntary) regulation of free market activity.

---

5 Corporate governance

Introduction

Although shareholders own a company, the responsibility for directing and controlling it rests largely with the board of directors. In the UK, a series of high-profile corporate scandals in the 1980s and 1990s led to a range of corporate governance controls.

KEY TERM

CORPORATE GOVERNANCE is the system by which companies and other entities are directed and controlled.

(CIMA Official Terminology)

Corporate governance concerns **shareholders** (the owners) and **directors** (the management), as between them they direct and control the company. It also concerns the **stakeholders** of non profit making organisations; this is because the principles apply to these organisations as well as companies.

Sometimes, particularly in **smaller businesses**, companies are owned and managed by the **same people**. This is the situation where people form a company to carry out their own business, buy the shares and appoint themselves as directors.

In other, mainly **bigger, companies**, the directors and shareholders are **different sets of people**. Often in larger companies quoted on stock exchanges, shareholders purchase shares as an investment and may have very little personal contact with the company. Directors are employed for their management expertise and have no other connection with the company.

There is a key difference between these two types of organisation, which is known as the '**knowledge gap**' or 'agency problem'. In the owner-managed company, as the directors and shareholders are the same people, they have access to the same information and are in a position to direct company policy. In the other company, the shareholders do not have access to day to day company management information and therefore have to rely on the directors to act in their interest.

5.1 Stakeholders

Stakeholders are persons or groups that have a **legitimate interest in a business's conduct** and whose concerns should be addressed as a matter of principle. Many stakeholder groups have influence over the way in which organisations are managed and operated. They can therefore be fundamental to corporate governance.

Stakeholder needs analysis is used by an organisation to identify key stakeholders and what their needs are. Questionnaires, focus groups and interviews can be used to investigate stakeholder interests.

KEY TERMS

STAKEHOLDERS are those persons and organisations that have an interest in the strategy of an organisation.
(CIMA Official Terminology)

STAKEHOLDER THEORY states that shareholders should not be the sole focus of an organisation's attention, but that it should be accountable to all stakeholders.

There are three broad types, or **constituencies**, of stakeholder in an organisation:

- **Internal** stakeholders such as employees and management
- **Connected** stakeholders such as shareholders, customers, suppliers and financiers
- **External** stakeholders such as the community, government, trade unions and pressure groups

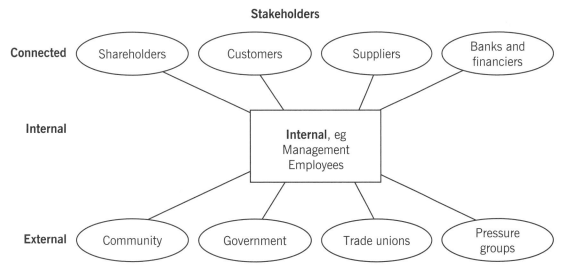

The extent to which external stakeholders are interested and recognised is linked in some ways to the size of the organisation. For example, the policies and actions of **larger organisations** are more likely to be of interest to **national governments** and even **international bodies** than are those of smaller organisations.

Stakeholders may also be analysed into those who have a **formal contractual relationship** with the organisation and those who do not. These two groups are called **primary** and **secondary** stakeholders. Internal and connected stakeholders fall into the primary category, while external stakeholders are secondary stakeholders.

It is important for management to **consider stakeholders** when determining corporate goals, objectives and strategy for two reasons.

Firstly, certain stakeholder groups that hold **power** in the organisation might be able to disrupt or prevent certain policies being carried out. For example, staff may go on strike and suppliers may choose not to supply the organisation if they do not agree with its activities.

Secondly, the organisation may **legitimise its goals** if it discusses them with those affected. In other words, the organisation can demonstrate that its goals have been agreed on by not just the senior management team and therefore the decision may not be questioned by others.

5.1.1 Stakeholder conflict

Stakeholders are mostly interested in the success of the business, and this creates a **common goal** between them. However, they may pursue their own interests in certain circumstances, and these interests may be incompatible with the interests of other stakeholder groups, creating conflict between them.

Examples of **conflicting interests** include:

(a) Shareholders demanding rising profits and customers wanting higher-quality (more costly) products

(b) Employee demand for pay rises against the need for management to maximise profit (perhaps at least in part to achieve their bonuses)

(c) The community wanting minimal environmental impact from the organisation but shareholders wanting the least costly option for disposing of waste chosen

(d) Directors possibly recommending that the business is taken over by another but shareholders wanting to remain independent

Directors usually give priority to those stakeholders which have the most **power**, but decisions are usually a **compromise** between the various stakeholder groups. Mendelow classifies stakeholders on a matrix whose axes are **power** (or influence) and degree of **interest** in the organisation's activities. These factors help define the type of relationship the organisation should seek with its stakeholders.

Level of interest

		Low	High
Power/influence	**Low**	A	B
	High	C	D

(a) **Key players** are found in segment D. Any strategy must be **acceptable** to them, at least. An example would be a major customer. These stakeholders may **participate** in decision making.

(b) Stakeholders in segment C must be **treated with care**. While often passive, they may be capable of moving to segment D. They should, therefore, be **kept satisfied**. Large institutional shareholders might fall into segment C.

(c) Stakeholders in segment B do not have great ability to influence strategy, but their views can be important in **influencing more powerful stakeholders**, perhaps by lobbying. They should therefore be **kept informed**. Community representatives and charities might fall into segment B.

(d) **Minimal effort** should be expended on segment A. An example might be a contractor's employees.

Internal stakeholder groups are likely to have both more influence and more interest than external groups. Coalitions of stakeholder groups are likely to have more influence than single stakeholders or small uniform groups.

5.2 Failures of corporate governance

Though mostly discussed in relation to quoted companies, governance is an issue **for all organisations**. An increasing number of **high-profile corporate scandals** and collapses, including Polly Peck International, BCCI and Maxwell Communications Corporation, prompted the development of governance codes in the early 1990s. However, scandals since then, such as Parmalat and Enron, have raised questions about further measures that may be necessary. These scandals have highlighted the need for guidance to tackle the various **risks and problems** that can arise in organisations' systems of governance.

5.2.1 Domination by a single individual

A feature of many corporate governance scandals has been boards dominated by a single senior executive with other board members merely acting as a rubber stamp. Sometimes the single individual may bypass the board to action their own interests. The report on the UK Guinness case suggested that the Chief Executive Ernest Saunders paid himself a substantial reward without consulting the other directors. The presence of non-executive directors on the board is felt to be an important safeguard against domination by a single individual.

5.2.2 Lack of involvement of board

Boards that meet irregularly or fail to consider systematically the organisation's activities and risks are clearly weak. Sometimes the failure to carry out proper oversight is due to a **lack of information** being provided.

5.2.3 Lack of adequate control function

An obvious weakness is an ineffective **internal audit function**, since this is one of the most important aspects of internal control. Another important weakness is a **lack of adequate technical knowledge** in key roles, for example in the audit committee or in senior compliance positions. A rapid turnover of staff involved in accounting or control may suggest inadequate resourcing and the constant change will make control more difficult.

5.2.4 Lack of supervision

Employees who are not properly supervised can create large losses for the organisation through incompetence, negligence or fraudulent activity. The behaviour of Nick Leeson, the employee who caused the collapse of Barings Bank, was not challenged because he appeared to be successful, whereas he was using unauthorised accounts to cover up his large trading losses. Leeson was able to do this because he was in charge of both dealing and settlement, a systems weakness or **lack of segregation of key roles** that has also featured in other financial frauds.

5.2.5 Lack of independent scrutiny

External auditors may not carry out the necessary questioning of senior management because of fears of losing the audit and internal audit may avoid awkward questions because the Chief Financial Officer determines their employment prospects. Often, corporate collapses are followed by criticisms of external auditors where poorly planned and focused audit work failed to identify illegal use of client monies.

5.2.6 Lack of contact with shareholders

Board members may be out of touch with the **interests and views** of shareholders. One possible symptom of this is the payment of remuneration packages that do not appear to be warranted by results. Equally, the directors may choose to pursue their own interests and ignore the requirements of the shareholders.

5.2.7 Emphasis on short-term profitability

Emphasis on short-term results can lead to the **concealment** of problems or errors, or **manipulation** of accounts to achieve desired results.

5.2.8 Misleading accounts and information

Often, misleading figures are symptomatic of other problems (or are designed to conceal them). In many cases, poor-quality accounting information is a major problem if markets are trying to make a fair assessment of the company's value. Giving out misleading information was a major issue in the UK's Equitable Life scandal where the company gave contradictory information to savers, independent advisers, media and regulators.

5.3 Benefits of improving corporate governance

5.3.1 Risk reduction

Clearly, the ultimate risk is of the organisation **making such large losses** that **bankruptcy** becomes inevitable. The organisation may also be closed down as a result of **serious regulatory breaches**, for example misapplying investors' monies. Proper corporate governance reduces such risks by aligning directors' interests with the company's strategic objectives and by providing measures to reduce fraud.

5.3.2 Performance

Performance should improve if **accountabilities** are made clear and directors' motivation is enhanced by performance-related remuneration. Also, the extra breadth of experience brought by non-executive directors and measures to prevent domination by a single powerful figure should improve the quality of decision making at board level.

5.3.3 External support

External perceptions of the company should be enhanced. This can have wide-ranging benefits:

- Improved ability to raise finance
- Improved corporate image with public and government
- Improved relations with stakeholders such as customers and employees

5.4 The UK Corporate Governance Code (an example)

The **UK Corporate Governance Code**, like other governance codes, is government led. This means the need for the Code was identified by the Government and authority to create the rules was delegated to a relevant body. The Code applies to listed companies in the UK, although smaller companies that are outside the FTSE 350 can take a more flexible approach to applying the Code. These companies must either comply with the Code or explain any departures from it in a note to their financial statements ('**comply or explain**'). The approach taken by the **UK Corporate Governance Code** is one based on a **framework of best practice principles**.

The key principles of the UK Code are explained briefly below.

5.4.1 Leadership

Every company should be headed by an **effective board**. The board consists of the Chairman, Chief Executive, executive directors and non-executive directors (NEDs).

A '**senior independent director**' should be appointed out of the NEDs and act as a point of contact for shareholders who wish to raise issues that concern them.

A company's **annual report** should identify the **Chairman**, the **Deputy Chairman** (where there is one), the **Chief Executive**, the **Senior Independent Director** and the **chairmen** and **members of the board committees**. It should also set out the number of meetings of the board and those committees and individual attendance by directors.

The roles of **Chairman** and **Chief Executive** should not be exercised by the same individual. The Chairman runs the board and the Chief Executive runs the operations of the company. The Chairman should be independent (see below) when appointed.

If the board decides that the roles of Chief Executive and Chairman should be held by the same individual, it should consult major shareholders in advance, setting out its reasons.

Executive directors are involved in the day to day management of the company and may have titles that describe their function – such as Finance Director. The main role of **NEDs** is to attend board and board committee meetings and constructively challenge and help develop proposals on strategy.

The board should include sufficient **NEDs**. What is '**sufficient**' in terms of number of NEDs depends on the company. In larger companies, NEDs should make up half the board (excluding the Chairman), but in small companies only two NEDs are required.

NEDs should as far as possible be **independent**. This means that they must not:

- Have been an employee of the company for five years prior to appointment
- Have had a material interest in the company in the last three years
- Have share options or a company pension
- Have close links with other directors or senior employees
- Serve for more than nine years
- Hold cross-directorships (two or more directors sitting on the board of the same company)

5.4.2 Effectiveness

The board should have an appropriate **balance of skills, experience, independence and knowledge**.

There should be a formal and transparent procedure for the appointment of new directors via a **nomination committee**. This committee should ensure that appointments to the board are based on finding the best person for the job (ie on merit). Over 50% of this committee must be made up of NEDs.

The board should undertake a formal **annual evaluation** of its performance.

All directors should receive an induction on joining the board and should **regularly update** and refresh their **skills** and **knowledge**. Directors should be submitted for re-election at regular intervals.

The board should be supplied in a timely manner with **information** in a form and of a quality appropriate to enable it to discharge its duties.

The board should include an **appropriate combination** of executive and non-executive directors such that no individual or small group of individuals can dominate.

5.4.3 Accountability

The board should **present a balanced and understandable assessment of the company's position and prospects**. The board is responsible for determining the nature and extent of risks it is willing to take to achieve strategic objectives.

The board should establish an **audit committee** of at least three (or in the case of smaller companies two) independent NEDs. At least one member of the audit committee should have recent and relevant financial experience.

The **main role** and **responsibilities** of the **audit committee** should include monitoring the integrity of accounting policies and financial statements, reviewing the company's internal controls and risk management, reviewing the work and effectiveness of the internal audit function, monitoring the external

auditor's independence and objectivity, shortlisting external audit firms when a change is needed and being available for internal and external auditors to speak to.

5.4.4 Remuneration

Director remuneration should be **sufficient** to attract, retain and motivate **directors of the quality required**, but should not be more than is necessary. A significant proportion of executive directors' remuneration should be linked to corporate and individual performance.

There should be a formal and transparent procedure for developing policy on executive remuneration and for fixing the remuneration of individual directors. No director should be involved in deciding their own remuneration; rather, a **remuneration committee** consisting of NEDs should set director pay.

5.4.5 Relations with shareholders

There should be a **dialogue with shareholders** based on the mutual understanding of objectives. The board as a whole has responsibility for ensuring that a satisfactory dialogue with shareholders takes place. The **Annual General Meeting** (AGM) has a key role to play in this.

5.5 Sarbanes-Oxley Act 2002 (US Corporate Governance)

The UK's '**best practice**' approach to corporate governance differs from that of the US where corporate governance rules are a **legal requirement** under the **Sarbanes-Oxley Act 2002**, with penalties for failure to comply.

The US rules restrict the **non-audit services** that an auditor can provide to their client and make it a legal requirement for companies to have an **audit committee**. In terms of reporting, companies must detail all **balance sheet financing** and include statements concerning the organisation's **internal control systems**.

Exam skills

Learn the **principles of good corporate governance** rather than the specific requirements of the UK Corporate Governance Code or any other country-specific regime.

Corporate governance appears on a number of syllabuses within the CIMA qualification; for example, you will come across it again when you study E2.

Further details of the UK Corporate Governance Code (including the principles) are available on the web. Visit **www.frc.org.uk**

Section summary

Corporate governance is the system by which companies and other entities are directed and controlled.

Stakeholders are persons or groups that have a **legitimate interest in a business's conduct** and whose concerns should be addressed as a matter of principle.

Since their interests may be widely different, **conflict between stakeholders** can be quite common.

The **UK Corporate Governance Code** sets out standards of best practice in relation to issues such as board composition, remuneration and accountability.

6   Ethical behaviour

Introduction

Ethics refer to a code of **moral principles** that people follow with respect to what is right or wrong. Ethical principles are not necessarily enforced by law, although the law incorporates moral judgements (eg theft is wrong ethically, and is also punishable legally).

Companies have to follow **legal standards**, or else they will be subject to fines and their officers might face similar charges. Ethics in organisations relate to **business practice** and **social responsibility**. Increasingly, consumers and businesses prefer to purchase from and do business with organisations with high ethical standards.

6.1 Ethical decisions

A number of factors might be considered when determining whether something is ethically right or wrong:

- **Values** – such as rights and obligations from society
- **Principles** – such as CIMA's ethical principles
- **Motivation** – the reasons why a person acted as they did
- **Consequences** – does the outcome of an action justify how it was carried out?

There are a range of approaches that can be taken when making ethical decisions:

- **Egoists** look after their own needs when making a decision.

- **Pluralists** consider whether other stakeholders are compromised by a decision.

- **Absolutists** are concerned about whether a course of action is fundamentally incorrect – for example, is it against the law?

- **Consequentialists** will focus on the consequences of a decision before determining a course of action.

- **Utilitarians** seek to maximise the overall benefit to society when making a decision.

6.1.1 Ethics in organisations

Organisations are coming under increasing pressure to adopt an ethical approach towards:

- **Stakeholders** (employees, customers, competitors, suppliers and society as a whole)
- **Environmental issues** (such as pollution and recycling)
- **The disadvantaged**
- Dealings with **unethical companies or countries**

This pressure may come from:

- **Government**
- UK and European **legislation**
- **Treaty obligations** (such as the Kyoto protocol)
- **Consumers**
- **Employers**
- **Pressure groups**

To be effective, a code of ethics will have to be incorporated into the entire culture of the organisation. Its ethical views can therefore directly impact on the mission statement and strategy adopted by the organisation.

6.2 Ethics in business practice

KEY TERM

ETHICS IN BUSINESS: 'The application of ethical values to business behaviour.' (*CIMA Official Terminology*)

Businesses have ethical values, based on the **norms** and **standards** of **behaviour** that their leaders believe will best help them express their identity and achieve their objectives. Some of these ethical values may be **explicit**; for example, expressed in a mission statement or in employee training programmes. Others may be **unwritten rules and customs** that form part of the organisation's culture: 'the way we do things around here'.

Business life is a fruitful source of **ethical dilemmas** because its whole purpose is material gain, the making of profit. Success in business requires a constant, avid search for potential advantage over others and businesspeople are under pressure to do whatever yields such advantage.

For **organisations**, good **business ethics** is increasingly being seen as a key factor driving profitability in the longer term because it supports good corporate governance and demonstrates to society that the organisation is being well run. This should help reassure shareholders and other investors, and help attract employees who want to work in an ethical environment.

At the level of an **individual**, expectations have developed in recent years. **Employees** are increasingly not willing to be party to unethical business practices and **customers** are actively seeking out ethical products and services, even if they have a higher cost.

The table below summarises **three elements** to ethics.

Element	Explanation
I	Ethics concern an individual's professional responsibility to act.
DO	Ethics concern the 'real-world' practical actions an individual can take. It is important to consider how an individual acts and not always what they do.
BEST	Ethics concern choices between different courses of action. These may involve taking a course of action which is less unpalatable than another.

6.2.1 An issue of trust

Whatever the situation, there is a public expectation that organisations will act ethically. This is known as the **'Trust me'** model and was the case for many years when most businesses were owned by families. Times have changed and most companies are now run by directors and managers rather than fathers and sons. The model changed to **'Involve me'** as more evidence is needed of an organisation's ethical credentials.

In recent times, trust in businesses has fallen and increasingly more evidence is required to demonstrate it.

The **'Show me'** stage required some demonstration of trust, **'Prove to me'** required independent verification and assurance and the final stage of **'Obey me'** would exist when the law creates legislation to cure instances of unethical behaviour. We are some way off this point currently. What caused this trust to disintegrate? Since the 1980s, the UK has seen a procession of corporate disasters, including the names of Barings Bank, Polly Peck and Maxwell.

In an attempt to counter this lack of trust, many corporations developed general **corporate ethics statements** or more detailed ethical rules (**corporate codes of ethics**). Many organisations have created **ethical strategies** and **policies** and provide **guidance** and **training** for their employees. The strategy is set by the leadership and feeds into all areas of the business, becoming part of the cultural DNA of the organisation.

6.3 CIMA's Ethical Guidelines

All CIMA members and registered students are subject to **CIMA's Ethical Guidelines**.

These **guidelines** make it clear that individuals must:

- Observe the highest standards of conduct and integrity
- Uphold the good standing and reputation of the profession
- Refrain from any conduct which might discredit the profession

As an accountant, a key role of a CIMA member is to act in the **public interest**. This means acting in a manner that supports the common good, or welfare, of society. This is a special role, because it is in addition to any duty the accountant owes to their employers or clients.

In particular, members should pay attention to the **fundamental principles** given in the Introduction and the discussion of objectivity and the resolution of ethical conflicts that appear in Part A. Despite being aimed at accountants, these guidelines are **equally relevant** to **any employee** or **manager** within an organisation and are discussed briefly below.

Ethical behaviour and CIMA's Ethical Guidelines are core to the CIMA qualification and feature in many of the syllabuses.

CIMA's Ethical Guidelines are examinable. You should download a copy from the CIMA website (www.cimaglobal.com).

6.3.1 Fundamental principles

The **fundamental principles of CIMA's Ethical Guidelines** are:

(a) **Integrity**. This is more than not telling lies – professional accountants must not be party to anything which is deceptive or misleading. You should be straightforward, honest and truthful in all professional and business relationships.

(b) **Objectivity**. This is founded on fairness and avoiding all forms of bias, prejudice and partiality.

(c) **Professional competence and due care**. Individuals must ensure they remain up to date with current developments and are technically competent. Those working under your authority must also have the appropriate training and supervision.

(d) **Confidentiality**. Employers and clients are entitled to expect that confidential information will not be revealed without specific permission or unless there is a legal or professional right or duty to do so.

(e) **Professional behaviour**. Accountants should behave in such a way as to protect the reputation of the professional and the professional body, and comply with relevant laws and regulations.

6.3.2 Ethical conflicts

Resolution of **ethical conflicts** is also covered by CIMA's guidance. The possibility of such conflicts arising is discussed. Potentially difficult situations include:

- Pressure from an overbearing supervisor
- Pressure from a friend or relation
- Divided loyalties

A CIMA member or student should act responsibly, honour any legal contract of employment and conform to employment legislation.

When dealing with an **ethical dilemma**, an individual should consider:

- Whether more information or evidence is required
- Whether there is an internal system in place for dealing with ethical concerns

- Whether it is necessary or important to pass the matter up the organisation's hierarchy (including the audit committee)

- Whether to obtain professional advice or consult CIMA

In cases where the CIMA member/student is encouraged or required to act illegally, resignation may be the only option (if discussion fails to resolve the situation).

Section summary

Businesses have ethical values, based on the **norms** and **standards** of **behaviour** that their leaders believe will best help them express their identity and achieve their objectives.

All CIMA members and registered students are subject to **CIMA's Ethical Guidelines**.

---

7 Corporate social responsibility (CSR)

The traditional view of business is that **companies** have the sole **objective of maximising profits** for shareholders and that social responsibility has no part to play in business decision making. In recent times, however, this view has shifted towards **corporate social responsibility (CSR) related strategies** that may offer a business a number of advantages. The main benefits are to improve the organisation's **image in society** and create a **long-term bond with customers**. Other advantages include the following:

Advantages of CSR strategies	
Attractive to like-minded, high-quality employees	Differentiation from competitors
May reduce packaging costs and environmental taxes	Creates new markets for goods and services and attracts new, like-minded customers
Improves image of firm/brand	Positive impact on profitability if sales increase and costs fall

7.1 Caroll and Buchholtz's layers of CSR

Caroll and Buchholtz argued that there are **four main 'layers' of CSR**.

7.1.1 Economic responsibilities

Companies have **economic responsibilities** to shareholders demanding a good return, to employees wanting fair employment conditions and to customers seeking good-quality products at a fair price. Businesses are formed to be **properly functioning economic units** and so economic responsibilities form the basis of all other responsibilities.

7.1.2 Legal responsibilities

Since **laws codify society's moral views**, obeying them must be the foundation of compliance with social responsibilities. Although in all societies corporations will have some legal responsibilities, there is perhaps more emphasis on them in continental Europe than in the Anglo-American economies. In Anglo-American economies the focus of discussion has often been whether many legal responsibilities are unnecessary burdens on business.

7.1.3 Ethical responsibilities

These are responsibilities that require corporations to act in a **fair and just way** even if the law does not compel them to do so. If customers demand this, acting ethically may be as much a business decision as a moral one.

7.1.4 Philanthropic responsibilities

According to Carroll and Buchholtz, these are **desired** rather than being required of businesses. They include charitable donations, contributions to local communities and providing employees with the chances to improve their own lives.

While CSR principles tend to be similar the world over, there are differences in application. For example, in **the US** the approach of many businesses is to make **charitable donations**, but in **Europe** the focus tends to be on **investing in communities** and having **responsible business practices**. Although some investment is needed when implementing a CSR policy, most firms see them as profitable in the long term as customers expect companies to be socially responsible, and if they're not they will spend their money elsewhere.

7.2 Corporate citizenship

The concept of **corporate citizenship** provides a different perspective on organisations and society. It seeks to explain what determines how much and in what ways organisations engage with society. Again, there are different views of how far it should extend.

7.2.1 Limited view

This is based on **voluntary philanthropy** undertaken in the organisations' interests. The main stakeholder groups that the corporate citizen engages with are local communities and employees. Citizenship in action takes the form of limited focus projects.

7.2.2 Equivalent view

This is based on a wider general definition of **citizenship** that is partly voluntary and partly imposed. The organisation focuses on a broad range of stakeholders and responds to the demands of society. Self-interest is not the primary motivation; instead the organisation is focused on **legal requirements** and **ethical fulfilment**.

7.2.3 Extended view

This view is based on a partly voluntary and partly imposed view of **active social and political citizenship**. Corporations must respect citizens' rights, particularly as governments have failed to provide some necessary safeguards. Given this, corporations can make a big impact since they are the most powerful institutions in society. Again the focus is on a wide range of stakeholders.

Under the extended view, **organisations will promote**:

(a)   **Social rights**, by provision (for example decent working conditions)

(b)   **Civil rights**, by intervening to promote citizens' individual rights themselves or to pressurise governments to promote citizens' rights

(c)   **Political rights**, by channelling (allowing individuals to promote their causes by using corporate power)

Many companies now produce **Corporate Responsibility Policies (CRPs)** and **Corporate Responsibility Reports (CRRs)** to demonstrate their commitment to being a 'good corporate citizen'.

7.3 Corporate (social) responsibility policies

KEY POINT

Corporate (social) responsibility policies explain the organisation's approach to helping the community and reducing the environmental impact of the organisation.

These policies must be consistent with the overall aims of the organisation, and should not be overstated in an attempt to paint a 'better' image. Exaggerated claims are likely to harm an organisation in the eyes of the public.

7.4 Corporate Responsibility Reports (CRRs)

KEY POINT

These reports include figures or statistics covering areas such as the organisation's carbon footprint and impact on the environment. These can be added to more conventional assessments such as staff turnover to provide a wide-ranging picture of the organisation.

Corporate values also guide staff as to the expectations that employers have regarding their behaviour. The aim is to end up with consistent behaviour across the workforce in terms of personal conduct and professionalism. These policies are enforced on a voluntary basis and results are monitored through audits, surveys and interviews.

It is important that all employees, especially **line managers**, follow the policies laid down by the organisation's leadership. The media is quick to pick up on any ethical failings by employees, often resulting in adverse publicity for the organisation.

7.5 CSR stances

Different organisations take very different stances on social responsibility, and their different stances will be reflected in how they manage such responsibilities.

Johnson, Scholes and Whittington identify four CSR stances, which reflect a progressively more inclusive list of stakeholder interests:

- Laissez-faire
- Enlightened self-interest (long-term shareholder interest)
- Multiple stakeholder obligations
- Shaper of society

Laissez-faire

Organisations which adopt a laissez-faire stance take the view that an organisation's only responsibilities are the **short-term interests of shareholders**, and to make a profit, pay taxes and provide jobs.

Organisations adopting this view believe that it is government's role to prescribe, through legislation and regulation, the constraints which are placed on businesses in their pursuit of economic efficiency. Laissez-faire organisations will meet these minimum obligations but no more.

Enlightened self-interest (long-term shareholder interest)

The rationale behind the 'enlightened self-interest' stance is that there can be a long-term benefit to shareholders from well-managed relationships with other stakeholders. Therefore, the justification for social action is that it makes good business sense.

There are two reasons why an organisation might take a wider view of ethical responsibilities when considering the longer-term interest of shareholders:

(a)   The organisation's **corporate image** may be enhanced by an assumption of wider responsibilities. The cost of undertaking such responsibilities may be justified as essentially promotional expenditure.

(b)   The responsible exercise of corporate power may prevent a build-up of social and political **pressure for legal regulation**. Freedom of action may be preserved and the burden of regulation lightened by acceptance of ethical responsibilities.

For example, in 2012 in the UK, following a downturn in its profits, the supermarket giant Tesco sought to reinvent its business to persuade people that it isn't simply a money-making machine, but also has 'a softer side'. To this end, the Chief Executive Philip Clarke said that 'We will do more to ensure that Tesco is valued and trusted in local communities all around the world for doing the right thing' – although critics were quick to point out that this is the same company which has been squeezing farmers and other suppliers for years to extract the best price it can for its customers.

Multiple stakeholder obligations

Organisations adopting this stance accept the **legitimacy of the expectations of stakeholders other than shareholders** and build those expectations into the organisation's stated purposes. Such organisations recognise that, without appropriate relationships with groups such as suppliers, employers and customers, they would not be able to function.

However, organisations adopting a 'multiple stakeholder obligations' stance also argue that performance should not be measured simply through the financial bottom line. They argue that the key to long-term survival is dependent on social and environmental performance as well as economic (financial) performance, and therefore it is important to take account of the views of stakeholders with interests relating to social and environmental matters.

Shaper of society

Shapers of society regard financial considerations as being of secondary importance to changing society or social norms. For such organisations, ensuring that society benefits from their actions is more important than financial and other stakeholder interests.

7.6 Against CSR

Milton Friedman argued against CSR along the following lines:

(a)   Businesses do not have responsibilities; only people have responsibilities. Managers in charge of corporations are responsible to the owners of the business, by whom they are employed.

(b)   These employers may have charity as their aim, but 'generally [their aim] will be to make as much money as possible while conforming to the basic rules of the society, both those embodied in law and those embodied in ethical custom'.

(c)   If the statement that a manager has social responsibilities is to have any meaning, 'it must mean that he is to act in some way that is not in the interest of his employers'.

(d)   If managers do this they are, generally speaking, spending the owners' money for purposes other than those they have authorised; sometimes it is the money of customers or suppliers that is spent and, on occasion, the money of employees. By doing this, the manager is, in effect, both raising taxes and deciding how they should be spent, which are functions of government, not of business. There are two objections to this:

  (i)   Managers have not been democratically elected (or selected in any other way) to exercise government power.

  (ii)   Managers are not experts in government policy and cannot foresee the detailed effect of such social responsibility spending.

Friedman argues that the social responsibility model is politically collectivist in nature and deplores the possibility that collectivism should be extended any further than absolutely necessary in a free society.

A second argument against the assumption of CSR is that the **maximisation of wealth is the best way that society can benefit from a business's activities**.

(a) Maximising wealth has the effect of increasing the tax revenues available to the State to disburse on socially desirable objectives.

(b) Maximising shareholder value has a 'trickle down' effect on other disadvantaged members of society.

(c) Many company shares are owned by pension funds, whose ultimate beneficiaries may not be the wealthy anyway.

7.7 Arguments in favour of CSR

Despite Friedman's arguments against it, there are a number of reasons why CSR can be strategically beneficial for businesses:

Customer expectations – There is an increasing expectation from consumers and other stakeholders that businesses will act in a more socially responsible manner. From, for example, the food they eat, to the coffee they drink and the clothes they wear, consumers are becoming more aware of the origins of the everyday things they buy, and they want to buy products that are responsibly sourced.

Given that one of the key success factors for a business is the ability to offer customers what they want, then offering products and services which are deemed to be socially responsible could help boost sales.

In this respect, CSR could provide opportunities to enter new markets or develop new products – for example, in the way that Toyota developed the 'Prius' hybrid car.

Brand name – Being seen as socially responsible can help enhance a business's reputation and therefore its brand. Customers may prefer to deal with a business they feel is socially responsible rather than with one which is not. Therefore, CSR could actually be a source of differentiation for a business.

Lower environmental costs – If firms improve the efficiency of their energy usage, for example, then as well as making lower emissions they will also have lower cost bases. If firms can achieve a lower cost base through the efficient use of resources, this could help them create (or improve) their competitive advantage.

More generally, firms could also find it to be less costly to regulate their own activities voluntarily than ignore social responsibility in the short term and then having to comply with statutory regulations (in the form of taxes or fines, for example) which may be imposed on them later.

Trading opportunities – If firms are perceived as not being socially responsible, they may find it harder to attract trading partners, or support from nations and local communities where they might want to invest.

Access to staff – Similarly, the way firms are perceived to treat their staff may affect their ability to attract staff. For example, firms that are perceived to offer good working conditions are more likely to be able to attract a higher calibre of staff than firms which are perceived to offer unfavourable working conditions. In turn, a firm which is able to attract (and retain) high-quality staff may be able to generate competitive advantage over a firm which is less able to attract good-quality staff.

Investment and funding – A firm's reputation may also affect its ability to attract finance, particularly from ethical investors. For example, obtaining a listing on the FTSE4Good (index of companies that meet globally recognised corporate responsibility standards) is likely to help a firm attract finance from ethical investors.

Sustainable business – Taken collectively, the arguments in favour of CSR suggest that a socially responsible business is likely to be able to operate for longer in society than a less responsible one. In turn, if the business can expect more years of cash flows in the future, it might be reasonable to expect the value of the company to be higher than that of one whose future is perceived to be less secure.

7.8 Other strategies for social responsibility

Proactive strategy	A strategy which a business follows where it is prepared to take full responsibility for its actions. A company which discovers a fault in a product and recalls the product without being forced to, before any injury or damage is caused, acts in a proactive way.
Reactive strategy	This involves allowing a situation to continue unresolved until the public, government or consumer groups find out about it.
Defence strategy	This involves minimising or attempting to avoid additional obligations arising from a particular problem.
Accommodation strategy	This approach involves taking responsibility for actions, probably when one of the following happens: • Encouragement from special interest groups • Perception that a failure to act will result in government intervention

Section summary

Corporate social responsibility is an organisation's obligation to maximise shareholder benefits while minimising the negative effects of its actions. It is not the same as ethical behaviour, although the two are related.

Chapter Summary

Quick Quiz

1   Which of CIMA's Ethical Principles is founded on fairness and avoiding all forms of bias, prejudice and partiality?

    A   Objectivity
    B   Integrity
    C   Professional behaviour
    D   Confidentiality

2   The primary consequence of an increase in a nation's interest rates is:

    A   To make imports more expensive
    B   To make borrowing more expensive
    C   To make imports cheaper
    D   To make borrowing cheaper

3   Which of the following is an external stakeholder?

    A   Shareholders
    B   Customers
    C   Suppliers
    D   Pressure groups

4   Which of the following is **not** an example of a corporate governance failure?

    A   Domination by a single individual
    B   Lack of contact with shareholders
    C   Strong corporate finance controls
    D   Short-term profitability being pursued

5   Charitable donations are an example of which layer of corporate social responsibility according to Caroll and Buchholtz?

    A   Economic
    B   Legal
    C   Ethical
    D   Philanthropic

Answers to Quick Quiz

1   A   Objectivity is founded on fairness and avoiding all forms of bias, prejudice and partiality.

2   B   An increase in interest rates makes company and individual borrowing more expensive.

3   D   Pressure groups are external stakeholders. The others are connected stakeholders.

4   C   Strong corporate finance controls would be an example of good corporate governance.

5   D   Charitable donations are an example of the philanthropic layer of corporate social responsibility according to Caroll and Buchholtz.

Now try these questions from the Practice Question Bank	Number
	6, 7, 8, 9, 10

MANAGING THE FINANCE FUNCTION

Part B

THE FINANCE FUNCTION

It is important to understand why accounts and reports are prepared. This chapter introduces some basic ideas about accounts and gives an indication of their purpose.

The main focus of the chapter, however, is on the components of the finance function, the information the components produce, and the roles that they fulfil in the organisation.

Topic list	Learning outcomes	Syllabus references	Ability required
1 The purpose of the finance function	B1(a)	B1(i), B1(ii), B1(iii), B1(iv), B1(v)	application
2 Financial accounting and company secretarial	B1(a), B1(b), B2(a)	B1(ii), B1(vi), B1(ix), B2(i)	analysis
3 Management accounting	B1(a), B1(b), B2(a)	B1(iv), B1(v), B1(vii), B2(ii), B2(iv), B2(v), B2(vi)	application
4 Treasury management	B1(a), B1(b), B2(a)	B1(iii), B1(viii), B2(iii)	application
5 Internal audit	B1(a), B1(b), B2(a)	B1(i), B1(x), B2(vii)	application
6 Conflict	B1(c)	B1(xi)	application
7 Contemporary developments in the finance function	B2(b)	B2(viii) to B2(xiii)	comprehension

Chapter Overview

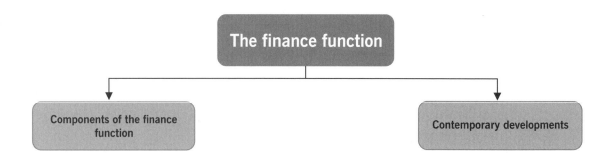

1   The purpose of the finance function

Introduction

Accounting is a way of recording, analysing and summarising transactions of a business.

1.1 What is accounting?

The accounting function is part of the broader business system, and does not operate in isolation. It handles the financial operations of the organisation, but also provides information and advice to other departments. It also provides **stewardship and control** of the organisation's **physical and financial resources**.

Accounts are produced to aid management in planning, control and decision making and to comply with statutory regulations. **The accounting system must be adequate to fulfil these functions**. An organisation's accounting systems are affected by the nature of its business transactions and the sort of business it is.

Factor	Example
Size	A small business like a greengrocer will have a simple accounting system, where the main accounting record will probably be the till roll. A large retail business, such as a chain of supermarkets, will have elaborate accounting systems covering a large number of product ranges and sites.
Type of organisation	A service business might need to record the time employees take on particular jobs. Accounting on a job or client basis might also be a feature of service businesses. A public sector organisation, such as a government department, may be more concerned with the monitoring of expenditure against performance targets than recording revenue. A manufacturing company will account for both unit sales and revenue, but needs to keep track of costs for decision-making purposes and so forth.
Organisation structure	In a business managed by area, accounts will be prepared on an area basis. In a functional organisation, the accounts staff are in a separate department.

Be aware that accounting work has to comply with a wide range of **regulations** to avoid penalties, including laws such as the Companies Act. As a result, it tends to be rather formalised and procedural in order to make sure that nothing is overlooked. Organisations often lay down their accounting rules and procedures in writing, and this may form part of an organisation manual or procedures manual.

1.2 The need for accounts

Renaissance scholar Luca Pacioli wrote the first printed explanation of double-entry bookkeeping in 1494. Double-entry bookkeeping involves entering every transaction as a **debit** in one account and a corresponding **credit** in another account, and ensuring that they 'balance'. Pacioli's description of the method was widely influential.

The first English book on the subject was written in 1543. The practice of double-entry bookkeeping has barely changed since then and is standard across the world, based on the concept that every transaction has a dual effect that balances to zero.

The original role of the **accounting function** was to record financial information and this is still its main focus.

Why do businesses need to produce accounts? If a business is being run efficiently, why should it have to go through all the bother of accounting procedures in order to produce financial information?

A business should produce information about its activities because there are various groups of people who want or need to know that information. This sounds rather vague: to make it clearer, we should look more closely at the classes of people who might need information about a business. We also need to think about what information is of particular interest to the members of each class.

Large businesses are usually of interest to a greater variety of people than small businesses, so we will consider the case of a large public company whose shares can be purchased and sold on the stock exchange.

1.3 Users of financial statements and accounting information

The people who might be interested in financial information about a large public company may be classified as follows:

(a) **Managers of the company**. These are people appointed by the company's owners to supervise the day to day activities of the company. They need information about the company's financial situation as it is currently and as it is expected to be in the future. This is to enable them to manage the business efficiently and to take effective control and planning decisions.

(b) **Shareholders of the company**, ie the company's owners. They will want to assess how effectively management is performing its stewardship function. They will want to know how profitably management is running the company's operations and how much profit they can afford to withdraw from the business for their own use.

(c) **Trade contacts**, including suppliers who provide goods to the company on credit and customers who purchase the goods or services provided by the company. **Suppliers** will want to know about the company's ability to pay its debts; **customers** need to know that the company is a secure source of supply and is in no danger of having to close down.

(d) **Providers of finance to the company**. These might include a bank which permits the company to operate an overdraft, or provides longer-term finance by granting a loan. The bank will want to ensure that the company is able to keep up with interest payments, and eventually to repay the amounts advanced.

(e) **Tax authorities**, which will want to know about business profits in order to assess the tax payable by the company.

(f) **Employees of the company**. They should have a right to information about the company's financial situation, because their future careers and the size of their wages and salaries depend on it.

(g) **Financial analysts and advisers**, who need information for their clients or audience. For example, stockbrokers will need information to advise investors in stocks and shares; credit agencies will want information to advise potential suppliers of goods to the company; and journalists need information for their reading public.

(h) **Government and their agencies**. Governments and their agencies are interested in the allocation of resources and therefore in the activities of enterprises. They also require information in order to provide a basis for national statistics.

(i) **The public**. Enterprises affect members of the public in a variety of ways. For example, enterprises may make a substantial contribution to a local economy by providing employment and using local suppliers. Another important factor is the effect of an enterprise on the environment, for example as regards pollution.

Accounting information is organised into financial statements to satisfy the **information needs** of these different groups. Not all will be equally satisfied.

Managers of a business need the most information, to help them take their planning and control decisions; and they obviously have 'special' access to information about the business, because they can get people to give them the types of statements they want. When managers want a large amount of information about the costs and profitability of individual products, or different parts of their business, they can arrange to obtain it through a system of cost and management accounting.

In addition to management information, financial statements are prepared and perhaps published for the benefit of other user groups.

(a)   The **law** provides for the provision of some information. For example, in the UK, the Companies Act requires every company to publish accounting information for its shareholders; companies must also file a copy of their accounts with the Registrar of Companies, so that any member of the public who so wishes can go and look at them.

(b)   The **tax authorities** will receive the information they need to make tax assessments.

(c)   A **bank** might demand a forecast of a company's expected future cash flows as a pre-condition of granting an overdraft.

(d)   The **professional accountancy bodies** have been jointly responsible for issuing **accounting standards** and some standards require companies to publish certain additional information. Accountants, as members of these professional bodies, are placed under a strong obligation to ensure that company accounts conform to the requirements of the standards.

(e)   Some companies provide, voluntarily, specially prepared financial information for issue to their employees. These statements are known as **employee reports**.

Exam alert

You may be asked about what information would be needed by managers, employees or shareholders.

1.3.1 Non-commercial undertakings

It is not only businesses that need to prepare accounts. **Charities and clubs**, for example, prepare financial statements every year. Accounts also need to be prepared for **government** (public sector organisations).

1.4 Qualities of good accounting information

You should be able to identify the qualities of good accounting information.

Below are some features that accounting information should have if it is to be useful.

(a)   **Relevance**. The information provided should satisfy the needs of information users. In the case of company accounts, clearly a wide range of information will be needed to satisfy a wide range of users.

(b)   **Comprehensibility**. Information may be difficult to understand because it is skimpy or incomplete, but too much detail is also a defect which can cause difficulties of understanding.

(c)   **Reliability**. Information will be more reliable if it is independently verified. The law requires that the accounts published by limited companies should be verified by auditors, who must be independent of the company and must hold an approved qualification.

(d)   **Completeness**. A company's accounts should present a rounded picture of its economic activities.

(e)   **Objectivity**. Information should be as objective as possible. This is particularly the case where conflicting interests operate and an unbiased presentation of information is needed. In the context of preparing accounts, where many decisions must be based on judgement rather than objective facts, this problem often arises.

Management are often inclined to paint a rosy picture of a company's profitability to make their own performance look impressive. By contrast, auditors responsible for verifying the accounts are inclined to take a more prudent view so that they cannot be held liable by, say, a supplier misled into granting credit to a shaky company.

(f) **Timeliness**. The usefulness of information is reduced if it does not appear until long after the period to which it relates, or if it is produced at unreasonably long intervals. What constitutes a long interval depends on the circumstances; management of a company may need very frequent (perhaps daily) information on cash flows to run the business efficiently, but shareholders are normally content to see accounts produced annually.

(g) **Comparability**. Information should be produced on a consistent basis so that valid comparisons can be made with information from previous periods and with information produced by other sources (for example the accounts of similar companies operating in the same line of business).

1.5 The components of the accounting function

In many organisations the head of the accounting structure is the **Finance Director**. The Finance Director has a seat on the **board of directors** and is responsible for all accounting matters and for broad financial policy.

The Finance Director may have one or more **deputies** below them, each of whom are responsible for one component of the accounting function. The components of the accounting function are set out below:

(a) **Financial accounting**

Usually headed by a **Financial Controller**:

- Routine accounting
- Providing accounting reports for other departments
- Cashiers' duties and cash control

(b) **Management accounting**

Management accounting is such an important function that a **Management Accountant** is often appointed with status equal to the Financial Controller and separate responsibilities.

- Cost accounting
- Budgets and budgetary control
- Financial management of projects

(c) **Treasury**

A very large organisation might have a **Treasurer** in charge of treasury work.

- Raising funds by borrowing
- Investing surplus funds on the money market or other investment markets
- Cash flow control

(d) **Internal audit**

Internal auditors may also work in very large organisations. Their roles include:

- Checking that business units comply with internal and external regulations
- Prevention, detection and avoidance of fraud

You should note that the **boundary of each deputy's authority may be blurred**. For example, the Financial Controller and Treasurer may have a role to play in budgeting as well as the Management Accountant.

Also, some of these functions may be brought together under a single job description, particularly in smaller businesses. For example, there may be one person who does the job of a financial accountant and a cost accountant.

Section summary

Accounting is a way of recording, analysing and summarising transactions of a business.

The components of the accounting function are: **financial accounting**, **management accounting**, **treasury** and **internal audit**.

2 Financial accounting and company secretarial

Introduction

The role of financial accountants is to assist in the publication of an organisation's financial statements to external parties.

2.1 Financial accounting

KEY TERM

FINANCIAL ACCOUNTING is mainly a method of reporting the results and financial position of a business in its financial statements.

It is not primarily concerned with providing information towards the more efficient conduct of the business. Although financial accounts are of interest to management, their principal function is to satisfy the information needs of persons not involved in the day to day running of the business.

This is particularly clear in the context of the published accounts of limited companies. **Accounting standards** (and company law) prescribe that a company should **produce accounts to be presented to the shareholders**. There are usually detailed regulations on what the accounts must contain and this enables shareholders to assess how well the directors (or management board) have run the company. The UK's Companies Act states that financial statements should give a **true and fair view** of the state of the company's affairs.

Shareholders often apply **financial ratios**, such as the three below, to analyse how profitable a company is and how well it is being run.

$$\text{Earnings per share (EPS)} = \frac{\text{Profit after tax (less preference dividends)}}{\text{Weighted average number of ordinary shares in issue}}$$

EPS is a measure of how much profit is attached to each company share.

$$\text{Price/earnings (P/E) ratio} = \frac{\text{Share price}}{\text{Earnings per share}}$$

The P/E ratio indicates the relationship between share price and earnings. A high P/E ratio suggests that shareholders are prepared to pay a high price for shares now because they expect future earnings to rise.

$$\text{Dividend yield} = \frac{\text{Dividend per share}}{\text{Current share price}} \times 100\%$$

The dividend yield shows the percentage return that a shareholder receives on their investment. Investors often choose to invest in companies that pay high dividends compared to their share price.

Other third parties who also need information about a company include: suppliers, customers, employees, the Government and banks. Their information needs are satisfied, wholly or in part, by the company's published financial statements.

Financial reporting is not an optional extra. The published accounts are an important source of communication with outsiders. Reported levels of profit determine the return that investors can receive. They also indirectly affect the company's cost of capital by affecting the share price.

2.2 Business transactions and financial accounts

All financial statements are based on information stored within an organisation's **information system**.

As a first stage, **transactions** such as sales to customers and purchases from suppliers are recorded. The **sales day book** (or receivables ledger) is a list of all sales invoices. The **purchase day book** (or payables ledger) is a list of all purchase invoices.

When **payments** are received from customers or paid to suppliers, they are recorded in the **cash book** (a list of payments in and out of the organisation's bank account). When small amounts of cash are paid or received (for example for buying tea and coffee for staff), this is usually recorded in a **petty cash book**.

Once recorded, transactions filter through to the **ledger accounts** and the **general ledger**. It is on the balances of these accounts at the end of the financial year that the financial statements are based. At this stage, other accounting entries (known as **journal entries**) can be entered by senior accounting staff. These entries are used to record **non-routine transactions** that fall outside the ledger system, to **correct errors** in ledger accounts, or make other **adjustments**. Accruals and prepayments are also examples of journal entries.

The following diagram shows a simplified flow of information relating to transactions. Journal entries will be recorded in the general ledger, outside of this system.

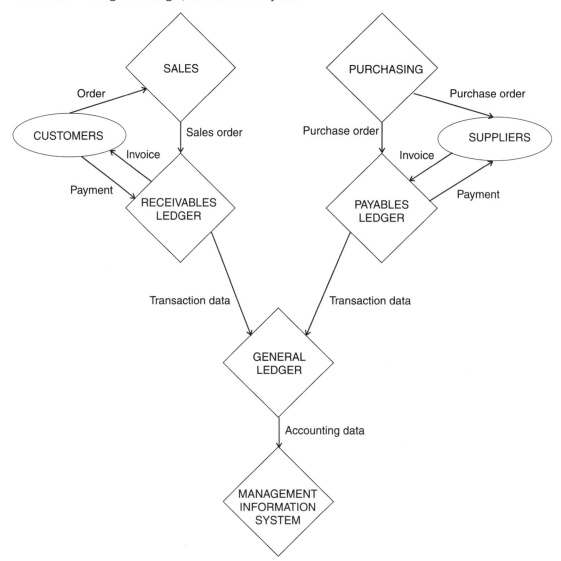

The main **financial statements** produced from the information system by the financial accountants are as follows:

- The statement of profit or loss
- The statement of financial position
- The statement of cash flows

2.3 The statement of profit or loss

The **statement of profit or loss** is a record of income generated and expenditure incurred over a given period. For a limited liability company it will be made up for the period of a year, commencing from the date of the previous year's accounts. The statement shows whether the business has more income than expenditure (a profit) or vice versa (a loss) during a period.

Organisations which are not run for profit (charities etc) produce a similar statement called an **income and expenditure account** which shows the surplus of income over expenditure (or a deficit where expenditure exceeds income).

2.4 The statement of financial position

The **statement of financial position** is a list of all the assets owned by a company and all the liabilities owed by it at a particular date. It also shows the amount of capital that its owners (the shareholders) have invested in it (known as shareholders' equity).

Assets are the business's resources eg buildings to operate from, plant and machinery to manufacture goods, inventory to sell and IT equipment for its employees. These are all resources which it uses in its operations. Also, it may have bank balances, cash and amounts of money owed to it. These provide the funds it needs to carry out its operations and are also assets. It may owe money to the Government, to the bank or to suppliers; these are **liabilities**.

2.5 The statement of cash flows

The **statement of cash flows** shows sources of cash generated during a period and how these funds have been spent. It therefore gives an indication of the solvency of the business at a particular moment in time.

2.6 Integrated reporting

Integrated reporting involves an organisation divulging **other relevant information** that might be of interest to its stakeholders, above and beyond the three statements that make up the financial statements. Examples of additional information reported include reports on **ethics** and **corporate responsibility**, **risk** and **risk management** and **sustainability performance**.

2.7 Company secretarial

There are a number of **important administration roles** that companies need to perform. They are usually in relation to **filing statutory returns** and very often the duties will be delegated to the finance team. The specific company secretarial duties are determined by the directors of the company. Common duties that are performed include:

- Establishing and maintaining the company's statutory registers
- Filing accurate returns with the Company Registrar on time
- Organising and taking minutes at company and board meetings
- Ensuring that accounting records meet statutory requirements
- Ensuring that annual accounts are prepared and filed in accordance with statutory requirements

- Monitoring non accountancy related statutory requirements of the company (such as health and safety rules or employment law)

- Signing company documents as may be required by law

Section summary

Financial accounting is a method of recording and reporting an organisation's transactions in order to provide a picture of its financial position and performance.

The **transactions** of the organisation are recorded in an information system which is used to produce the financial accounts.

A number of **company secretarial roles** could be delegated to the finance team.

3 Management accounting

Introduction

The role of management accountants is to provide a range of information that is used for management decision making and control.

KEY TERM

MANAGEMENT (OR COST) ACCOUNTING is a management information system which analyses data to provide information as a basis for managerial action. The concern of a Management Accountant is to present accounting information in the form most helpful to management.

The **Management Accountant** works closely with the policy making, strategy and management process. An example of cost reduction can be used to illustrate this.

If management set as a strategy that an organisation should **reduce costs** by x% then the Management Accountant will have a role to play in analysing and suggesting ways that this can be achieved. Once a course of action is decided, the Management Accountant may be involved in setting goals and objectives in the form of a budget. Once the plan is set, they will monitor and report on performance; if performance is not as expected they will look into why this is the case and suggest what remedial action can be taken.

Examples of **reports** under the remit of the **Management Accountant** include the following:

- Cost schedules
- Budgets
- Variance reports

3.1 Cost schedules

Cost schedules are lists of expenses incurred by manufacturing units when producing products. They are also known as standard cost cards and are needed at regular intervals to enable managers to keep a check on what the business is spending. Standard cost cards may record:

- Direct material costs
- Direct labour costs
- Variable costs
- Fixed overheads

Schedules may also be split by **product or process**, depending on the level of detail required by management. For example, if a business makes cars, then the overall cost of producing a car can be broken down by each part that the car is made from and the cost of performing the process to build the

car. By listing the cost of each part or process a quite detailed analysis of the overall cost of the car can be achieved. The **types of decision** that can be assisted by cost schedules include:

- Breakeven (how many products to make in order to cover costs?)
- Key-factor analysis (such as whether to produce products in-house or outsource production)
- Pricing (how much to sell products for in order to maximise profits?)
- Investment appraisal (for example, should new equipment be purchased?)

3.2 Budgets

Most businesses will prepare a **budget**, a plan of revenues and expenses that the organisation expects for a forthcoming period. For example, a budget may be for the year ahead, and show projected sales, costs involved in generating those sales, overheads and projected profits. Budgets may be produced for the business as a whole and for individual departments.

Budgets can be useful for a number of reasons:

(a) **Co-ordination** – ensures managers work together in the best interests of the organisation

(b) **Responsibility** – sets out which managers are responsible for controlling which costs and authorises them to do so

(c) **Utilisation** – helps managers make efficient and effective use of the resources under their control

(d) **Motivation** – helps to motivate managers to act in the best interests of the organisation by aligning their goals with those of the business

(e) **Planning** – managers are forced to look to the future, identify opportunities and threats and consider ways of tackling them

(f) **Evaluation** – forms a basis for the appraisal of managers

(g) **Telling** – the plans are communicated to individuals within the business so that all know what they are expected to do

It should be noted that several of these uses (in particular, motivation and planning) are only relevant if managers are involved in the budgeting process, rather than where managers have budgets imposed on them.

3.3 Variance (performance) reports

The **cost schedules should be compared to budget** and any differences accounted for. These differences are called variances and the variance report details the differences between actual and budgeted costs, and explains any material variances. Variance reports and analysis can also be used in a similar way in relation to revenue and sales (by analysing differences between actual and budget revenue).

Once variances are identified, **action** can be taken to stop the repeat of adverse variances and to encourage more instances of favourable variances in the future. The goal is to take action to bring **actual results** back into line with what was budgeted or, if possible, to improve them. **Forecasts** can be made during the financial year where budgets are adjusted for actual results and predicted outcomes from corrective action.

Using an example of a car maker: if the cost of certain parts and processes is greater than budget, then steps can be taken to reduce them and therefore keep the overall cost of producing the car down. It is important that **performance reports** are made regularly and are usually on a **monthly basis**. This allows the Management Accountant time to produce the information, but it is not too long after the event for any remedial action to be taken.

The comparison of **forecasted results** against budget is an example of a **feedforward control system** (so that corrective action can be taken during the financial period). By contrast, a **feedback control system** just compares actual historic results against budget.

Exam alert

It is important that you understand the distinction between management accounting and financial accounting. The accounting statements drawn up by a Management Accountant are often prepared and presented very differently from those of the financial accountant. You should bear in mind the different reasons for preparing management and financial accounts, and the different people to whom they are addressed. The following summary shows the key points for both management and financial accounting:

Management accounting

- Internal use
- Planning and control
- No legal requirements
- Management decide on report content and format
- Financial and non-financial information (such as productivity and quality reports)
- Historic and forward-looking information

Financial accounting

- External use
- Recording financial performance
- Legal and regulatory requirements (limited companies must produce financial accounts)
- Format and content must follow accounting standards and company law
- Financial information
- Historical information

Section summary

Management accounting involves analysing data to provide information as a basis for managerial action.

Reports are used for **internal purposes only** and contain **financial** and **non-financial information**.

4 Treasury management

Introduction

Treasury management is a separate discipline from both management accounting and financial accounting, although in a small organisation the three roles may be carried out by the same person.

The Treasury Manager (or Treasurer) is responsible for **raising finance** and **controlling financial resources**, including the following decisions:

- Should the firm borrow from a bank or raise funds by issuing shares?
- How much should be paid as a dividend?
- Should the firm spend money on new machinery?
- How much credit should be given to customers?

The Treasury Manager is responsible for **collecting all necessary information** to enable the best use to be made of the **organisation's assets**. Assets should only be purchased if they will **add value** to the business's operations and once purchased this should be **cost effective** and **contribute to effective business operations**.

4.1 The role of the Treasurer

The key roles of the Treasurer are as follows:

(a) **Working capital (liquidity) management**

Working capital (or liquidity) management involves making sure that the organisation has the **liquid funds** it **needs** to sustain its day to day operations and does not run out of cash.

(b) **Funding (cash) management**

Treasurers monitor **cash balances** on a daily basis and line up short-term funding (such as overdrafts) if required. They need to know where funds are obtainable, for how long, at what interest rate, whether security would be required or not and whether interest rates would be fixed or variable. They are also responsible for preparing the **cash budget**.

(c) **Currency (foreign exchange) management**

For companies which have international operations, a Treasurer should monitor relevant **foreign exchange rates** and conduct the organisation's currency transactions to minimise losses caused by movements in currency markets.

(d) **Corporate finance**

In cash-rich companies, the Treasurer will be heavily involved in the **investment of surplus funds** to earn a good yield until they are required again for another purpose. A good relationship with one or more banks is desirable. The overall objective is to maximise gains from investments and minimise any interest costs.

(e) **Tax management**

The treasury team has a role to play in ensuring that the business legally minimises the amount of tax that it has to pay.

4.1.1 Working capital management

An organisation's **working capital** is its **inventory**, **receivables**, **payables** and **cash**. It is the lifeblood of the business because capital is converted into cash. Cash is needed for the business to pay its debts as they fall due and therefore it is important that there is little or no delay in generating it.

Cash is created when products and services are sold to customers. Sales are often on credit, but the customer will at some point pay the company in cash. Because raw materials have to be purchased from creditors and the business has other costs that have to be paid for, cash will also leave the business.

Working capital reports are needed to manage cash inflows and outflows.

Inventory reports show the value of materials and finished products held in stock and the length of time they have been held for. Holding large amounts of inventory reduces the availability of cash because it is tied up in assets. Holding small amounts of inventory minimises holding costs and risk of the inventory becoming obsolete. The business should monitor inventory to make sure it is converted into finished products and cash as soon as possible.

Receivables reports show how much customers owe the business and how long the debt has been outstanding. Like inventory, holding large amounts of receivables reduces the availability of cash because it is tied up in the asset, but it keeps the customer happy because they like credit. Keeping the level of receivables as low as possible minimises the risk of debts going unpaid. By analysing receivables, decisions can be taken over which debts should be chased up.

Payables reports show how much the business owes its suppliers and how long debts have been outstanding. Delaying paying debts increases the availability of cash because it is not paid until necessary. However, paying quickly keeps the supplier happy and they may offer discounts to encourage this. The business should pay its debts, but not so early that it does not make use of periods of credit, or so late that it faces legal action for not paying what it owes. Late payment should be avoided because it damages relationships with suppliers, meaning they will not want to supply the business in future.

Cash reports show how much cash and liquid assets the business has. It is important to ensure sufficient cash is available as required to pay business expenses and other commitments, because this will keep creditors happy. Small cash balances are good provided that excess cash is being invested elsewhere to earn profit. Reports should highlight if cash shortages might occur so action can be taken (such as extending an overdraft) to prevent the business running out of cash.

4.1.2 Funding (cash) management

The **sources of finance** for businesses can be split into two main types: **debt** and **equity**.

In simple terms, **debt** is money lent to the organisation by a third party such as a bank on the agreement that it will be repaid with interest. Examples of lending methods are overdrafts, bank loans, bonds, debentures and money from venture capitalists.

From the point of view of the lender, debt can be **secured** on company assets such as property or plant and equipment and takes priority over the repayment of equity in the event of a liquidation. This means that it may be seen as a safer option than equity. Debt also means the lender gets a **guaranteed source of income** (interest), whereas there is no guarantee a company will pay dividends. From the point of view of the borrower, interest payments are a **tax deductible expense** and **must be paid** each year. Because of the lower risk to the lender, it can be a cheaper source of finance.

Equity is a stake in the ownership of a business that is usually represented by **shares**. A return in the form of a **dividend** may be (but **does not have to be**) paid every year to each shareholder. Unlike debt, shares are not secured on company assets and are attractive to borrower companies that do not own many assets. However, they are seen as a **higher risk** than debt finance and so it may be harder to attract investors. It should be remembered that, with equity, the organisation effectively gives away a share of its business to the investor. This does not happen with debt.

A key role of a Treasurer is to balance the amount of debt and equity within their organisation. The gearing ratio is used to analyse levels of debt. A highly geared company is seen as high risk because it must maintain high levels of compulsory interest payments. Companies that have low gearing are seen as lower risk because dividend payments are voluntary.

$$\text{Gearing} = \frac{\text{Long-term debt}}{\text{Shareholders' funds}} \times 100$$

4.1.3 Currency (foreign exchange) management

A company (such as a multinational) which is involved in **international transactions** faces the possibility of exposure to **foreign exchange risk**; the values of assets and liabilities denominated in one currency will change with fluctuations in that currency's exchange rate against another currency.

For example, a UK company may buy goods on 1 March from a US company and payment is due on 1 June. The goods cost $500,000 and at the exchange rate on 1 March, the cost in UK £ is £350,000. There is a risk that when the payment is due in June, the cost in UK £ may increase due to a change in exchange rates to, say, £385,000. To counter this risk, it may be possible for the company to enter a forward exchange contract on 1 March to buy $500,000 on 1 June at the current exchange rate and therefore fix the UK £ cost of £350,000.

4.1.4 Tax management

The Treasurer has a duty to help directors **maximise post-tax profits** for shareholders and this means to mitigate (minimise) tax charges as far as possible. However, there is a limit to how far the Treasurer and the directors can go when doing this.

Legitimate application of the rules of the tax regime in order to reduce tax payments is known as **tax avoidance** and this is perfectly legal. However, many tax avoidance schemes go against the spirit of the law, or what the Government intended, and may be viewed as immoral by some.

Tax evasion is the illegal reduction of tax liability by misleading the tax authorities, so that the true state of the organisation's tax affairs is hidden.

Tax mitigation is similar to tax avoidance, but schemes are designed to be within the spirit of the law as well as being legal.

Section summary

The Treasury Manager (or Treasurer) is responsible for **raising finance** and **controlling an organisation's financial resources**.

---

5   Internal audit

Introduction

Internal auditors are employees of the company whose duties are fixed by management and who report on the effectiveness of internal control systems. Their main concern is to ensure that internal and external rules are being complied with, and to prevent and detect fraud.

KEY TERM

CIMA defines INTERNAL AUDIT as 'an independent appraisal activity established within an organisation as a service to it. It is a control which functions by examining and evaluating the adequacy and effectiveness of other controls; a management tool which analyses the effectiveness of all parts of an entity's operations and management'.   (CIMA's *Management Accounting Official Terminology*)

The work of the internal audit often involves **investigating accounting sub-systems** to ensure transactions are recorded correctly and that they have not been tampered with. Internal auditors also **audit the business's operations** to give assurance that business objectives are valid, control information is reliable, and that activities are effective, efficient and economic. In recent years, the role of many internal auditors has expanded to helping to set **corporate objectives** and designing and monitoring **performance measures** to ensure these objectives are met.

5.1 Scope of internal audit

The scope of the work done by an internal audit team is determined by the **organisation's management**. There is **no legal requirement** for a business to have an internal audit department and there are no legal specifications regarding what the department should do if one is in place.

The main driver for internal audit is that of **corporate governance codes**. These codes have played a key role in the development of internal audit because they require directors to ensure they have adequate **internal control systems** in place to understand and mitigate risk in their organisation. The codes also generally say that if a company does not have an internal audit department then it should **review annually** whether it needs one. If a company does have an internal audit function then it should employ **experienced** and **suitably qualified staff** and annually review the scope of its work, authority and resources.

Roles that come under the remit of **internal audit** include:

- **Reviewing internal controls**, **risk management systems** and financial reports
- **Managing the data** used by management to identify risks
- **Identifying** methods for **prioritising** and **managing** risks
- **Reporting** on how effective **risk management controls** are
- **Prevention** and **detection of fraud** and **intentional misstatements** in financial statements

Internal audit will only be successful if the department is **appropriately staffed** and **funded**. Even though internal auditors are not as **independent** as external auditors, they are expected to act objectively as if

they were independent. This can make their role difficult, especially if they uncover fraud or misstatements and **fear internal repercussions** on their career if they report it.

These issues can be mitigated by the use of **audit committees** which set the work of the internal audit, receive their work, ensure the department has the resources it needs, and has a strong voice at board meetings.

5.1.1 Fraud and internal audit

As mentioned above, one of the roles of internal audit is to **prevent** and **detect fraud** and **intentional misstatements**. Fraud is a **criminal activity** and can be described as **'theft by deception'**. In regards to misrepresentation in financial statements, fraud is the use of deception to gain an **unjust** or **illegal advantage**, for example by falsifying documents, ignoring deliberate errors and suppressing relevant information.

Fraud can have a number of **impacts** on a business. The primary effect is a **loss of assets** or **financial difficulties** that may occur following the fraud. This may lead to **reduced confidence of shareholders** and the **collapse of the company** if the fraud is severe and widespread. **Fines** may also be imposed by authorities if the organisation did not follow certain rules and regulations, designed to help prevent fraud.

For a fraud to occur, **three prerequisites** are usually required to be present. These are **dishonesty** (a lack of integrity or honesty in the people committing the fraud), **opportunity** (usually created by weak internal controls) and **motivation** (the rewards of the fraud outweigh the risk of being caught).

Factors that contribute to an **increased chance of fraud** or misstatement can be split between causes and symptoms of fraud:

Causes of fraud

(a)   **Low staff morale** – unhappiness can create the motivation to defraud

(b)   **Lack of monitoring and control systems** – controls need to be reviewed and monitored in order for fraud to be detected

(c)   **Lack of segregation of duties** – increases the opportunity for fraud if tasks are not shared

(d)   **Unnecessarily complex corporate structures** – increases the opportunity for staff to hide fraud by making it harder for transactions to be traced

(e)   **Domination of management by one person or a small group** – dominant individuals may avoid controls and procedures

Symptoms of fraud

(a)   **Staff not taking leave or holiday** – may be a sign that staff do not want others to find out what they have been doing

(b)   **Strange transactions** – for example, cash payments to staff or transfers to unnamed bank accounts may be a sign that the transaction is fraudulent

(c)   **Payments being made out of proportion to work done** – this may be a sign of fraud

(d)   **Lavish lifestyles of employees** – staff living beyond their means may mean they are defrauding the company, or may need to do so in future if their funds run out

It should be noted that **good design of business systems** helps to prevent as well as detect fraud. If systems are poorly designed they will not be effective at either preventing or detecting fraudulent activity.

Section summary

Internal audit involves investigating accounting sub-systems to ensure transactions are recorded correctly and that they have not been tampered with and to audit the business's operations to give assurance that business objectives are valid, controls are adequate and reliable, and that activities are effective, efficient and economic.

6 Conflict

Introduction

Conflict between the departments of a finance function can be caused when the interests of each team are at odds with each other.

Most of the time, the various parts of an organisation's finance function will work in harmony. This is because they are **interdependent**; in other words, each part of the finance function is mutually dependent on the others. They all share resources and information, and produce information that should be consistent and reflected in the reports and information they produce. The various teams may also help each other out in busy periods.

However, there are times when the interests of each team may conflict. This is because in certain circumstances they may act **independently**. An example of this is the internal audit team. They are expected to act independently of the other finance teams and must do this to ensure their work is objective. If they find errors or fraud within the finance function they must report it.

Other sources of conflict are related to the point of view taken by each team and their own objectives. For example, the Management Accountant may be focused on **short-term objectives** such as reducing costs and increasing profit. These short-term objectives may conflict with the **organisation's long-term objectives** held by the treasury team. The treasury team may take a long-term view when making investments in new assets. A conflict may occur between the Management Accountant and Treasurer if the management requests a new asset that will help reduce costs in the short term, if the purchase does not meet the Treasurer's criteria for long-term profitability and the request is refused.

Conflict may also be created in the **application of accounting standards**, especially where there is some degree of debate about how a particular transaction should be treated. The Financial Accountant may treat a transaction as **revenue based** but a Management Accountant may treat the transaction as **capital based**. A conflict will be created because there will be a difference in the profits that each accountant reports.

As well as **conflict between finance teams**, there may be **conflict between the finance function and other departments** within an organisation. These conflicts can also be caused by **interdependence** and **independence**. For example, the work of the finance department is affected, and affects the work of other parts of the organisation, such as where financial reports affect the public relations team. The finance team must remain independent in order for the accounts to give a true and fair view, but this may conflict where there is pressure from other departments to give a different view. Such pressures are likely to increase as finance becomes a business partner (see later). For example, a Divisional Management Accountant may be under pressure to do what their division wants, as well as what the financial accountants might want.

Section summary

There is the **potential for conflict** between members of the finance function as well as between the finance function and other parts of the organisation.

Conflict is often caused by **interdependence** and **independence**.

7 Contemporary developments in the finance function

Introduction

The rapidly changing business environment has led to a number of developments in how accountants and finance functions operate. Increasingly, hybrid accountants are needed who can combine accountancy skills and commercial awareness as their role moves towards business support, rather than traditional accounting. As a consequence, accountants are becoming integrated into departments across organisations, rather than just being employed in finance teams.

The **main drivers for change** in finance functions include:

(a) **Technology**

Systems, such as management information systems, allow users across an organisation to have access to information and analysis previously provided by management accountants.

(b) **Management**

Responsibility for business performance has increasingly been delegated from head office to local business units and this has reduced the role of management accountants in budgeting. However, management accountants are now becoming a strategic link between the business unit and the board of directors.

(c) **Competition**

Increased competition has created a need for accountants to move their focus from short-term profit to long-term performance and adopt a greater strategic view. This has been driven by greater external information and competitor analysis which has created the role of the strategic management accountant (see later).

7.1 The finance function and market orientation

The traditional finance function is organised as a process-driven **bureaucracy**. Transactions are recorded and reports are generated at regular intervals. Authorisation for new asset purchases and other investments must be applied for and granted following set procedures.

However, in recent times there is a trend in organisations to move to a market orientation. We shall consider this concept when we study marketing later on; however, in general terms, this means that an organisation or function is built around the needs of the **customer**.

For an **in-house finance function**, this means the team provides a service to other parts of the organisation, its customers. For example, it provides an investment appraisal service to departments wishing to purchase new assets or management reports to operational managers who wish to monitor the performance of their departments.

The **cost of the finance function** might be split equally across all departments, or a charge may be made each time a service is performed. This means the service provided by the finance team is a commodity like other services the business may receive and the information will have a quantifiable value.

The main point to take from this is that the role of the accountant has moved from **bureaucratic transaction processing** to a **value-adding market orientation** where the accountant is involved in transforming business processes.

It may be discovered that services provided by the finance function could be obtained for a cheaper cost by offshoring or outsourcing the work.

7.2 Offshoring and outsourcing

KEY TERMS

OFFSHORING is the relocation of some part of an organisation's activities to another country.

OUTSOURCING involves an organisation subcontracting business activities to external providers. These providers may be in the same country as the organisation, or based overseas.

Developments in technology have made offshoring and outsourcing feasible in many situations. These technological advances permit business processes (such as the finance function) to be split up and performed in several locations. Communication devices such as smartphones and computers allow people in various locations to work together and to share information.

7.2.1 Offshoring

Offshoring could involve locating a department (such as the finance department) in another country, or using an external company based in another country (referred to as 'offshore outsourcing'). **Near-shoring** is a form of offshoring but the department is relocated to a country within the region of the business. For example, a UK-based company may relocate a service to mainland Europe.

The most common motivation for offshoring is to make **cost savings** by taking advantage of lower labour and/or other costs.

Managing operations based in another country involves a number of **challenges**:

- Risks associated with currency exchange rates and political and economic stability of the offshore country

- Loss of skills and jobs in the home country

- Exercising control from a distance and security of sensitive information

- Cost savings and efficiency improvements may be slow to accrue or may not be realised at all

- Dealing with cultural, time zone and language differences

Offshoring has grown significantly in many **developing countries** in recent years. It is popular due to the creation of new jobs and improvements in technological infrastructure and in education and skills that are created. However, some nations have voiced concerns over wages, working hours and other issues regarding the treatment of employees.

India is one popular offshoring country – for example, many UK banks and other large companies now have service centres based in India.

7.2.2 Outsourcing

Generally speaking, outsourcing is appropriate for **peripheral, non-core activities**. To outsource strategic or **core competences** could lead to loss of competitive advantage and risk the collapse of the whole organisation.

Outsourcing of **non-core activities** is widely acknowledged as having the potential to achieve important cost savings. However, it can be difficult to distinguish between core and non-core competences.

Threshold competences are activities that an organisation must possess in order to be a realistic competitor in a market. Outsourcing may be the only way for some organisations to obtain this type of competence.

Cox categorises competences into three groups:

Cox's types of competence
Core competences are those that result in competitive advantage. They should not be outsourced. Product design is an example.
Complementary competences aren't core themselves, but are connected or essential to core competences. These may be outsourced, but only to trusted key suppliers with whom a strategic relationship is formed. In many industries and organisations, the IT function is a complementary competence.
Residual competences aren't in any way core and are suitable for outsourcing. The payroll function is an example.

Quinn and Hilmer developed three tests that can be used to identify an organisation's core competences:

Quinn and Hilmer's core competence tests
Does the competence allow entry into a number of markets?
Does the competence make a substantial contribution to a customer's perceived benefits of a product?
Is the competence difficult for a competitor to copy?

If the answer to the questions is yes, then it is likely that the competence is core. Applying these tests to a finance function, it is likely that finance will not be classified as a core competence.

Quinn and Hilmer also identified three tests to establish whether an activity should be outsourced.

Quinn and Hilmer's tests to establish whether an activity should be outsourced
Potential for competitive advantage. The lower the potential for competitive advantage, the more suitable an activity is for outsourcing.
Strategic risk (or vulnerability) and the need for flexibility. Where strategic risk is high, or where an organisation is vulnerable, the activity should be kept in-house. However, where strategic risk is low and the need for flexibility is high, then the activity should be outsourced on a short-term contract.
Transaction costs. The level of transaction costs should be input into the decision.

Question 3.1	Offshoring and outsourcing

Learning outcomes B2(xi)

Explain the differences between offshoring and outsourcing. **(4 marks)**

7.2.3 Transaction costs

A **transaction cost** is incurred by an organisation as a consequence of having a business activity performed by a third party. Such costs arise from activities associated with the arrangement, for example creating product specifications, managing quality and co-ordinating delivery and manufacturing operations. **Standard products** which are mass produced may have **low transaction costs** due to the standardisation of design. However, **non-standard products** may have high transaction costs which can be classified as:

(a)   **Search and information costs**. These are the result of determining which products are needed and selecting a supplier at an appropriate cost and quality.

(b)   **Bargaining costs**. These result from negotiating a deal with the supplier and completing any legal formalities such as drawing up contracts.

(c)   **Policing and enforcement costs**. These are the costs of monitoring whether the supplier adheres to the terms of the contract and taking appropriate legal action if they do not.

7.2.4 Transaction cost theory

According to Williamson, an organisation has a choice of whether to produce goods itself (by owning assets and running the production process) or to buy in the use of another organisation's assets to produce the goods for it. There are **three aspects** to the make or buy decision:

(a)   **Uncertainty** – Uncertainty in the business environment makes it difficult to arrange long-term contracts and therefore it is more likely for a process to be undertaken in-house.

(b)   **Frequency** – Work is more likely to be outsourced if it is infrequent or unlikely to reoccur.

(c)   **Asset specificity** – Where the assets required are specific to the transaction then the process should be taken on in-house as the corresponding transaction costs will be high.

Williamson suggests that the main concern in the decision is asset specificity which can be classified into six main types.

Type of asset specificity	Description
Site specificity	Some sites, such as factories, are immobile and therefore specific to a certain location.
Physical asset specificity	Customised assets, or those with limited other uses, have lower alternative use values. This means they are more specific to the task.
Human asset specificity	Workers acquire knowledge or skills that are specific to their role. This knowledge or skill has a higher value within the activity (and therefore within an organisation) rather than outside it.
Brand name capital specificity	A brand name may become so associated with an activity or process that it cannot be used in other activities or for other customers.
Dedicated asset specificity	This is similar to physical asset specificity but relates to assets acquired solely for work undertaken for a specific customer.
Temporal specificity	Some activities, such as those involving perishable goods, are so time specific that an alternative processor is unlikely to be found in time if the current supplier fails.

7.2.5 Advantages and disadvantages of outsourcing

The **advantages** of outsourcing are as follows:

(a)   Outsourcing can remove uncertainty about cost, as there is often a long-term contract where services are specified in advance for a fixed price.

(b)   Long-term contracts (maybe up to ten years) encourage planning for the future. The organisation can focus on its core business.

(c)   It can save on costs by making use of a supplier's economies of scale, reduced headcount, reduced research and development costs and reduced capital spending on equipment.

(d)   It can increase effectiveness and quality of output where the supplier deploys higher levels of expertise.

(e)   Access to specialist knowledge and innovations in technology is made possible, and easier, if the organisation is experiencing a skills shortage. A specialist company can share staff with specific expertise between several clients.

(f)   Flexibility (contract permitting). Resources may be able to be scaled up or down depending on demand. In the long term, the organisation may be able to switch suppliers to match cost and quality requirements.

Some possible **disadvantages** are outlined below:

(a)   Difficulties negotiating and managing a service level agreement that meets the organisation's needs.

(b)   There are cost implications to consider – for example, the supplier will need to make a profit, which may result in outsourcing being more expensive than doing the work internally. Transaction costs will also arise as a consequence of the outsourcing arrangement.

(c)   It can lead to loss of control, particularly over quality and continuity of supply.

(d)   It means giving up an area of threshold competence that may be difficult to reacquire. The organisation may become out of touch with new developments resulting in a lack of in-house knowledge.

(e)   The same outsourcing service is likely to be available to competitors. There is a risk of confidential information being leaked.

(f)   Potential damage to employee morale due to redundancies and impact on corporate culture.

7.2.6 Shared servicing

An alternative to outsourcing is shared servicing, where shared service centres consolidate the **transaction-processing activities** of many operations within a company. Shared service centres aim to achieve significant cost reductions while improving service levels through the use of standardised technology and processes and service level agreements. For example, a multinational business may use shared servicing in its head office to process all transactions incurred by its overseas operations.

Advantages to using this approach include:

(a)   **Reduced headcount** due to economies of scale resulting from the single location centre

(b)   Associated **reduction in premises** and other overhead costs

(c)   Knowledge sharing should lead to an **improvement in quality** of the service provided

(d)   Allows **standard approaches** to be adopted across the organisation leading to more consistent management of business data

7.2.7 The finance function as business partner

The finance function has faced pressures to become **more actively involved** in business operations. Many finance functions have therefore refocused their roles as business partners, adopting a more **commercial, action-orientated approach**. This means management accountants need to gain a broad knowledge of the business they work for, participating as full members of operational teams and bringing financial expertise to the management process. They are also expected to **integrate management accounting information** with **strategic management accounting data**.

Strategic management accounting data has sources both external and internal to the business, is forward looking (as well as being historical), and includes non-financial information as well as financial.

Important areas where the finance function's role has developed have included:

*   Providing more useful information on business units, projects, products and customers
*   Supplying business cases for new investments
*   Giving support in helping operational managers understand the information provided
*   Collaborating in strategic planning and budgeting
*   Designing information systems that provide greater support for operational managers

One example of where finance functions have been expected to assume a more active role is **investment appraisal**. Accountants are now often required to do more than state that the proposal does not meet financial criteria; they are expected to help develop and refine proposals.

7.2.8 Problems with the business partner model

Over the last couple of years the business partner model has in turn faced criticism. Critics have questioned the **identification** of the finance function with **operational viewpoints** and the **loss of independence** of the finance function that has arisen from finance staff reporting to, and being accountable to, operational managers.

Critics also claim that the finance function has become too greatly diverted from delivering basic controls and safeguards and functions, providing prudent financial management and ensuring the **true and fair view** is given. The finance function has, critics suggest, lost sight of its role in governance and failed to protect shareholder and public interest.

7.2.9 Independent business partner

A new independent business partner model has therefore emerged, not losing sight of co-operation with operational managers, but also having at its heart **strict controls**, **safeguarding of assets** and **effective reporting**.

The independent business partner model stresses that the finance function should seek to **add** value, but its role is not to **create** value. The creation of strategy, ideas and opportunities is the responsibility of the operational departments. Finance's role is to **assess** and **validate** these ideas, taking a commercial view, but also ensuring that business plans and strategy are rigorously reviewed and challenged if necessary. Finance must also **review actual performance** rigorously and be prepared to challenge better than expected, as well as worse than expected, performance in order to minimise the risks of overstatement as well as understatement.

7.2.10 Business partners and change

It is important that business partners are **informed of any changes** to the finance team because changes to processes will have an impact on them. If the finance function is offshored or outsourced then new relationships will need to be established. The support and understanding of business partners is important for changes to be successful.

7.3 The finance function and Business Process Re-engineering (BPR)

The operation of the finance function may be transformed using Business Process Re-engineering (BPR).

KEY TERM

BUSINESS PROCESS RE-ENGINEERING is the fundamental rethinking and radical redesign of business processes to achieve dramatic improvements in critical contemporary measures of performance, such as cost, quality, service and speed.   (Hammer and Champy (2001))

As the definition states, BPR involves **fundamental** changes in the way an organisation, or part of it, operates. Other key words from the definition are '**radical**', '**dramatic**' and '**process**'.

(a) **Fundamental** and **radical** indicate that BPR assumes nothing; it starts by asking basic questions such as 'why do we do what we do', without making any assumptions.

(b) **Dramatic** means that BPR should achieve 'quantum leaps in performance', not just marginal, incremental improvements.

(c) A **process** is a collection of activities that takes one or more kinds of input and creates an output. For example, recording business transactions in the accounting system results in data that is used in management reports.

The **application of BPR to the finance function** will mean **identifying work processes** that are necessary and which add value. Next comes **process rationalisation** where non value adding activities are discarded. Following that, new, **efficient processes are designed** and documented for future reference. Finally comes **process reassembly** where the new processes are implemented.

7.3.1 Four themes of BPR

Hammer and Champy identify four themes of BPR:

(a) **Process reorientation**. There should be a focus on resources, tasks and constraints.
(b) **Creative use of IT** should be explored.
(c) **Ambition**. Don't be restricted by current ways of working. Think widely and ambitiously.
(d) Challenge and **break rules**. Think radically. Old rules may not apply to new processes.

7.3.2 Limitations of BPR

Some BPR projects have **failed to bring the benefits expected**. To succeed, a BPR initiative requires sustained management **commitment** and leadership, **realistic scope** and expectations, and a **willingness to change**.

BPR has become associated with narrow targets such as **reductions in staff numbers** and other **cost-cutting** measures. Some companies, attracted by the latest high-tech gadgetry, believed they could enhance their performance solely by redeploying office automation systems (and laying off workers) rather than through the much harder task of significant organisational process redesign, which may involve neither IT investment nor redundancies, just the better use of people.

CASE STUDY

Example of BPR

A company employs 25 staff to perform the standard accounting task of matching goods received notes with orders and then with invoices. A process review established that 50% of employee time was spent trying to match the 20% of document sets that do not agree.

One way of improving the situation would be to computerise the existing process to facilitate matching. This would help, but BPR would go further.

A BPR approach may question why **any** incorrect orders are accepted. To enable incorrect orders to be identified before being accepted, all orders could first be entered into a computerised database. When goods arrive, they either agree to goods that have been ordered (as recorded in the database) or they don't.

Goods that agree to an order are accepted and paid for. Goods that are not agreed are sent back to the supplier. Time is not wasted trying to sort out unmatched documents.

Gains would include staff time saved, quicker payment for suppliers, lower stocks, and lower investment in working capital.

Section summary

The role of the **finance function** is increasingly seen as providing a **service** to internal customers and acting as a **business partner** for operating units within an organisation.

The finance function may be **offshored** or **outsourced** to reduce company costs.

Business Process Re-engineering (BPR) can radically change the way the finance team does its work.

Chapter Summary

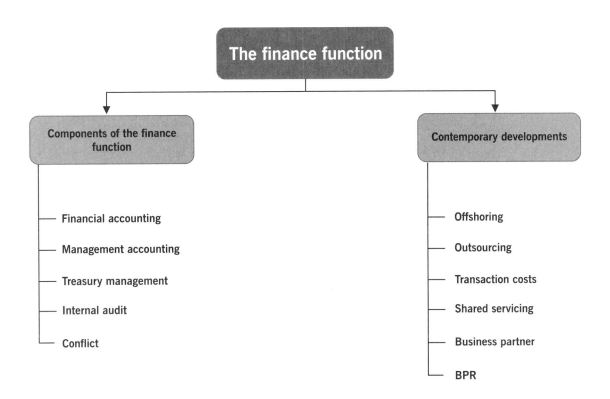

Quick Quiz

1   Accounting journal entries are recorded in which of the following?

   A   The sales day book
   B   The general ledger
   C   The purchase day book
   D   The management information system

2   The person responsible for cost accounting is most likely to be the company treasurer. Is this true or false?

3   Internal auditors are employed by:

   A   The company that they audit
   B   An independent auditing/accounting firm
   C   Either A or B

4   Which of the following ratios analyses the level of debt within an organisation?

   A   Gearing
   B   Dividend yield
   C   Price/earnings
   D   Earnings per share

5   Minimising an organisation's tax liability by operating within the letter and spirit of the law is known as:

   A   Tax avoidance
   B   Tax mitigation
   C   Tax evasion
   D   Double taxation

Answers to Quick Quiz

1	B	Journals are entered into the general ledger.
2	False	Cost accounting is usually done by the Management Accountant.
3	A	Internal auditors are employees of the company that they audit.
4	A	The gearing ratio compares the level of debt and equity within an organisation.
5	B	Tax mitigation involves minimising tax liability through schemes that operate both within the letter and spirit of the law. Tax avoidance operates within the law but not the spirit of the law. Tax evasion is outside the law.

Answers to Questions

3.1 Offshoring and outsourcing

Offshoring is the relocation of some part of an organisation's activities to another country.

Outsourcing involves an organisation subcontracting business activities to external providers. These providers may be in the same country as the organisation, or based overseas.

Now try these questions from the Practice Question Bank	Number
	11, 12, 13, 14, 15

MANAGING TECHNOLOGY AND INFORMATION

Part C

THE TECHNOLOGY AND INFORMATION FUNCTION

 In this chapter we introduce **information systems** and explain their role within organisations.

In particular, we are interested in how developments in technology have provided organisations with **new ways of working** and how IT-enabled **'transformations'** have led to new forms of organisation, both **real** and **'virtual'**.

New technologies are providing valuable additional information to managers to help support their decision making.

Big Data is one key example, and we consider its main principles. However, it is an important part of the CIMA syllabus and we will revisit it again in later chapters.

Topic list	Learning outcomes	Syllabus references	Ability required
1 The role of information systems in organisations	C1(a)	C1(i)	demonstrate
2 Data and information	C1(a)	C1(i)	demonstrate
3 Types of information systems	C1(a), C1(b), C2(a)	C1(i), C1(v), C2(ii)	demonstrate
4 System architecture and data flows	C2(a)	C2(iv)	explain
5 Emerging trends in information systems	C1(a), C1(b), C2(b)	C1(ii), C1(v), C2(x)	demonstrate
6 Big Data	C2(a), C2(b)	C2(v), C2(vi), C2(xii)	explain
7 IT-enabled transformation	C1(b), C2(b)	C1(iii), C1(v), C2(xi)	demonstrate
8 IT and new forms of organisation	C1(b)	C1(iii), C1(iv), C1(v)	demonstrate

Chapter Overview

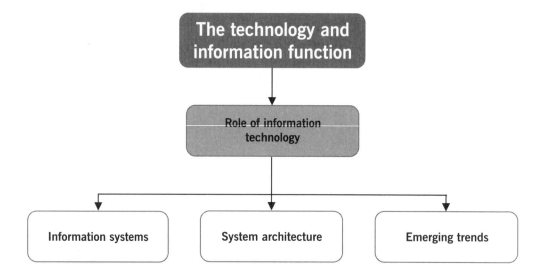

1 The role of information systems in organisations

Introduction

In this section we look at the role information systems play in organisations. Two main roles can be identified:

- **Support operations** through the processing and storing of transactions

- **Support managerial activities** such as decision making, planning, performance measurement and control

Organisations need **information systems** to enable them to **capture** and **generate the information** that **managers need** for planning, control and decision-making purposes. We shall consider these needs further later in this chapter when we look at the types of information system.

Information systems also have more **general roles** to play within an organisation. For example, they **improve communication**, allow **better operations** and **manufacturing**, **enhance products** and **services** provided and provide opportunities to **reduce costs**.

KEY POINT

Organisations **require information** for a range of purposes:

- Recording transactions
- Decision making
- Planning
- Performance measurement
- Control

1.1 Recording transactions

Information about **each business transaction or event** is required for a number of reasons. Documentation of transactions can be used as **evidence** in a case of dispute. There may be a **legal requirement** to record transactions, for example for accounting and audit purposes. Detailed information on production costs can be built up allowing a better **assessment of profitability**.

1.2 Decision making

Information is also required to make **informed decisions**. Information and information systems enable **informed decisions** to be made. **Information** used by information systems may be classified as **internal** and **external**.

1.3 Planning

Planning requires knowledge of, among other things, available **resources**, possible **timescales** for implementation and the likely **outcome under alternative scenarios**. Information systems can provide a number of **planning tools**.

1.4 Performance measurement

Just as individual operations need to be controlled, so overall performance must be measured in order to enable **comparisons against budget or plan** to be made. This may involve the collection of information on, for example, costs, revenues, volumes, timescale and profitability. The **collection**, **analysis** and **presentation** of such data can be performed by information systems.

1.5 Control

Once a plan is implemented, its actual performance must be controlled. Information is required to assess **whether it is proceeding as expected** or whether there is some unexpected deviation from the plan. It may consequently be necessary to take some form of corrective action. Information systems can be used to **monitor** and **control the outcomes of plans**.

2   Data and information

Introduction

When discussing information systems the terms data and information often crop up. It is worth defining these terms.

- **Data** consists of raw, unprocessed facts and figures.

- **Information** is data that has been processed in a way that makes it meaningful for planning or decision making.

The process of **turning data into information** involves a number of stages.

 STEP 1   Data collection

Data gathering from internal and external sources.

 STEP 2   Data evaluation

The data collected is examined and filtered. Irrelevant data may be deleted or ignored.

 STEP 3   Data analysis

Data collected is compared against benchmarks or yardsticks, for example actual versus budget.

 STEP 4   Interpretation

Data is considered, interpreted and meaning added, for example an explanation as to why actual differs from budget.

 STEP 5   Reporting

Information is distributed to those who require it, for example as a report sent out as an email attachment.

There are **costs** associated with **developing** and **running** the **system** required to convert data into information – for example costs associated with system design, purchasing, housing and testing equipment, and operating costs such as electricity and staff salaries.

It is important that such costs do not exceed the **value of the information** created by the system. Information may have an intrinsic value and may be sold, but it may also have a value to the organisation in terms of creating competitive advantage, cost control and reduction, improving corporate decision making and strategy (such as marketing decisions).

2.1 Internal data and information

This is data and information that is held within the organisation's own files. The following are examples of internal information.

2.1.1 Accounting records

Accounts receivable ledgers, **accounts payable** ledgers, **general ledgers** and **cash books** etc hold information that may be of great value outside the accounts department – for example, sales information for the marketing function.

2.1.2 Personnel records

Information about **personnel** will be held, possibly linked to the **payroll** system. Additional information may be obtained from this source if, say, a project is being costed and it is necessary to ascertain the availability and rate of pay of different levels of staff, or the need for and cost of recruiting staff from outside the organisation.

2.1.3 Production data

Much information will be produced by a **production** department about machine capacity, fuel consumption, movement of people, materials, work in progress, set-up times, maintenance requirements and so on.

2.1.4 Timesheets

Many **service** businesses, notably accountants and solicitors, need to keep detailed records of the **time spent** on various activities, both to justify fees to clients and to assess the efficiency and profitability of operations.

2.2 External data and information

Organisations often need to collect information concerning environmental factors. The following table describes some of these factors using PEST analysis.

Factor	Comment
Political/legal	National or local politics may affect how an organisation operates. Changes in legislation may put new responsibilities or liabilities on an organisation.
Economic	Economic factors affect an organisation's finances such as the availability of loans and sales levels.
Social	Society's views may put pressure on how the organisation is run, for example pressure to reduce environmental pollution.
Technological	Technological advances may affect an organisation's production and/or management processes. Technology may also allow the development of new products and services which were not previously possible.

Organisations may also require external information relating to:

(a) **Competitors** – how successful are they, are they developing new products?

(b) **Customers** – what are their needs, how large is the potential market, are there any new market segments?

(c) **Suppliers** – what are their prices, what is the quality of their products like, are there any new potential suppliers in the market?

Formal collection of data from outside sources includes the following:

(a)   A company's **tax specialists** will be expected to gather information about changes in tax law and how this will affect the company.

(b)   The company's **legal expert** or **company secretary** would collect relevant information relating to any new legislation on health and safety at work, or employment regulations.

(c)   **Research and development** (R&D) work often relies on information about other R&D work being done by another company or by government institutions.

(d)   **Marketing managers** need to know about the opinions and buying attitudes of potential customers. To obtain this information, they might carry out market research exercises.

KEY TERM

The phrase ENVIRONMENTAL SCANNING is often used to describe the process of gathering external information from a wide range of sources.

Sometimes additional external information is needed, requiring an active search outside the organisation.

The following **additional external sources** may be identified – the Government, advice or information bureaux, consultancies, newspaper and magazine publishers, specific reference works which are used in a particular line of work, libraries and information services, and customer or supplier systems can be a source of information, for instance via electronic data interchange (EDI), and web-based sources of information are becoming ever more important.

2.2.1 Informal data and information gathering

Informal gathering of data and information from the environment goes on all the time, when employees learn **what is going on in the world around** them – perhaps from trade magazines, newspapers, websites, television reports or meetings with business associates.

Knowledge, skills and experience developed by members of staff is collectively known as the organisation's **human capital**. This contrasts with **structural capital** which comprises assets such as patents and client lists that the business owns.

2.3 The qualities of information

To be useful, information requires a number of specific qualities. The mnemonic ACCURATE, shown in the following table, is a useful way of remembering them.

Information systems should aim to produce information that possesses these qualities.

Quality	Example
Accurate	Figures in a report should add up, the degree of rounding should be appropriate, there should be no typos, items should be allocated to the correct category, assumptions should be stated for uncertain information. Must be **reliable**.
Complete	Information should include everything relevant to the decision being considered. If relevant, comparative information should be included. Information should be **consistent**, for example it should be collected on the same basis each time, to allow for meaningful **comparison**. Excessive information should be avoided.
Cost effective	It should not cost more to obtain the information than the **benefit** derived from its use. Information collection and analysis should be **efficient**. Presentation should be clear, such that users do not waste time working out what the information means.
Understandable	The **needs of the user** are paramount. The information must be easy to read and well presented.

Quality	Example
Relevant	Information that is **not needed** for a decision should be omitted. All significant information that is relevant to the decision being considered should be included.
Accessible	The **choice of medium** to provide the information should be appropriate (face to face, email, letter, written report) and consider the needs of the user.
Timely	The information should be available **when it is needed** and in time for required action to be effective.
Easy to use	As well as being **understandable** (clear and well presented) and **accessible** (correct choice of medium) the information should be presented in a manner that the user can **easily use** or pass on as required.

Section summary

Information systems play a key role within organisations. In particular they are used in **planning**, **controlling**, **recording transactions**, **performance measurement** and **decision making**.

Data consists of raw, unprocessed facts and figures. **Information** is data that has been processed in a way that makes it meaningful for planning or decision making.

Information used by organisations comes from a variety of **internal** and **external sources**.

Information systems should provide information that possesses certain specific **qualities** (ACCURATE).

3 Types of information systems

Introduction

There are a large **range of information systems** available to an organisation, with different purposes. In this section we shall look at common forms of information system and, later, some **recent trends** and **developments in information systems**.

3.1 Information systems at different organisational levels

The term **information system (IS)** is a general concept that refers to the provision and management of information to support the running of the organisation. Most ISs utilised in a business context today rely on **information technology (IT)** which is the hardware infrastructure that supports the IS.

Exam alert

You must be aware of the difference between ISs and IT. ISs provide management information and assist with business operations. IT is the underlying hardware equipment that the system is built on.

Organisations require different types of IS to provide information at **different levels** of the organisation, and in a range of functional areas.

Organisational level	System purpose and features	Examples
Strategic	**Purpose**: To help senior managers with long-term planning **Time focus**: Long term **Coverage**: Whole organisation **Uncertainty and subjectivity**: High **Accuracy**: Less critical than at other levels	Key ratios and performance indicators Ad hoc market analysis Strategic plans
Management or tactical	**Purpose**: To help middle managers monitor and control **Time focus**: Short to medium term **Coverage**: Department(s) or function(s) **Uncertainty and subjectivity**: Moderate **Accuracy**: Moderate level, not as detailed as operational level	Variance analyses Exception reports
Operational	**Purpose**: To process transactions and help operational managers track the organisation's day to day operational activities **Time focus**: Immediate **Coverage**: Specific activities **Uncertainty and subjectivity**: Low **Accuracy**: A high level of accuracy is required	Transaction listings Daily receipts and payments Real-time production data Debtors and creditors listings

Different types of ISs exist with different characteristics, reflecting the different roles they perform. The most common are described below.

3.2 Transaction Processing Systems (TPSs)

KEY TERM

A TRANSACTION PROCESSING SYSTEM (TPS) performs and records routine transactions.

TPSs are used for **routine tasks** in which data items or transactions must be processed so that operations can continue. TPSs support most business functions in most types of organisation. TPSs are sometimes referred to as **Data Processing Systems (DPSs)**.

The following table shows a range of TPS applications.

Transaction Processing Systems				
	Sales/ marketing systems	Manufacturing/ production systems	Finance/ accounting systems	Human resources systems	Other types (eg university)
Major functions of system	• Sales management • Market research • Promotion pricing • New products	• Scheduling • Purchasing • Shipping/ receiving • Engineering • Operations	• Budgeting • General ledger • Billing • Management accounting	• Personnel records • Benefits • Salaries • Labour relations • Training	• Admissions • Student academic records • Course records • Graduates

| Transaction Processing Systems | | | | |
Sales/ marketing systems	Manufacturing/ production systems	Finance/ accounting systems	Human resources systems	Other types (eg university)
Major application systems				
• Sales order IS • Market research system • Pricing system	• Materials resource planning • Purchase order control • Engineering • Quality control	• General ledger • Accounts receivable/ payable • Budgeting • Funds management	• Payroll • Employee records • Employee benefits • Career path systems	• Registration • Student record • Curriculum/ class control systems • Benefactor IS

3.3 Management Information Systems (MISs)

KEY TERM

MANAGEMENT INFORMATION SYSTEMS (MISs) convert data from mainly internal sources into information (eg summary reports, exception reports). This information enables managers to make timely and effective decisions for planning, directing and controlling the activities for which they are responsible.

An MIS provides **regular reports** and **access** to the organisation's current and historical performance.

MISs usually **transform data** from **underlying TPSs** into summarised **files** that are used as the basis for management reports.

MISs have the following characteristics:

- Support **structured** decisions at operational and management control levels
- Designed to report on **existing** operations
- Have **little analytical capability**
- Relatively **inflexible**
- Have an **internal** focus

3.4 Executive Information Systems (EISs)

KEY TERM

An EXECUTIVE INFORMATION SYSTEM (EIS) pools data from internal and external sources and makes information available to senior managers in an easy to use form. EISs help senior managers make strategic, unstructured decisions.

An EIS should provide senior managers with easy access to key **internal** and **external** information. The system summarises and tracks strategically critical information, possibly drawn from internal MISs and DSSs (see below), but also including data from **external sources** eg competitors, legislation and external databases such as Reuters.

EISs are sometimes referred to as **Executive Support Systems** (ESSs). An ESS/EIS is likely to have the following **features**:

- Flexibility
- Quick response time
- Sophisticated data analysis and modelling tools

A model of a **typical EIS** follows.

An EIS

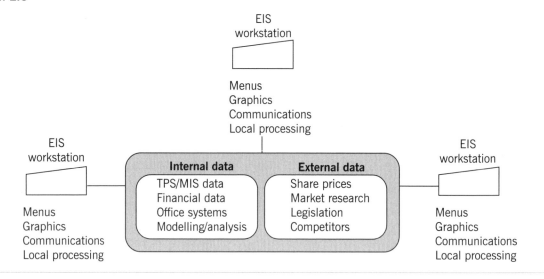

3.5 Decision Support Systems (DSSs)

KEY TERM

DECISION SUPPORT SYSTEMS (DSSs) combine data and analytical models or data analysis tools to support semi-structured and unstructured decision making.

DSSs are used by **management to assist in making decisions** on issues which are subject to high levels of uncertainty. They are intended to provide a wide range of alternative information gathering and analytical tools with a major emphasis on **flexibility** and **user friendliness**.

DSSs have more **analytical power** than other systems, enabling them to analyse and condense large volumes of data into a form that aids managers' decision making. The objective is to allow the manager to consider a number of **alternatives** and evaluate them under a variety of potential conditions.

3.6 Knowledge Work Systems (KWSs)

KEY TERMS

KNOWLEDGE WORK SYSTEMS (KWSs) are ISs that facilitate the creation and integration of new knowledge into an organisation.

KNOWLEDGE WORKERS are people whose jobs primarily involve creating new information and knowledge. They are often members of a profession, such as doctors, engineers, lawyers and scientists.

KWSs help **knowledge workers** create new knowledge and expertise. Examples include:

- Computer Aided Design (CAD)
- Computer Aided Manufacturing (CAM)
- Specialised financial software that analyses trading situations

3.7 Office Automation Systems (OASs)

KEY TERM

OFFICE AUTOMATION SYSTEMS (OASs) are computer systems designed to increase the productivity of data and information workers.

OASs **support the major activities** performed in a typical office such as document management, facilitating communication and managing data.

Examples include:

- Word processing, desktop publishing, presentation software
- Digital filing systems
- Email, voice mail, videoconferencing (or teleconferencing)
- Groupware (calendars, address books and journals), intranets, extranets, schedulers
- Spreadsheets, desktop databases

3.8 Expert systems

KEY TERM

EXPERT SYSTEMS are a form of DSS that allow users to benefit from expert knowledge and information. Such systems consist of a **database** holding specialised data and **rules** about what to do in, or how to interpret, a given set of circumstances.

For example, many financial institutions now use expert systems to process straightforward **loan applications**. The user enters certain key facts into the system such as the loan applicant's name, their most recent addresses, their income, monthly outgoings and details of other loans. The system will then:

(a)   **Check the facts** given against its database to see whether the applicant has a good credit record.

(b)   **Perform calculations** to see whether the applicant can afford to repay the loan.

(c)   **Match up other criteria** such as whether the security offered for the loan or the purpose for which the loan is wanted is acceptable and appropriate to the applicant's risk profile. The system makes these judgements based on previous experience (as represented within the system).

A decision is then suggested, based on the results of this processing. This is why it is possible to get a loan or arrange insurance **over the telephone**. In the past it would have been necessary to go and speak to a bank manager or send details to an actuary and then wait for them to come to a decision.

Exam skills

Do not just learn what these systems are – you need to understand which levels of an organisation's hierarchy would use them and how they support its operations.

There are many other **business applications** of expert systems:

(a)   **Legal** advice

(b)   **Tax** advice

(c)   **Forecasting** of economic or financial developments, or of market and customer behaviour

(d)   **Surveillance**, for example of the number of customers entering a supermarket to decide when more checkouts need to be opened – or of machines in a factory, to determine when they need maintenance

(e)   **Diagnostic systems** to identify causes of problems, for example in production control in a factory, or in healthcare

(f)   **Project management**

(g)   **Education** and **training**, diagnosing a student's or worker's weaknesses and providing or recommending extra instruction as appropriate

An organisation can use an expert system when a number of **conditions** are met:

(a) The problem is **reasonably well defined**.

(b) The expert can define some **rules** by which the problem can be solved.

(c) The problem cannot be solved by **conventional** transaction processing or data handling.

(d) The **expert could be released** to more difficult problems. Experts are often highly paid, meaning the value of even small time savings is likely to be significant.

(e) The **investment** in an expert system is **cost-justified**.

| Question 4.1 | Expert systems |

Learning outcomes C1(a)

Explain why organisations use expert systems for decision-making tasks which humans are naturally better able to perform than computers. **(5 marks)**

3.9 Internet, intranets and related technologies

Organisations are increasingly using the **internet**, **intranets** and **extranets** to **disseminate information**.

(a) The **internet** describes a system of computers and networks that use the standard internet protocol suite (TCP/IP) to connect between each other globally. The majority of computers and networks around the world are connected – for example, privately owned computers, academic, business, and government networks. As well as connections, the internet contains information and provides a structure to provide services such as email and file sharing.

(b) An **intranet** is like a mini version of the internet. Organisation members use networked computers to access information held on a server. The user interface is a browser – similar to those used on the internet. The intranet offers access to information on a wide variety of topics.

(c) An **extranet** is an intranet that is accessible to **authorised outsiders**, using a valid username and password. The username will have access rights attached, determining which parts of the extranet can be viewed. Extranets are becoming a very popular means for business partners to exchange information.

KEY TERMS

The INTERNET describes a system of computers and networks that use the standard internet protocol suite (TCP/IP) to connect between each other globally.

An INTRANET is a private network inside a company or organisation accessed through web browser like software. Intranets are for the use of staff only; they are not accessible by the public. Intranets are used to provide and distribute information.

An EXTRANET allows customers and suppliers to gain limited access to an intranet in order to enhance the speed and efficiency of their business relationship. Put another way, it is an intranet that allows some access by authorised outsiders.

3.10 Databases

KEY TERMS

A DATABASE is a collection of data organised to service many applications. The database provides convenient access to data for a wide variety of users.

A DATABASE MANAGEMENT SYSTEM (DMS) is the software that centralises data and manages access to the database. It enables numerous applications to utilise the same files.

The term '**database system**' is used to describe a wide range of systems that utilise a central pool of data.

Example of a database system

```
                    ┌──────────────────┐
                    │    INPUT DATA    │
                    └──────────────────┘
                             ▲
                             │
                             ▼
   ┌──────────────────┐           ┌──────────────────┐
   │    DATABASE      │           │                  │
   │   MANAGEMENT     │◄────────► │    DATABASE      │
   │     SYSTEM       │           │                  │
   └──────────────────┘           └──────────────────┘
                             ▲
                             │
                             ▼
                    ┌──────────────────┐
                    │   APPLICATION    │
                    │    PROGRAMS      │
                    └──────────────────┘
```

| SALES APPLICATIONS STATISTICS ETC | BRANCH AND PERSONNEL STATISTICS ETC | STAFF PAYROLL ANALYSIS ETC | OTHER APPLICATIONS |

3.10.1 The characteristics of a database system

The way in which data is held on a system affects the ease with which the data is able to be accessed and manipulated. A database system has the following characteristics:

(a)   **Shared**. Different users are able to access the same data for their own processing applications. This removes the need to hold the same data in different files.

(b)   **Controls** to preserve the **integrity** of the database.

(c)   **Flexibility**. The database system should provide for the **needs of different users**, who each have their own processing requirements and data access methods. The database should be capable of **evolving** to meet **future** needs.

3.10.2 Database queries

A database can be interrogated by a **query language**. A query language is a formalised method of constructing queries in a database system. The language provides a way of asking a database for data. Some query languages are also able to make changes within the database. SQL, short for **Structured Query Language**, is a popular language.

Databases connected to a **web server** are able to be accessed by people outside the organisation through their web browser. Microsoft ADO is an example of a **database connectivity component** that enables this functionality. Potential customers are able to view product and service information and, if the site is enabled for e-commerce, make a purchase.

3.10.3 Advantages of database systems

The **advantages** of a database system include the following:

(a) Avoidance of **unnecessary duplication** of data (data redundancy) brings time and efficiency savings and **reduced storage costs**.

(b) Data is looked upon as serving the **organisation as a whole**, not just individual departments. The database concept encourages management to regard data as a resource that must be **properly managed**.

(c) The installation of a database system encourages management to **analyse data**, relationships between data items, and how data is used in different applications.

(d) **Consistency** (data integrity) – because data is only held once, the possibility of departments holding conflicting data on the same subject is reduced.

(e) Data on file is **independent** of the user programs that access the data. This allows **greater flexibility** in the ways that data can be used. New programs can be easily introduced to make use of existing data in a different way. More than one user can use the information at any one time.

(f) Developing **new application programs** with a database system is easier because the programmer is not responsible for the file organisation.

3.10.4 Disadvantages of database systems

The **disadvantages** of database systems relate mainly to security and control:

(a) There are problems of **data security** and **data privacy**. There is potential for unauthorised access to data. Administrative procedures for data security must supplement software controls. Staff training may be required.

(b) Since there is only one set of data, it is essential that the data should be **accurate** and free from corruption. This process is known as **data cleansing**.

(c) There may be disputes over who '**owns**' the data and has the right to decide how it is maintained.

(d) Since data is held once, but its use is widespread, the impact of **system failure** would be greater. A contingency plan in case of data loss is required.

(e) If an organisation develops its own database system from scratch, **initial development costs** will be high.

Section summary

Different types of information system exist with different characteristics, reflecting the different roles they perform.

Organisations are increasingly using **intranets, extranets** and **database systems** to manage and provide access to data and information.

4 System architecture and data flows

Introduction

- **Topology** refers to how a computer network is physically arranged.

- A **local area network (LAN)** is a system of linked personal computers (PCs) and other devices such as printers.

- A **wide area network** is a network of computers which are dispersed on a wider geographical scale than LANs.

- Centralised **network architecture** involves all processing being carried out on one or more processors at a single central location.

- **Distributed network architectures** spread the processing power throughout the organisation at several different locations.

KEY TERM

The term NETWORK is a general term used to describe any computing system that includes CONNECTED computers.

A computer **network** is made up of a number of connected computers and other devices, for example a number of connected PCs and printers. Networks are popular because they provide a number of users with access to **resources** (eg data files, printers and software).

4.1 Network topology

KEY TERM

TOPOLOGY refers to how a computer network is physically arranged.

4.1.1 Topology in network design

The virtual shape or structure of a network is called topology and this refers to how the machines are connected. This shape does not necessarily correspond to the actual physical layout of the devices on the network. For example, the computers on a small enterprise LAN may be physically arranged in a circle in an office, but it would be highly unlikely to find a ring topology there.

Network topologies can be any of the following basic types: bus, ring, star, tree or mesh.

More complex networks can be built as hybrids of two or more of the above basic topologies.

Network topology	Type of topology
Bus topology This topology was fairly popular in the early years of networking. Bus networks use a common backbone to connect all devices. A single cable – the backbone – functions as a shared communication medium that devices attach or tap into with an interface connector.	**Bus topology**

Network topology	Type of topology
Star topology and extended star topology One of the most popular technologies for Ethernet LANs is the star and extended star topology. The star topology is made up of a central connection point that is a device such as a hub, switch or router, where all the cabling segments meet. Devices typically connect to the hub with Unshielded Twisted Pair Ethernet. Increasingly WiFi is used on small networks instead of cables for communication to the hub. Because each computer is connected to the central device with its own cable, when that cable has a problem only that computer is affected; the rest of the network remains operational.	**Star topology** 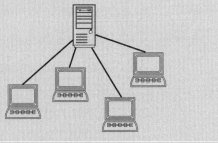
The extended star topology has one or more repeaters between the central node (the 'hub' of the star) and the peripheral or 'spoke' nodes, the repeaters being used to extend the maximum transmission distance of the point to point links between the central node and the peripheral nodes.	**Extended star topology** 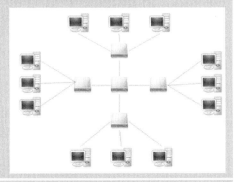
Tree topology Tree topologies can be viewed as a collection of star networks arranged in a hierarchy. In a building-wide network the use of routers creates a type of tree topology. The tree has individual peripheral nodes (leaves) which are required to transmit to and receive from one other node only and are not required to act as repeaters or regenerators. Unlike the star network, the functionality of the central node may be distributed. If a link connecting a leaf fails, that leaf is isolated; if a connection to a non-leaf node fails, an entire section of the network becomes isolated from the rest.	**Tree topology** 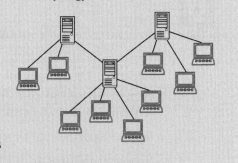
Mesh topology Unlike each of the previous topologies, messages sent on a mesh network can take any of several possible paths from source to destination. A mesh network in which every device connects to every other is called a full mesh. However, partial mesh networks also exist in which some devices connect only indirectly to others. The internet is a packet-switching network with a distributed mesh topology. Information travels in packets across a network that consists of multiple paths to a destination. Networks are interconnected with routers, which forward packets along paths to their destinations. The mesh topology provides redundant links. If a link fails, packets are routed around the link along different paths.	**Mesh topology** 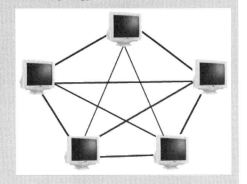

4.2 Centralised and decentralised systems

KEY POINT

An information system or department may be centralised or decentralised.

A **centralised information system** or department involves all functions being based out of a single central location, such as head office.

A **decentralised information system** or department involves functions being spread out throughout the organisation's locations.

There is **no single 'best' structure**, so an organisation should consider the merits of each.

4.2.1 Advantages of centralisation

Advantages of a **centralised system** or **department** include the following:

(a) Assuming centralised processing is used, there is only one set of files. Everyone uses the same data and information.

(b) It gives better security/control over data and files. It is easier to enforce standards.

(c) Head office is in a better position to know what is going on.

(d) There may be economies of scale available in purchasing computer equipment and supplies.

(e) Computer staff are in a single location, and more expert staff are likely to be employed. Career paths may be more clearly defined.

4.2.2 Disadvantages of centralisation

Disadvantages of a **centralised system** or **department** include the following:

(a) Local offices might have to wait for IS/IT services and assistance.
(b) Reliance on head office. Local offices are less self-sufficient.
(c) A system fault at head office will impact across the organisation.

4.2.3 Advantages of decentralisation

Advantages of a **decentralised system** or **department** include the following:

(a) Each office can introduce an information system specially tailored for its individual needs. Local changes in business requirements can be taken into account.

(b) Each office is more self-sufficient.

(c) Offices are likely to have quicker access to IS/IT support/advice.

(d) A decentralised structure is more likely to facilitate accurate cost/overhead allocations.

4.2.4 Disadvantages of decentralisation

The **disadvantages** of a **decentralised system** or **department** include the following:

(a) Control may be difficult, as uncoordinated ISs may be introduced.

(b) Self-sufficiency may encourage a lack of co-ordination between departments.

(c) There is increased risk of data duplication, with different offices holding the same data on their own separate files.

The term system architecture is often used to describe the way in which the various components of an IS are linked together. In the following paragraphs we discuss the theory behind centralised and distributed systems. However, in reality many systems include elements of both.

4.2.5 Centralised network architecture

KEY TERM

A CENTRALISED ARCHITECTURE can be defined as 'processing performed in one computer or in a cluster of coupled computers in a single location'.

Centralised network architectures use a centralised file server to provide the majority of services to the workstations on the network. The workstations are often said to be clients of the file server. File and print services are easily the most popular but may be augmented with communication, directory, backup and a number of other services.

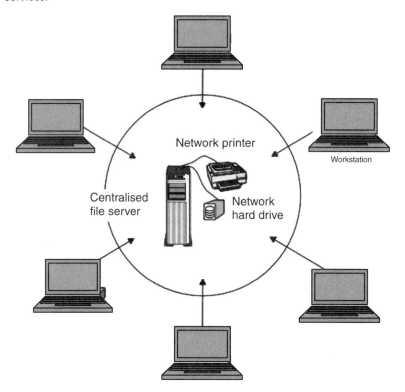

High security installations may require that the PCs used do not have any CD drives, storage media or USB ports. Email access should not be allowed on the workstations as files could be attached to emails and sent outside the organisation.

Centralised architectures could be based in a single location or spread over multiple locations. For example, both a LAN and a wide area network (WAN) could utilise a centralised architecture.

Advantages of centralised architectures include the following:

(a) There is one set of files on the centralised file server so that everyone uses the same data and information.

(b) It gives better security/control over data and files and automatic backup. It is easier to enforce standards centrally and easier to support.

(c) Head office (where the computer is usually based) is able to control computing processes and developments.

(d) An organisation might be able to afford a very large central computer, with extensive processing capabilities that smaller 'local' computers could not carry out.

(e) There may be economies of scale available in purchasing computer equipment and supplies.

The main **disadvantages** of centralised architectures include the following:

(a)   This type of system is not particularly flexible. Resources must be placed on the server to be shared. For example, a file produced by one user must be transferred to the server before it can be made available to other users.

(b)   Local offices might experience processing delays or interruptions.

(c)   Reliance on head office. Local offices rely on head office to provide information they need.

(d)   If the central computer or cluster breaks down, or the software develops a fault, the entire system goes out of operation.

(e)   Processing speed can deteriorate as more users log onto the system.

4.2.6 Decentralised or distributed network architectures

KEY TERM

DISTRIBUTED ARCHITECTURES spread the processing power throughout the organisation at several different locations. With modern distributed systems, the majority of processing power is held on numerous PCs spread throughout the organisation.

An example of a distributed architecture, with a combination of standalone PCs and networks spread throughout an organisation, is shown in the following diagram:

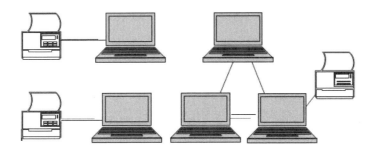

Key features of distributed architectures:

(a)   Many computers have their own processing capability.
(b)   Some sharing of information is possible via communication links.
(c)   The systems are often more user friendly than centralised systems.
(d)   End users are given responsibility for, and control over, programs and data.

Advantages of distributed architectures:

(a)   There is greater flexibility in system design. The system can cater for both the specific needs of each local user of an individual computer and also for the needs of the organisation as a whole, by providing communications between different local computers in the system.

(b)   Since data files can be held locally, data transmission is reduced because each computer maintains its own data files which provide most of the data it will need. This reduces the costs and security risks in data transmission.

(c)   There is an improvement in the speed of processing as standalone computers are not affected by the workload of others.

(d)   There is a possibility of a distributed database. Data is held in a number of locations, but any user can access all of it for a global view.

(e)   The effect of breakdowns is minimised, because a fault in one computer will not affect other computers in the system.

(f)   It allows for better local control over the physical and procedural aspects of the system.

(g)   It may facilitate greater user involvement and increase familiarity with the use of computer technology.

Disadvantages of distributed architectures:

(a)   There may be some duplication of data on different computers, increasing the risk of data inaccuracies. Data can diverge so that there can be several different versions of what should be the same information.

(b)   A distributed network can be more difficult to administer and to maintain, as several sites require access to staff with IT skills. Backup protocols are more difficult to manage as many people have to back up their local data reliably.

(c)   An increasingly significant disadvantage of distributed architectures is security. This includes the introduction of malware and making the unauthorised copying of data onto memory sticks and the like. Even computers isolated from the internet can be infected with malware, eg the stuxnet worm, which was specifically written to be spread by memory sticks.

4.2.7 Grid computing

In this approach, distributed computing environments pool the processing power of many computers.

One possible business application involves making use of spare processing time on client machines across the network to make more efficient use of computing resources. This **grid computing** model has been used for heavy number-crunching in scientific research and in a limited way in some corporate applications such as data mining and CAD. Grid computing is also used by some financial services and scientific firms to utilise the processing power available on employees' PCs.

4.2.8 Cloud computing

Wikipedia defines **cloud computing** as the delivery of computing as a service rather than a product, whereby shared resources, software and information are provided to computers and other devices as a utility (like the electricity grid) over a network (typically the internet).

People who have an email account with a web-based email service like Hotmail, Yahoo! Mail or Gmail will have already used some form of cloud computing. Instead of running an email program on your computer, you log in to a web email account remotely. The software and storage for your account exists on the service's computer cloud – not on your computer. Processing is also performed in the cloud. Google is one of the most prominent companies offering software as a free online service to billions of users across the world. The internet giant hosts a set of online productivity tools and applications in the cloud such as email, word processing, calendars, photo sharing and website creation tools. Apple is also now offering a cloud computing facility that allows synchronisation of a user's various Apple devices so that the same information is automatically available on all of them.

Dropbox is another popular service used to transfer files between users and devices. It is in some ways similar to Apple's iCloud except that it works with a wider range of devices, including Windows, Macintosh, Linux, iPad/iPhone and Android.

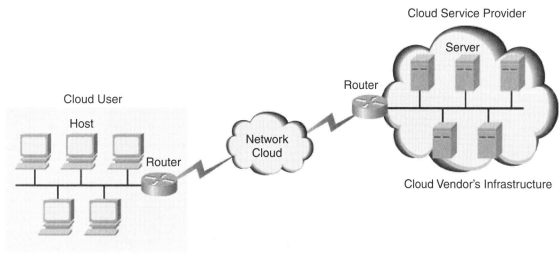

Enterprise

A cloud can be private or public. A **public cloud** sells services to anyone on the internet. (Currently, Amazon Web Services is the largest public cloud provider.) A **private cloud** is a proprietary network or a data centre that supplies hosted services to a limited number of people. When a service provider uses public cloud resources to create their private cloud, the result is called a virtual private cloud. Private or public, the goal of cloud computing is to provide easy, scalable access to computing resources and IT services.

A cloud service has distinct characteristics that differentiate it from traditional hosting:

(a)   It is sold on demand, typically by the minute or the hour. You pay for cloud services only when you use them, either for the short term (for example, for processing time) or for a longer duration (for example, for cloud-based storage or vault services). Cloud computing involves shifting the bulk of the costs from **capital expenditures** (or buying and installing servers, storage, networking and related infrastructure) to an **operating expense** model, where you pay for usage of these types of resources.

(b)   It is elastic – a user can have as much or as little of a service as they want at any given time. Cloud computing allows for the expansion and reduction of resources according to specific service requirement. For example, a large number of server resources may be required only for the duration of a specific task.

(c)   The service is fully managed by the provider (the consumer needs nothing but a personal computer and internet access).

(d)   The service is 'on-demand' and 'self-service'. This means it is available all the time and the user operates the service themselves.

4.3 Area networks

One way to distinguish between the different types of computer network designs is by their scope or scale. For historical reasons, the networking industry refers to nearly every type of design as some kind of area network. LANs and WANs were the original categories of area networks, while the others have gradually emerged over many years of technology evolution.

4.3.1 Local area network (LAN)

A **LAN** connects network devices over a relatively short distance. A networked office building, school or home usually contains a single LAN, though sometimes one building will contain a few small LANs (perhaps one per room), and occasionally a LAN will span a group of nearby buildings.

In addition to operating in a limited space, LANs are typically owned, controlled and managed by a single person or organisation.

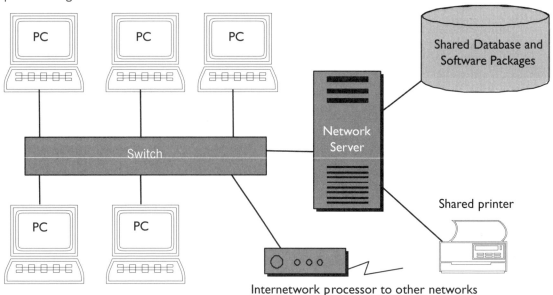

Internetwork processor to other networks

A LAN configuration typically consists of:

(a) A **file server** – stores all the software that controls the network, as well as the software that can be shared by the computers attached to the network.

(b) A **workstation** – computers connected to the file server (Macs or PCs). These are less powerful than the file server.

(c) **Cables** – used to connect the network interface cards in each computer.

4.3.2 Wide area network (WAN)

A **WAN** is a computer network that spans a relatively large geographical area. Typically, a WAN consists of two or more LANs. Computers connected to a WAN are often connected through public networks, such as the telephone system. They can also be connected through leased lines or satellites. Numerous WANs have been constructed, including large corporate networks, military networks, banking networks, universities, stock brokerage networks and airline reservation networks. Some WANs are very extensive, spanning the globe, but most do not provide true global coverage. Organisations supporting WANs using the internet protocol are known as Network Service Providers. These form the core of the internet, which is the largest WAN in existence.

A WAN is a geographically dispersed collection of LANs. A network device called a router connects LANs to a WAN.

The **main differences** between a LAN and a WAN are as follows:

(a) The **geographical area** covered by a WAN is greater, not being limited to a single building or site.
(b) WANs will send data over commercial **telecommunications links**.
(c) WANs will often use a **larger computer** as a file server.
(d) WANs will often be larger than LANs, with **more terminals or computers** linked to the network.
(e) A WAN can link two or more LANs, using **gateways**.

4.3.3 Virtual Private Network

A **Virtual Private Network (VPN)** is a network technology which gives the owner the ability to share information with others on the network by means of a private, exclusive link that is created by a method other than permanent hard-wires or leased lines.

A VPN is usually set up using the internet. Before the internet, computers in different offices, cities or even countries could only talk to each other like people could – through telephone lines. For computer A to talk to computer B, there had to be a physical wire connection that would last for the duration of the call. For security reasons, you would want to make sure that only your two computers used that line, so you would contract with a vendor to 'lease' that circuit. With the advent of the internet, connections no longer needed to be based on a fixed connection. As long as each computer has access to the internet, information can be shared using local Internet Service Provider (ISP) circuits. Each time the computers connect, a very different route could be used through the internet. This is why the way VPN works is considered a 'virtual' network; the entire connection is not hard-wired.

There are four critical functions in a VPN:

(a)   Authentication – validates that the data was sent from the sender

(b)   Access control – limiting unauthorised users from accessing the network

(c)   Confidentiality – preventing the data from being read or copied as it is being transported

(d)   Data integrity – ensuring that the data has not been altered

Advantages of VPN include the following:

(a)   **Security** – VPNs provide the highest level of security by using advanced encryption and authentication protocols that protect data from unauthorised access. The data is not only encrypted, but is also encapsulated, meaning it is sent in its own private 'tunnel' or connection across the internet. No one can see the data and, even if they could, they could not decipher or change it.

(b)   **Cost savings** – VPNs enable organisations to use the global internet to connect remote offices and remote users to the main corporate site, thus eliminating expensive dedicated WAN links.

(c)   **Scalability** – Because VPNs use the internet infrastructure within ISPs and devices, it is easy to add new users. Corporations are able to add large amounts of capacity without adding significant infrastructure.

(d)   **Compatibility with broadband technology** – VPN technology is supported by broadband service providers such as Digital Subscriber Line (DSL) – a local telephone network – and cable, so mobile workers and telecommuters can take advantage of their home high-speed internet service to access their corporate networks.

Industries that may use a VPN include:

(a)   **Healthcare**: enables the transferring of confidential patient information within the medical facilities and healthcare provider

(b)   **Manufacturing**: allows suppliers to view inventory and allows clients to purchase online safely

(c)   **Retail**: able to securely transfer sales data or customer information between stores and the headquarters

(d)   **Banking/Financial**: enables account information to be transferred safely within departments and branches

(e)   **General business**: communication between remote employees can be securely exchanged

4.3.4 Other types of area networks

While LAN, WAN and VPN are by far the most popular network types mentioned, you may also commonly see references to the following:

(a) **Wireless Local Area Network** – a LAN based on WiFi wireless network technology (see below).

(b) **Storage Area Network** – connects servers to data storage devices through a technology like Fibre channel.

(c) **System Area Network** – links high-performance computers with high-speed connections in a cluster configuration. Also known as **Cluster Area Network**.

(d) **Client-server networks** – these consist of two kinds of computer. The clients are usually computer workstations sitting on the desks of employees in an organisation. The servers are usually more powerful computers and are held in a central location or locations within an organisation.

(e) **Peer to peer networks** – these have workstations connected to each other but do not have servers. Files can be shared between workstations, and a printer connected to one workstation can be accessed by another workstation. Peer to peer networks are often much simpler to set up than client/server networks. However, they lack some of the advantages normally associated with networks such as centrally managed security and ease of backing up files.

4.3.5 WiFi and wireless technology

WiFi or Wireless Fidelity is a technology that facilitates the mobile use of laptop computers and personal handheld devices away from the home or office. WiFi networks are created through an array of hundreds and even thousands of local 'hotspots' throughout metropolitan areas.

Initially, hotspots were rare but can now be found in most major airports, hotels, bookstores, coffee houses, shopping centres and even car dealerships.

Some cities are partnering with ISPs to build wireless networks that blanket every inch of their city. This new technology removes the need to be near a localised hotspot and provides wireless access to all residents and businesses within the city limits, including open spaces such as parks and highways.

Mobile devices also have certain drawbacks:

Keyboards on handheld mobile devices are small and so can be difficult to use. It is possible to get around this by choosing one with a stylus, which can be quicker than typing or using a touch screen. The larger-size tablet is more comfortable for users, similar to working on a laptop or desktop PC. It has the capability to be used in a docking station so that it can be used with a mouse and keyboard and the screen size is easy to read. A clip-on keyboard is available for many tablets.

Laptops, netbooks and smartphones have security issues – eg they are easy to steal or lose. When using mobile devices it is important to ensure that employees are aware of their responsibilities and the need to keep both mobile devices and business information secure. If using public WiFi to access the internet, it may not always be possible to find a secure and available network. This may prevent access to business information when required.

There are costs involved in setting up the equipment and training required to make use of mobile devices. Mobile IT devices can expose valuable data to unauthorised people if the proper precautions are not taken to ensure that the devices, and the data they can access, are kept safe.

5   Emerging trends in information systems (ISs)

> **Introduction**
>
> In recent years information systems and technology have continued to develop rapidly. Three trends in IS have emerged as being popular with many types of organisation. These are **enterprise-wide systems**, **knowledge management systems** and **customer relationship management systems**.

5.1 Enterprise-wide systems

KEY TERM

ENTERPRISE-WIDE SYSTEMS are designed to **co-ordinate** all **business functions**, **resources** and **information**, wherever they are geographically.

Under an enterprise-wide system, each business area (such as accounts, HR, production and sales) is provided with a system that fulfils its needs; however, each module shares a **common database** that is the basis of all the information within the organisation.

The central database allows each business area to **access** and **update information** in **real time** and this means that information is **easy to share**, **available** to all business areas and, above all, **reliable**.

In some enterprises, even though the system spans the whole organisation, individual locations have their own specific data processing capability via a direct link to the central database. This is known as **Distributed Data Processing**. The link is provided by a **network** – a connection between devices that allows them to communicate. The two main types of network are **LANs** and **WANs**.

The difference between the two is where the **networked devices are located**. LANs are often found within an office and are often used to connect printers and other peripherals to computers. WANs are used when the devices are dispersed geographically – even around the world.

Enterprise resource planning (ERP) software is an example of an enterprise-wide system. A relatively recent development has been the development of **web-based enterprise-wide software**. To access these systems requires only a computer with an internet connection and a web browser. The application is web based, so the distance between the user and the data is irrelevant. The use of web-based software is sometimes referred to as **cloud computing**.

5.2 Knowledge management systems

KEY TERM

KNOWLEDGE MANAGEMENT SYSTEMS (KMSs) record and store the knowledge held within an organisation.

Information held on a KMS is easily accessed and shared by employees. Examples of information held in a KMS include facts, solutions to problems, relevant legislation and intellectual property.

A KMS is primarily of benefit to **knowledge-based organisations**, such as those involved in R&D or providing services such as legal advice. This is because their information is best suited to storing and sharing by a database. We have already seen examples of **KMSs**. These include extranets and intranets, groupware and LANs and WANs.

Benefits of a KMS include:

(a)   **Valuable data is preserved** for the future and not lost, for example, when an employee leaves.

(b)   The data is **easily shared**.

(c)   **Data duplication** (or data redundancy) is **avoided**.

(d)   It allows employees to 'get up to speed' on knowledge quickly and easily and this may **reduce the time they need to spend training**.

5.3 Customer relationship management systems

KEY TERM

CUSTOMER RELATIONSHIP MANAGEMENT (CRM) systems are software applications which specialise in providing information concerning an organisation's products, services and customers.

Most CRM systems are based on a **database** which stores data about customers such as their **order history** and **personal information** such as address, age and any marketing feedback they have provided. These systems allow a personalised service to be provided to the customer as well as a swift reply to their queries. They can be a **cost-effective solution** because, although they can be made **bespoke**, there are plenty of **off the shelf packages** that can be used instead.

CRM systems are often used by customer-facing staff who handle **customer enquiries**, **orders** or **complaints** and who need to understand the customer's immediate needs and provide an appropriate response. By providing a CRM, **motivation** can be increased in customer-facing staff who feel they are properly equipped to do their job.

The **benefits of CRM systems** are in regards to **customer retention** and **targeted marketing**. Better understanding of the customer, and being able to deal with them as an individual, should help generate customer loyalty. Since the needs of the customer are appreciated, marketing material can be better targeted. For example, products aimed at, say, female customers between the ages of 18 and 29 can be sent only to those customers, rather than male customers, or female customers in other age groups that would not welcome the marketing material. This has two main benefits: customers only receive appropriate marketing material, and the business makes more effective use of its marketing budget. Such increased control and management of organisational resources can be a source of **competitive advantage** over competitors who do not have a CRM system.

There are a number of criticisms of CRM systems, although most can be applied to any new system (not just CRMs).

- **Cost of purchasing the system** (can be expensive if bespoke)

- **Additional costs** (such as purchasing new hardware or other systems in order to use the CRM)

- **Opportunity costs** (money used on the CRM system could be spent on other projects)

- **Staff costs** (training costs, getting staff support and costs to the business of the disruption of introducing a CRM)

- **Effect on business processes** (which may have to be changed to fit the system)

- **Effect on customer relationship strategy** (software takes over, rather than supports, the strategy)

5.4 Web 2.0, the networked enterprise and e-commerce

Two other trends are increased business use of Web 2.0 applications and increased use of e-commerce.

5.4.1 Web 2.0 and social media

KEY TERM

WEB 2.0 APPLICATIONS are 'second generation' internet-based services. These sites usually include tools that let people collaborate and share information online. These may be used as part of a CRM system.

Examples of Web 2.0 applications include **blogs** (short for web log), **RSS** feeds, **wikis** and **YouTube** (although there is some debate as to whether YouTube qualifies as Web 2.0 as, although users upload to it, and access content from it, they don't download from it).

Social networking (or social media) sites such as **Facebook** and **Twitter** are also part of the Web 2.0 movement, and are increasingly being used by businesses. They are frequently used to monitor customer feedback and to influence sales by providing online content. We shall consider social media in more detail later on when we study marketing.

5.4.2 Benefits of using social media

The benefits to an organisation of using social media include:

- **Advertising and branding** – Notification of product offers and new offerings can easily be circulated to those who receive Facebook and Twitter updates. These platforms can also be used to develop a brand, for example by customers posting pictures of their favourite products.

- **Customer feedback** – Social media enables a business to listen to its customers, for example by observing Facebook comments or reviews of its products.

- **Communication with employees and clients** – Social media and other online platforms can be used to host meetings, make presentations and provide other information to staff and clients.

- **Recruitment** – Job adverts can be placed on social media.

- **Selection** – Candidates' social media profiles (such as Facebook and LinkedIn) can be analysed during the selection process.

5.4.3 The networked enterprise

According to McKinsey, a new breed of business organisation has developed – the **networked enterprise**. This type of business uses Web 2.0 technology to connect the work of the organisation's employees with those of stakeholders such as customers and suppliers. There are three types of networked enterprise which reflect the level of which the organisation has embraced the technology:

(a) **Internally networked organisations**. These businesses use Web 2.0, but limit its reach to within the organisation only, usually to interactions between employees. The benefits of using Web 2.0 technology in this way is to promote flexible operations, improve the ease of sharing information between all levels of the business and allow tasks to be tackled in a project-based manner.

(b) **Externally networked organisations**. These businesses extend the use of Web 2.0 technology beyond the organisation to include interactions with customers and other business partners. Despite a number of benefits such as improved communication with customers and suppliers, research suggests that the flexibility seen in internally networked organisations is reduced when the business becomes externally networked.

(c) **Fully networked enterprises**. These organisations apply Web 2.0 technology in revolutionary ways. Such businesses lead the way in developing and applying technology that connects the organisation with its stakeholders. Web 2.0 is almost fully integrated into the day to day operations of the business and this promotes high levels of collaboration between employees, customers and suppliers by breaking down barriers to the flow of information.

5.4.4 E-commerce and e-business

KEY TERMS

E-COMMERCE is the use of electronic techniques, including the internet, to buy and sell products and services.

E-BUSINESS is the use of electronic techniques, including the internet, to transform key business processes.

E-commerce (the selling of goods or services over the internet) has developed alongside CRM systems. The trend is towards providing the customer with a **unique shopping experience** that is tailored to their needs. The view and products presented to a customer is geared to their individual tastes, based on their profile and past behaviour on the site.

Most **organisations** have e-commerce capability on their website. Many have gone further; for example, Amazon suggests potential purchases for customers when they log on. These suggestions are driven by the customer's previous orders and their history of viewing products. Berens (2006) identifies the following points to consider when building a website with e-commerce capability:

(a)   Ensure transactions are **secure**, and tell customers they are. Customer trust is essential.

(b)   Comply with all applicable consumer, privacy and data protection legislation.

(c)   Have clear **terms of use** for the site.

(d)   Don't require customers to provide excessive amounts of information, as this may deter them.

(e)   Maintain **ongoing communication** with willing customers, for example by email.

Benefits to a business of using **e-commerce** include: improved marketing and decision making through the collection of sales and customer data, increased sales as customers increasingly look to the internet to purchase goods, and reduced costs as it is cheaper to operate a website than a physical shop.

Despite the benefits of e-commerce, some organisations face a number of **challenges** when adopting it. For example, they may lack the necessary in-house skills to develop the website, it may be expensive to set up and maintain the trading platform, it may be difficult to integrate back-office and fulfilment systems, there may be security concerns and certain staff may be unhappy or unwilling to work with the new system.

The term **e-business** refers to the transformation of an organisation's operations and processes through internet technology. It has a wider meaning than e-commerce, because it covers not only buying and selling but also servicing customers and collaborating with suppliers.

There are four types of e-business which are categorised according to which party initiates the transaction and which delivers the goods or services.

*   **B2B** – business to business transactions (where transactions are only between business organisations)

*   **B2C** – business to consumer transactions (such as Amazon)

*   **C2B** – consumer to business transactions (which the consumer 'names their price' for goods or services)

*   **C2C** – consumer to consumer transactions (such as eBay)

5.4.5 Digital markets and digital goods

The development of e-commerce has led to digital markets and goods.

A **digital market** is a segment of a business's overall market that is found online rather than in the real world. It may include, for example, an internet shop that supplies physical products and services, or digital-only content known as digital goods.

Digital goods have no physical presence and can be transferred from the seller to buyer almost instantaneously over the internet. Examples of digital goods include music, movies, books and magazines. The main issue for sellers of digital goods is to ensure that it has a suitable online presence to attract customers and deliver the product effectively. Apple's iTunes software is a good example of how digital goods (music, movies and apps) can be advertised and sold.

Exam skills

You may have a good understanding of many of the emerging technologies that we cover in this and the previous chapter. Do not hesitate to apply this knowledge in the exam if the opportunity arises.

Section summary

Enterprise-wide systems are designed to **co-ordinate** all **business functions**, **resources** and **information**.

The purpose of **knowledge management systems (KMSs)** is to record and store the knowledge held within an organisation.

Customer relationship management (CRM) systems are software applications which specialise in providing information concerning an organisation's products, services and customers.

Web 2.0 applications are second-generation internet-based services. These sites usually include tools that let people collaborate and share information online.

E-commerce (the selling of goods or services over the internet) continues to grow rapidly.

6 Big Data

Introduction

Big Data is an emerging technology that has implications across all business departments. It involves the collection and analysis of large amounts of data to find trends, understand customer needs and help organisations to focus resources more effectively.

6.1 Big Data

'Big Data is a popular term used to describe the exponential growth and availability of data, both structured and unstructured. Big Data may be as important to business and society as the internet has become.'   (SAS, www.sas.com)

'Big Data' can also be used to describe **large volumes of data** such as Petabytes and Exabytes. For comparison, there are 1,024 Gigabytes in a Terabyte, 1,024 Terabytes in a Petabyte and 1,024 Petabytes in an Exabyte.

6.2 What is it?

In a commercial setting 'Big Data' is used to identify trends that may exist in vast quantities of data in the pursuit of value creation. Historically, organisations have been restricted as to the amount of data that they can process due to the storage limitations of existing computer systems.

Big Data management is a term relating to the storage and administration of large volumes of data in all forms. Once stored, Big Data analytics are used to analyse the data to identify relationships, patterns and other correlations in order to develop corporate strategy to improve profitability. Big Data analytics are often developed using Hadoop – an open source programming tool which is designed to process vast amounts of data held on multiple servers.

Due to the emergence of 'cloud-based' data storage providers and improved computer technologies, these problems are gradually being overcome.

In March 2014 the BBC's Matthew Wall reported on the growing emphasis that big business is now placing on the role of 'Big Data'.

CASE STUDY   **It's not big, it's just bigger**

Laurie Miles, Head of Analytics for Big Data specialist SAS, explains 'the term Big Data has been around for decades, and we've been doing analytics all this time. It's not big, it's just bigger'. Miles highlights that for many years organisations held traditional structured data, which could be neatly stored and organised in databases. However, over the last 20 years the rise of the internet has led to a 'proliferation of so-called

unstructured data generated by all our digital interactions, from email to online shopping, text messages to tweets, Facebook updates to YouTube videos'. This has resulted in increasingly large and complex data sets, which have become harder to analyse. It is predicted that 90% of all the data in existence today has been created in the past few years.

The big challenge

The challenge for big business has been to capture and analyse these vast quantities of data which may be of use in a commercial context. Miles notes 'data is only as good as the intelligence we can glean from it, and that entails effective data analytics and a whole lot of computing power to cope with the exponential increase in volume'.

Wall reports a significant number of large entities have already turned to 'Big Data analytics' with the aim of gaining a competitive advantage over their rivals. Proponents of 'Big Data analytics' argue that the insights gained may lead to improvements throughout the entire organisation. 'Practically, anyone who makes, grows and sells anything can use Big Data analytics to make their manufacturing and production processes more efficient and their marketing more targeted and cost effective'.

The article draws an important distinction between the roles of 'Big Data analytics' and historic data analysis. 'Big Data' is not just about understanding historic business intelligence, but instead combines several 'real-time' data sets which make it increasingly useful to big businesses.

The big questions

It should be noted that the rise of 'Big Data' has had its implications. Organisations looking to exploit the opportunities presented have encountered a significant shortage of individuals with the required skills in the job market to analyse the data. As Duncan Ross, Director of Science at Teradata, highlights, 'Big Data needs new skills, but the business and academic worlds are playing catch up. The job of the data scientist didn't exist five years or ten years ago.'

Questions have also been raised over who ultimately owns the data that organisations hold and who is responsible for keeping such data safe from hackers. Does it belong to the individual or customer, the company, the service provider hosting the data or the national jurisdiction where the data is held? Such questions are unlikely to go away in the short term – as Miles highlights, it is a 'legal minefield'.

Adapted from an article:

'Big Data: Are you ready for blast-off?' by Matthew Wall (March 2014) published on the BBC website; www.bbc.co.uk

6.3 The three Vs

Big Data has a role to play in information management. Laney suggests that Big Data can be defined by considering the three Vs: volume, velocity and variety.

	Comment
Volume	The volume of data generated is a key feature of Big Data. The quantity of data now being produced is being driven by social media and transactional-based data sets recorded by large organisations, for example data captured from in-store loyalty cards and till receipts. Data is also now being derived from the increasing use of 'sensors' in business and even outside of business (for example the use of data from traffic control systems to identify traffic jams).
Velocity	Velocity refers to the speed at which 'real-time' data is being streamed into the organisation. To make data meaningful it needs to be processed in a reasonable time frame.
Variety	Modern data takes many different forms. Structured data may take the form of numerical data whereas unstructured data may be in the format of email or video. This presents a challenge for organisations as processing varied forms of data requires significant investment in people and IT infrastructure.

6.4 Big Data, digitisation and decision making

There are numerous uses of Big Data in the business context. At this stage we shall consider how it is relevant to businesses' **decision making**.

A business makes all kinds of decisions every day; for example, should it enter a new market, redesign its packaging, reorganise the sales team or keep the organisation the same. Such decisions are often more **complicated** than they first appear because many factors will come into play to determine whether or not the decision will be successful. In very complex decisions, some factors are beyond the knowledge of those taking them.

The key role of Big Data is to **analyse all relevant information** and to generate a **predictive model** of what the outcome of the decision will be. Only data that has been **digitised**, or in a digital form, can be analysed (for example from social media, audio/video content, financial data, GPS data, banking transactions and web server logs).

6.4.1 Big Data and business value

Business value is measured in many ways, such as profit, shareholder value, brand value and intellectual value. Big Data can be used to **analyse opportunities** to increase revenue and reduce costs, thereby increasing profit. For example, a holiday company can use Big Data to analyse trends in where tourists are visiting in order to improve the range of holiday locations that it offers. It can reduce its offering in unpopular areas and increase its offering of popular areas and increase its revenue.

6.4.2 Big Data and the customer

Understanding the customer is a key benefit of **Big Data analytics**. We shall consider this further in the marketing part of the syllabus but, by understanding the customer, the business can respond to their needs and tailor the **customer experience** to be more personal and therefore improve customer loyalty.

6.4.3 Big Data and corporate strategy

To be successful, Big Data must fit into the organisation's overall **corporate strategy** and be used to help drive what the strategy is. After identifying how business value can be improved, and the requirements of the customer, **business priorities** can be determined – for example, which markets or customers are the most important in terms of increasing business value. Once the priorities are established, the organisation should analyse its **current capability** to meet the priorities. Decisions can be taken, based on data, that are most appropriate and have the best **predicted chance of success**. Since business decisions are based on data and expected outcomes, they can be **measured** in a similar way to management accounting variances. For example, if a decision to enter the ice cream market was taken because summer temperatures were expected to rise to a certain level, then the success or failure of the decision might be related to the actual temperature level.

Big Data is a key source of **innovation**, helping to create **new products** and **services**. Volume and velocity of data helps speed up **decision making**. This means that Big Data can help create new **sources of income** for a business and contribute to an improvement in the organisation's **competitive advantage**.

6.5 Effect of Big Data on decisions

The **key effects of Big Data on decisions** can be summarised as follows:

(a)   Decisions can be made quickly.

(b)   Businesses can respond earlier to environmental changes and be more flexible in their response.

(c)   Decisions can be based on current situation but also have an element of taking potential future situations into account.

(d)   Decisions are made on hard data evidence that can be quantified.

(e)   Decisions can be made on a collaborative basis because data is easily shared and converted from one form into another.

(f)   'Outside the box' decisions are more likely because all factors are taken into account, not just the ones managers think of.

6.6 Benefits of Big Data analytics

There are a number of potential benefits to organisations undertaking Big Data analytics.

Benefits	Comment
Examine vast quantities of data relatively quickly	Big Data analytics allows for large quantities of data to be examined to identify trends and correlations eg shopper buying habits.
Improves organisational decision making	Better data analysis helps management to take advantage of current social trends by introducing new products to meet customers' needs.
Greater focus on the individual customer	Organisations can target special offers or discounts directly to individual customers to entice repeat business.
Cost reduction	Improved data about customers and internal operations may help to reduce costs. This is illustrated in the following case study.

CASE STUDY

Big Data in action

In May 2013 Tesco, the market-leading supermarket chain in the UK, unveiled plans to save €20m a year by exploiting the use of 'Big Data analytics' to help ensure that its in-store refrigerators operate at the right temperature. A report by Computerweekly.com highlighted the findings of a joint project between Tesco Ireland and IBM aimed at 'optimising the performance of its in-store refrigerators'. The project used highly sophisticated computer systems to analyse Tesco's refrigeration data and identified that, 'without realising it, many Tesco stores in Ireland were running their refrigerators at a lower temperature than necessary'. John Walsh, Tesco's energy and carbon manager in Ireland, noted, 'ideally, we keep our refrigerators at between −21°C and −23°C, but in reality we found we were keeping them colder. That came as a surprise to us'.

Tesco was able to capture this data from in-store sensors which monitor the performance of individual refrigeration units. The sensors then process the data in real time, and display the results on a Google map which shows the performance of refrigerators in more than 120 Irish stores.

As the article highlights, Tesco has achieved maintenance cost savings as engineers are now able to investigate potential faults remotely, 'diagnose the problem and turn up with the right part. Previously, engineers would turn up to the store, diagnose the problem and have to return to the depot to collect the equipment they needed'.

Adapted from an article:

'Tesco uses big data to cut cooling costs by up to €20m' by Bill Goodwin (May 2013) published on the Computerweekly.com website; www.computerweekly.com

6.7 Criticisms of Big Data

An article in the *Financial Times* entitled 'Big data: are we making a big mistake?' raised a number of criticisms over the ability of Big Data to deliver the anticipated benefits.

Critics argue:

(a)   Big Data is simply a buzzword, a vague term that has turned into an obsession in large organisations and the media. Very few examples exist where analysing vast amounts of data has resulted in significant new discoveries.

(b)   There is a focus on finding correlations between data sets and less of an emphasis on causation. Critics suggest that it is easier to identify correlations between two variables than to determine what is actually causing the correlation.

Other issues relating to Big Data include:

*   **Security and data protection** – To store and protect vast amounts of personal information is difficult and comes with great risk.

*   **Privacy** – Have customers consented to data about them being captured and stored?

*   **Personnel issues** – The availability of suitably qualified employees to capture, maintain and analyse Big Data may be difficult and expensive. A change in corporate culture may be needed to make the most of the opportunities Big Data brings.

*   **Information** – There may be technical difficulties involved when integrating new Big Data systems with existing technology. Also, could valuable time be wasted collecting data that has no value to the organisation? Just because information can be collected doesn't mean it has to be collected.

Exam skills

Big Data is a new area of the CIMA syllabus and you should consider it highly examinable. It is important to keep your eye out for articles on the subject in *Financial Management*.

Section summary

A company's response to the environment is influenced by its complexity and its dynamism. The value of forecasts varies according to these factors.

An organisation should plan to obtain **strategic intelligence** as a basis for future strategies. Internal and external databases should be maintained and the data they contain assessed and applied.

Big Data analytics is a term used to describe the extraction of meaning from vast quantities of data. Organisations are particularly interested in identifying trends and correlations in the data that they collect and store with the aim of putting this to commercial use.

Laney suggests that Big Data is comprised of three Vs (volume, velocity and variety).

Big Data analytics is now being used by a number of organisations in competitor analysis.

Although the rise of Big Data analytics brings benefits, critics argue that it simply represents the latest buzzword and has not delivered the groundbreaking discoveries initially thought possible.

7 IT-enabled transformation

Introduction

Information technology and information systems allow an organisation **to transform how it does business**. **A dependence on IT commits an organisation to continual change**. The pace of technological change is rapid. Computer systems – both hardware and software – are likely to be superseded after a few years.

In this section we consider how IT enables an organisation to transform itself.

7.1 IT as an enabler of change

IT may be the **driving force** or **trigger of organisational change**. Even when IT is not a significant factor in the actual change, it can play an important part in the change management process.

The **benefits an IT strategy** can bring to an organisation are numerous. For example, it may:

- Develop business opportunities
- Improve operational productivity and performance
- Create competitive advantage
- Enable structural change (such as employees working at home)
- Bring congruency to corporate goals

The table below indicates the numerous ways in which **IT may enable change** within an organisation.

IT's possible role in organisational change	Comment
The type of products or services that are made and sold	For example, companies like Sony manufacture home computers, Virgin has an ISP business. **Technological changes** affect many products, for example the introduction of tennis and squash rackets with graphite frames.
The way in which products are made	There is a continuing trend towards computer aided design and manufacture. **CAD** can be used to create designs which can be quickly amended. **CAM** involves the use of software to control machine tools and related machinery. **Computer-Integrated Manufacturing (CIM)** involves using computers to control the production process. CAD and CAM are integrated, and the flow of data and processing of material is controlled. CAD and CAM have **changed the methods and cost profiles** of many manufacturing processes as they increase the organisation's flexibility to meet customer requirements and reduce mistakes and therefore wastage. The techniques used to **measure and record costs** have also adapted to the use of IT.
The way in which employees are mobilised	The use of IT encourages delayering of organisational hierarchies and greater **workforce empowerment** and skills. Using technology frequently requires changes in working methods. **Remote working** is the ability of employees to work from a number of locations rather than in a single office – for example, working at home or while travelling on business. This ability has been driven by wireless and cloud technology and mobile devices such as laptop computers. Businesses that introduce remote working often see productivity improvements and increased commitment from employees. Very often staff turnover falls, as does absenteeism. Remote working may be attractive to higher-calibre employees. However, there could be problems associated with loss of control and co-ordination of staff, negative effects on corporate culture, and increased costs as new equipment is required. **Hot desking** involves employees working at a business location, such as a head office or factory, but unlike a traditional workplace they do not have a fixed desk. Instead, they use a desk that is free when they arrive for work. The organisation provides banks of desks that may include computers for the employees to access the IS, or may be clear for employees to bring laptops with them. When used in combination with remote working, the employer can reduce the amount of workspace needed by employees and reduce costs, or use the space more productively for other uses. Hot desking is not always popular with employees because staff often prefer to have their own space, and it may not always be practical, especially if employees are required to attend the office every day.
The way in which services are provided	High-street banks encourage customers to use 'hole in the wall' cash dispensers, or telephone or internet banking. Most larger shops now use **Electronic Point of Sale terminals** at cash desks. Many organisations use **e-commerce** – selling products and services over the internet.

IT's possible role in organisational change	Comment
To enable change	IT can produce dramatic changes in individual businesses and whole industries. For example, competition in the airline industry has intensified due to ISs that allow easy fare comparison and booking. IT can be both a **cause** of major changes in doing business and a **response** to them.
To aid communication and co-ordination	Co-ordination is essential when introducing change. IT can facilitate this through the use of email, project management software, an intranet and groupware (such as Microsoft Outlook).
As a source of unity and structure	In times of restructuring, ISs can be a visible sign of the new situation. For example, an organisation-wide network, perhaps with an intranet, provides evidence of and encourages acceptance of the new situation.

7.2 Degrees of transformation

The diagram below illustrates **five different degrees of IT-enabled change**.

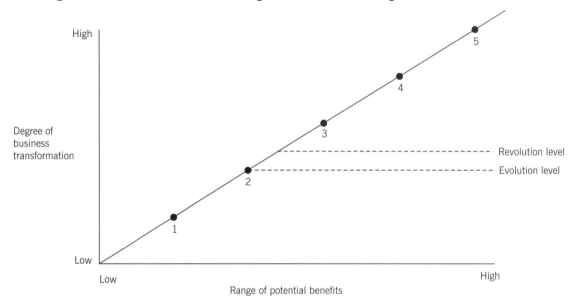

Level	Name	Description
1	Localised exploitation (automation)	Existing IT is used to re-engineer high-value business areas
2	Internal integration	Integrate business operations into a smooth process using IT capabilities
3	Business Process Re-engineering	Use IT to enable the redesign of key business processes to provide future capabilities
4	Business network redesign	The business network and IT are used to develop new products and services
5	Business scope redefinition	Organisational scope, and that of business partners, is redefined by what is possible using IT

Learning outcome C1(iii)

Velospeed designs, manufactures and distributes bicycles.

Designs are drawn by hand. These are passed to skilled workers who construct the bicycle frame by hand using traditional materials such as steel. Some customers have reported quality problems with frames.

The frame is the only part that Velospeed builds itself. Wheels, gears, brakes and pedals are each sourced from individual suppliers.

Orders for these parts are made over the telephone, recorded on paper and filed in a storage cabinet. The company has problems in retrieving and analysing cost data for management reports.

Required

Advise Velospeed as to how information technology could transform its business.   **(9 marks)**

Section summary

IT may **enable an organisation to transform** how it does business. In particular:

- The type of products or services that are made and sold
- The way in which products are made
- The way in which employees are mobilised
- The way in which services are provided
- To enable change
- To aid communication and co-ordination
- As a source of unity and structure

8   IT and new forms of organisation

Introduction

As we have seen, IT can affect an organisation in many ways including **changing the way it does its business**. As a consequence, IT has allowed different types of organisation to emerge. Some examples of **emerging types of organisation** are described below.

8.1 Virtual organisations

The global explosion of IT has led to the creation of **virtual teams, virtual companies and virtual supply chains**.

8.1.1 Virtual teams

Virtual teams are groups of people who aren't based in the same office or organisation (and may even be in different areas of the world) but who:

- Share information and tasks (eg technical support provided by a supplier)
- Make joint decisions (eg on quality assurance or staff training)
- Fulfil the collaborative (working together) function of a team

Technology has facilitated this kind of collaboration, simulating team working through the use of **teleconferencing, videoconferencing, networked computers** and the **internet**.

(a) Dispersed individuals and units can use such technology to **access** and **share** product, customer, inventory and delivery information (eg using web-based databases and data tracking systems).

(b) **Electronic meeting sites and systems** allow virtual meeting participants to talk and listen to each other while sharing data and using electronic 'white boards' on their PCs.

This has enabled organisations to:

(a) **Outsource** areas of organisational activity to other organisations and freelance workers (even 'offshore' in countries where skilled labour is cheaper) without losing control or co-ordination.

(b) **Organise 'territorially'** without the overhead costs of local offices and without the difficulties of supervision, communication and control. Dispersed centres are linked to a 'virtual office' by communications technology and can share data freely.

(c) **Centralise** shared functions and services (such as data storage and retrieval) without the disadvantages of 'geographical' centralisation, and with the advantages of decentralised authority. Databases and communications (email) create genuine sharing of, and access to, common data.

(d) **Adopt flexible cross-functional and multiskilled working** by making expertise available across the organisation. A 'virtual team' co-opts the best people for the task – regardless of location.

Forming a virtual team is different to forming a team based in a single location. The main issue is the **lack of face to face contact**. This makes it difficult for team members to bond and build trust, share knowledge, establish a hierarchy and team processes, and support morale. Cultural differences between team members may create misunderstandings that damage working relationships.

Skyrme (1997) developed a number of **principles** regarding **virtual teams**. These principles suggest that:

(a) The team should develop a sense of purpose, support members and build high levels of trust.

(b) Team members should give back what they get in terms of support, information and knowledge.

(c) Teams should be small and multi-disciplined.

(d) Communication – there should be frequent communication, where emails are used they should only have one topic per email, emails should be used to summarise face to face meetings and should be informal.

8.1.2 Virtual companies and Virtual Supply Chains

KEY TERMS

A VIRTUAL COMPANY is a collection of separate companies, each with a specific expertise, which work together, sharing their expertise to compete for bigger contracts/projects than would be possible if they worked alone.

A traditional SUPPLY CHAIN is made up of the physical entities linked together to facilitate the supply of goods and services to the final consumer.

A VIRTUAL SUPPLY CHAIN (VSC) is a supply chain that is enabled through e-business links, for example the web and extranets.

A relatively recent development is the **virtual company**. This is created out of **a network of alliances and subcontracting arrangements**. It is as if most of the activities in a particular **value chain** are conducted by different organisations, even though the process is loosely co-ordinated.

For example, assume an organisation produces small toys. It could in theory outsource:

- The **design** to a consultancy
- **Manufacturing** to a subcontractor
- **Delivery** arrangements to a specialist logistics organisation
- **Debt collection** to a bank
- **Filing, tax returns, bookkeeping** to an accountancy firm

The **virtual company** relies on technology such as **remote networking**, the **internet** and **extranets**. Many companies have become, or are becoming, more '**virtual**'. They are developing into looser affiliations of companies, organised as a supply network. **VSC** networks have two types of organisation: producers and integrators.

(a)   **Producers** produce goods and services. Producers must focus on delivery to schedule and within cost. The sales driver within these companies is on ensuring that their capacity is fully sold. Producers are often servicing multiple chains, so managing and avoiding capacity and commercial conflicts becomes key.

(b)   **Integrators** manage the supply network and effectively 'own' the end customer contact. The focus of the integrating organisation is on managing the end customer relationship. This includes synchronising the responses and performance of network functions and members. Many of the most popular internet companies are integrators in virtual companies, for example Amazon.com and Lastminute.com. These organisations 'own' **customer contact** and manage customer relationships for a range of producers.

8.2 Advantages of virtual operations

Virtual operations have various **advantages**:

- Flexibility and speed of operation
- Low investment in assets and hence less risk involved
- Injection of market forces into all the linkages in the value chain

8.3 Disadvantages of virtual operations

But there are some **disadvantages**:

- Organisations must be complementary and form close relationships if the venture is to succeed.

- Quality may be a problem owing to a loss of control.

- The suppliers/resources may also be available to rival operations.

- If customers recognise the virtual characteristics it may negatively affect their perception of the service or product.

Section summary

The **global explosion** of information technology has led to the creation of virtual teams, companies and supply chains.

Virtual teams are interconnected groups of people who may not be in the same office or organisation.

A **virtual company** is a collection of separate companies, each with a specific expertise, which work together to compete for bigger contracts/projects than would be possible if they worked alone.

A **Virtual Supply Chain (VSC)** is a supply chain that is enabled through e-business links, for example the web or extranets.

Chapter Summary

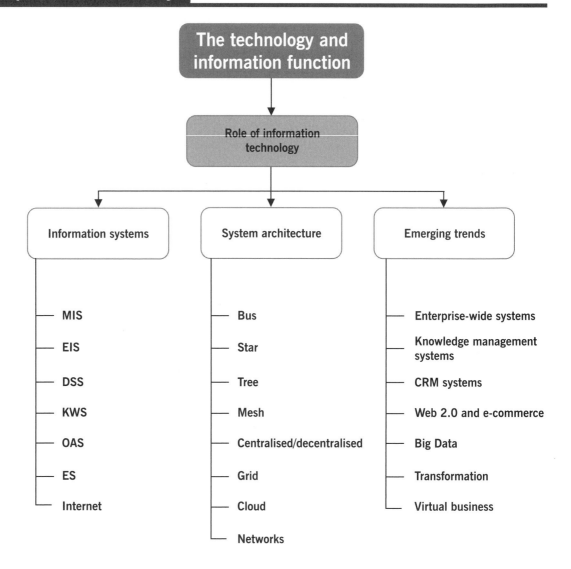

Quick Quiz

1. Which of the following is not a type of information system?

   A   EIS
   B   MIS
   C   DSL
   D   OAS

2. A private network inside an organisation that is accessed through web browser like software is known as:

   A   Internet
   B   Extranet
   C   Intranet
   D   Privatenet

3. Which type of system is designed to co-ordinate all an organisation's functions, resources and information?

   A   A knowledge management system
   B   A customer relationship system
   C   An expert system
   D   An enterprise-wide system

4. Web 2.0 applications have what purpose?

   A   To engage the customer in the organisation
   B   To reduce the number of customer complaints
   C   To increase an organisation's sales
   D   To increase the speed of product delivery to the customer

5. Briefly explain what a virtual company is.

Answers to Quick Quiz

1.   C   DSL (Digital Subscriber Line) is a communications technology. The others are: Executive Information System, Management Information System and Office Automation System.

2.   C   A private network inside an organisation that is accessed through web browser like software is known as an intranet.

3.   D   An enterprise-wide system is designed to co-ordinate all an organisation's functions, resources and information.

4.   A   Web 2.0 applications allow the customer to interact with the organisation with the purpose of engaging them in the organisation.

5.   A virtual company is a collection of separate companies, each with a specific expertise, which work together to compete for bigger contracts/projects than would be possible if they worked alone.

Answers to Questions

4.1 Expert systems

The primary reason has to do with the relative costs. A 'human' expert is likely to be more expensive either to employ or to use on a consultancy basis.

Secondly, enshrining an expert's accumulated wisdom in a computer system means that this wisdom can be accessed by more people. Therefore, the delivery of complicated services to customers, decisions on whether or not to extend credit and so forth can be made by less experienced members of staff. If a manufacturing company has a complicated mixture of plant and machinery, then the repair engineer may accumulate a lot of knowledge over a period of time about the way it behaves. If a problem occurs, the engineer will be able to make a reasoned guess as to where the likely cause is to be found. If this accumulated expert information is made available to less experienced staff, it means that some of their learning curve is avoided.

An expert system is advantageous because it saves time, like all computer systems (in theory at least), but it is particularly useful as it possesses both knowledge and limited reasoning ability.

4.2 IT transformation

IT could transform Velospeed in three main areas.

The way in which bicycles are made

The current labour-intensive process of manufacture can be made more efficient. Computer Aided Design (CAD) can be used to allow efficient and accurate design, rather than relying on hand drawings which may contain inaccuracies or be unclear.

Computer-Integrated Manufacturing (CIM) could be used to change the manufacturing process of the bike frames. Data from the design can be fed into an automated system that cuts and forms the metal into frames. This will ensure consistent standards of production and will reduce labour costs.

The types of bicycle which are made

The use of modern production methods will facilitate a move to new types of material in the bicycle frame. Materials not suitable for use under manual methods, such as carbon-fibre, may be used.

The combination of state of the art design technology and modern materials permit new types of product to be made. For example, professional race bikes, which need to be aerodynamic and extremely light, could be produced.

To aid communication and co-ordination

Velospeed could change its paper-based ordering and filing system to one which is based on an enterprise-wide system. Orders could be made electronically over the internet and invoices posted to an accounting system, perhaps using EDI.

Data could be stored in a database, and reports extracted. This will result in more accurate and consistent reports, as all systems will use the same source information.

Now try these questions from the Practice Question Bank	**Number**
	16, 17, 18, 19, 20

SYSTEM IMPLEMENTATION AND BUSINESS STRATEGY

 In this chapter we move on from looking at the role of information systems to looking at their **implementation** and **alignment with business strategy**.

Implementing a system involves a number of stages, each of which is vital if the completed system is to be a success. We shall see that a key cause of information system failure is **user resistance** – we look at a number of ways to overcome or prevent this.

Later we consider how **aligning** a new information system with the organisation's overall business strategy can help make the system a success and even be a source of **competitive advantage**.

5

Topic list	Learning outcomes	Syllabus references	Ability required
1 System implementation	C2(a), C2(b)	C2(i), C2(vii), C2(viii)	comprehension
2 Information technology (IT) and change management	C2(b)	C2(vii)	comprehension
3 Introducing the change	C2(b)	C2(vii)	comprehension
4 System evaluation	C2(a)	C2(i)	comprehension
5 System maintenance	C2(a)	C2(vii)	comprehension
6 System outsourcing	C2(b)	C2(ix)	comprehension
7 Aligning systems with business strategy	C1(a)	C1(i)	application
8 Privacy and security	C2(a)	C2(iii)	comprehension
9 Ethics and social issues of information systems	C1(b)	C1(vi)	application

Chapter Overview

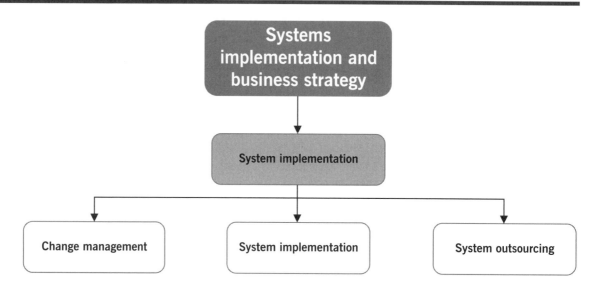

1 System implementation

Introduction

Implementation is part of the systems development cycle, or systems development life cycle (SDLC). The main stages of the SDLC are **Planning, Analysis, Design, Development** and **Implementation**.

The **planning stage** includes a **feasibility study** into relevant technical, operational, economic and social factors. A **cost-benefit analysis** may be used to check that the costs of the new system do not exceed the benefits. At this stage, the costs and benefits are estimated.

Costs of a new system can be divided into **initial costs** and **running costs**; these include system design, purchase of equipment, purchase or development of software, testing and implementation, training, staff costs to operate and maintain the system, consumables associated with the system and support costs for the developers or in-house information technology (IT) team.

Benefits of a new system include better quality of information, efficient operations, increased capacity, cost savings (labour), improved access to information across the organisation, better communications, improved customer service, and potential competitive advantage.

System analysis determines the system's purpose and the features and procedures required in it. The future users of the new system should have the opportunity to provide their input, to ensure the new system satisfies their needs.

After system requirements have been documented, work can begin on **system design**. Here the component parts of the system (its hardware and software) are decided upon and purchased. The **systems development** stage follows and involves writing software and integrating it with hardware.

Implementation comes next. This is the process the E1 syllabus focuses on – we cover this in detail in this chapter.

Following implementation comes **system review and maintenance**. Where appropriate, the outcomes of both feed back into the planning stage and the cycle starts again.

The main steps in the **implementation** of an information system are as follows:

(a) **Installation** of the hardware and software
(b) **Testing**
(c) **Staff training** and production of **documentation**
(d) **File conversion**
(e) **Changeover**

The items in the list above **do not** necessarily happen in a set **chronological order** and some may be done at the same time – for example, staff training and system testing can be part of the same operation. The requirements for implementation vary from system to system.

1.1 Installation

Installing a mainframe computer or a large network is a major operation that is carried out by the **manufacturer/supplier**. If just a few PCs are being installed in a small network, this may be able to be performed by non-specialists.

Most new software is provided on CD-ROM or DVD and may be able to be installed by non-specialists, depending on the complexity of the system and the checks required to ensure it is operating correctly.

1.2 Testing

A system must be thoroughly tested before implementation, to prevent the system 'going live' with faults that might prove costly. The scope of tests and trials will vary with the size and complexity of the system. To ensure a coherent, effective approach to testing, a testing strategy should be developed.

A **testing strategy** should cover the following areas.

Testing strategy area	Comment
Strategy approach	A testing strategy should be formulated that details the approach that will be taken to testing, including the tests to be conducted and the testing tools/techniques that will be used.
Test plan	A test plan should be developed that states what will be tested, when it will be tested (sequence), and the test environment.
Test design	The logic and reasoning behind the design of the tests should be explained.
Performing tests	Detailed procedures should be provided for all tests. This explanation should ensure tests are carried out consistently, even if different people carry out the tests.
Documentation	It must be clear how the results of tests are to be documented. This provides a record of errors, and a starting point for error correction procedures.
Retesting	The retest procedure should be explained. In many cases, after correction all aspects of the software should be retested to ensure the corrections have not affected other aspects of the software.

Four **stages of testing** can be identified as:

- System logic
- Program testing
- System testing
- User acceptance testing

1.2.1 Testing system logic

Before any programs are written, the **logic** devised by the systems analyst should be checked. This process often involves the use of flowcharts or data flow diagrams. Both tools involve the manual plotting of different types of data and transactions through the system. The object is to ensure that all possibilities have been catered for and that the processing logic is correct. When all results are as expected, programs can be written.

1.2.2 Program testing

Program testing involves processing **test data** through all system programs. Test data should be of the type that the program will be required to process and should include invalid/exceptional items to test whether the program reacts as it should.

Program testing should cover the following areas:

- Input validity checks
- Program logic and functioning
- Interfaces with related modules/systems
- Output format and validity

The testing process should be **fully documented** – recording data used, expected results, actual results and action taken. This documentation may be referred to at a later date, for example if program modifications are required. Two types of program testing are **unit testing** and **unit integration testing**.

1.2.3 Unit testing and unit integration testing

KEY TERMS

UNIT TESTING means testing one function or part of a program to ensure it operates as intended.

UNIT INTEGRATION TESTING involves testing two or more software units to ensure they work together as intended. The output from unit integration testing is a debugged module.

Unit testing involves detailed **testing of part of a program**. If it is established that a program is not operating as intended, the cause of the error must be established and corrected. Automated diagnostic routines that step through the program line by line may be used to help this process.

Test cases should be developed that include test data (inputs), test procedures, expected results and evaluation criteria. Sets of data should be developed for both unit testing and integration testing. Cases should be developed for all aspects of the software.

1.2.4 System testing (overall system testing)

When it has been established that individual programs and interfaces are operating as intended, **overall system testing** should begin. System testing has a wider focus than program testing. System testing should extend beyond areas already tested, to cover:

- Input documentation and the practicalities of input eg time taken
- Flexibility of the system to allow amendments to the 'normal' processing cycle
- Ability to produce information on time
- Ability to cope with peak resource requirements eg transaction volumes
- Viability of operating procedures
- Ability to produce information on time

System testing will involve testing both before installation (known as **off-line testing**) and after implementation (**on-line testing**). As many problems as possible should be identified before implementation, but it is likely that some problems will only become apparent when the system goes live.

1.2.5 User acceptance testing

KEY TERM

USER ACCEPTANCE TESTING is carried out by those who will use the system to determine whether the system meets their needs. These needs should have previously been stated as acceptance criteria.

The purpose of **user acceptance testing** is to establish whether **users are satisfied that the system meets the system specification** when used in the actual operating environment. Users process test data, system performance is closely monitored and users report whether they feel the system meets their needs. Test data may include some historical data, because it is then possible to check results against the 'actual' output from the old system.

It is **vital that users are involved** in system testing to ensure the system operates as intended when used by the people expected to utilise it. Any problems identified should be corrected – this will improve system efficiency and should also encourage users to accept the new system.

1.2.6 Types of test

To ensure as many scenarios as possible are tested, testing should include the following **types of test**:

(a)   **Realistic tests**. These involve using the system in the way it will be used in reality – ie the actual environment, users and types of data.

(b)   **Contrived tests**. These are designed to present the system with unusual events to ensure these are handled correctly, for example that invalid data is rejected.

(c)   **Volume tests**. These present the system with large numbers of transactions to see how the system copes.

(d)   **Acceptance tests**. These are undertaken by users to ensure the system meets user needs.

1.2.7 Limitations of testing

The presence of '**bugs**' or errors in the vast majority of software/systems show that even the most rigorous testing plan is unlikely to identify all errors. The **limitations of software testing** are outlined below.

Limitation	Comment
Poor testing process	The test plan may not cover all areas of system functionality. Testers may not be adequately trained. The testing process may not be adequately documented.
Inadequate time	Software and systems are inevitably produced under significant time pressures. Testing time is often 'squeezed' to compensate for project overruns in other areas.
Future requirements not anticipated	The test data used may have been fine at the time of testing, but future demands may be outside the range of values tested. Testing should allow for future expansion of the system.
Inadequate test data	Test data should test 'positively' – checking that the software does what it should do, and test 'negatively' – that it doesn't do what it shouldn't. It is difficult to include the complete range of possible input errors in test data.
Software changes inadequately tested	System/software changes made as a result of testing findings or for other reasons may not be adequately tested as they were not in the original test plan.

1.3 Training

Staff training in the use of a new system is essential if the system is to meet its full potential. Training should be provided to **all staff** who will use the system. Training should **focus on the specific tasks the user is required to perform**, such as entering an invoice or answering a query. There are a range of options available to deliver training, as shown below.

Training method	Comment
Individual tuition 'at desk'	A trainer could work with an employee observing how they use a system and suggesting possible alternatives.
Classroom course	The software could be used in a classroom environment, using 'dummy' data.
Computer-based training	Training can be provided using CDs, DVDs, over an intranet or via an interactive website.
Case studies and exercises	Regardless of how training is delivered, it is likely that material will be based around a realistic case study relevant to the user.
Software reference material	Users may find online help, built-in tutorials and reference manuals useful.

The **training method** applicable in a given situation will **depend on the following factors**:

- Time available
- Software complexity
- User skill levels
- Facilities available
- Budget

User documentation may be used to **explain** the system to users. Much of this information **may be available online** using context-sensitive help eg 'Push F1 for help'.

1.4 File conversion

KEY TERM

FILE CONVERSION means converting **existing files** into a format suitable for the new system.

Most computer systems are based around files containing **data**. When a new system is introduced, files must be created that conform to the requirements of that system. The various scenarios that **file conversion** could involve are outlined in the following table.

Existing data	Comment
Held in manual (ie paper) files	Data will be keyed into the new system – probably via input forms, so that data entry operators have all the data they require in one document. This is likely to be a time-consuming process.
Held in existing computer files	How complex the process is in converting the files to a format compatible with the new system will depend on technical issues and the coding systems used. It may be possible to automate much of the conversion process.
Held in both manual and computer files	Two separate conversion procedures are required.
Existing data is incomplete	If the missing data is crucial, it must be researched and made available in a format suitable for the new system – or suitable for the file conversion process.

The **file conversion process** is shown below; the diagram assumes original data is held in manual files.

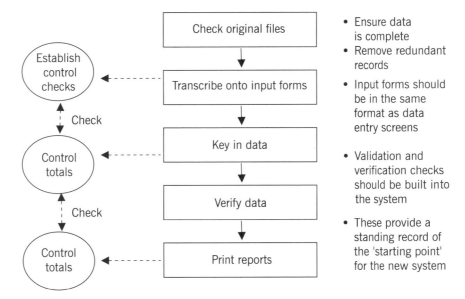

It is essential that the 'new' converted files are **accurate**. Various controls can be utilised during the conversion process.

(a)   **One to one checking** between records on the old and new systems.

(b)   **Sample checking**. Selecting and checking a sample of records. This is used if there are too many records to check individually.

(c)   **Built-in data validation** routines in automated conversion processes.

(d)   **Control totals** and **reconciliations**. These checks could include checking the total number of records, and the value of transactions.

Exam alert

You may find it useful to remember the main system implementation stages as **FITT**: **F**ile conversion, **I**nstallation, **T**esting, **T**raining and documentation.

1.5 Changeover

Once the new system has been fully and satisfactorily tested, the final stage of implementation, **changeover**, can begin. There are **four approaches to system changeover**; each varies in terms of time required, cost and risk.

- Direct ('Big Bang') changeover
- Parallel running
- Pilot operation
- Phased or modular implementation

1.5.1 Direct ('Big Bang') changeover

The old system is **completely replaced** by the new system **in one move**. This may be unavoidable where the two systems are substantially different, or where the costs of parallel running are too great.

While this method is comparatively **cheap** and convenient, it is **risky** (system or program corrections are difficult while the system has to remain operational). The new system should be introduced during **a quiet period**, for example over a bank holiday weekend or during an office closure.

A **direct changeover** is often used where there is:

- Complete confidence in the new system
- A need to overcome a reluctance to 'let the old system go'
- A need to implement the system before staff have a chance to object
- A need on cost or convenience grounds to avoid running two systems

1.5.2 Parallel running

The **old and new** systems are **run in parallel** for a period of time. They both process current data which enables cross-checking to be made. This method provides a **degree of safety** should there be problems with the new system. However, if there are differences between the two systems, cross-checking may be difficult or impossible.

Parallel running **delays** the actual implementation of the new system, which may be perceived as a **lack of confidence** in the system. Also, **more staff** are required to cope with systems running concurrently. This cautious approach, if adopted, should be properly planned, and the **plan should include**:

(a)   A firm **time limit** on parallel running
(b)   Details of **cross-checking** procedures
(c)   Instructions on how **errors** in the old system are to be dealt with
(d)   Instructions on how to report and act on **any major problems** in the new system

1.5.3 Pilot operation

Pilot operation involves selecting **part** or **parts of an organisation** (eg a department or branch) to operate the new system in parallel with the existing system. When the branch or department piloting the system is satisfied with it, they cease to use the old system. The new system is then piloted in another area of the organisation.

Pilot operation is **cheaper** and **easier to control** than running the whole system in parallel, and provides a **greater degree of safety** than a direct changeover.

1.5.4 Phased or modular changeover

Phased or **modular changeover** involves **selecting a complete section of the system** for a direct changeover, eg in an accounting system the payables ledger. When this part is running satisfactorily, another part is switched – until eventually the whole system has been changed. A phased series of direct changeovers is less risky than a single direct changeover, as any problems and disruption experienced should be isolated in an area of operations.

1.5.5 Advantages and disadvantages

The advantages and disadvantages of the various changeover methods are outlined below.

Method	Advantages	Disadvantages
Direct ('Big Bang') changeover	Quick Minimal cost Minimises workload	Risky Could disrupt operations If fails, will be costly
Parallel running	Safe, built-in safety Provides a way of verifying results of the new system	Costly, two systems need to be operated Time consuming Additional workload
Pilot operation	Less risky than direct changeover Less costly than complete parallel running	Can take a long time to achieve total changeover Not as safe as complete parallel running
Phased or modular changeover	Less risky than a single direct changeover Any problems should be in one area – other operations unaffected	Can take a long time to achieve total changeover Interfaces between parts of the system may make this impractical

CASE STUDY

Facing frequent outages in the Digital Subscriber Line (DSL) network serving 50-plus corporate-owned gyms, Gold's Gym's management knew it was time for a significant upgrade. After looking into the various options they opted to replace DSL with a carrier-provided voice Voice over Internet Protocol (VoIP) service.

If they had to do this again, however, they would take a more phased approach. 'We tried the big-bang theory, doing everything at once,' a spokesman said. That decision was driven by business needs, because the DSL network was so unreliable, and because the supplier was urging Gold's to sign a contract that included every gym. 'I think we should've done two or three gyms first, and made sure they worked OK, before we did the rest.' This would have reduced system downtime.

Adapted from Case study: VoIP implementation – The problems of the 'big bang' approach, Paul Desmond, *PC Advisor*

Section summary

The main stages in the **implementation** of a computer system are:

- **Installation** of the hardware and software
- **Testing**
- **Staff training** and production of **documentation**
- **File conversion**
- **Changeover**

2 Information technology (IT) and change management

Introduction

Any change, such as the introduction of a new information system, involves structural and behavioural factors which may result in **resistance from individuals** to that change. Many new systems fail not because of hardware or software problems, but because the users themselves are against it.

This section considers what causes user resistance and how it can be **overcome** or **prevented** by management action.

2.1 How change affects individuals

Before looking at the causes of user resistance we must first consider how change **affects individuals**.

Change may affect individuals in several areas:

(a)   There may be **physiological** changes in a person's life, both as the natural product of development, maturation and ageing, and **as the result of external factors**. For example, a change in the pattern of shift working may temporarily throw the individual's eating, waking and sleeping routine out of synchronisation with the body's sense of time.

(b)   **Circumstantial** changes – living in a new house, establishing new relationships, working to new routines – will involve letting go of things, perhaps 'unlearning' old knowledge, and learning new ways of doing things.

Above all, change affects individuals **psychologically**.

(a)   It may create **feelings of disorientation** before new circumstances have been assimilated.

(b)   **Uncertainty may lead to insecurity**. This is especially acute in changes involving work, where there can be very great pressures for continuity and fast acclimatisation.

(c)   The secure basis of **warm, accepting relationships may be uprooted** – the business of forging new relationships can be fraught with personal insecurity.

2.1.1 Types of change experience

Four types of **change experience** have been identified (Torrington and Weightman (1994)).

Type	Comment	Reaction
Imposition	Initiated and driven by someone else	Resistance
Adaptation	A change in attitude or behaviour as a result of changes by others	Uncertainty
Growth	A response to opportunities	Delight
Creativity	The individual instigates and controls the change process	Excitement

2.1.2 Reactions to proposed change

There is a range of other possible reactions to a proposed change:

(a)   **Acceptance** – whether enthusiastic espousal, co-operation, grudging co-operation or resignation

(b)   **Indifference** – usually where the change does not directly affect the individual: apathy, lack of interest, inaction

(c)   **Passive resistance** – refusal to learn, working to rule

(d)   **Active resistance** – deliberate 'spoiling', go-slows, deliberate errors, sabotage, absenteeism or strikes

John Hunt highlights a number of responses that may not **look** like resistance on the face of things, but are **behaviours aimed at reinforcing the status quo**. There are a number of responses that the manager should learn to recognise:

(a) **Pleas of ignorance** ('I need more information')

(b) **Delayed judgement** ('Let's wait and see ...'), perhaps stalling for time with comparisons ('There are other ways ...')

(c) **Defensive stances** ('This isn't going to work', 'It'd be too expensive', 'It's the wrong time to ...')

(d) The **display of various personal insecurities** ('I won't be able to cope', 'I won't see my team any more', 'We won't have control over our planning any more', 'Why can't we just go on as we are?'); fear, anxiety, resentment at the manner of change, frustration at perceived losses

(e) **Withdrawal**, or **disowning of the change** ('Oh well. On their heads be it', 'I'm not interested in flexitime anyway')

2.2 Problems in the design stage

One common cause of dissatisfaction with new information systems is **insufficient user involvement** when establishing requirements for the new system.

Other **common causes of dissatisfaction** with information systems (ISs) include the following:

(a) IS project managers are often **technicians**, not managers. Technical ability for IS staff is no guarantee of management skill – an individual might be a highly proficient analyst or programmer, but **not a good manager**.

(b) The project manager may accept **an unrealistic deadline** where the timescale is fixed early in the planning process. User demands may be accepted as deadlines before sufficient consideration is given to the realism of this.

(c) **Poor or non-existent planning** is a recipe for disaster. Unrealistic deadlines would be identified much earlier if a proper planning process was undertaken.

(d) A lack of **monitoring** and **control**.

(e) Users **change their requirements**, resulting in changes to the system as it is being developed.

(f) **Poor timetabling and resourcing**. It is no use being presented on Day 1 with a team of programmers when there is still systems analysis and design work to do. The development and implementation of a computer project may take a considerable length of time (perhaps two years for a relatively large installation). Major projects require formal planning and scheduling.

2.3 Problems in the development process

Problems that occur when implementing a new IS can usually be traced to **deficiencies in the development process**.

The table that follows outlines some common mistakes that adversely affect the implementation process, and the systems development stage or activity they relate to.

Stage/activity	Problems
Analysis	The problem the system is intended to solve is not fully understood.
	Investigation of the situation is hindered by insufficient resources.
	User input is inadequate through either lack of consultation or lack of user interest.
	The project team is unable to dedicate the time required or insufficient time spent planning the project.
Design	Insufficient user input.
	Lack of flexibility. The organisation's future needs are neglected.
	The system requires unforeseen changes in working patterns.
	Failure to perform organisation impact analysis. An organisational impact analysis studies the way a proposed system will affect organisation structure, attitudes, decision making and operations. The analysis aims to ensure the system is designed to best ensure integration with the organisation.
	Organisational factors sometimes overlooked include: • Ergonomics (including equipment, work environment and user interfaces) • Health and safety • Compliance with legislation • Job design • Employee involvement
Programming	Insufficient time and money allocated to programming.
	Programmers supplied with incomplete or inaccurate specifications.
	The logic of the program is misunderstood.
	Poor programming technique results in programs that are hard to modify.
	Programs are not adequately documented.
Testing	Insufficient time and money allocated to testing.
	Failure to develop an organised testing plan.
	Insufficient user involvement.
	User management do not review and sign off the results of testing.
Conversion	Insufficient time and money allocated to data conversion.
	Insufficient checking between old and new files.
	The process is rushed to compensate for time overruns elsewhere.
Final implementation	Insufficient time, money and/or appropriate staff mean the process has to be rushed.
	Lack of user training increases the risk of system underutilisation and rejection.
	Poor system and user documentation.
	Lack of performance standards to assess system performance against.
	System maintenance provisions are inadequate.

2.4 Dealing with user resistance

We now look at two models relevant to dealing with user resistance.

2.4.1 Lewin/Schein: Unfreeze, Move, Refreeze

In the words of John Hunt (*Managing People at Work*): 'Learning also involves re-learning – not merely learning something new but trying to unlearn what is already known.' This is the thinking behind Lewin/Schein's **three-stage approach** to changing human behaviour, which may be depicted as follows.

UNFREEZE		**MOVE**		**REFREEZE**
existing behaviour	→	attitudinal/behavioural change	→	new behaviour

Unfreeze is the most difficult (and in many cases neglected) stage of the process, concerned mainly with **selling** the change, and with giving individuals or groups a **motive** for changing their attitudes, values, behaviour, systems or structures. If the need for change is immediate, clear and perceived to be associated with the survival of the individual or group (for example change in reaction to an organisation crisis), the unfreeze stage will be greatly accelerated. Routine changes may be harder to sell than transformational ones, if they are perceived to be unimportant and not survival based.

Changing organisational **culture** is perhaps hardest of all, especially if it involves changes to long-held cultural values.

Unfreezing processes require four things: a trigger, someone to challenge and expose the existing behaviour pattern, the involvement of outsiders and alterations to the power structure.

Move is the second stage. It is mainly concerned with identifying what the new, desirable behaviour or norm should be, communicating it and encouraging individuals and groups to 'own' the new attitude or behaviour. This might involve the adoption of a new culture. To be successful, the new ideas must be shown to work.

Refreeze is the final stage, implying consolidation or reinforcement of the new behaviour. Positive reinforcement (praise and reward) or negative reinforcement (sanctions applied to those who deviate from the new behaviour) may be used.

This model is based on the view that change is **capable of being planned**. You should note that this is not always possible.

2.4.2 Lewin's force field analysis

Force field analysis consists of identifying the factors that promote or hinder change. In order for change to be successfully implemented, driving forces need to be exploited and the effect of restraining forces need to be reduced, such that the driving forces for change outweigh those forces resisting change.

Examples of driving forces
Perceived improvements to organisational performance
Necessary in order to keep up with competitors
Improved profitability and employee bonuses
Dislike of old system
Better information and work processes
New challenges and improved motivation

Examples of restraining forces
Job security fears
Happy with old system
Lack of understanding of need for change
Fears over poor implementation process
Employee loss of control over how they work
Lack of training and fears over difficulty of using new system

2.4.3 Dealing with resistance

Kotter and Schlesinger (1979) identified six methods of dealing with **resistance to change** and **restraining forces**. They are:

(a)   **Education** and **communication**. This method is effective where the cause of the resistance is lack of information about the change.

(b)   **Participation** and **involvement**. Where those affected by the change have the power to resist it, this method reduces the resistance by taking their views into account.

(c)   **Facilitation** and **support**. Where the cause of the resistance is anxiety and insecurity, support such as training is effective.

(d)   **Negotiation** and **agreement**. Compensating those who lose out (for example redundancy packages) may be appropriate in some instances.

(e)   **Manipulation** and **co-optation**. This method involves the presentation of partial or misleading information to those resisting change or 'buying off' the main individuals who are at the heart of the resistance.

(f)   **Explicit** and **implicit coercion**. This involves the use or threat of force to push through the change. A very last resort if parties are operating from fixed positions and are unwilling to move.

The final two options raise ethical and legal issues. They also risk alienating people, making the change even less likely to be accepted.

The six approaches are not intended to be used separately in isolation – a **combination** of them is likely to be required. Remember that people may disguise their real reason for opposing change (such as possible loss of influence or status) with technical objections.

Exam alert

Exam questions may test potential strategies for overcoming resistance to change and identifying which would be most appropriate in given situations.

Question 5.1	Resistance to change

Learning outcome C2(vii)

Which of Kotter and Schlesinger's six methods of dealing with resistance to change is best suited to a situation where resistance is caused by a lack of information about the change?

A   Education and communication
B   Negotiation and agreement
C   Manipulation and co-optation
D   Explicit and implicit coercion   **(2 marks)**

Section summary

User resistance is a key cause of information systems failure.

Theories that may help when considering how to **overcome user resistance** include:

- Lewin/Schein's unfreeze, move, refreeze
- Kotter and Schlesinger's six methods of dealing with resistance

3 Introducing the change

Introduction

Rather than dealing with resistance to change after it has occurred, a better approach is to try to **prevent resistance before it occurs**.

Several theories have been developed that aim to help managers deal with change more effectively so that resistance is prevented or at least minimised.

3.1 Pace, Manner and Scope

There are **three important factors** for managers to consider when **introducing change**:

- The **pace** of change
- The **manner** of change
- The **scope** of change

3.1.1 Pace

The more **gradual** the change, the more time is available for questions to be asked, reassurances to be given and retraining (where necessary) embarked upon. People can get used to the idea of new methods and become acclimatised at each stage.

(a)   Presenting the individuals concerned with change as a *fait accompli* may avoid resistance at the planning stage, but may result in resistance surfacing later – probably strengthened by resentment.

(b)   **Timing** will also be crucial. Those responsible for change should be sensitive to incidents and attitudes that might indicate that 'now is not the time'.

3.1.2 Manner

The manner in which a change is put across (**communicated**) is very important. The need for change must be made clear, fears soothed, and if possible the individuals concerned positively motivated to embrace the changes as their own.

(a)   **Resistance should be welcomed and confronted**, not swept under the carpet. Talking through areas of conflict may lead to useful insights and the adaption of the programme of change to the company's advantage. Repressing resistance will only send it underground.

(b)   **There should be free circulation of information** about the reasons for the change, its expected results and likely consequences. That information should appear sensible, clear, consistent and realistic. There is no point issuing information which will be seen as a blatant misrepresentation of the situation.

(c)   **The change must be sold to the people concerned**. Objections must be overcome, but it is also possible to get people behind the change in a positive way. If those involved understand that there is a real problem which poses a threat to the organisation and themselves, and that the solution is a sensible one and will solve the problem, there will be a firm rational basis for implementing change. It may even be possible to get staff excited by the change, by emphasising the challenge and opportunity and perhaps by offering rewards and incentives.

(d)   **Individuals must be helped to learn**; that is, to change their attitudes and behaviours. Few individuals will really be able to see the big picture in a proposed programme of change. In order to put across the overall objective, the organisation should use **visual aids** to help conceptualise. Learning programmes for any new skills or systems necessary will have to be designed according to the abilities of the individuals concerned.

(e)   The effects of **insecurity** and **resentment** may be lessened if people are **involved** in the planning and implementation of the change, so that it is not perceived to have been imposed from above.

3.1.3 Scope

The scope or **extent of the change** is important and should be reviewed. Total transformation will create greater insecurity – but also provides the opportunity for greater excitement – than moderate innovation.

There may be **hidden changes** to take into account. For example, a change in technology may necessitate changes in work methods, which may in turn result in the breaking up of work groups. Management should be aware of how many various aspects of their employees' lives they are proposing to alter – and therefore on how many fronts they are likely to encounter resistance.

3.2 Commitment, co-ordination and communication

Commitment, **co-ordination** and **communication** are often cited as playing an important role in the context of introducing any form of change.

(a)   **Commitment.** Commitment to the change must be universal. Senior management must ensure adequate resources are provided (people, money, time etc) to achieve change.

(b)   **Co-ordination.** To implement change successfully requires co-ordination. This involves ensuring those involved in the process work in an efficient and effective way towards an agreed common goal. This requires planning and control.

(c)   **Communication.** Successful change requires good communication. The right people must communicate the right things at the right time and in the right way. Good communication early in the process should ensure all are aware of what the process hopes to achieve. Communication during the process should aid co-ordination and maintain momentum. Upon completion, communication is likely to focus on ensuring there is no return to the previous behaviour – and a review of the process itself to see if any lessons may be learnt.

3.3 Successful implementation of information systems (ISs)

A recurring theme when examining the reasons for **IS failure** is user resistance. Three types of theory explain the causes of user resistance against new ISs together with how they are overcome (Markus 1983 and David and Olsen 1985).

Theory	Description	Overcoming the resistance
People-oriented	User resistance is caused by factors internal to users as individuals or as a group. For example, users may not wish to disrupt their current work practices and social groupings.	User training. Organisation policies. Find 'change champions' who already see the benefits of the system and can persuade others who are resisting. User involvement in system development.
System-oriented	User resistance is caused by factors inherent in the new system design, relating to ease of use and functionality. For example, a poorly designed user interface will generate user resistance.	User training and education. Improve the user interface. Ensure users contribute to the system design process. Ensure the system 'fits' with the organisation.
Interaction	User resistance is caused by the interaction of people and the system. For example, the system may be well designed but its implementation will cause organisational changes that users resist eg reduced chance of bonuses, redundancies, monotonous work.	Reorganise the organisation before implementing the system. Redesign any affected incentive schemes to incorporate into the new system. Promote user participation and encourage organisation-wide teamwork. Emphasise the benefits the system brings.

Section summary

It is better for the organisation to **prevent or minimise resistance** occurring in the first place. Theories aimed at achieving this include:

- Pace, manner and scope
- Commitment, co-ordination and communication

4 System evaluation

Introduction

A system should be **reviewed** after implementation, and periodically when in operation, so that any unforeseen problems may be resolved and to confirm that it is achieving the desired results. The system should have been designed with clear, specified **objectives**, and justification in terms of **cost-benefit analysis** or other **performance criteria**.

4.1 Cost-benefit review

A cost-benefit review is similar to a cost-benefit analysis, except that **actual** data can be used. For instance when a large project is completed, techniques such as **discounted cash flow appraisal** can be performed **again**, with actual figures being available for much of the expenditure.

Question 5.2	Cost-benefit review

Learning outcome C2(i)

A cost-benefit review might categorise items under the five headings of **direct benefits**, **indirect benefits**, **development costs**, **implementation costs** and **running costs**.

Required

Give two examples of items which could fall to be evaluated under each heading.   **(5 marks)**

4.2 Measuring system performance

KEY TERM

METRICS are quantified measurements used to measure system performance.

The use of metrics enables some aspects of **system quality** to be **measured**. Metrics may also allow the early identification of problems – for example, by highlighting instances of system failure, the causes of which may then be investigated.

Metrics should be carefully thought out, objective and **stated clearly**. They must measure significant aspects of the system, be used consistently and agreed with users. **Examples** of metrics include system response time, the number of transactions that can be processed per minute, the number of bugs per hundred lines of code and the number of system crashes per week.

Many facets of system quality are not easy to measure **statistically** (eg user friendliness). Indirect measurements such as the number of calls to the helpdesk per month can be used as an indication of overall quality/performance.

4.3 Performance reviews

Performance reviews can be carried out to look at a wide range of system functions and characteristics. They will vary in content from organisation to organisation, but may include the following:

(a) The **growth** rates in file sizes and the number of transactions processed by the system. Trends should be analysed and projected to assess whether it is likely there will be problems with lengthy processing time or an inefficient file structure due to the volume of processing.

(b) The **staffing** requirements of the system, and whether they are more or less than anticipated.

(c) The identification of any **delays** in processing and an assessment of their consequences.

(d) An assessment of the efficiency of **security** procedures, in terms of number of breaches, or number of viruses encountered.

(e) A check of the **error rates** for input data. High error rates may indicate inefficient preparation of input documents, an inappropriate method of data capture or poor design of input media.

(f) An examination of whether **output** from the computer is being used for a good purpose. (Is it used? Is it timely? Does it go to the right people?)

(g) Operational **running costs** can be examined to discover any inefficient programs or processes. This examination may reveal excessive costs for certain items although in total costs may be acceptable.

4.4 Post-implementation review

A **post-implementation review** establishes whether the objectives and targeted performance criteria have been met, and if not, why not, and what should be done about it. In appraising the operation of the new system immediately after the changeover, comparison should be made between **actual and predicted performance**.

This will include:

(a)   Consideration of **throughput speed** (time between input and output)
(b)   Use of computer **storage** (both internal and external)
(c)   The number and type of **errors/queries**
(d)   The **cost** of processing (data capture, preparation, storage and output media, etc)

A special **steering committee** may be set up to ensure that post-implementation reviews are carried out, although the **internal audit** department may be required to do the work of carrying out the reviews.

The post-implementation measurements should **not be made too soon** after the system goes live, or else results will be abnormally affected by 'teething' problems, lack of user familiarity and resistance to change. A suitable period is likely to be between one month and one year after completion (the appropriate length of time will depend on the role of the system, and how complex it is).

 Post-implementation audits may be examined in E2 with regard to project management.

4.4.1 The post-implementation review report

The findings of a post-implementation review team should be formalised in a **report**.

(a)   A **summary** of their findings should be provided, emphasising any areas where the system has been found to be **unsatisfactory** so the organisation can learn from its mistakes.

(b)   A review of **system performance** should be provided. This will address the matters outlined above, such as run times and error rates and whether it meets users' needs.

(c)   A **cost-benefit review** should be included, comparing the forecast costs and benefits identified at the time of the feasibility study with actual costs and benefits.

(d)   **Recommendations** should be made as to any **further action** or steps which should be taken to improve performance. It will also make recommendations on how the project was managed to help future initiatives.

4.5 Reasons for system failure

The performance review may conclude that the project has failed. **Common causes** often cited include:

- Poor planning and co-ordination
- Unrealistic schedules and deadlines
- Poor project control
- Lack of user involvement
- Project complexity
- Lack of support from senior management
- Insufficient skills within the workforce to deliver a successful project

Section summary

After implementation the system should be **evaluated** to see if it is a success and whether there are any lessons to be learned.

Evaluation often takes the form of a **cost-benefit review** or **performance measurement** using metrics or other measurable features of the system.

A **post-implementation review** compares actual and expected performance levels and is a formal report that should be compiled after a suitable period of time following implementation.

5   System maintenance

Introduction

After implementation, the system will require **regular maintenance** if it is to continue operating as expected and to develop with the organisation.

There are **three types of systems maintenance**.

KEY TERMS

CORRECTIVE MAINTENANCE is carried out when there is a systems failure of some kind, for example a defect in processing or in an implementation procedure. Its objective is to ensure that systems remain operational.

PERFECTIVE MAINTENANCE is carried out in order to perfect the software, or to improve it so that processing inefficiencies are eliminated and performance is enhanced.

ADAPTIVE MAINTENANCE is carried out to take account of anticipated changes in the processing environment. For example, new taxation legislation might require changes to be made to payroll software.

Corrective maintenance usually consists of action in response to a **problem**.

Perfective maintenance consists of making enhancements requested by **users** to improve or extend the facilities available. The user interface may be amended to make software more user friendly.

There are many examples of **adaptive maintenance**, for example:

(a)   The system needs minor modifications to cope with changes in the computer user's procedures or volume of business.

(b)   The system can benefit from advances in computer hardware technology without having to switch to another system altogether.

5.1 The causes of system maintenance

Besides environmental changes, **three factors** contribute to the need for maintenance.

Factor	Comment
Errors	However diligently a system is tested, it is likely that **bugs** will exist in a newly implemented system. These require fixing.
Poor documentation	If old systems are accompanied by poor documentation, or even a complete lack of documentation, they may be difficult to understand. It is difficult to update or maintain these systems. Programmers may opt instead to patch up the system with new applications using newer technology.

Factor	Comment
Changes in requirements	Although users should be consulted at all stages of systems development, problems may arise after implementation, for example users may have found it difficult to express their requirements, or have not participated fully in development.
	Cost constraints may have meant that certain requested features were not incorporated. Time constraints may have meant that requirements suggested during development were ignored in the interest of prompt completion.

5.1.1 Testing the effect of changes

A problem with systems development and maintenance is that it is **hard to predict all the effects of a change** to the system. A 'simple' software change in one area of the system may have unpredicted effects elsewhere. It is important therefore to carry out **regression testing**.

KEY TERM

REGRESSION TESTING involves the retesting of software that has been modified to fix 'bugs'. It aims to ensure that the bugs have been fixed **and** that no other previously working functions have failed as a result of the changes.

Regression testing involves **repeating system tests** that had been executed correctly before the recent changes were made. Only the changes expected as a result of the system maintenance should occur under the regression test – other changes could be due to errors caused by the recent change.

Problems with regression testing include deciding on the **extent of testing** required, **envisaging all areas** possibly affected, and **convincing users** and **programmers** that the **tests are necessary**.

5.2 Hardware maintenance

Provision must also be made to ensure computer hardware is maintained. A **hardware maintenance contract** should specify service response times in the event of a breakdown, and include provision for temporary replacement equipment if necessary. Maintenance services may be provided by the computer manufacturers or suppliers, or by a third-party maintenance company.

Section summary

Corrective maintenance is carried out when there is a systems failure of some kind, for example a defect in processing or in an implementation procedure. Its objective is to ensure that systems remain operational.

Perfective maintenance is carried out in order to perfect the software, or to improve it so that processing inefficiencies are eliminated and performance is enhanced.

Adaptive maintenance is carried out to take account of anticipated changes in the processing environment. For example, new taxation legislation might require changes to be made to payroll software.

6   System outsourcing

Introduction

We shall now consider the **application of outsourcing** to **information systems**.

There are four **broad classifications** of IT outsourcing.

Classification	Comment
Ad hoc	The organisation has a short-term requirement for increased IT skills. An example would be employing programmers on a short-term contract to help with the programming of bespoke software.
Project management	The development and installation of a particular project is outsourced – for example, a new accounting system. This approach is sometimes referred to as **systems integration**.
Partial	Some services are outsourced. Examples include hardware maintenance, network management and ongoing website management.
Total	An external supplier provides the vast majority of an organisation's IS services. For example, a third party owns or is responsible for IT equipment, software and possibly staff.

6.1 Levels of service provision

The degree to which the provision and management of IS services are transferred to the third party varies according to the situation and the skills of both organisations.

(a) **Timeshare**. The vendor charges for access to an external processing system on a time-used basis. Software ownership may be with either the vendor or the client organisation.

(b) **Service bureaux** usually focus on a specific function. Traditionally bureaux would provide the same type of service to many organisations, eg payroll processing. As organisations have developed their own IT infrastructure, the use of bureaux has decreased.

(c) **Facilities management (FM)**. The terms 'outsourcing' and 'facilities management' are sometimes confused. FM traditionally involved contracts for premises-related services such as cleaning and site security.

In the context of IS, FM involves an **outside agency** managing the organisation's IS facilities. All equipment usually remains with the client, but the responsibility for providing and managing the specified services rests with the FM company. FM companies operating in the UK include Accenture, Cap Gemini, EDS and CFM.

CASE STUDY

The retailer Sears outsourced the management of its vast IT and accounting functions to Accenture. First-year savings were estimated to be £5 million per annum, growing to £14 million in the following year, and thereafter. This is clearly considerable, although reorganisation costs relating to redundancies, relocation and asset write-offs are thought to be in the region of £35 million. About 900 staff were involved: under the transfer of undertakings regulations (which protect employees when part or all of a company changes hands), Accenture was obliged to take on the existing Sears staff. This provided new opportunities for the staff who moved, while those who remained at Sears were free to concentrate on strategy development and management direction.

6.2 Developments in outsourcing

Outsourcing arrangements are becoming increasingly flexible to cope with the ever-changing nature of the modern business environment.

Examples of outsourcing arrangements include:

(a) **Multiple sourcing**. This involves outsourcing different areas of the IS function to a range of suppliers. Some suppliers may form alliances to present a stronger case for selection.

(b) **Incremental approach**. Organisations progressively outsource selected areas of their IS function. Possible problems with outsourced services are solved before progressing to the next stage.

(c) **Joint venture sourcing**. This term is used to describe an organisation entering into a joint venture with a supplier. The costs (risks) and possible rewards are split on an agreed basis. Such an arrangement may be suitable when developing software that could be sold to other organisations.

(d) **Application Service Providers (ASPs)**. ASPs are third parties that manage and distribute software services and solutions to customers across a wide area network. ASPs could be considered the modern equivalent of the traditional computer bureaux.

6.3 Managing outsourcing arrangements

Managing outsourcing arrangements involves deciding **what** will be outsourced, **choosing and negotiating** with **suppliers** and **managing the client-vendor relationship**.

6.3.1 Deciding what to outsource

When **considering** whether to outsource a particular service, the following issues are relevant:

(a) **Strategic importance** of system. If the decision relates to an IS, strategic ISs are generally not suited to outsourcing as they require a high degree of specific business knowledge that a third-party IT specialist cannot be expected to possess.

(b) Is the function and/or system **relatively isolated**? Functions that have only **limited interfaces** are most easily outsourced, eg payroll.

(c) **Is there enough in-house system knowledge to manage the outsourced service agreement**? If an organisation knows very little about a particular technology it may be difficult to know what constitutes good service and value for money. It may be necessary to recruit additional **expertise** to manage the relationship with the other party.

(d) Are the **organisation's requirements likely to change**? Organisations should avoid tying themselves into a long-term outsourcing agreement if requirements are likely to change.

(e) **Communication with employees**. Once the decision to outsource has been taken it is important for employees to be kept informed of the reasons behind the decision and how it may impact on them. If redundancies are planned then this should be managed sensitively.

6.3.2 Choosing and negotiating with suppliers

The organisation should draw up a shortlist of potential suppliers and invite them to bid for the outsource contract by an **invitation to tender**. The choice of outsource supplier should be made based on clearly defined criteria and the organisation should also make **background checks** into the supplier's finances, seek references from its other clients and check its legal history for any litigation against it. Any potential supplier should be sympathetic to the organisation's culture and ethics and be willing to put mechanisms in place to ensure the satisfaction of the organisation's customers.

A contract known as a **Service Level Contract** or **Service Level Agreement** (SLA) should be drawn up that sets out the terms and conditions of the arrangement.

The **key elements of the contract** are described below.

Contract element	Comment
Service level	The contract should clearly specify minimum levels of service to be provided. Penalties should be specified for failure to meet these standards. Relevant factors will vary depending on the nature of the services outsourced but could include: • Response time to requests for assistance/information • System 'uptime' percentage • Deadlines for performing relevant tasks
Exit route	Arrangements for an exit route, addressing how the transfer to another supplier or the move back in-house would be conducted.
Timescale	When does the contract expire? Is the timescale suitable for the organisation's needs or should it be renegotiated?
Software ownership	Relevant factors include: • Software licensing and security • If the arrangement includes the development of new software, who owns the copyright?
Dependencies	If related services are outsourced, the level of service quality agreed should group these services together.
Employment issues	If the arrangement includes provision for the organisation's IT staff to move to the third party, employer responsibilities must be specified clearly.

Once the arrangement has been established, **handover** should take place at an appropriate time either directly or be phased in.

6.3.3 Managing the client–vendor relationship

It is important for the organisation to build a **strong relationship** with its outsource supplier, perhaps through the use of a **relationship manager** responsible for **monitoring the costs** of the agreement and checking that the **terms and conditions** of the SLA are adhered to. Any issues arising should be dealt with appropriately. The closeness of the relationship would depend on the nature of the function being outsourced.

If full **FM** is involved and almost all management responsibility for IS lies with the entity providing the service, then a close relationship between the parties is necessary (a '**partnership**'). Factors such as organisation culture need to be considered when entering into such a close and critical relationship.

On the other hand, if a relatively **simple function** such as payroll were outsourced, such a close relationship with the supplier would not be necessary. A 'typical' supplier–customer relationship is all that is required.

6.4 Advantages of outsourcing arrangements

The **advantages** of outsourcing are as follows.

(a)   Outsourcing can remove uncertainty about **cost**, as there is often a long-term contract where services are specified in advance for a **fixed price**. If computing services are inefficient, the costs will be borne by the outsourcing company. This is also an incentive to the third party to provide a high-quality service.

(b)   Long-term contracts (maybe up to ten years) encourage **planning** for the future.

(c)   Outsourcing can bring the benefits of **economies of scale**. For example, an outsourcing company may conduct research into new technologies that benefits a number of its clients.

(d)   A specialist organisation is able to retain **skills and knowledge**. Many organisations would not have a sufficiently well-developed IS department to offer IS staff opportunities for career development. Talented staff would leave to pursue their careers elsewhere.

(e)   New skills and knowledge become available. A specialist company can **share** staff with **specific expertise** (such as programming in HTML to produce web pages) between several clients. This allows the outsourcing company to take advantage of new developments without the need to recruit new people or retrain existing staff, and without the cost.

(f)   **Flexibility** (contract permitting). Resources may be able to be scaled up or down depending on demand. For instance, during a major changeover from one system to another the number of IT staff needed may be twice as large as it will be once the new system is working satisfactorily.

An outsourcing organisation is more able to arrange its work on a **project** basis, whereby some staff will expect to be moved periodically from one project to the next.

6.5 Disadvantages of outsourcing arrangements

Some possible **drawbacks** are outlined below.

(a)   It is arguable that information and its provision is **an inherent part of the business and of management**. Unlike office cleaning, or catering, an organisation's IS services may be too important to be contracted out. Information is at the heart of management.

(b)   A company may have highly **confidential information** and to let outsiders handle it could be seen as **risky** in commercial and/or legal terms.

(c)   Information strategy can be used to gain **competitive advantage**. Opportunities may be missed if a third party is handling IS services, because there is no onus upon internal management to keep up with new developments and have new ideas. Any new technology or application devised by the third party is likely to be available to competitors.

(d)   An organisation may find itself **locked into** an unsatisfactory contract. The decision may be very difficult to reverse. If the outsourcing company supplies unsatisfactory levels of service, the effort and expense the organisation would incur to rebuild its own computing function or to move to another provider could be substantial.

(e)   The use of outsourcing does not encourage **awareness** of the potential costs and benefits of IS within the organisation. If managers cannot manage in-house IS resources effectively, then it could be argued that they will not be able to manage an arrangement to outsource effectively either.

6.6 ISs and broader management operations

The ISs within an organisation should complement and **support other functional areas** such as finance, human resources and marketing. For example, an intranet facilitates the sharing of information.

Effective ISs and information management **contribute towards the attainment of organisational goals**. To best achieve this, **a cohesive IS strategy** should be developed that supports the organisation's overall strategy.

As with any expenditure, the **benefits** of ISs should be **greater than their costs**.

Section summary

Four broad **types of information systems outsourcing are ad hoc**, **project management**, **partial** and **total**.

Examples of **outsourcing arrangements** include **multiple sourcing, incremental approach, joint venture sourcing** and **Application Service Providers (ASPs)**.

7 Aligning systems with business strategy

Introduction

An organisation's **information systems (ISs)** should **support** the **overall strategy of the business**.

A **firm's strategy** is built in three layers:

- **Corporate** (what products to make or markets to be in)
- **Business** (how to increase sales or profitability of a product)
- **Functional** (the strategy of a business function such as HR or Marketing)

Therefore a firm's **IT strategy** is a **functional strategy**, although due to its revolutionary nature it can also become a **business strategy**, for example where IT can improve efficiency or sales (such as through e-commerce).

The **identification of business needs** and the IT framework to satisfy them is at the **heart of a strategy for ISs**. However, this is not always feasible, especially if an organisation's use of technology has grown in a haphazard fashion. The purpose of the strategy in this situation may be to impose some sort of order on a disorganised situation.

We shall begin by looking at the **effect** ISs have on an industry.

7.1 The effect of ISs on an industry

Porter and Millar state that ISs have the potential to **change the nature of competition** within an industry.

The ways in which ISs can **impact an industry** according to Porter and Millar are as follows:

- Change the industry structure
- Create new businesses and industries
- Be used to create competitive advantage

7.2 Changing the industry structure

Porter's five forces model can be used to analyse the effect of ISs on an industry.

Porter identified **five competitive forces** operating in a competitive environment.

(a) The threat of **new entrants**
(b) The bargaining power of **suppliers**
(c) The bargaining power of **customers**
(d) The threat of **substitute** products/services
(e) The **existing competitive rivalry** in the industry

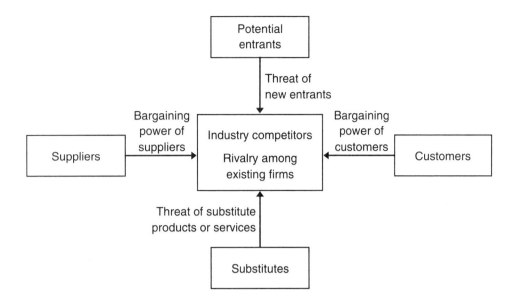

7.2.1 New entrants

ISs can have two possible roles in relation to **barriers to entry**:

(a) **Defensively**. ISs can increase economies of scale, raise the capital cost of entry (by requiring an investment in ISs) or effectively colonise distribution channels by tying customers and suppliers into the supply chain.

(b) **Offensively**. ISs can leap over entry barriers. An example is the use of telephone banking, which sometimes obviates the need to establish a branch network.

7.2.2 Suppliers

Supplier power can derive from various factors such as geographical proximity and the fact that the organisation requires goods of a certain standard in a certain time.

The bargaining power of suppliers can be **eroded** by ISs in three ways.

(a) By **increasing competition** between suppliers. ISs can provide a purchases database, which enables easy scanning of prices from a number of suppliers.

(b) Suppliers' power can be **shared**. An example is using Computer Aided Design (CAD) to **design components in tandem with suppliers**. Such relationships might be developed with a few key suppliers. The supplier and the organisation both benefit from performance improvement.

(c) Suppliers can be **integrated**, in purely administrative terms, by a system of **electronic data interchange (EDI)**. This involves the creation of **standardised electronic documents** (such as order forms) that can be transmitted between supplier and customer to save duplication of effort in terms of getting the information into each computer system.

7.2.3 Customers

The bargaining power of **customers** can be affected by using ISs to '**lock them in**'.

(a) ISs can **raise switching costs** in cash terms, and in terms of operational inconvenience. An example is where ISs provide a distribution channel for certain services (eg airline tickets). Another example comes from the computer industry itself. Until the advent of the PC, most computers were run with proprietary software; in other words, you could not run ICL software, say, on IBM mainframes. This made any switch in supplier (of hardware or software) too much trouble to contemplate.

(b)   Customer ISs can enable a **thorough analysis of marketing information** so that products and services can be **tailored to the needs** of certain market segments.

7.2.4 Substitutes

ISs have the following relationships to existing and substitute products and services.

(a)   In some cases, the IS itself is the **'substitute'**. PC-based word processing packages were originally a substitute for typewriters; e-commerce is a substitute for a high street shop.

(b)   Technology is the basis for **new leisure activities** (eg computer games). Alternatively, IT-based systems can imitate existing goods (eg electronic keyboards imitating pianos).

(c)   Technology can **add value to existing services** by allowing more detailed analysis, by generating cost advantages, or by extending the market.

7.2.5 Rivalry

ISs can be used to compete – as a source of **competitive advantage** (see below).

Porter's five forces is another important strategy for analysing an organisation's environment. Be prepared to use it again as it is relevant to other CIMA papers.

7.3 Using ISs for competitive advantage

As the importance of information has increased, organisations have realised that **ISs** can be used as a source of **competitive advantage**.

Where the majority of organisations in an industry use ISs for competitive advantage, or the industry is based on ISs to a large extent, there may be a **competitive necessity** to use it.

KEY TERM

COMPETITIVE ADVANTAGE is a profitable and sustainable position. It exists in the minds of customers, who believe the value they will receive from a product or service is greater than both the price they will pay and the value offered by competitors.

7.3.1 Generic strategies for competitive advantage

Porter proposes **three generic strategies** for achieving competitive advantage:

(a)   **Cost leadership** means being the lowest-cost producer in the industry as a whole. A cost leadership strategy seeks to achieve the position of lowest-cost producer in the industry.

(b)   **Differentiation** is the exploitation of a product or service which the industry as a whole believes to be unique. A differentiation strategy assumes that competitive advantage can be gained through **particular characteristics** of a product or service.

(c)   **Focus** involves a restriction of activities to only part of the market (a segment or niche) through:

    (i)   Providing goods and/or services at lower cost **to that segment** (**cost-focus**)
    (ii)   Providing a differentiated product or service to that segment (**differentiation-focus**)

Cost leadership and differentiation are **industry-wide** strategies. Focus involves segmentation – pursuing **within the segment** a strategy of cost leadership or differentiation. Examples of how ISs can **support** each of these strategies are shown in the following table.

Strategy	How IS can support the strategy
Cost leadership	By facilitating reductions in cost levels, for example by reducing the number of administration staff required.
	Allowing better resource utilisation, for example by providing accurate stock information allowing lower 'buffer' inventories to be held.
	Using ISs to support just-in-time (JIT) and advanced manufacturing systems.
Differentiation	Differentiation can be suggested by an IS, perhaps in the product itself or in the way it is marketed, for example moving away from paper-based products to electronic.
Focus	ISs may enable a more customised or specialised product/service to be produced.
	ISs also facilitate the collection of sales and customer information that identifies targetable market segments.

7.4 Porter's value chain

Porter analyses the various activities of an organisation into a **value chain**. This is a model of value activities (which procure inputs, process them and add value to them in some way, to generate outputs for customers) and the relationships between them.

The value chain is usually applied in relation to **operations management**. We are considering it briefly here as it can be applied to IS strategy as well.

Value chain analysis can be used to assess the impact of ISs, and to identify **processes where it could be used to add value**. The activities and how ISs can benefit them are described below.

7.4.1 Logistics

In both **inbound** logistics and **outbound** logistics, ISs can have an impact.

(a)   **Inbound logistics**. The use of inventory control systems such as MRP, MRPII, ERP and JIT.

(b)   **Warehousing**. The use of barcodes facilitates accurate inventory data.

(c)   It is possible to create computer models, or **virtual warehouses**, of inventory held at different locations.

7.4.2 Marketing

Marketing and services can be made more effective by **customer databases** enabling market segmentation.

(a)   Buying and analysing a mailing list is a more precise method of targeting particular groups of consumers than television advertising.

(b)   A variety of market research companies use ISs to monitor consumers' buying habits.

(c)   Supermarkets can use automated EPOS systems to have a precise hour by hour idea of how products are selling to enable speedy ordering and replenishments.

Customer relationship management systems can encourage closer customer relationships.

7.4.3 Support activities

As far as **support** activities are concerned, ISs have some impact.

(a)   **Procurement**. ISs can automate some purchasing decisions. Paperwork can be saved if the organisation's purchase systems are linked directly to the sales order systems of some suppliers (eg by EDI).

(b) **Technology development**. **CAD** is, in a number of areas, an important influence.

    (i)   **Drafting**. CAD produces engineer's drawings, component design, layout (eg of stores, wiring and piping) and electronic circuit diagrams in complex systems.

    (ii)   **Updating**. It is easy to change design in CAD systems and to assess ramifications of any changes. Some CAD systems have archive data (eg for reference).

    (iii)   CAD enables modelling to be **checked** without the necessity of producing working prototypes. Some 'stress testing' can be carried out on the model.

(c) There is perhaps less impact on **human resources**. However, HR applications include the maintenance of a skills database, staff planning, computer-based training, time attendance systems, payroll systems and pension systems.

7.5 ISs and strategy – other writers

7.5.1 Ward and Griffiths

Ward and Griffiths suggested four ways that ISs could be used for competitive advantage:

(a) Linking the organisation to customers or suppliers
(b) Creating effective integration of the use of information in a value-adding process
(c) Enabling the organisation to develop, produce, market and distribute new products or services
(d) Giving senior management information to help develop and implement strategy

7.5.2 Clegg

Clegg (2003) stated that an organisation's **information strategy** is a plan for ensuring that information is appropriate, accurate, available, timely and effective. A starting point for achieving this could be the organisation reviewing its information for duplication or errors, or taking a 'blank page' approach and simply deciding its information requirements from scratch.

He emphasised that information strategy should not be left in the hands of IT experts. It's the managers within the organisation who know what information they require.

7.5.3 Boomer

Boomer (2007) identified a number of issues relevant when planning ISs.

Strategic issues relevant when planning ISs:

- The corporate plan and the organisation's priorities expressed in it
- How technology could be used to meet corporate objectives
- Trends in the use of IT in the organisation's industry and in other industries

Tactical issues relevant when planning ISs:

- What skills and abilities do people within the organisation possess?
- How are ISs and IT resources managed? Is outsourcing used – and should it be?
- What is the budget and timescale?

Question 5.3	Five forces

Learning outcome C1(i)

Using each of Porter's five forces, identify and briefly explain five ways that information systems could be used to create a competitive advantage for an organisation that manufactures wooden furniture for sale through a chain of its shops.   **(10 marks)**

Section summary

The ways in which **ISs can impact an industry** according to Porter and Millar are: **change the industry structure, create new businesses and industries** and **be used to create competitive advantage**.

Porter identified **five competitive forces** operating in a competitive environment.

Porter proposes **three generic strategies** for achieving competitive advantage: **cost leadership, differentiation** and **focus**.

Value chain analysis can be used to assess the impact of ISs and to identify **processes where they could be used to add value**.

8   Privacy and security

Introduction

Most of the advances in technology and information systems that we have seen in this chapter rely on the internet as a means of communication. However, establishing internet links makes organisations vulnerable to **privacy** and **security risks**. Therefore suitable systems, policies and procedures should be implemented to minimise them.

Computer systems are exposed to privacy and security risks. Some of the main risks are explained below.

Privacy and security risks	
Risk	**Explanation**
Hackers and eavesdroppers	Hackers attempt to gain unauthorised access to computer systems. They may attempt to damage a system or steal information. Hackers use tools like electronic password generators which enable rapid multiple password attempts.
	Data that is transmitted across telecommunications links is exposed to the risk of being intercepted or examined during transmission (eavesdropping).

Privacy and security risks	
Risk	**Explanation**
Viruses	A virus is a small piece of software which performs unauthorised actions and which replicates itself. Viruses may cause damage to files or attempt to destroy files and damage hard disks. When transmitted over a network such as the internet, into a 'clean' system, the virus reproduces and infects that system.
	Types of virus:
	Email viruses spread using email messages and replicated by mailing themselves to addresses held in the user's contacts book.
	Worms copy themselves from machine to machine on a network.
	Trojans or Trojan horses are hidden inside a 'valid' program but perform an unexpected act. Trojans therefore act like a virus, but aren't classified as a virus as they don't replicate themselves.
	Trap doors are undocumented access points to a system allowing controls to be bypassed.
	Logic bombs are triggered by the occurrence of a certain event.
	Time bombs are triggered by a certain date.
Hoaxes	An associated problem is that of hoax virus warnings. There are a vast number of common hoaxes, most of which circulate via email. Many are a variation of one of the most 'popular' early hoaxes – the Good Times hoax. This hoax takes the form of a warning about viruses contained in email. People pass along the warning trying to be helpful, but they are in fact wasting the time of all concerned.
Denial of service attack	Another threat to websites is the 'denial of service attack'. This involves an organised campaign to bombard a site with excessive volumes of traffic at a given time, with the aim of overloading the site.
Natural disasters	Fires, floods and other natural events may damage the place where the system is stored. It is important for the organisation to protect the system by selecting a suitable location and environment to house it. Backups should be taken regularly and be stored in a separate location so that the system can be restored if necessary. Steps should be taken to prevent risks as far as possible, for example by installing sprinkler systems and locating the system on a high floor to avoid flooding.
Hardware and software failure	Systems may malfunction for a number of reasons. This risk can be minimised by designing them to cope with extreme volumes of demand. Backups will enable the system to be restored if it does fail.
Human error	Operators may accidentally damage or delete information held on the system. This risk can be minimised by staff training and in-built protections, such as only allowing certain individuals to alter or amend information.
Operator injury	Repetitive strain injury (RSI) is a risk faced by computer operators. This risk can be minimised through the design of workstations and the office environment.

 A number of websites provide information on hoaxes and 'real' viruses – for example www.sophos.com. If you receive a warning of a virus or the promise of rewards for forwarding an email to a number of others, this is a good place to look to establish if the warning is a hoax or not.

8.1 Minimising privacy and security risks

The risks concerned with hackers, eavesdroppers and viruses can be minimised through a variety of **controls** that provide network and communications security.

8.1.1 Anti-virus software

The main protection against viruses is **anti-virus software**. Anti-virus software, such as McAfee and Norton, searches systems for viruses and removes them. Anti-virus programs include an auto-update feature that downloads profiles of new viruses, enabling the software to check for all known or existing viruses. Very new viruses may go undetected by anti-virus software (until the anti-virus software vendor updates their package – and the organisation installs the update).

Additional precautions include **disabling external media** to prevent viruses entering an organisation via external storage devices. However, this can disrupt work processes. At the very least, organisations should ensure all files received via external media and email are virus checked.

8.1.2 A firewall

External email links can be protected by way of a **firewall** that may be configured to virus check all messages, and may also prevent files of a certain type being sent via email (eg .exe files, as these are the most common means of transporting a virus). Firewalls can be implemented in both hardware and software, or a combination of both. A firewall disables part of the telecoms technology to prevent **unauthorised intrusions**. However, a determined hacker may well be able to bypass this.

8.1.3 Encryption

Data that is transmitted across telecommunications links is exposed to the risk of being **intercepted or read during transmission** (known as 'eavesdropping'). Encryption is used to reduce this risk and involves scrambling the data at one end of the line, transmitting the scrambled data, and unscrambling it at the receiver's end of the line. A person intercepting the scrambled data is unable to make sense of it.

8.1.4 Electronic signatures

One way of providing **electronic signatures** is to make use of what is known as **public key** (or asymmetric) cryptography signatures. Public key cryptography uses two keys – public and private. The private key is only known to its owner and is used to scramble the data contained in a file. The received **'scrambled' data** is checked against the original file using the public key of the person who signed it. This check confirms the file could only have been signed by someone with access to the private key. If a third party altered the message, the fact that they had done so would be easily detectable.

An alternative is the use of encryption products which support key recovery, also known as **key encapsulation**. These products incorporate a **Key Recovery Agent** (KRA) which allows the authorised user to unscramble data by approaching the KRA with an encrypted portion of the message.

8.1.5 Authentication

Authentication is a technique of making sure that a message has come from an **authorised sender**. Authentication involves adding extra data in a form previously agreed between sender and recipient.

8.1.6 Dial-back security

Dial-back security operates by requiring the person wanting access to dial into the network **and identify themselves first**. The system then dials the person back on their authorised number before allowing access.

8.2 General and application controls

There are two main types of control designed to safeguard information stored in a system, and ensure it is processed accurately and only used by those who are authorised.

8.2.1 General controls

General controls are often **physical restrictions** on who can access and use information held in the system. There may be personnel controls, such as internet use policies, segregation of duties and levels of access based on seniority which may be protected by passwords and lock-outs. Equipment may also be physically protected by locks, doors and cages.

8.2.2 Application controls

These are controls to ensure the **accuracy and validity of data**. For example, there may be checks on who can access and amend the data, completeness checks built into the system to ensure all expected information is provided and validity checks to ensure the data being entered is in the expected form (eg to stop words being entered where numbers are expected).

8.3 Data Protection Act (DPA) 1998

An **individual's privacy** relates to their right to control how personal information held about them is disseminated and used by others. In the UK, the relevant legislation is the **Data Protection Act (DPA) 1998**. This is an attempt to protect the **individual**. The terms of the Act cover data about individuals – not data about **corporate bodies**.

8.3.1 Definitions of terms used in the Act

In order to understand the Act it is necessary to know some of the technical terms used in it.

Personal data is information about a living individual, including expressions of opinion about them. Data about organisations is not personal data.

Data users are organisations or individuals who control personal data and the use of personal data.

A **data subject** is an individual who is the subject of personal data.

8.3.2 The data protection principles

The **UK DPA** includes eight **data protection principles** with which data users must comply.

DATA PROTECTION PRINCIPLES

Schedule 1 of the Act contains the data protection principles.

1   Personal data shall be processed fairly and lawfully in accordance with the Act.

2   Personal data shall be obtained only for one or more specified and lawful purposes, and shall not be further processed in any manner incompatible with that purpose or those purposes.

3   Personal data shall be adequate, relevant and not excessive in relation to the purpose or purposes for which they are processed.

4   Personal data shall be accurate and, where necessary, kept up to date.

5   Personal data processed for any purpose or purposes shall not be kept for longer than is necessary for that purpose or those purposes.

6   Personal data shall be processed in accordance with the rights of data subjects under this Act.

7   Appropriate technical and organisational measures shall be taken against unauthorised or unlawful processing of personal data and against accidental loss or destruction of, or damage to, personal data.

8   Personal data shall not be transferred to a country or territory outside the European Economic Area unless that country or territory ensures an adequate level of protection for the rights and freedoms of data subjects in relation to the processing of personal data.

The Act has two main aims:

(a)   To protect **individual privacy**. Previous UK law only applied to **computer-based** information. The 1998 Act applies to **all personal data, in any form**.

(b)   To **harmonise data protection legislation** so that, in the interests of improving the operation of the single European market, there can be a **free flow of personal data** between the member states of the EU.

8.3.3 The rights of data subjects

The Act establishes the following rights for data subjects:

(a)   A data subject may seek **compensation** through the courts for damage and any associated distress caused by the **loss**, **destruction** or **unauthorised disclosure** of data about himself or herself or by **inaccurate data** about himself or herself.

(b)   A data subject may apply to the courts for **inaccurate data** to be **put right** or even **wiped off** the data user's files altogether. Such applications may also be made to the Registrar.

(c)   A data subject may obtain **access** to personal data of which he or she is the subject. (This is known as the 'subject access' provision.) In other words, a data subject can ask to see his or her personal data that the data user is holding.

(d)   A data subject can **sue** a data user for any **damage or distress** caused by personal data about him or her being **incorrect** or **misleading** as to matter of **fact** (rather than opinion).

8.3.4 The Privacy and Electronic Communications (EC directives) Regulations 2003

These regulations are derived from electronic communications **(EC) directives** with the intention of protecting individuals and organisations from receiving **spam** (unsolicited electronic communications).

Most **e-marketing activities** are covered (such as email and SMS messages) and such communications are only permitted if the recipient has **'opted in'** to receive them. For the sender, this means having to obtain consent from the recipient before contacting them for the **first time**. The sender must also **identify themselves** in any direct marketing communication and provide a **valid reply email address**.

Permission is also deemed granted where a person is an **existing customer** (and has already provided their contact details) or where they have **emailed** or sent a **text enquiry** directly to the organisation.

All communications must provide a **free 'unsubscribe' service** and a fine of £5,000 may be imposed on the sender of any unlawful communications.

The regulations also impose certain controls on the use of **cookies** which are used to store information about website visitors.

Section summary

Computer systems with links to other systems such as the **internet** are exposed to privacy and security risks.

The **key privacy** and **security risks** come from **hackers** and **eavesdroppers, viruses, hoaxes** and **denial of service attacks**.

Organisations can take various **measures** against privacy and security risks, including **anti-virus software, firewalls, encryption, electronic signatures, authentication** and **dial-back security**.

The **Data Protection Act 1998** provides individuals with some protection regarding how data held about them is used.

9 Ethics and social issues of information systems

Introduction

A review of the literature on ethical and social issues surrounding systems identifies five moral dimensions of the information age: information rights and privacy, property rights, accountability and control, system quality and quality of life.

9.1 Introduction

KEY TERM

ETHICS can be defined as the principles of right and wrong that can be referenced by individuals in making a personal decision or judgement. Often these references are made from a combination of sources.

ISs have the ability to affect individuals, companies, cultures and countries instantaneously. This heightens the need to take ethical issues into account because damage can be done instantly.

There are several professional bodies that publish codes of conduct or guidelines for their members with reference to the use of IT, but a generic set of guidelines would contain the following:

- Avoid harm to others
- Be honest and trustworthy
- Contribute to society and human wellbeing
- Honour property rights including copyrights and patents
- Access computing resources only when authorised
- Respect the privacy of others

The majority of professional bodies add to this generic list and propose specific guidelines relating to the appropriate profession.

9.2 The five moral dimensions of the information age

ISs raise new ethical questions for both individuals and societies because they create opportunities for intense social change, and thus threaten existing distributions of power, money, rights and obligations. The development of IT will produce benefits for many, and costs for others. In this situation, what is the ethical and socially responsible course of action?

The principles which guide a manager's decision making are important to all affected. Computer ethics involve questions related to the use of technology and its social impact.

A review of the literature on ethical and social issues surrounding systems identifies five moral dimensions of the information age:

(1)   Information rights and obligations; essentially, this relates to privacy
(2)   Property rights
(3)   Accountability and control
(4)   System quality
(5)   Quality of life

The five moral dimensions should constantly be reviewed by all organisations in an attempt to create policies and codes of practice that will encourage all employees to recognise the need to act in an ethical manner.

9.2.1 Information rights and obligations: privacy

Privacy is the claim of individuals to be left alone, free from surveillance or interference from other individuals or organisations, including the State. Claims to privacy are also involved at the workplace. Millions of employees are subject to electronic and other forms of high-tech surveillance. Information technology and systems threaten individual claims to privacy by making the invasion of privacy cheap, profitable and effective.

Some countries have a set of principles governing the collection and use of information about individuals. The five fair information practices principles are:

(1)   Individuals have rights of access, inspection, review and amendment to systems that contain information about them.

(2)   There must be no use of personal information for purposes other than those for which it was gathered without prior consent.

(3)   There should be no personal record systems whose existence is secret.

(4)   Governments have the right to intervene in the information relationships among private parties.

(5)   Managers of systems are responsible and can be held accountable and liable for the damage done by systems.

Despite growing concerns about privacy, some would argue that it is often in a person's best interests to reveal rather than withhold private information. For example, credit could not be provided if borrowers were unwilling to release the relevant personal information to allow their creditworthiness to be assessed, and fair decisions concerning personal taxation could not be made if lawful personal data was not provided by the appropriate people.

Whatever the privacy debate, privacy protection is very important, and is likely to become more so as developments mean that new classes of data and actions must be considered to effectively ensure the privacy of individuals. Hussain and Hussain (1992) describe two important privacy issues:

(a)   **Fair use**: the concept of data privacy that would only allow data to be used in support of the organisation's specific business mission. This would require an organisation to seek an individual's permission before passing personal data on to others. Data use is complex; it seems legitimate to use personal data for marketing purposes, perhaps to direct advertising efforts. However, once such personal data is gathered it describes individuals in ways that can have less savoury use, such as for political harassment, or to allow criminals to identify lucrative (or soft touch) targets.

(b)   **Gatekeeping**: the restricted access to services, privileges, benefits or opportunities on the basis of certain data values. Some gatekeeping seems inevitable, and acceptable; entry to a university permitted by a points system based on exam results is one such example and a point-scoring system for credit provision is another. However, the same principle can be used to keep out 'trouble makers', and then the central issue becomes: whose definition of trouble maker?

9.2.2 Internet challenges to privacy

Every day, internet users are giving out personally identifiable information unknowingly. With the technology available today, and especially in relation to **Big Data**, users' every action online is being recorded without their explicit permission. The chief issue of internet surfing privacy is choice and awareness. In today's competitive world, collection of consumer data helps companies survive and thrive. But the question is the manner in which such information is collected. The internet privacy violators include cookies, web bugs, spyware and smart tags.

Cookies – An internet cookie is a packet of information sent by a server to a browser, which is then sent by the browser each time it accesses the server. Cookies are typically used to authenticate a registered user of a website, personalise the site, maintain an online shopping cart, etc. Originally developed by Netscape, cookies offer convenience to the visitor if care is taken by the website. One of the controversies surrounding cookies is their ability to build a personal profile of the user's browsing and purchasing habits.

Spyware – Some companies place spyware through their software installations, usually without the user's permission. It can pass on information about software, browsing habits and purchasing habits of the user to the company's data collection facilities. It also has the capability to take names, credit card details and other personal information. The information gathered by such companies is usually sold and combined with other databases to build a profile of individual web users. This profile is mainly used for direct marketing purposes.

Web bugs – Web bugs are graphics on a web page or in an email message that are designed to monitor who is reading the web page or email message. A web bug is often invisible as its size is only 1 pixel by 1 pixel. It is represented as HTML IMG tags. Any graphics used for monitoring is a web bug. Not all invisible gif images are web bugs, as some are used for alignment purposes. Web bugs are also known as clear gifs, 1 by 1 gifs or invisible gifs.

Ad networks use web bugs to add information to a personal profile of what sites a person is visiting. This information is stored in a database belonging to the ad network. This in turn determines what banner ad the user is shown. Web bugs are also used to gather statistics about web browser usage and independent accounting of the number of people who have visited a particular website. Web bugs can be found by using the HTML source of a web page. The web bug is usually loaded from a different server than the rest of the page.

9.2.3 Property rights

Intangible property created by individuals or corporations, which is subject to protection, includes trade secrets, copyright (books, music, films, newspapers and so on) and patents. Information technologies pose a severe challenge to existing intellectual property regimes. Digital media differs from other traditional forms of media in terms of ease of replication, ease of transmission and ease of alteration. How will traditional intellectual property rights be protected in a digital society in which tracing and accounting for ownership is difficult, and ignoring such property rights is so easy?

Contemporary ISs have challenged existing law and social practices that protect private intellectual property, which is subject to a variety of protections under three different legal traditions: trade secrets, copyright and patent law. In the case of computer software, the question here becomes what an individual, or organisation, can own – ideas, media, source code, object code? A related question is whether owners and users should be constrained in their use or access. **Copyright law** has been invoked in an attempt to protect those who develop software from having it copied. Unquestionably, the hours spent in program development should be protected from piracy but many believe that copyright laws can cause more harm than good. Part of the problem lies in the uniqueness of software, its ease of dissemination and the possibility of exact replication. It does not quite fit with the current categories and conventions regarding ownership.

9.2.4 Accountability and control

These are the mechanisms for assessing responsibility for decisions made and actions taken. Who can and will be held accountable and liable for harm done to the individual? If a machine injures a person and the machine is controlled, in part, by software, who should be held accountable? Should an electronic service provider be held responsible for the broadcasts made by its clients of, for example, offensive or pornographic materials? The central ethical issue here is whether individuals and organisations that create, produce and sell systems are morally responsible for the consequences of their use.

In general, it is very difficult to hold software producers liable for their products when:

- Some software may be part of a machine
- Some software acts more like a book storing and displaying information
- Software is a service (ATM)

Liability of electronic information services

- Are such services liable for the content of their transmissions?

- Telephone companies are not liable for their transmissions because they are regulated 'common carriers'.

- Radio and television are liable.

- What should we do with respect to the internet?

- What happens when one company provides telephone, cable and internet access services over one wire?

9.2.5 System quality

What standards of data and system quality should we demand to protect individual rights and the safety of society? A balance has to be struck between endless testing to create a perfect system, and the delay in implementing a new system that might be beneficial to users. Data quality is a major concern. What is an acceptable, technologically feasible level of system quality? There are grey areas, such as what if some system errors are correctable only at very great expense, an expense so great that pursuing this level of perfection is not feasible economically?

For example, although software companies try to debug their products before releasing them to the marketplace, they knowingly ship faulty products because the time and cost of fixing all minor errors would prevent these products from ever being released. Three principal sources of poor system performance are software bugs and errors, hardware or facility failures due to natural or other causes, and poor input data quality. Unfortunately, there is a technological barrier to perfect software, and users must be aware of the potential for catastrophic failure. The software industry has not yet arrived at testing standards for producing software of acceptable but not perfect performance.

Although software bugs and facility catastrophe are likely to be widely reported in the press, by far the most common source of business system failure is data quality. Few companies routinely measure the quality of their data but studies of individual organisations report data error rates ranging from 0.5% to 30%. For example, a manufacturer attempted to reorganise its customer files by customer number only to discover the sales staff had been entering a new customer number for each sale because of special incentives for opening new accounts. One customer was entered 7,000 times. The company scrapped the software project after spending $1 million.

The central quality-related ethical issue raised by ISs is at what point should anyone release software or services for consumption by others? At what point can a person conclude that the software or service achieves an economically and technologically adequate level of quality?

9.2.6 Quality of life

The negative social costs of introducing information technologies and systems are rising along with the power of the technology. Many of these negative social consequences are not violations of individual rights, nor are they property crimes. Nevertheless, they can be extremely harmful to individuals and societies. The negative consequences of ISs include the following:

(a) **Monitoring** – much of the decentralisation of decision making has been ineffective; modern communication systems allow remote parts of a business to be monitored and controlled from the centre. There is an argument that remote parts can be constantly watched by the central core.

(b) **Rapidity of change** and the more efficient global marketplace mean that businesses now no longer have the necessary time to adjust to change. News of change is broadcast instantaneously.

(c) **Boundaries** between family, work and leisure – the 'work umbrella' extends far beyond the eight-hour day because of the 'do anything anywhere' computing environment.

(d) **Dependence** and vulnerability – businesses, schools, the government and private institutions are dependent on ISs. Should we be worried that there are no regulatory or standard-setting forces in place like in other public utility technologies?

(e) **Employment** – trickle-down technology: new technologies, originally expensive and used in developed countries, become cheaper through improved design and mass production, and are then used widely in less developed countries, often displacing workers in what were labour intensive industries.

(f) **Equity and access** – increasing racial and social class divisions. Do all members of society have equal access to IS/IT?

(g) **Health risks** such as RSI, computer vision syndrome, video display terminal radiation and Technostress.

(h) **Computer crime** and abuse – technologies including computers create new valuable items to steal, new ways to steal them and new ways to harm others. Abuse is the commission of acts involving a computer that may not be illegal but are considered unethical (eg spam).

Examples of internet crime and abuse:

- **Hacking** – access to proprietary data
- **Jamming** – also called Denial of Service – tie up host computer
- **Malicious software** – viruses disable computer
- **Sniffing** – intercept data passing through system eg credit card data
- **Spoofing** – fraudulent misrepresentation

9.3 Technology and ethics

There are four major technology and system trends that have heightened concern about ethical issues.

(1) The **doubling of computing power** every 18 months has helped the proliferation of ISs. As a result, our dependence on systems and our vulnerability to system errors and poor data quality has increased. Public concern has heightened over our growing dependence on some critical systems but standards for ensuring the accuracy and reliability of ISs are not universally accepted or enforced.

(2) Advances in **data storage techniques** and rapidly declining storage costs have been responsible for the multiplying of databases on individuals – employees, customers and potential customers maintained by private and public organisations. These advances in data storage have made the routine violation of individual privacy both cheap and effective. Already massive data storage systems are cheap enough for regional and even local retailing firms to use in identifying customers, a simple application of Big Data.

(3)   Advances in **data mining techniques** for large databases is a third technological trend that heightens ethical concerns, because they enable companies to find out much detailed personal information about individuals. With contemporary IS technology, companies can assemble and combine the many pieces of information stored by you on computers much more easily than in the past. Think of all the ways you generate computer information about yourself: credit card purchases, telephone calls, magazine subscriptions, video rentals, mail-order purchases, banking records, and local, state and federal government records (including court and police records). Put together and mined properly, this information could reveal not only your credit information but also your police record, your tastes, your associations and your leisure interests. Companies with products to sell purchase relevant information from these sources to help them more finely target their marketing campaigns. For example, if you buy expensive merchandise from one catalogue, the catalogue company might sell your name to another retailer. In most countries this is illegal unless permission is obtained from the user, but websites often require the user to take some action (such as ticking a box) to prevent permission being given, and it is not always obvious that this should be done.

(4)   **Advances in networking**, including the internet, promise to greatly reduce the costs of moving and accessing large quantities of data, and open the possibility of mining large pools of data remotely using small desktop machines, permitting an invasion of privacy on a scale precision never before imaginable.

Section summary

The **five moral dimensions of the information age** should constantly be reviewed by all organisations in an attempt to create policies and codes of practice that will encourage all employees to recognise the need to act in an ethical manner.

Chapter Summary

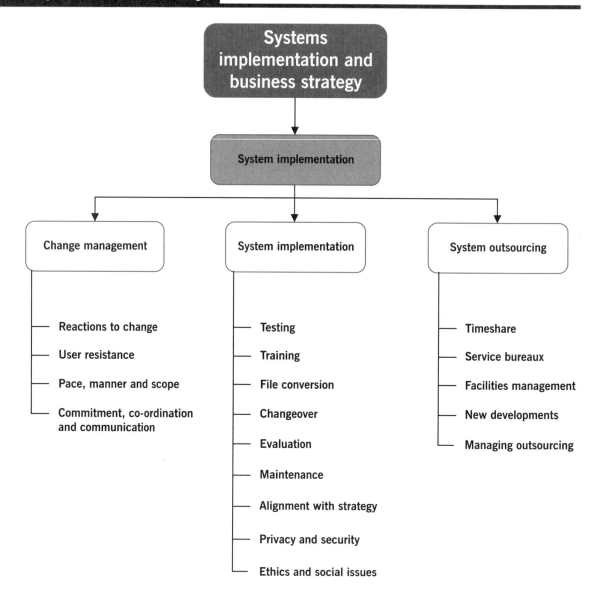

Quick Quiz

1   Which of the following is the final step in Lewin and Schien's three-stage model of change?

    A   Refreeze
    B   Move
    C   Unfreeze
    D   Fix

2   Which of the following describes corrective maintenance?

    A   Maintenance carried out when there is a systems failure
    B   Maintenance carried out to perfect the system
    C   Maintenance carried out to adjust the system for changes in the processing environment
    D   Maintenance carried out to improve user friendliness

3   How does a cost-benefit review differ from a cost-benefit analysis?

4   Which level of service provision by an IS outsourcing organisation is described below?

    'The vendor charges for access to an external processing system on a time-used basis.'

    A   Service bureaux
    B   Timeshare
    C   Facilities management
    D   Processing rental

5   Who developed the five forces model that can be used to analyse the effect of information systems on an industry?

    A   Lewin
    B   Schein
    C   Porter
    D   Clegg

Answers to Quick Quiz

1. **A**   The final stage in Lewin and Schien's three-stage model of change is refreeze.

2. **A**   Option B is perfective maintenance, C is adaptive maintenance, D is also perfective maintenance.

3.   The review uses actual data. The analysis relies on estimates.

4. **B**   Timeshare is where the vendor charges for access to an external processing system on a time-used basis.

5. **C**   Porter developed the five forces model.

Answers to Questions

5.1 Resistance to change

A   Education and communication is effective where the cause of the resistance is lack of information about the change.

5.2 Cost-benefit review

Direct benefits might include reduced operating costs, for example lower overtime payments.

Indirect benefits might include better decision making and the freeing of human 'brainpower' from routine tasks so that it can be used for more creative work.

Development costs include systems analysts' costs and the cost of time spent by users in assisting with fact-finding.

Implementation costs would include costs of site preparation and costs of training.

Running costs include maintenance costs, software leasing costs and ongoing user support.

5.3 Five forces

The following are just some ideas that are possible – you may have thought of others.

Potential entrants

Technology can reduce the labour cost of manufacturing and speed up the production process so that substantial economies of scale are created. This may mean that new entrants cannot compete with the organisation on cost.

Suppliers

The organisation can store price, and other data, regarding suppliers on a database. This will allow it to quickly scan which suppliers provide the best deal, increasing the competition between them and therefore reducing their bargaining power.

Customers

The organisation can store marketing data that it collects from its customers on a database. This information can be analysed and used to improve the targeting of the marketing effort, therefore reducing customer bargaining power.

Substitutes

The organisation can develop a website and an in-store product database that allows customers to analyse and compare the products that are on offer – for example by colour, size and style. Such value-added activities can help reduce the threat of substitutes.

Industry rivalry

Porter proposed three strategies for competitive advantage: cost leadership, differentiation and focus.

We have already seen how ISs can help the organisation compete on cost. Differentiation can be achieved through the provision of the website and in-store database – not all the organisation's competitors will provide this.

ISs can also help focus the organisation's activities by allowing it to trade under two different brands on the internet. For example, one brand could compete on cost – this would sell cheaper products. Another brand could compete on product differentiation such as stylish or luxury products. Each brand could have a separate website and be marketed differently, even though the organisation that manufactures their products is the same.

Now try these questions from the Practice Question Bank	Number
	21, 22, 23, 24, 25

OPERATIONS MANAGEMENT

Part D

OPERATIONS MANAGEMENT AND THE ORGANISATION

In this chapter we begin our study of **operations management** by discussing what it is and the important role it plays in organisations.

We then continue by considering an organisation's broad **operations strategy**. This is concerned with how the

organisation **structures itself** and its **relations with suppliers** to meet the needs of the customer.

Finally, we look at the issues of **corporate social responsibility** (CSR) and **sustainability in operations management**. These are recent developments that many organisations are under pressure from customers to address.

Topic list	Learning outcomes	Syllabus references	Ability required
1 Operations management	D1(a), D1(b)	D1(i), D1(v)	application
2 Operations strategy	D1(a), D1(b), D2(a), D2(b)	D1(i), D1(ii), D1(iii), D1(iv), D1(v), D2(i), D2(ii), D2(iii), D2(ix)	application
3 Corporate social responsibility (CSR) and sustainability in operations management	D1(b)	D1(vi)	application

Chapter Overview

1 Operations management

Introduction

The overall objective of operations is to use a **transformation process** to add value and create **competitive advantage**. It involves taking input resources and transforming them into outputs of products or services for customers. Operations management involves the design, implementation and control of these processes.

KEY TERM

OPERATIONS MANAGEMENT is concerned with the transformation of 'inputs' into 'outputs' that meet the needs of the customer.

1.1 The operations function

Organisations will invariably have an **operations function**. The operations function might be considered as one of the three traditional 'core functions':

(a) **Operations**. This is responsible for fulfilling customer orders and requests through production of the goods or services, and for delivery of products or services to the customer.

(b) **Marketing and sales**. This is responsible for identifying customer needs and, perhaps more significantly, for communicating information about the organisation's products or services to customers so as to procure sales orders.

(c) **Product and service development**. This is responsible for designing new products and services that will meet customer needs, to generate sales orders.

There are also **support functions** within an organisation that help the core functions to operate effectively. Traditionally, support functions might include accounting, HR and IT. However, what is actually a core function or a support function will depend on the particular organisation. For example, organisations that rely heavily on technology (eg the use of Computer Aided Manufacturing) may consider IT a core function.

The functions within an organisation **overlap**, and for any particular task or process input is often required from more than one core function or support function.

The core functions: examples		
	Publishing company	**Hotel**
Operations	Editing Printing Distribution	Reservations Housekeeping Building maintenance Catering
Marketing and sales	Advertise through trade magazines Book fairs Negotiate sale of rights Sell into bookshops and other outlets	Advertise across media Liaise with tour operators, travel agents and booking agents
Product/ service development	Commission new titles Vet submitted scripts Develop new media forms, eg internet delivery	Develop accommodation offerings, creative ambience, catering and ancillary facilities such as gym, business centre, conference facilities, entertainment Devise new packages Identify new locations

At its simplest, operations management tries to ensure that organisations are run as **efficiently** as possible.

1.2 The transformation process model

An operation takes **input resources** and, through one or more **processes**, **transforms** these into **outputs**. Input resources are transformed in the process into a product or service that satisfies customer needs. This generalised concept of the transformation process model applies to all processes and may be depicted as follows.

Transformation processes

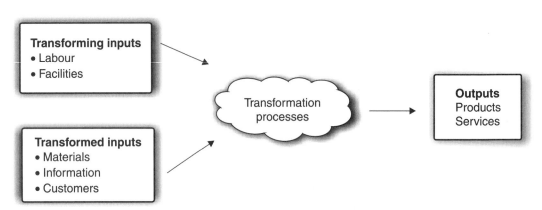

The **transformation process** could be a **physical transformation**, a **change in nature or form** (for example, a transformation of data into information), a **change in location**, a **change in ownership** or, in the case of customers, a **psychological change** (eg giving enjoyment).

Inputs to the transformation process can be categorised as either transformed resources or transforming resources.

(a)   **Transformed resources** are manipulated and formed into a different condition by the process. These resources can be materials, information or customers themselves.

(b)   **Transforming resources** are the resources that are used to alter the condition of the transformed resources. These consist of the workforce of the organisation and facilities such as buildings, equipment and vehicles.

Here are some **practical examples of the transformation process**.

(a)   In a manufacturing process, inputs of raw materials and components are manipulated into a finished product. The **output** is the **product**. This is then distributed to the customer.

(b)   In the legal profession, a client seeks clarification about a legal problem. A lawyer holds a meeting with the client and provides the necessary advice. The **output** is an **informed client**.

(c)   In the rail industry, rail service providers take customers, and use their workforce and facilities (eg trains) to deliver the customers from one location to another. The **output** is a **relocated customer**.

(d)   In banking, instructions from a customer (information) are processed using the facilities of the bank, and the instructions are carried out, for example by the transfer of money. The **output** is the **completed transfer**.

(e)   In the entertainment industry, the customer might be provided with entertainment input such as a comedian telling a joke. The **output** is an **entertained customer**.

1.2.1 Product and service outputs

Many operations produce a **mixture** of product and service outputs. Remember also that in many countries the service economy may be more significant than the manufacturing economy. Here are some examples of the close interrelationships between service and manufacturing operations.

(a)   The **manufacture of machine tools** is primarily concerned with the output of products. However, the organisation will also provide training and technical support services to customers.

(b)   An **education and training organisation** might provide lectures, tutorials and workshops. The service may include the provision of products in the form of study notes or books. It might also provide an online helpline.

(c)   A **restaurant** provides products in the form of food and drink. However, for the customer an essential ingredient of going to a restaurant is usually the overall dining experience that includes the enjoyment obtained from the service style, entertainment and general ambience.

1.2.2 The four Vs of operations

Another method of analysing the differences between transformational processes is by using the **four Vs**.

V	Description
Volume	The volume of units produced. High volume usually means capital intensive, low volume usually means labour intensive.
Variety	Whether the operation handles a number of different inputs or produces a range of different outputs.
Variation in demand	Demand for same operations may be seasonal or regular peaks and dips in demand may be experienced.
Visibility	The degree to which business operations are visible to the customer.

Section summary

Operations is a **core** part of any organisation.

The **transformational process model** describes how **inputs** are converted through **processes** into **outputs**.

2   Operations strategy

Introduction

Organisations may employ one or more of a number of **operations strategies** to improve their processes and as a source of competitive advantage over competitors. Common strategies involve what is known as the **value chain** and **supply chain management**. This is the view that an organisation is one link in a chain that aims to turn raw materials into what the customer wants. As a result, all links in the chain benefit.

2.1 The value chain

KEY TERM

VALUE CHAIN. 'Sequence of business activities by which, in the perspective of the end-user, value is added to the products or services produced by an entity.'   *(CIMA Official Terminology)*

In Porter's analysis, **business activities** are **not** the same as **business functions**.

(a)   **Functions** are the familiar departments of a business (eg production function, the finance function) and reflect the formal organisation structure and the distribution of labour.

(b)   **Activities** are what actually goes on, the work that is done. Activities are the means by which an organisation creates value in its products – sometimes referred to as **value activities**. Activities incur costs and provide a product or service which earns revenue.

An example should make this clear. An organisation needs many inputs of resources to function. It needs to secure resources from the environment. This activity can be called **procurement**. However, procurement will involve more departments than purchasing; for example, the accounts department will certainly be involved and possibly production and quality assurance.

Organisations **create value** for their buyers by **performing these activities**. The ultimate value a firm creates is measured by the amount customers are willing to pay for its products or services above the cost of carrying out value activities. A business is profitable if the realised value to customers exceeds the collective cost of performing the activities.

There are two points to note here:

(a) **Customers purchase value**, which they measure by comparing an organisation's products and services with similar offerings from competitors.

(b) **The business creates value** by carrying out its activities either more efficiently than other businesses, or combined in such a way as to provide a unique product or service.

Porter's value chain is a model of value activities (which procure inputs, process them and add value to them in some way, to generate outputs for customers) and the relationships between them.

Porter's Value Chain

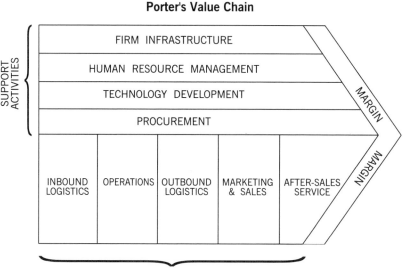

2.1.1 Primary activities

Porter distinguished between **primary activities** and **support activities**.

Primary activities are those directly related with production, sales, marketing, delivery and services.

The diagram shows **five primary activities**:

(a) **Inbound logistics** are those activities involved with receiving, handling and storing inputs to the production system.

(b) **Operations** are those activities which convert resource inputs into a final product. In a manufacturing business, this is relatively easy to identify as the factory. In a service company, operations include those activities which make up the basic service.

(c) **Outbound logistics** are those activities relating to storing the product and its distribution to customers.

(d) **Marketing and sales** are those activities that relate to informing customers about the product, persuading them to buy it, and enabling them to do so.

(e) **After-sales service** includes activities such as installing products, repairing them and providing spare parts.

2.1.2 Support activities

Support activities are those which provide purchased inputs, human resources, technology and infrastructural functions to support the primary activities.

(a)   **Procurement** consists of those activities which acquire the resource inputs to the primary activities (eg purchase of materials, subcomponents, equipment).

(b)   **Technology development** (in the sense of apparatus, techniques and work organisation). These activities are related to both product design and to improving processes and/or resource utilisation.

(c)   **Human resource management** is the activities of recruiting, training, developing and rewarding people.

(d)   **Firm infrastructure**. The systems of planning, finance, quality control and management are activities which Porter believes are crucially important to an organisation's strategic capability in all primary activities.

2.1.3 Other elements

Furthermore, in addition to the categories described above, Porter identifies three further types of activity:

(a)   **Direct activities** are concerned with adding value to inputs.

(b)   **Indirect activities** enable direct activities to be performed (eg maintenance, sales force administration).

(c)   **Quality assurance**. This type of activity monitors the quality of other activities, and includes inspection, review and audit (eg the quality of the financial records).

Linkages connect the interdependent elements of the value chain together. They occur when one element of the value chain affects the costs or effectiveness of another. They require co-ordination.

(a)   More costly product design, or better quality production, might reduce the need for after-sales service.

(b)   To deliver goods on time requires smooth functioning of operations, outbound logistics and service activities such as installation.

Question 6.1	Activities

Learning outcome D1(ii)

Which of the following is a support activity in the value chain?

A   Inbound logistics
B   Human resource management
C   Marketing and sales
D   Service   **(2 marks)**

2.2 The value system

Activities that add value do not stop at the organisation's boundaries. For example, when a restaurant serves a meal, the quality of the ingredients – although they are chosen by the cook – is determined by the grower. The grower has also added value, and the grower's success in growing produce of good quality is as important to the customer's ultimate satisfaction as the skills of the chef. Consequently, a company's value chain is connected to what Porter describes as a **value system**.

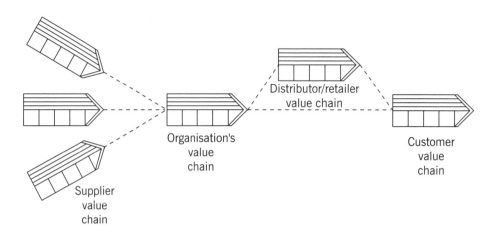

As well as managing its own value chain, a business can secure **competitive advantage** by managing the linkages with its suppliers and customers. A company can create competitive advantage by making best use of these links. An example is a **just-in-time system** where close integration of the organisation's operations with those of its suppliers is essential.

2.3 Purchasing and supply chain management

KEY TERM

SUPPLY CHAIN MANAGEMENT is concerned with the flow of goods and services through the supply chain with the aim of making the firm more competitive.

(Cousins)

The nature of **purchasing** has changed dramatically over recent years. Historically, it was viewed as a **clerical function** related to the day to day purchase of goods (a **contractual approach**). High importance was placed on price, quality and timely delivery and the meeting of contractual specifications. However, this has changed in recent years.

Purchasing today, in most organisations, is viewed as a strategically important function that impacts significantly on **organisational performance**. Organisations are increasingly seeking strong, long-term relationships with their suppliers (a **relational approach**). A degree of control is sought over the supply process and businesses actively manage the number of suppliers they use, implement outsourcing arrangements as necessary and consider developing strategic partnerships where appropriate.

2.3.1 What caused the need for closer supply chain links?

Christopher (2005) identified a number of factors:

- Shorter product life cycles requiring more efficient supply pipelines
- Increasingly global supply chains requiring greater co-ordination
- A move towards more flexible organisations that partner with others (organisational integration)
- More demanding customer service standards

2.3.2 Effective supply chain management

Supply chain management is concerned with the flow of goods and services through the supply chain. Ultimately, the goal is to contribute to customer **satisfaction**.

Porter recognised that management of the supply chain and supply network could be a source of **competitive advantage**. He referred to the position of firms in supply chains and networks in relation to their proximity to the customer. If a firm is closer to the customer than another, it is '**downstream**' of it. If a firm is further away from the customer than another, it is '**upstream**' of it.

Supply chains today must be **responsive** and **reliable**. The relationships between members must demonstrate a high degree of **mutual understanding**. Integration between the organisation and other chain members, both upstream and downstream, should be facilitated by **integrated information systems**.

2.3.3 Reck and Long

Reck and Long (1988) devised a model that aimed to provide an insight into the evolution of the purchasing function. Their **strategic positioning tool** identified a four-phase **development of procurement** within organisations.

The phases of Reck and Long's strategic positioning tool	
Phase	**Comment**
1 Passive	• Purchasing reacts to requests from other departments. • The focus is on efficient transaction processing.
2 Independent	• A more professional approach to purchasing is taken. • During this phase, the importance of negotiation with suppliers to securing the best prices for individual products/services purchased is recognised. • Often includes IT improvements and the creation of a purchasing manager position to manage supplier negotiations.
3 Supportive	• The potential for purchasing to support wider organisational goals is recognised. • This phase is often characterised by a centralised purchasing department with organisation-wide buying policies and systems. • The emphasis is co-ordination and compliance with centrally negotiated contracts. • The importance of careful supplier selection is recognised. • Policies and procedures for supplier management are developed.
4 Integrative	• Purchasing is now fully integrated in the major business activities of the organisation. • Proactive purchasing strategies are developed and followed. • Purchasing is part of the firm's strategic planning process and purchasing strategy is aligned with corporate goals and strategy. • The alignment of purchasing strategy with overall organisational goals and strategy often leads to new requirements in suppliers' performance and capabilities. • Suppliers are viewed as partners and supplier management is viewed as relationship management. • Today, closely linked or joint communication and information systems would facilitate this relationship.

2.3.4 Cousins

Cousins (2000) conducted a 12-month research project to investigate the level of **strategic maturity** in the purchasing function of UK/European companies. In particular, the research aimed to establish the level of collaboration between leading UK companies (ie suppliers) and their major customers. The research looked at a range of interconnected aspects considered important when looking at how an organisation deals with relationships relevant to overall strategy and supply strategy.

These aspects are shown in the diagram below.

Cousin's Strategic Supply Wheel

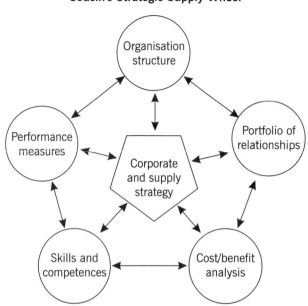

The research revealed that all the aspects identified and shown in the **Strategic Supply Wheel** are interconnected. Cousins stated that it was clear that a focus on any one area (eg relationship development) would be to the detriment of another area (eg performance measures). Organisations need to **balance** these resources and issues.

The research also examined the '**relationship type**', using a simple classification of '**opportunistic**' (low level of co-operation with the supplier) versus '**collaborative**' (high level of co-operation). The results showed that the more collaborative the relationship, the greater the degree of strategic alignment required (between overall strategy and purchasing strategy).

An '**opportunistic**' (or '**competitive**') approach is one where suppliers are selected on price and is based on the power and threat of the purchasing organisation to switch suppliers and insist on heavy penalty clauses in supply contracts. There is little trust between the parties and very little information passes between them (as the buyer seeks to retain as much power in the relationship as possible). This means that the true potential of the arrangement can never be exploited.

A '**collaborative**' approach is based on the customer and supplier working together to provide a package that best meets the needs of the market. The end result should be that both parties increase their market share. Such relationships are long-term partnerships where both parties work together when designing products and overcoming problems. In this regard, the purchasing organisation may offer sole supply contracts in return for the supplier's commitment.

2.4 Supply chain networks

KEY TERM

A SUPPLY CHAIN NETWORK is an interconnecting group of organisations which relate to each other through linkages between the different processes and activities involved in producing products/services to the ultimate consumer.

Increasingly, organisations are recognising the need for and benefits of establishing **close links** with companies in the supply chain. Historically, businesses in the supply chain have operated relatively **independently** of one another to create value for an ultimate customer. Independence was maintained through holding buffer stocks and managing lead times. There was very little control over other channel members, and no wider perspective on the system as a whole.

Market and competitive demands are now, however, **compressing lead times** and businesses are reducing inventories and excess capacity. Linkages between businesses in the supply chain must therefore become much tighter. This new condition is shown in the '**integrated supply chain**' model (the second model in the following diagram).

There seems to be increasing recognition that, in the future, it will be **whole supply chains** which will compete and not just individual organisations.

Traditional and integrated supply chain models

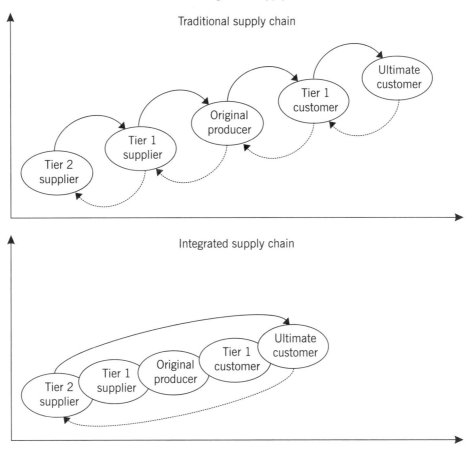

The aim is to co-ordinate the whole chain, from raw material suppliers to end customers. The chain should be considered as a **network** rather than a **pipeline** – a network of vendors support a network of customers, with third parties such as transport businesses helping to link the companies. In marketing channels, organisations have to manage the trade-off between the desire to remain **independent and autonomous**, and the need to be **interdependent and co-operative**.

KEY TERMS

INDEPENDENCE: each channel member operates in isolation and is not affected by others, so maintains a greater degree of control.

INTERDEPENDENCE: each channel member can affect the performance of others in the channel.

If the supplier 'knows' what its customers want, it does not necessarily have to guess, or wait until the customer places an order. It will be able to better plan its own delivery systems. The potential for using the **internet** to allow customers and suppliers to acquire up to date information about forecasted needs and delivery schedules is a recent development, but one which is being used by an increasing number of companies. Some supply chain relationships are strengthened and communication facilitated through the use of **extranets** (intranets accessible to authorised outsiders).

2.4.1 Implications for supply chain management

Supply chain management involves optimising the activities of companies working together to produce goods and services. The trend towards closer links with suppliers and the development of supply chain networks has implications for supply chain management.

(a) **Reduction in customers served**. For the sake of focus, companies might concentrate resources on customers of high potential value.

(b) **Price and inventory co-ordination**. Businesses co-ordinate their price and inventory policies to avoid problems and bottlenecks caused by short-term surges in demand, such as promotions.

(c) **Linked computer systems**. Closer links may be facilitated through the use of **Electronic Data Interchange**, for example to allow paperless communication, billing and payment and through the use of a computer **extranet**.

(d) **Early supplier involvement** in product development and component design.

(e) **Logistics design**. Hewlett-Packard restructured its distribution system by enabling certain product components to be added at the distribution warehouse rather than at the central factory. For example, user manuals which are specific to the French market would be added at the French distribution centre.

(f) **Joint problem solving**.

(g) **Supplier representative on site**.

The business case for supply chain management is the **benefit** to **all** the **participants** in terms of the performance objectives of speed, dependability and cost.

Performance objective	Example
Speed	Plumbers need to manage their supply chains to ensure they are able to get hold of parts such as water tanks, boilers and valves so they can respond quickly to customer emergencies.
Dependability	A mail order business promises delivery within ten days of receipt of order. It will need to ensure good supply chain management to fulfil its promise.
Cost	A company providing mortgages will need to manage its supply chain with great skill, with one of its objectives being to obtain the cheapest sources of finance in keeping with the profile and risks of their mortgage lending.

Businesses that are perceived by customers and potential customers to excel at delivering the desired performance objectives are likely to derive a **competitive advantage**.

2.5 Demand networks

Demand networks are a recent evolution of supply chains. The key difference between them is how they are formed.

KEY POINT

In a traditional **supply chain**, producers form links between themselves in order to produce a product that the customer wants at an appropriate selling price and cost to the producer. The chain is formed to '**push**' the product out into the market.

By contrast, products produced by **demand networks** are '**pulled**' into existence in response to demand signals. Organisations within a demand network share information and collaborate to produce a product or service the market is demanding.

A **demand network** is the result of companies **evolving** internally (or within their departments) and externally (with their partners). This evolution is a four-stage process.

Reacting

Departments optimise their operations to meet demand. Reacting organisations cannot sense demand or tie it into corporate strategy – they simply react to market conditions.

 Anticipating

Anticipating companies have developed internally to **respond to long- and short-term demand**. They often use lean production or Six Sigma (see later) to bring order to their operations. They can anticipate upstream demand (the demand which is coming to them) but not downstream demand.

 Collaborating

Collaborating organisations have established **external relationships** with business partners that allow **intelligence** to be gathered on downstream demand. This allows better forecasting and adjustment of plans.

 Orchestrating

Supply and demand have evolved into a **flow of information** throughout the network. Companies plan new products and product life cycles, and can begin to influence demand patterns. Production decisions are based on costs and profitability.

Demand network evolution

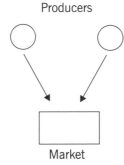

Reacting
Producers estimate demand and push products to market

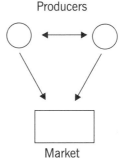

Anticipating
Some communication between producers. The product continues to be pushed to market

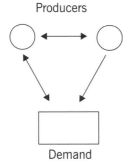

Collaborating
Use of intelligence allows the market to be manipulated – the pull process begins

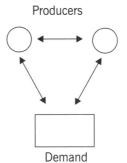

Orchestrating
Producers are fully networked and can control the pull process

To create **competitive advantage**, organisations within a demand network have to manage **three factors**:

- **Alignment** – of shared incentives
- **Agility** – to respond to demand quickly
- **Adaptability** – to adjust the structure of the supply chain to meet demand

Exam alert

Exam questions may test your understanding of a range of operations' strategies.

2.6 Supply portfolios and sourcing strategies

Organisations may use a number of suppliers for their raw materials, and there is a range of possible **strategies** open to an organisation when deciding who it will purchase its supplies from. For example:

(a)   Certain suppliers may produce a **better quality** of product.

(b)   Some suppliers may be **cheaper on price**.

(c)   Suppliers may also be selected from **a number of countries** to guard against the risk of supplies from one country being affected by circumstances such as bad weather.

(d)   Suppliers are of **different sizes** so buyers can match order sizes to appropriate suppliers (ie small suppliers may not be suitable for larger orders).

(e)   **Expertise** varies between suppliers so building relationships with a number of them can help the buyer make more **informed choices**.

The **mix of suppliers should be optimised** so that the organisation maximises the benefits it offers and minimises any risks involved in supply – the result is a **supply portfolio**.

The following strategies may be followed when deciding on a **supply strategy**.

Supply sourcing strategies	
Option	**Comment**
Single	**Description** • The buyer chooses one source of supply **Advantages** • Stronger relationship with the supplier • Possible source of superior quality due to increased opportunity for a supplier quality assurance programme • Facilitates better communication • Economies of scale • Facilitates confidentiality • Possible source of competitive advantage **Disadvantages** • Vulnerable to any disruption in supply • The buyer is dependent on the supplier • Supplier power may increase if no alternative supplier • The supplier is vulnerable to shifts in order levels

Supply sourcing strategies	
Option	**Comment**
Multiple	**Description** • The buyer chooses several sources of supply **Advantages** • Access to a wide range of knowledge and expertise • Competition among suppliers may drive the price down • Supply failure by one supplier will cause minimal disruption – it is easy to switch between suppliers **Disadvantages** • Not easy to develop an effective quality assurance programme • Suppliers may display less commitment • Economies of scale are neglected
Delegated	**Description** • A supplier is given responsibility for the delivery of a complete sub-assembly. For example, rather than dealing with several suppliers a 'first-tier' supplier would be appointed to deliver a complete sub-assembly (eg a PC manufacturer may delegate the production of keyboards) **Advantages** • Allows the utilisation of specialist external expertise • Frees up internal staff for other tasks • The purchasing entity may be able to negotiate economies of scale **Disadvantages** • Quality control is difficult to maintain • Loss of confidentiality if products use trade secrets • Competitors may utilise the same external organisation so it is unlikely to be a source of competitive advantage
Parallel	**Description** • Parallel sourcing involves mixing/combining the other three approaches to maximise the benefits of each **Advantages** • If used correctly should provide an efficient/effective strategy • Supplier failure will not halt production • Price competition is created between suppliers **Disadvantages** • Can be complicated to manage • Quality control is difficult to maintain

Question 6.2 | Sourcing and supplier performance

Learning outcome D1(iii)

(a) List four methods organisations use to source materials. **(4 marks)**

(b) Which method would you recommend to an organisation whose product is based on a trade secret and relies on quality for competitive advantage? **(1 mark)**

(c) List four criteria that could be used to assess supplier performance. (**Hint**. Come up with these yourself based on what you have read and your own experience when you order a product or service.) **(4 marks)**

2.7 Reverse logistics

We have already seen from Porter's value chain that **outbound logistics** concerns the **delivery of products to the customer**. **Reverse logistics** is exactly the opposite – **receiving products back from the customer**. While this commonly includes the return of faulty or unwanted goods (such as from warranty claims, following installation problems, or e-commerce customers returning goods according to a returns policy), reverse logistics also involves the return of **used products**.

Examples of reverse logistics include the **return of printer toners** so that they can be refilled and sold again, **cars and machinery** that are **leased** have to be returned after the leasing period is complete, and **products** used for **demonstration purposes** will also find their way back to the seller.

It is important for organisations to plan how to handle the return of goods and ensure that where possible they are **recycled** into new products, **refurbished** and sold again or **disposed of** appropriately. Accordingly, production processes should be developed so that recycled materials can enter the production process at an appropriate point and separate production lines are available for product refurbishment. These production lines should be able to deal with a range of possible repairs.

A key part of any operations policy is to **reduce the level of returns** and make the **returns process** as **efficient** as possible. To do this, the organisation must seek the **root cause of returns** and focus on minimising them. It should also separate reverse logistics from forward logistics. To make the process efficient, the organisation can create **profit centres** to maximise the income from returned goods and use state of the art technology (such as enterprise resource planning) to support processes. Centralising the returns centre and outsourcing the returns process are other options.

2.8 Information flows across supply chains and networks

For supply chains and networks to operate successfully, information must flow smoothly between all participating organisations. One way of analysing and representing information flows is with the use of **process maps**. Process maps are a **diagrammatic representation** of a process. A number of techniques or notations may be used to produce a process map.

2.9 Process mapping

Process mapping aims to **identify** and **represent** the **steps** and **decisions** involved in a process, in diagrammatic form.

Process maps:

- Describe the flow of materials, information and documents
- Display the tasks contained within the process
- Show that the tasks transform inputs into outputs
- Indicate the decisions that need to be made
- Demonstrate the relationships and dependencies between the process steps

There are many types of **process maps** (also known as process charts) and many charting conventions. Two **common types** of process map are:

- A **'basic' flowchart** – which provides a basic 'bird's eye' view

- A **deployment chart** – which provides an overview and also indicates where or by whom actions are performed

Process maps should be simple enough for the process under review to be understood by almost anyone, even someone unfamiliar with the process.

2.9.1 Why process map?

Process maps are **important** for several reasons.

(a) Changing systems and working methods without understanding the underlying processes can lead to costly mistakes. It can also create conditions that make it difficult for staff to work effectively.

(b) If organisations don't understand a process they will not be able to manage it effectively – and if they cannot manage a process they cannot improve it.

(c) Process mapping enables businesses to clearly define current processes, identifying problem areas such as bottlenecks, delays and waste. This knowledge provides a solid basis from which to develop solutions and plan new improved processes.

(d) Process mapping enables an organisation to:

   (i)   Establish what is currently happening and why

   (ii)   Measure how efficiently the process is working

   (iii) Gather information to understand where waste and inefficiencies exist and their impact on employees, customers and/or partners

   (iv) Develop new, improved processes to reduce or eliminate inefficiency

(e) Some benefits of process mapping include:

   (i)   Identifying opportunities to standardise and simplify processes

   (ii)   Identifying areas of inefficiency and waste such as duplication of effort

   (iii) Identifying potential bottlenecks or pinch points (which could lead to delays and any inefficiencies resulting from those delays)

   (iv) Providing management with an overall understanding of how the processes under their control operate

   (v)   Allowing workers to better understand their role and how their work fits into the organisation's operations

   (vi) Providing support to new initiatives such as lean production and customer satisfaction improvements

2.9.2 Process map types and symbols

Two common types of process map are a basic flowchart and a deployment flowchart.

(a) **Basic process map flowchart**

   Process map flowcharts set out the sequence of activities and decision points. They illustrate the main steps and decisions in the process. Labels showing the type and level of staff doing each step can be added if required.

(b) **Deployment process map flowchart**

Deployment process map flowcharts are similar to basic process maps, but also show who does what, including interactions between the parties involved. This type of chart is sometimes referred to as a 'swim lane' chart – as the page is divided into vertical lanes for each person or party involved.

2.9.3 Process map flowcharting symbols

Below are examples of **commonly used flowcharting symbols**. You should remember though that different people and organisations may use different symbols, or may use only some of the symbols below. Factors such as the complexity of the process being modelled and simple personal preference play a part.

Flowcharting symbols

Start/End

This symbol marks the starting or ending point of the system.

Action or process

A box can represent a single step ('add two cups of flour'), or an entire sub-process ('make bread') within a larger process.

Document

A printed document or report. This symbol is not always used – it depends on the level of detail required in the model.

Decision

A decision or branching point. Lines representing different decisions emerge from different points of the diamond.

Input/ Output

Represents material or information entering or leaving the system, such as customer order (input) or a product (output). Again, the use of this symbol is not consistent – some people may identify a customer placing an order at a retail counter as an action – others may identify it as input.

Flow

This arrow indicates the sequence of steps and the direction of flow.

2.9.4 Constructing a process flowchart

Maps are most easily produced using relatively specialised software, for example Microsoft Visio. General purpose software packages such as Word, Excel and PowerPoint can also be used.

 Organise the sequence by working down rather than across.

 Having thought through the main 'steps' of the process, flowchart them in the sequence they are performed.

 Use rectangles for 'tasks' and diamonds for 'decisions'. Use connecting arrows between boxes to represent the direction of the sequence.

 Concisely describe each task or decision in its own box. Boxes may be numbered and a key provided where the activity is described in more detail.

 If the process includes decision points, this will normally imply some 'return-routing' causing some boxes to have more than one input. 'Return routing' or 'loops' often indicate an inefficiency or waste.

 Decisions usually (but not always) pose questions answerable by 'Yes' or 'No'. Structure questions so that the preferred answer is 'Yes'.

 Conventions include drawing the 'Yes' route out of the bottom of the diamond (ie normal flow downward through the chart) and the 'No' route as a line to the side of the box).

2.9.5 A simple process flowchart

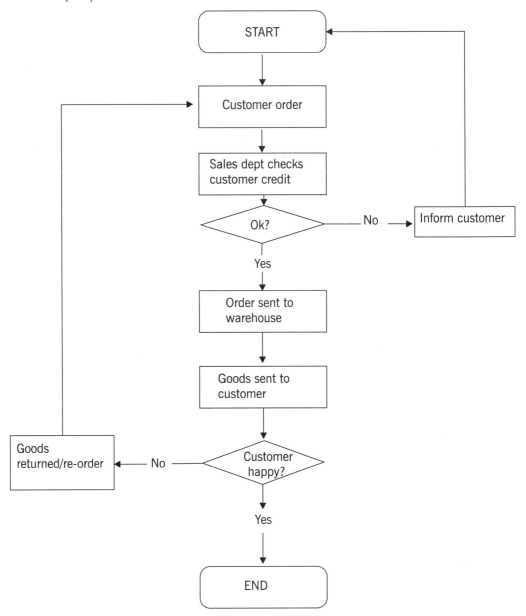

2.9.6 Constructing a deployment flowchart

Deployment flowcharts include a 'department' or 'unit' dimension along the top of the chart. They may include individuals, groups, departments, agencies, organisations and functions – whatever 'units' are involved in the process.

The following should be considered when **constructing deployment flowcharts**:

- Draw vertical lines to separate the functional boundaries.

- When the flow moves from one function to another, this is ideally denoted by a horizontal line.

- Apart from the horizontal moves between functions, aim when possible to sequence activities from top to bottom.

- Always connect symbols with arrows indicating the direction of flow.

2.9.7 A simple deployment flowchart

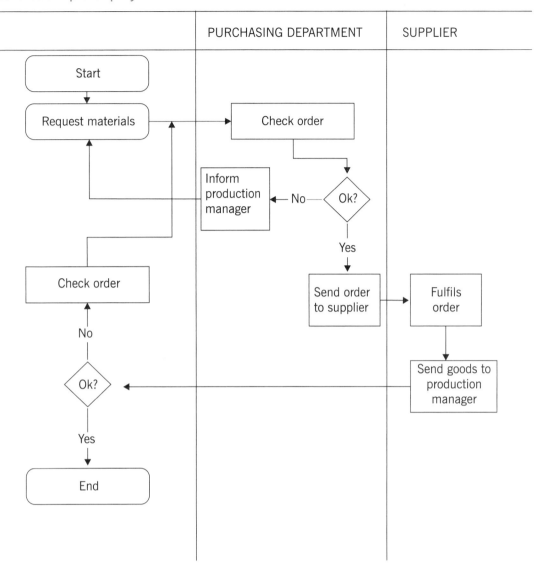

It may be useful to also use the D symbol to indicate any delays in the process, particularly at the boundaries between agencies or sections.

2.10 Process design

Process mapping is also often used to build a prototype model when designing **organisational processes**.

Bowhill (2008) saw process design as a way of **highlighting inefficiencies and designing improved processes** that ultimately led to increased customer satisfaction.

An important technique that an organisation can use to identify inefficiencies is **benchmarking**.

2.10.1 Benchmarking

Benchmarking is the analysis of performance compared with a similar activity elsewhere. **Types of benchmarking** include:

- **Internal benchmarking** – comparison against the best elsewhere in the organisation
- **Competitive benchmarking** – comparison against the best elsewhere in the industry
- **Inter-industry benchmarking** – comparison against the best functional area in any industry

Other **management techniques** covered elsewhere in this book could be used to improve processes – for example, supply chain management, total quality management, Kaizen and Business Process Re-engineering.

2.11 Operations strategy – Brown

Brown (2001) identified six items to consider when devising an organisation's operations strategy.

Item	Comment
Capability required	What is it that the organisation wants to 'do' or produce?
Range and location of operations	How big and/or widespread does the organisation want to be?
Investment in technology	How will processes and production be performed?
Strategic buyer–supplier relationships	Who will be key strategic partners?
New products/services	How long will the business be able to keep doing what it does? What are the expected product life cycles?
Structure of operations	How will staff be organised and managed?

2.12 General points

Operations strategy theories are simply illustrations of approaches to operations strategy formulation. In broad terms, **strategy formulation** in practice will include many of the **following concepts**:

(a)   Setting **operational objectives** that are consistent with the organisation's overall business strategy.

(b)   Translating **business strategy** or **marketing strategy** into **operations strategy**, by means of identifying key competitive factors.

(c)   Assessing the relative importance of different **competitive factors**.

(d)   Assessing current operational performance by **comparison** with the performance of **competitors**.

(e)   Using the idea of a clean-slate or 'green-field' approach to strategy selection. Managers are asked to consider how they would ideally design operations if they could **start again from scratch**. The ideal operations design is then compared with actual operations, and important differences identified. Strategy decisions are then taken to move actual performance closer towards the ideal.

(f)   Formulating strategy could be based on other types of **gap analysis**, such as comparing what the market wants with what the operation is actually achieving, and taking decisions aimed at closing the significant gaps.

(g)   Emphasising the iterative process of strategy selection. Strategies should be **continually reviewed, refined and redeveloped** through experience and in response to changes in the environment.

Section summary

Porter saw organisations as **value chains** that are made up of different processes. A competitive advantage can be gained by ensuring these processes are efficient.

Organisations can become part of a larger **supply chain**. They purchase from suppliers and sell to other organisations which are buyers. Eventually raw materials are converted into what the end customer wants.

Supply chains are a source of **competitive advantage** as each organisation works towards a common goal.

Demand networks are an evolution of supply chains. They are formed by demand acting as a stimulus to produce a product.

Supply portfolios are the mix of suppliers selected by an organisation to balance the benefits and risks involved in relying on them.

Process maps can be used to present the processes involved in supply chains and networks.

3 Corporate social responsibility (CSR) and sustainability in operations management

3.1 Sustainability

KEY TERM

SUSTAINABILITY is a long-term programme involving a series of sustainable development practices, aimed at improving organisational efficiency, stakeholder support and market edge.

(Goldsmith and Samson (2004))

KEY POINT

In relation to the world's resources, sustainability has been defined as ensuring that development meets the needs of the present without compromising the ability of future generations to meet their own needs.

For organisations, **sustainability** involves developing strategies that balance environmental, economic and social needs. The eventual aim is that the organisation only **uses resources at a rate that allows them to be replenished**, and that **emissions of waste are at a level the environment is able to absorb**. Let's examine three aspects of Goldsmith and Samson's definition above.

3.1.1 Sustainability and efficiency

Sustainable efficiency practices for organisations are **reducing waste**, **using less energy** and **recycling**.

3.1.2 Sustainability and stakeholder support

Sustainable practices that might **gain stakeholder support** include **reducing greenhouse gas emissions**, **employee cycle schemes**, encouraging **employee flexible working** (reduce commuting), **reduced business travel**, **utilise technology** eg web conferencing, and sourcing from **green suppliers**.

3.1.3 Sustainability and market edge

Sustainable practices that could provide '**market edge**' include **innovation**, **supply chain improvements**, and **research and development** (eg greener motor vehicles).

3.2 Sustainability considerations

There are five **sustainability considerations** relevant to operations management.

3.2.1 Sustainable for whom

This issue concerns **which species** (other than humans) are to be sustained, the level of world population that should be sustained and the needs of developing countries. An operations management consideration is whether organisations should source products from developing nations or look to the tried and tested industries of developed countries.

3.2.2 Sustainable in what way

This concerns what sustainability is about: is it about the environment, employees or economic factors?

(a) **Ecological sustainability** concerns the preservation of the environment so it can function as naturally as possible. The operations management issue is whether organisations should continue production processes which are harmful to the environment, or should they look for less harmful (but possibly more expensive) alternatives?

(b) **Social sustainability** is about personal growth and development. For organisations the issue is whether or not employees should be treated like robots by requiring them to perform repetitive tasks, or should they be given scope to develop their abilities and perform a wide range of production roles?

(c) **Economic sustainability** is about producing goods and services that people want while maximising the organisation's profitability. The operations issue here is to ensure the organisation produces products and services that its customers want while minimising waste to maximise profit.

3.2.3 Sustainable for how long

The issue here is **generational equity**. This is about ensuring future generations can enjoy the same environmental conditions as the current generation, and that social welfare is maintained or increased. The main operations management concern is the use of **natural materials**. As the world has finite resources, production levels cannot be sustained forever. Therefore organisations need to plan their use of resources carefully, especially the rate at which they use them up. They should also look for new ways of producing the products that people want, as well as looking for sustainable resources.

3.2.4 Sustainable at what cost

There is a **balance** to be found between **preserving the environment** and **natural resources** with the need to **produce goods** and **services**. The operations management issue concerns **sourcing materials** which balance the need for sustainability with the need to produce goods and services. For example, organisations can look at substituting some raw materials with sustainable alternatives or look to produce products using more sustainable processes.

3.2.5 Sustainable by whom

Ideally the **whole world** will take responsibility for sustainability, but this is unlikely due to a lack of meaningful international agreements. The operations management issue is that **organisations** must take on responsibility for sustainability themselves rather than waiting for legal regulation.

3.3 Impacts of sustainability

Sustainability may impact an organisation in several ways. These include:

(a) **Quality** – By attempting to reduce waste and rework, an organisation may also improve the efficiency of its production process and improve the quality of its output.

(b) **Process and product design** – Improvements in operational efficiency should be designed into the production process. Products should be designed to minimise the amount of resources needed to produce them. Where waste is created, it should be recycled where possible.

(c) **Supply chain** – An organisation implementing sustainability will look to purchase materials from sustainable sources, and select suppliers that share its objectives and, if possible, are located the minimum possible distance away from it. The World Fairtrade Organisation tries to support such activities by promoting sustainability, fair working conditions and a fair price for producers.

CASE STUDY

In the year since Comerica Bank opened its first **L**eadership in **E**nergy and **E**nvironmental **D**esign (LEED®) certified banking centre, the bank has received recognition for its progress in implementing its commitment to sustainability.

'Integrating green practices into the way we do business is a core commitment and allows us to enhance our performance as a company and **create long-term value for our stakeholders**,' said Richard J. Plewa, Comerica Bank's Chief Sustainability Officer.

In 2009, Comerica Bank was named to the following **sustainability leadership indices** in recognition of its recent sustainability successes:

The Carbon Disclosure Project's (CDP) Carbon Disclosure Leadership Index. The CDP represents 534 global investors responsible for the management of $64 trillion of assets.

For the second year in a row, Comerica was named to the CDP's Carbon Disclosure Leadership Index, which rates firms according to the level and quality of their disclosure and reporting on greenhouse gas emissions and climate change strategy. In 2009, Comerica's index score of 91 was top among S&P 500 companies.

Maplecroft Climate Innovation Leaders Index. The Maplecroft Index focuses on US companies with at least $1 billion of market capitalisation and identifies top performers in climate-related innovation and carbon management. Comerica was ranked number 61 overall and number 5 in the finance sector.

FTSE4Good Index. The FTSE4Good Index is a leading global responsibility investment index designed to measure the performance of companies that meet globally recognised corporate responsibility standards. Companies named in the FTSE4Good Index have demonstrated that they have put policies and management systems in place to help address relevant corporate responsibility risks as they pertain to social and environmental change. Comerica launched the following sustainability initiatives to **increase the efficiency of resources and decrease greenhouse gas emissions**:

Energy and Emissions. During 2009, Comerica implemented a range of initiatives to reduce energy use, corporate travel and the related greenhouse gas emissions. Total corporate emissions decreased by almost 5% from 2008 to 2009, partly reflecting the positive contributions of these initiatives.

Reducing Paper Use. Other initiatives implemented in 2009 were designed to reduce the use of paper throughout the company. Paper purchases were down by almost 19% for the year, a reduction of almost 6 million printed pages.

Greener Procurement. A Green Procurement Work Group was established in 2009 and a new Supplier Questionnaire & Scorecard was developed to help identify environmentally preferred providers of goods and services. Comerica plans to use this to improve the sustainability performance of its supply chain.

Eco-Friendly Buildings. All of Comerica's newly constructed banking centres in 2010 will have green features. Specifically, Comerica has five new banking centres that are LEED-certified by the US Green Building Council. Comerica is also seeking LEED certification for three additional banking centres opening in 2010. In addition, four existing Comerica buildings received Energy Star certification in 2009 from the US Environmental Protection Agency.

Sustainability Reporting. Comerica published its Inaugural Sustainability Report in September 2009. The report was based on the Global Reporting Initiative framework and included a wealth of information on Comerica's sustainability programmes and performance, including baseline environmental performance data against which future progress can be measured.

'We've been working hard to develop awareness of sustainability issues among our employees and to tap into the deep reservoir of creativity they possess when it comes to identifying better and more sustainable ways to operate,' noted Plewa. 'For example, on Earth Day 2010, Comerica teams sponsored and participated in a range of educational and service projects at Comerica locations and beyond.'

For more information visit www.comerica.com/sustainability

3.4 CSR and sustainability in operations management

CSR and **sustainability** initiatives will affect many aspects of a **business's operations** including:

- Design and delivery of products and services
- Capacity management
- Inventory management
- Quality management
- Supply chain management

3.4.1 Design and delivery of products and services

Operations should consider the **impact of products** and **services** at the **design stage** – for example, the benefits and costs on society and the environmental impact at all stages of a product or service's life. This means the resources used and waste created in the design and delivery stage, plus the use and eventual disposal of the product by the customer, should be considered. The provision of **recycling facilities** and information on materials used in a product are ways that a business can show social responsibility.

3.4.2 Capacity management

Waste and **energy use** by the organisation can be **minimised** if demand is managed and the organisation operates at an efficient level of capacity. This will mean that output meets actual demand and products or services will not be produced unnecessarily.

3.4.3 Inventory management

Inventory levels should be as **efficient as possible**. Storing materials for long periods of time is costly in terms of resources (such as energy) and potential wastage (if products have a limited life). Therefore operations should seek to hold the minimum levels of inventory.

3.4.4 Quality management

Poor quality results in **wasted resources** in terms of materials used in production and energy used in the production process. Therefore, operations should seek to minimise poor quality. If wastage does occur then materials should be recycled as much as possible and if necessary disposed in an environmentally friendly way.

3.4.5 Supply chain management

The design and **management of supply chains** can have a significant impact on the **resources used** in the production process and on society. Businesses should recognise that they have a responsibility to take appropriate steps to help reduce the environmental impact of their suppliers as well as themselves. Large organisations can show some social responsibility by using local suppliers where possible. This will help support the local economy and reduce the amount of resources used in transporting materials.

Section summary

Sustainability in operations is concerned with **efficient use of resources** and **minimising the effect** of an organisation's **activities** on **society** and the **environment**.

CSR and **sustainability** have impacts in all areas of **operations management**.

Chapter Summary

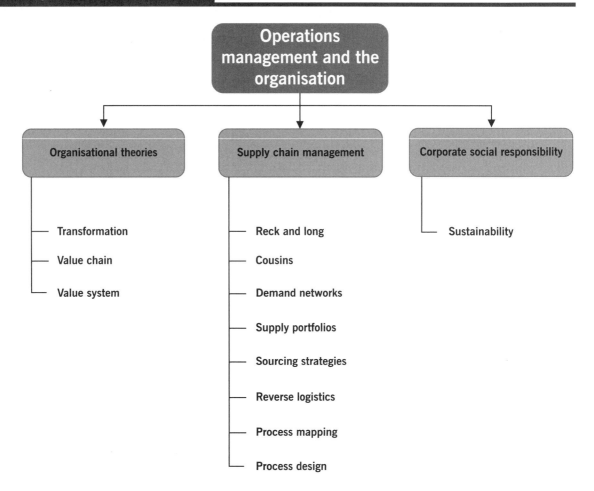

Quick Quiz

1   Which of the following is not one of the four Vs of operations?

     A   Volume
     B   Velocity
     C   Variety
     D   Visibility

2   Which of the following is a primary activity according to Porter's value chain?

     A   Firm infrastructure
     B   Technology development
     C   Procurement
     D   Marketing and sales

3   Who developed the strategic supply wheel?

     A   Porter
     B   Mintzberg
     C   Cousins
     D   Reck and Long

4   Organisations within a demand network need to manage which three factors to create a competitive advantage?

     A   Acceptability, agility and adaptability
     B   Agility, adaptability and access
     C   Adaptability, access and acceptability
     D   Alignment, agility and adaptability

5   List the six items Brown identified that should be covered by an organisation's operations strategy.

Answers to Quick Quiz

1   B   The four Vs are volume, variety, variation in demand and visibility.

2   D   Marketing and sales is a primary activity according to Porter's value chain.

3   C   Cousins developed the strategic supply wheel.

4   D   Organisations within a demand network need to manage alignment, agility and adaptability to create a competitive advantage.

5   Capability required, range and location of operations, investment in technology, strategic buyer–supplier relationships, new products/services and the structure of operations.

Answers to Questions

6.1 Activities

B   Human resource management is a support activity.

6.2 Sourcing and supplier performance

(a)   **Single sourcing** – the buyer chooses one source of supply.

      Multiple sourcing – the buyer chooses several sources of supply.

      Delegated sourcing – the buyer chooses a supplier to deliver a complete sub-assembly of part of the product.

      Parallel sourcing – the buyer mixes the other three approaches to maximise their benefits.

(b)   **Single sourcing**. This method allows a strong relationship to develop between buyer and supplier and helps to ensure confidential treatment of trade secrets and allows the development of a quality assurance programme.

(c)   **Quality** – whether the product or service is fit for purpose, defect rates.

      Flexibility and capability – is the supplier open to reasonable requests and able to meet them?

      Timeliness – is the product or service delivered on time?

      Price – value for money relative to competitors.

Now try these questions from the Practice Question Bank	Number
	26, 27, 28, 29, 30

QUALITY MANAGEMENT

A significant trend in all business sectors over recent years has been an increased **emphasis on quality**. In an increasingly **competitive** environment, quality is seen as vital to success.

As with many topics in this paper, you must learn the relevant theory but also be able to apply it to a practical situation. For example, a **theoretical** question may require you to evaluate various contemporary approaches to the management of quality – while a more **practical** question could ask you to identify and analyse problems with management of quality in an organisation described in the question.

The purposes of **external quality standards** (eg the various ISO standards appropriate to products and organisations) are also highly examinable.

We start this chapter by looking at the **concept** of quality, before moving on to the various **approaches** used to ensure quality in both the product or service produced and the systems used by the organisation.

Topic list	Learning outcomes	Syllabus references	Ability required
1 The scope of quality management	D2(b)	D2(ix)	comprehension
2 Quality management approaches	D2(b)	D2(ix)	comprehension
3 Total quality management (TQM)	D2(b)	D2(ix)	comprehension
4 Managing quality using TQM	D2(b)	D2(ix)	comprehension
5 Processes of continuous improvement	D2(b)	D2(ix)	comprehension
6 Lean production	D2(b)	D2(ix)	comprehension
7 International Organisation for Standardisation	D2(b)	D2(ix)	comprehension
8 Total productive maintenance (TPM)	D2(b)	D2(ix)	comprehension
9 The TQMEX model	D2(b)	D2(ix)	comprehension
10 Service quality	D2(b)	D2(ix)	comprehension

Chapter Overview

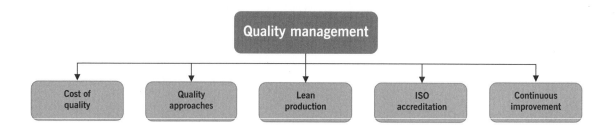

1 The scope of quality management

Introduction

In the modern commercial environment, there has been a change in emphasis **away from quantity** (produce as much as we can) **to quality** (produce the best we can). Customers have become more sophisticated and discerning. Poor-quality products and services are no longer tolerated.

Quality applies to both goods and services. Whether a customer goes shopping for food or visits a dentist, they expect a quality experience. More importantly, quality is increasingly a source of **competitive advantage**.

Quality is concerned with **'fitness for purpose'**. **Quality management** is concerned with ensuring that products or services meet their planned level of quality and conform to specifications.

KEY TERMS

QUALITY is 'the totality of features and characteristics of a product or service which bears on its ability to meet stated or implied needs'. (Holmes, 1992)

QUALITY MANAGEMENT is concerned with controlling activities with the aim of ensuring that products or services are fit for their purpose, and meet specifications. Quality management encompasses quality assurance and quality control.

QUALITY ASSURANCE focuses on the way a product or service is produced. Procedures and standards are devised with the aim of ensuring defects are eliminated (or at least minimised) during the development/production process.

QUALITY CONTROL is concerned with checking and reviewing work that has been done. Quality control therefore has a narrower focus than quality assurance.

1.1 Quality as a concept

Throughout this chapter, the following four themes reappear in relation to quality management:

(a) **Commitment**. A commitment to quality is required from top management down to the most junior-level employees.

(b) **Competence**. Employees must 'know what they are doing'. Training is important.

(c) **Communication**. The need for quality, and the benefits of quality, must be communicated throughout the organisation.

(d) **Continuous improvement**. Quality involves always looking to 'raise the bar'.

1.2 Quality control versus quality assurance

Traditional approaches to quality were focused on **inspection**. Modern approaches to quality focus on the **prevention** of defects through quality standards and processes.

1.2.1 Quality control

In the past, 'quality' usually meant **quality control** – which meant **inspection**. Inspection was usually carried out at three main points:

- Receiving inspection
- Floor or process inspection
- Final inspection or testing

The **problem** with this 'inspection' approach is that it allows for and often entails **built-in waste**.

(a) The inspection process itself does not add value. If it could be guaranteed that no defective items were produced there would be no need for a separate inspection function.

(b) The inspection function itself requires resources, both people and facilities.

(c) The production of substandard products is a waste of materials, machine time, human efforts and overheads.

(d) The production of defects is not compatible with newer production techniques such as just-in-time – there is no time for inspection.

(e) Working capital is tied up in inventory which cannot be sold.

(f) In a service industry, damage will have been done to customer relations before inspection takes place.

Quality control involves establishing standards of quality for a product or service, sampling output by inspection or testing, taking appropriate corrective action and testing output to ensure reoccurrences are detected.

1.2.2 Quality assurance

The demand for better quality has led to the acceptance of the view that quality management should aim to **prevent** defective production rather than simply detect it.

Most **modern approaches** to quality have therefore tried to assure quality in the **production process** (quality assurance) rather than inspecting goods or services after they have been produced.

The term '**quality assurance**' is used where a supplier guarantees the quality of goods or services they supply. Quality assurance programmes usually involve a close relationship between supplier and customer, which may extend to allowing customer representatives to view and/or monitor production procedures.

Quality assurance emphasises the **processes** and **procedures** used to produce a product or service – the logic being that if these are tightly controlled and monitored the resulting product and service will be high quality. As quality has been 'built in', the need for **inspection** after production should be **eliminated**.

Section summary

Most **modern approaches** to quality try to assure quality in the **production process** (quality assurance) rather than inspecting goods or services after they have been produced.

2 Quality management approaches

Introduction

For any **quality policy** to be successful, a suitable system should be developed and the levels of **quality measured** to enable the system's success to be monitored. In recent years a number of approaches to quality management have been developed.

2.1 Quality management

In general terms, any quality management system should involve the activities outlined below.

 Plan. Establish:

    (a)   **Standards** of quality for a product (eg a software package) or service (eg an IT helpdesk)

    (b)   **Procedures** or production methods that ought to ensure that these required standards of quality are met

 Devise suitable instruments and techniques to **monitor** actual quality.

 Compare actual quality with planned quality using quality measures.

 Take **control action** when actual quality falls below standard.

Quality auditing involves a systematic inspection to establish whether quality objectives are being met.

 Review the plan and standards to ensure continuous improvement.

The activities and steps above describe a **general approach** to quality management. In the following sections, we will look at some specific methodologies or approaches associated with quality.

2.2 Measuring quality

A number of methods of measuring quality have been developed, including **SERVQUAL, the balanced scorecard** and **value for money audits**.

2.2.1 SERVQUAL

SERVQUAL was developed in the 1980s by Zeithaml, Parasuraman and Berry as a method of **measuring quality in service organisations**. It was primarily concerned with measuring the gap between a customer's preconceived **expectations** and the **actual experience** they receive.

When it was first introduced, SERVQUAL **measured ten aspects of service quality** – understanding the customer, tangibles, courtesy, security, credibility, competence, communication, access, reliability and responsiveness. However, in the 1990s the model was refined and is now known as **RATER**.

Aspect	Description
Reliability	Employee ability to perform the service dependably and accurately
Assurance	Employee ability to inspire confidence and trust in the customer
Tangibles	The tangible environment – for example facilities, equipment and staff appearance
Empathy	The extent to which a caring, personal service is provided
Responsiveness	Employee willingness to help and respond to customer requests

SERVQUAL and RATER are not without their critics. Francis Buttle, for example, noted that the five aspects are not universals and that the model is not based on established economic, statistical or psychological theory.

2.2.2 Balanced scorecard

Deciding how to measure quality is an important aspect of quality management. **Quality measures** should cover **operational**, **financial** and **customer aspects**. One approach, originally developed by Kaplan and Norton (1990), is the use of a 'balanced scorecard'.

The balanced scorecard focuses on **four different perspectives**.

Perspective	Question	Explanation
Customer	What do existing and new customers value from us?	Gives rise to targets that matter to customers: cost, quality, delivery, inspection, handling and so on
Operational: internal operations	What processes must we excel at to achieve our financial and customer objectives?	Aims to improve internal processes and decision making
Operational: innovation and learning	Can we continue to improve and create future value?	Considers the business's capacity to maintain its competitive position through the acquisition of new skills and the development of new products
Financial	How do we create value for our shareholders?	Covers traditional measures such as growth, profitability and shareholder value but set through talking to the shareholder or shareholders direct

The scorecard is 'balanced' in the sense that managers are required to think in terms of **all four perspectives**, to prevent improvements being made in one area at the expense of another.

The types of measure which may be monitored under each of the four perspectives include the following. The list is **not exhaustive** but it will give you an idea of the possible scope of a balanced scorecard approach. The measures selected will vary considerably with the type of organisation and its objectives.

Perspective	Measures
Customer	• New customers acquired • Customer complaints • Customer satisfaction • Telephone response times • Delivery speeds
Operational: internal operations	• Quality control rejects • Productivity levels • Speed of producing management information • Streamlining/systems simplification
Operational: innovation and learning	• Training days for employees • Skills enhancement • Percentage of revenue generated by new products and services • Average time taken to develop new products and services
Financial	• Return on capital employed • Revenue growth • Cash flow • Earnings per share

2.2.3 Value for money (VFM) audit

Originally associated with the **public sector**, value for money (VFM) techniques are now increasingly being applied to private sector businesses.

The basic approach involves identifying and **measuring key aspects of performance**, such as money spent, inputs purchased, outputs and outcomes achieved.

The relationship between **money** spent and inputs purchased provides a measure of **economy**. The relationship between **inputs and outputs** provides a measure of **efficiency**. Comparing **outputs with outcomes** achieved provides a measure of **effectiveness**, eg ten clients serviced (output), nine 'extremely satisfied' clients (outcome).

2.3 Possible problems when attempting to measure quality

Measuring quality involves taking into account many **variables**, which can lead to problems.

Problem	Explanation
Conflicting measures	Some measures in the scorecard such as research funding and cost reduction may naturally conflict. It is often difficult to determine the balance which will achieve the best results.
Selecting measures	Not only do appropriate measures have to be devised but the number of measures used must be agreed. Care must be taken that the impact of the results is not lost in a sea of information.
Expertise	Measurement is only useful if it initiates appropriate action. Non-financial managers may have difficulty with the usual profit measures. With more measures to consider this problem will be compounded.
Interpretation	Even a financially trained manager may have difficulty in putting the figures into an overall perspective.
Too many measures	The ultimate objective for commercial organisations is to maximise profits or shareholder wealth. Other targets should offer a guide to achieving this objective and not become an end in themselves.

Section summary

Three methods of measuring quality include:

SERVQUAL – this can be used to measure quality in a service organisation. It measures the gap between customer expectations and their actual experience.

Balanced scorecards – these rate quality across four financial and non-financial perspectives.

Value for money audits – these identify and analyse key aspects of performance which are often related to economy, efficiency and effectiveness.

3   Total quality management (TQM)

Introduction

The development of **total quality management** (TQM) heralded a new era and philosophy of dealing with quality. Rather than 'firefighting' quality issues, the approach aims to **continuously improve** quality in all aspects of the organisation. **Customer satisfaction** is a key objective of TQM.

KEY TERM

TOTAL QUALITY MANAGEMENT (**TQM**) is the continuous improvement in quality, productivity and effectiveness obtained by establishing management responsibility for processes as well as output.

The **principles of TQM** evolved through a number of management theorists and 'quality gurus'; it is therefore an amalgamation of related but different ideas. Many principles involve **statistical process control** which is the application of statistics to quality control. The aim of this is to ensure that a finished product conforms to an 'ideal standard' and can be used where any deviation from the standard can be measured statistically.

3.1 Deming (TQM)

Deming (1982) is credited with the development of **TQM** in Japan. He took the view that as process variability (the amount of unpredictability in a process) decreases, quality and productivity increase. Quality can therefore be improved by reducing process variability.

His **14 points for quality improvement** stressed the need for statistical control methods, participation, education, feedback, openness and improvement.

(1) Create a constancy of purpose
(2) Adopt a new quality-conscious philosophy
(3) Cease dependence on inspection
(4) Stop awarding business on price
(5) Continuous improvement in the system of production and service
(6) Institute training on the job
(7) Institute leadership
(8) Drive out fear
(9) Break down barriers between departments
(10) Eliminate slogans and exhortations
(11) Eliminate quotas or work standards
(12) Give employees pride in their job
(13) Institute education and a self-improvement programme
(14) Put everyone to work to accomplish it

3.2 Ouchi (Theory Z)

Theory Z was devised by William Ouchi in the early 1980s. It emphasises the following **elements**:

- Interpersonal skills
- Building relationships
- Group interaction and decision making
- Participative management
- Free flow of information
- Trust
- Retention of hierarchical rules and control
- Formal procedures for planning and setting objectives

Theory Z combined aspects of **US management practice** (which Ouchi referred to as Theory A) and Japanese management practices (Theory J).

3.3 Juran (Fitness for use)

Juran (1988) argued that quality should focus on the role of the customer, both internal and external. This user-based approach to quality emphasises **fitness for use** (that is, a product or service is of good quality if it is fit for its intended use or purpose). Key projects should be identified to correct quality issues, rather than focus on worker motivation.

Juran emphasised that quality management should aim to ensure that the way in which work is performed (ie systems and processes) facilitates high-quality output. He developed the idea of internal, as well as external, customers because everyone affected by a product is a customer. He also believed 85% of quality problems were the result of ineffective systems.

3.4 Ishikawa (Quality circles)

Ishikawa (1985) stressed the importance of people and participation to improve quality. He is often credited with the idea of **quality circles**, and their use to achieve participation and overcome resistance to quality initiatives.

3.5 Crosby (Quality costs)

Crosby (1979) wrote about quality costs. Like other quality gurus, he argued for **worker participation** and the need to **motivate** individuals to do something about quality. His **'absolutes of quality management'** were:

(1)　Quality is conformance to requirements.
(2)　Prevention is required, not an appraisal of the costs of poor quality.
(3)　There should be zero defects in production.
(4)　Organisations should measure the cost or price of 'non-conformance'.
(5)　There is no such thing as a 'quality problem'.

3.6 Feignbaum (Total quality control)

Feignbaum (1961) believed that prevention is better than cure and that the design of systems used in the production process should reflect the need for, and enhance, quality.

3.7 The elements of TQM

TQM has been described as a natural extension of previous approaches to quality management, such as:

(a)　**Inspection**, ie inspecting output in order to detect and rectify errors.

(b)　**Quality control**, ie using statistical techniques to establish quality standards and monitor performance.

(c)　**Quality assurance**. This extended quality management to areas other than direct operations, and uses concepts such as quality costing, quality planning and problem solving.

The following **table of principles** should help you understand the key elements of TQM. Use the mnemonic **PRECEPT** to remember them.

Principle	Description
Prevention	Organisations should take measures that prevent poor quality occurring.
Right first time	A culture should be developed that encourages workers to get their work right first time.
Eliminate waste	The organisation should seek the most efficient and effective use of all its resources.
Continuous improvement	The Kaizen philosophy should be adopted. Organisations should seek to improve their processes continually.

Principle	Description
Everyone's concern	Everyone in the organisation is responsible for improving processes and systems under their control. There must also be a commitment to quality from senior management.
Participation	All workers should be encouraged to share their views and the organisation should value them.
Teamwork and empowerment	Workers across departments should form team bonds so that eventually the organisation becomes one.

Section summary

Total quality management (TQM) is the continuous improvement in quality, productivity and effectiveness obtained by establishing management responsibility for processes as well as output.

The key **principles of TQM** are: prevention, right first time, eliminate waste, continuous improvement, everyone's concern, participation and teamwork/empowerment.

4 Managing quality using TQM

Introduction

The introduction of TQM requires **new ideas** and methods of **managing quality** within an organisation. In particular, relationships between an organisation's departments and its culture are affected.

4.1 Internal customers and internal suppliers

In a TQM approach, **all parts** of the organisation are involved in quality issues and need to work together. Every person and every activity in the organisation affects the work done by others.

TQM promotes the concept of the **internal customer** and **internal supplier**. The work done by an internal supplier for an internal customer will eventually affect the quality of the product or service to the external customer.

Internal customers are therefore linked in **quality chains**. Internal customer A can satisfy internal customer B who can satisfy internal customer C who in turn can satisfy the external customer.

4.2 Service level agreements

Some organisations formalise the internal supplier–internal customer concept by requiring each internal supplier to make a **service level agreement** with its internal customer. A service level agreement is a statement of the standard of service and supply that will be provided to the internal customer and will cover issues such as the range of services supplied, response times and dependability.

Service level agreements have been criticised, however, for overformalising the relationship between the internal supplier and internal customer, therefore **creating barriers** to the development of a constructive relationship and **genuine co-operation** between them.

4.3 Quality culture

A purely **procedures-driven** approach is unlikely to secure a culture of quality. Interpersonal factors such as employee empowerment, teamwork and commitment are likely to be important considerations.

Every person within an organisation has an impact on quality and it is the **responsibility of everyone** to **get quality right**.

Individuals should be encouraged not just to comply with performance standards and procedures, but also to be proactive in improving their performance and the performance of others. This requires the **empowerment** of employees (covered in the next section). Customers are better served by employees who are in a position to make decisions in meeting their needs without having to obtain authorisation from others.

Team working skills are a key competence required of modern management. This recognises that employees are individuals with individual strengths and weaknesses. They need to work together to optimise their personal attributes for the collective benefit of the company.

Commitment is also important in achieving quality. This will require management to apply their skill in persuading and motivating staff into a true commitment to quality. Ultimately it is the employees who will have to deliver the quality.

4.4 Empowerment

KEY POINT

Empowerment recognises that employees are likely to know how best to perform their role and to improve quality. It contrasts with traditional **'top-down management'** which assumes that management is best qualified to make decisions.

Empowerment includes two key aspects:

(a)   Allowing workers to have the **freedom to decide how to do** the necessary work, using the skills they possess and acquiring new skills as necessary to be an effective team member

(b)   Making workers **responsible** for achieving production targets and for quality control

Empowerment may be more appropriate in **service organisations** where formal procedures might hamper the flexibility of employees responding quickly to a customer's needs. The concept of **empowerment** must be **embraced by management and staff at all levels** to be effective.

4.5 Continuous improvement or Kaizen

Quality management is not a one-off process but is the **continuous** examination and improvement of processes. This continuous improvement is sometimes referred to as 'Kaizen'. Some authors explain that Japan's competitive industrial success is a result of the implementation of the Kaizen concept.

Kaizen looks for uninterrupted **incremental change**. It can be implemented by improving every aspect of a business process in a step by step approach, while gradually developing employee skills through training, education and increased involvement.

The **principles** of **continuous improvement/Kaizen** are:

(a)   People are the most important organisational asset.
(b)   Processes should evolve by **gradual improvement** rather than radical change.
(c)   Improvement should be based on **statistical/quantitative evaluation** of process performance.
(d)   Resources, measurements, rewards and incentives all need to be **aligned**.
(e)   Continuous improvement enables **changing customer needs** to be taken into account.
(f)   Continuous improvement enables **new technologies** to be introduced.

Tools used in the **Kaizen process** include:

(a)   **The five why process**. This process seeks to identify the root cause of a problem by encouraging the employee to ask 'Why' to generate a symptom. This creates issues and questions and the process repeats until the solution or reason is discovered (often after five 'Whys'). This process was developed by Toyota.

BPP
LEARNING MEDIA

(b)   **Fishbone diagrams**. These are cause and effect diagrams used to analyse all causes (or inputs) that result in a single effect (or output). A map in the form of a Fishbone is created and the route of continuous improvement is drawn. Potential problems that may be encountered will 'splinter' off from the path.

(c)   **Plan-do-check-act (PDCA)**. The use of a PDCA cycle to encourage continuous improvement.

      Plan: Plan the process
      Do: Execute the process
      Check: Check the outcome of the process
      Act: Feedback to improve the process

(d)   **Pareto analysis (80/20 rule)**. Pareto analysis is based on the idea that 80% of an outcome is dependent on only 20% of the work (inputs or processes). Another way of looking at the rule would be to consider that 20% of output accounts for 80% of the overall revenue or value. In terms of quality, this means an organisation should focus its attention on the important 20% of factors that make up 80% of the overall quality. By doing so it will gain the most benefit from the minimum input.

4.6 Quality costs

The **cost of quality** may be looked at in a number of different ways.

Some argue that producing higher-quality output increases costs, as more expensive resources are likely to be required to achieve a higher standard.

Others argue that poor-quality output will lead to customer dissatisfaction, which generates costs associated with complaint resolution and loss of revenue as customers move to competitors.

There are **four types of quality cost** – prevention, appraisal/inspection, internal and external failure. Prevention and appraisal costs are known as **conformance costs**; internal failure and external failure costs are known as **non-conformance costs**.

Type of cost	Definition	Examples
Prevention cost	Costs incurred prior to making the product or delivering the service – to prevent substandard-quality products or services being delivered.	The cost of building quality into the product design or service design The cost of training staff in quality improvement and error prevention The cost of prevention devices (eg fail-safe features)
Appraisal cost or inspection cost	This is a cost incurred after a product has been made or service delivered, to ensure that the output or service performance meets the required quality standard or service performance.	The cost of inspecting finished goods or services, and other checking devices such as supplier vetting Customer or client feedback forms (although these may be a way of keeping service staff 'on their toes')

Type of cost	Definition	Examples
Internal failure cost	This is a cost arising from inadequate quality, where the problem is identified before the transfer of the item or service from the organisation to the customer or client.	Cost of materials scrapped due to inefficiencies in stockholding procedures
		Cost of materials and components lost during production or service delivery
		Cost of output rejected during the inspection process
		Cost of reworking faulty output
		Cost of reviewing product and service specifications after failures or customer dissatisfaction
		Losses due to selling faulty output cheaply
		Not charging for a service so as to pacify dissatisfied and angry customers or clients
External failure cost	This is a cost arising from inadequate quality, where the problem is identified after the transfer of the item or service from the organisation to the customer.	Cost of product liability claims from customers or clients
		Cost of repairing products returned by customers, including those forming part of service
		Cost of replacing substandard products including those included with a service
		Delivery costs of returned units or items
		Cost of the customer services section and its operations
		Loss of customer goodwill and loss of future sales

4.6.1 Traditional vs TQM approaches to quality costs

The **traditional approach to quality management** is that there is an optimal level of quality effort that minimises total quality costs, and that spending more in an attempt to improve quality beyond this point is not cost effective. Diminishing returns set in beyond the optimal quality level.

The **TQM philosophy** is different.

(a) **Failure and poor quality are unacceptable**. The inevitability of errors is not something that an organisation should accept. The target should be zero defects.

(b) Quality costs are difficult to measure, and **failure costs** in particular are often **seriously underestimated**. The real costs of failure include not just the cost of scrapped items and reworking faulty items or placating an unhappy customer or client. There is also all the management time spent sorting out problems and the loss of confidence between different parts of the organisation whenever faults occur.

(c) A TQM approach does not accept that the prevention costs of achieving **zero defects** become unacceptably high. If everyone in the organisation is involved in improving quality, the cost of continuous improvement need not be high.

(d) If an organisation accepts an **optimal quality level** that it believes will minimise total quality costs, there will be no further challenge to management to improve quality further.

The **TQM quality cost model** is based on the view:

(a) **Prevention costs and appraisal costs** are subject to management influence or control. It is better to spend money on prevention, before failures occur, than on inspection.

(b) **Internal failure costs and external failure costs** can be reduced through additional effort on prevention.

In other words, higher spending on prevention will eventually lead to lower total quality costs. The emphasis should be on **getting things right first time** and **designing quality** into the product or service.

4.7 Implementing TQM

The following structure may be used by an organisation looking to **implement a TQM approach**:

- Obtain **senior management support** and provide them with training on quality
- Form a **quality steering committee** to oversee the implementation
- **Communicate the change** down through the organisation's hierarchy to obtain employee support
- Form **quality circles** if appropriate
- **Record all actions** taken and **monitor progress** against expectations

4.8 Common reasons for failure of TQM initiatives

Participation is important in TQM, especially in the process of continuous improvement, where workforce views are valued. Management should encourage everybody to contribute.

Common reasons for failure in TQM programmes include:

(a) **Lack of management buy-in**. Managers continue to monitor, control and punish rather than being facilitators of open communication and worker involvement.

(b) **Tail-off**. After the initial enthusiasm, interest and support fades.

(c) **Deflection**. Other initiatives or problems take over from TQM.

(d) **Rejection**. TQM is not compatible with managers who feel their authority is threatened and make decisions with the aim of maintaining their position.

(e) General **cynicism** about quality and its role in fulfilling customer needs.

| **Question 7.1** | TQM and consistency |

Learning outcome D2(ix)

A key word in the TQM philosophy is **consistency**.

Briefly explain what in TQM needs to be consistent, and why consistency is important. **(4 marks)**

Section summary

In a TQM approach, **all parts** of the organisation are involved in quality issues, and need to work together. Every person and every activity in the organisation affects the work done by others.

Some organisations formalise the internal supplier–internal customer concept by requiring each internal supplier to make a **service level agreement** with its internal customer.

Kaizen is the **continuous** examination and improvement of existing processes.

There are four types of **quality costs** – **prevention**, **appraisal/inspection**, **internal failure** and **external failure**.

5 Processes of continuous improvement

Introduction

The concept of **Kaizen** and **continuous improvement** has led to the development of new management strategies and processes to handle it. **Multinational organisations**, often those which are American or Japanese, have been at the forefront of this development.

5.1 Quality circles

KEY TERM

A QUALITY CIRCLE is a team of workers from within the organisation which meets at intervals to discuss issues relating to the quality of the product or service produced.

A typical quality circle comprises employees from **many levels** of the organisation who meet regularly. The frequency of meetings varies across organisations – every three months would normally be sufficient.

Suggestions are encouraged regarding how the **product** or **service** produced could be made better, and how **processes** and **working practices** could be improved. Members are encouraged to analyse issues in a logical way.

Wider issues may also be discussed, as it is recognised that the complete working environment will affect quality levels. In some organisations this has led to quality circles having input on issues such as health and safety, employee benefits and bonuses, and training and education programmes.

5.1.1 Developing quality circles

An organisation can encourage the use of quality circles by:

(a) **Rewarding the circle** for suggestions that are implemented (eg a share of any savings made)

(b) **Providing a budget and support** to run the quality circle in terms of room provision, refreshments, staff to take minutes etc

(c) **Ensuring management are supportive** and prepared to act on useful suggestions from the circle

(d) **Providing an explanation** as to why **suggestions not implemented** were rejected

(e) **Management asking the circle** for **suggestions** and **comments** on specific issues and problems facing the company, without anticipating the outcomes

5.1.2 Benefits of quality circles

The **benefits of quality circles** include:

(a) Employee involvement improves morale.
(b) Practical improvements/solutions are likely as workers know the processes involved.
(c) Organisation unity is fostered as the circle includes all levels.
(d) Suggestions can result in valuable savings.
(e) A 'culture' of quality is fostered.

5.1.3 Drawbacks of quality circles

Possible **drawbacks** of quality circles include:

(a) Employee 'power' is hard to control.
(b) The scope of influence can become very wide.
(c) Rejected suggestions may cause resentment.
(d) Business practicalities (eg cost) may not be fully understood.

The concept of quality circles has expanded to now include groups drawn from **separate organisations** but with a common interest.

5.2 The 5Ss

Often associated with **lean production**, the overriding idea behind the 5Ss is that there is 'a place for everything and everything goes in its place'. Discipline, simplicity, pride, standardisation and repeatability are emphasised in the 5Ss as being critical to efficiency.

The 5Ss			Comment/meaning
Seiri	or	Structurise	Segregate or discard. Introduce order where possible.
Selton	or	Systemise	Arrange and identify for ease of use. Approach tasks systematically.
Seiso	or	Sanitise	Clean daily. Be tidy, avoid clutter.
Seiketsu	or	Standardise	Revisit each 'S' frequently. Be consistent in your approach.
Shitsuke	or	Self-discipline	Sustain via motivation. Do the above daily.

5.3 Six Sigma

KEY TERM

SIX SIGMA is a process designed to help organisations to focus on developing and delivering near-perfect products and services.

The expression is derived from the discipline of statistics. Sigma is a statistical measure of variation in output. A score of six times the Sigma within a specification means 99.999% of the manufactured items are within the specification (3.4 defects per million opportunities). A Three Sigma level of quality implies a 93.32% specification compliance (67,000 defects per million).

5.3.1 Elimination of defects

Six Sigma ensures the progressive **elimination of defects** by:

- Identifying the root causes of error
- Confirming the critical root causes
- Implementing corrective action

By minimising defects, **customer satisfaction** should improve and this should improve **profitability**. The thinking might be summarised as follows.

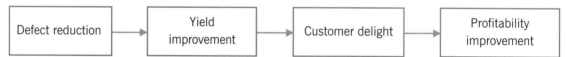

A key advantage of Six Sigma is that it can be implemented alongside other initiatives such as TQM and ISO 9000. However, Six Sigma is different in that it is **customer focused** rather than operations orientated. It looks at strategically critical outcomes that affect customer satisfaction.

The method was first devised by **Motorola** in the US in 1985 to help manufacture a virtually defect-free pager. The method has been successfully implemented by recognised corporations such as Polaroid, Kodak, and IBM. However, it was General Electric that propelled it to its current prominence and popularity.

5.3.2 Example of Six Sigma in practice

General Electric (GE) introduced Six Sigma and there are **three elements** to its approach.

(a)   **Delighting customers**

   (i)   The customer sets the quality standard, rather than some manager within the company.

(ii)   There is a focus on performance, reliability, price, delivery, service and transaction processing.

(b)   **Outside-in thinking**

        (i)   The company must be seen from the customer's perspective.

        (ii)   There is a need to understand what the customer is seeing and feeling as regards the company's processes.

        (iii)   Customer knowledge is used to improve company processes and add value.

(c)   **Leadership commitment**

        (i)   GE recognises that people are key to creating quality and generating results.

        (ii)   There is a commitment to providing opportunities for employees to develop themselves in the services they provide to customers.

        (iii)   There is a focus on ensuring employee training needs are satisfied.

CASE STUDY

Tiffinwallah system of Mumbai

The Tiffinwallah system in Mumbai, India, was singled out by Forbes Magazine as an outstanding example and awarded a Six Sigma grading.

Each day, 175,000 tiffins (lunchboxes) are delivered to offices and schools throughout Mumbai, and later returned home, by approximately 5,000 people called tiffinwallahs. Each tiffin holds a variety of dishes of food. Each tiffin is collected by a tiffinwallah and taken to one of Mumbai's suburban railway stations, where they are sorted. They are collected at the destination station and taken to the building.

There is a fairly simple method of coding which manages a very low failure rate. Each tiffinwallah does not have to deal with too many tiffin boxes. The tiffinwallahs make only one error in 16 million transactions. Statistically this represents 99.999% of correctness, thereby achieving Six Sigma.

Section summary

A **quality circle** is a team of workers from within the organisation which meets at intervals to discuss issues relating to the quality of the product or service produced.

The **5Ss** is a Japanese approach to quality that focuses on the five aspects of structurise, systemise, sanitise, standardise and self-discipline.

Six Sigma is a process designed to help organisations to focus on developing and delivering **near-perfect** products and services.

6   Lean production

Introduction

Lean production is a manufacturing methodology developed originally for Toyota. It is also known as the Toyota Production System. Its goal is 'to get the right things to the right place at the right time, the first time, while **minimising waste** and being open to change'.

KEY TERMS

LEAN PRODUCTION (sometimes referred to as lean manufacturing or lean process improvement) is a philosophy of production that aims to minimise the amount of resources (including time) used in all activities. It involves identifying and eliminating all non value adding activities.

LEAN SYNCHRONISATION is the application of lean techniques with the aim of producing products and services that deliver what customers want. For example, the right quantity of products is delivered at the right time, in the right location for the right price.

Lean production or lean process improvement involves the **systematic elimination of waste**, such as:

- **Overproduction** and early production
- **Waiting** – time delays, idle time, any time during which value is not added to the product
- **Transportation** – multiple handling, delay in materials handling, unnecessary handling
- **Inventory** – holding or purchasing unnecessary raw materials, work in process and finished goods
- **Motion** – actions of people or equipment that do not add value to the product
- **Overprocessing** – unnecessary steps or work elements/procedures (non added value work)
- **Defective units** – production of a part that is scrapped or requires rework

Ohno (an engineer) is generally credited with developing the principles of lean production. He argued that it **eliminated waste** and led to **improved product flow** and **improved quality**.

Lean production focuses on reducing system response time so that the **production system is capable of rapid change to meet market demands**.

6.1 Characteristics of lean production

The **characteristics of lean production** are:

- Integrated, single piece continuous workflow

- Integration of the whole value chain through partnerships with suppliers and distributors and continuous improvement

- Just-in-time processing

- Short order to ship cycle times synchronised with small batch production

- Production based on orders rather than forecasts (ie driven by customer demand – 'pull' – rather than production levels – 'push')

- Minimal inventories at each stage of the production process (zero inventories and zero waiting time)

- Quick changeovers of machines and equipment

- Production layout based on workflow

- Economies of scope (producing small batches of a variety of products from the same machine)

- Active involvement by workers in problem solving to improve quality and eliminate waste

- Defect prevention (rather than inspection and rework) by building quality into the process

- Team-based work with multiskilled staff empowered to make decisions

6.2 Applications of lean techniques

During the 1980s **lean production methods** were adopted by many manufacturing plants in the US and Europe, with varying degrees of success.

Recent years have seen a renewed interest in lean techniques, particularly since the reduction of inventory. Dell Computers and Boeing Aircraft have embraced the philosophy of lean production with great success.

Lean techniques are applicable not only in manufacturing, but **also in a service environment**. Every system contains waste (ie something that does not provide value to the customer).

Lean supply chains occur when lean techniques are applied in firms across the chain. This requires a high degree of trust and co-ordination. Integrated information systems would be required to ensure each organisation in the chain is aware of the activities of other chain members.

6.3 Lean synchronisation

Lean synchronisation involves the application of the techniques and ideas covered in this chapter with the purpose of **delivering to the customer exactly what they want**. This can be summarised as delivering the right quantity of the right product, at the right time, in the right location, for the right price.

The actual mix and application of techniques that an organisation uses will depend on the culture and nature of the organisation, the industry, and the strategy of the business. Lean synchronisation can be a very powerful tool to use – however, there are a number of barriers to its successful implementation.

6.3.1 Barriers to lean synchronisation

There are **three main barriers to successful lean synchronisation**.

The first barrier is a **failure of the organisation to eliminate waste**. Waste causes costs to rise and products to be delayed due to rework. It may also affect product quality.

The second barrier is a **failure to involve all the relevant people** involved in the operation. For any initiative to be successful there needs to be support and involvement from the leadership through to the shop floor. This is because all involved have a role to play in the success of the plan and if there are any weak links the venture will have limited or no benefit.

Finally, the third barrier is a **failure to adopt principles of continuous improvement**. The achievement of lean synchronisation requires a gradual process over a period of time rather than a one-time implementation and therefore organisations that do not embrace the principle of continuous improvement are unlikely to be successful.

6.4 Benefits of lean production

Supporters of lean production believe it enables a company to **deliver** on demand, **minimise** inventory, **maximise** the use of multiskilled employees, **flatten** the management structure and **focus** resources where they are most effective.

Other benefits include:

- Waste reduction (up to 80%)
- Production cost reduction (50%)
- Manufacturing cycle times decreased (50%)
- Labour reduction (50%) while maintaining or increasing throughput
- Inventory reduction (80%) while increasing customer service levels
- Capacity increase in current facilities (50%)
- Higher quality
- Higher profits
- Higher system flexibility
- More strategic focus
- Improved cash flow through increasing shipping and billing frequencies

6.5 Criticisms of lean principles

In many situations, organisations supposedly using **lean principles** have not experienced the improvements in productivity and profitability expected.

It is difficult to know whether this is due to shortcomings in the **lean philosophy** or whether the techniques involved are being interpreted and applied correctly.

For example, the **5Ss** concept should be used with the aim of creating a workplace with **real organisation** and **order** that creates pride by employees in their work, improves safety and results in better quality. However, in some organisations the 5Ss concept has become a cleaning and housekeeping exercise only.

Lean techniques should be seen and treated as outward signs of a more **fundamental approach** to **operations** and **quality**. Real improvements require a change in thinking and in **culture** – which are difficult to achieve.

There is often a **high initial investment** required to achieve lean production – for example in terms of training employees, acquiring new equipment for processes and reorganising factory floors. If the organisation is not 100% committed to the change, then it may not make sufficient investment to ensure success. Even where it does, the **benefits** achieved may be **outweighed by the costs**.

Many companies use lean manufacturing and Six Sigma techniques to **reduce costs**, rather than a fundamental commitment to eliminating waste and adding value.

6.6 World class manufacturing

In a **manufacturing environment** a commitment to quality (and the customer) may be referred to as 'world class manufacturing'. This approach involves a **focus on customer requirements** and ensuring products meet these requirements.

As customer requirements often change, **flexibility** in manufacturing operations is a key feature of world class manufacturing.

Three factors Japanese manufacturing organisations focused on that contributed to world class manufacturing are:

- Integrated operations processes enabling smooth production flow

- Team leaders that involved employees (team members) in quality issues and developed both their own and employees' problem-solving skills

- Tightly integrated value chains with close, productive relationships between supply chain partners

Section summary

The goal of **lean production** is 'to get the right things to the right place at the right time, the first time, while **minimising waste** and being open to change'.

In a **manufacturing environment** a commitment to quality (and to the customer) may be referred to as '**world class manufacturing**'.

7 International Organisation for Standardisation

Introduction

A number of organisations produce quality standards. The most widely used are those published by the **International Organisation for Standardisation (ISO)**.

The ISO 9000 quality standards have been adopted by many organisations worldwide.

ISO-issued standards are applicable to **many types of organisation** and they are updated periodically.

The ISO 9000:2000 series of standards consists of a number of primary standards: ISO 9000, ISO 9001, ISO 9004, ISO 19011 and ISO 140011.

(a)   **ISO 9001:2000** contains ISO's current quality management system requirements. This is the standard you need to use if you wish to become certified (registered).

(b)   **ISO 9000:2000 and ISO 9004:2000** contain ISO's quality management system guidelines. These standards explain ISO's approach to quality management presenting definitions and a set of guidelines for improving performance, but they are not intended to be used for certification purposes.

(c)   **ISO 19011** covers quality auditing standards.

(d)   **ISO 14001** relates to environmental management systems. It specifies a process for controlling and improving an organisation's environmental performance. Issues covered include:

(i)   Planning
(ii)   Policies on the environment
(iii)   Implementation and operation
(iv)   Reviews by management
(v)   Checking and taking corrective action

7.1 ISO certified/registered or ISO compliant?

KEY POINTS

> When a company claims that it is **ISO 9000 certified** or **registered**, it means that **an independent registrar** has audited its processes and certified that it meets the ISO requirements.
>
> When an organisation says that it is **ISO 9000 compliant**, it means that it has **met ISO's quality system requirements**, but has **not been formally certified** by an independent registrar. In effect, it is **self-certified.**
>
> Of course, official certification carries more weight in the marketplace.

The ISO 9000 standards are **process standards**, not product standards. Organisations are granted certified or compliant status on the basis that their **processes** rather than their products and services meet ISO 9000 requirements. The logic is that high-quality processes ensure high-quality output.

7.2 Criticisms of quality accreditation

Many writers and managers have criticised **formal quality schemes**. These criticisms tend to emphasise the following points:

(a)   Documentation is **expensive** (in terms of time) to produce.

(b)   Policies and procedures encourage **management by manual**, and **discourage innovation** and initiative.

(c)   The schemes **encourage bureaucracy**.

(d)   Formal methods may conflict with **working practices** in small and medium-sized organisations.

7.3 The European Foundation for Quality Management model

There are now many smaller self-assessment models for business/organisation improvement. In Europe, one of the most popular is the **European Foundation for Quality Management model**. This provides a **structured methodology for organisations** to measure their own performance in areas that are critical to businesses.

The model provides a basis for measurement of '**enablers**' (people, leadership, policies, strategies, processes, partnerships and resources) and '**results**' in relation to customers, people, society and performance indicators.

Criticisms of this and similar schemes include their **expense** (in terms of time) and the fact that scoring is largely **subjective**.

Section summary

ISO-certified organisations have had their **processes and procedures checked and verified** by an independent auditor.

ISO-compliant organisations **self-certify that they meet the ISO requirements**; however, such claims have not been verified.

8 Total productive maintenance (TPM)

Introduction

Quality issues do not just affect production processes. They filter into every part of the organisation, including the maintenance of production equipment. **Total productive maintenance** or **TPM** originated in Japan. It is defined as 'the productive maintenance carried out by all employees through small group activities'.

8.1 Five goals of TPM

The goals of TPM are:

(a) **Improve equipment effectiveness**. The goal should be to examine how the facilities of an operation are contributing to its effectiveness. Loss of effectiveness could be caused by defects, down-times and loss of operating speed.

(b) **Achieve autonomous maintenance**. The employees who use an item of equipment should be allowed to take on some of the responsibility for its maintenance. Specialist maintenance staff should be encouraged to take on the responsibility for improving maintenance performance.

(c) **Plan maintenance**. Maintenance should be planned, and the frequency and level of preventive maintenance and standards for condition-based maintenance should be specified.

(d) **Train all staff in maintenance skills**.

(e) **Achieve early equipment management**. This goal is linked to maintenance prevention, by which the causes of failure and the ease of maintenance of an item of equipment are considered at the design, manufacture, commissioning and installation stages, ie before the equipment is brought into operation.

8.2 Benefits of TPM

Benefits of TPM include:

- **Reduced** instances of **breakdowns**
- **Production consistency** and **uniform output**
- **Reduction** in **waste** and **cost of quality**
- **Improved accuracy** of **production schedules**
- Facilitation of an **on-time delivery**

One **possible approach** is shown in the steps below.

Step 1

Discover what the nature of the failure has been, its possible consequences, and the reasons why it has happened. Finding out the reason for a failure is not, at this stage, an in-depth investigation. Being aware of the reason for the failure can, however, help with making a decision about what the recovery procedure should be.

Step 2

Act by:

(i)   Telling people involved what you propose to do about the failure, for example by keeping customers informed

(ii) Containing the failure in order to stop the consequences from spreading

(iii) Following up to make sure that the containing action has been successful

---

Step 3

Learn. Use the failure as a learning opportunity, to find out in some depth why the failure occurred and 'engineering out' the cause to prevent it from happening again.

Step 4

Plan. Operations managers should incorporate the lessons learned from past failures to plan how they would deal with similar failures in the future. This involves identifying what failures might occur and their reasons and devising formal procedures to be followed if and when it **occurs**.

8.3 Business continuity

Business continuity is a term used to describe measures to help an operation **prevent or recover from failures**, and to continue operating in the event of a **disaster**. A disaster is a critical malfunction that stops normal operations (eg a key supplier going out of business, a major computer system failure, a bomb blast at a key location). One approach to **business continuity** planning is to:

(a)   **Identify and assess the risks** of various disasters happening.

(b)   **Identify core business processes**, and rank them in order of priority. Make sure that employees understand these priorities.

(c)   **Quantify recovery times**.

(d)   **Determine what resources will be needed** to carry out the recovery, and make sure that the resources will be available if and when required.

(e)   **Communicate** with everyone in the organisation and others involved in the recovery process to ensure they know what they will be required to do in the event of a disaster.

Section summary

Total productive maintenance is a policy that ensures quality is reflected in the maintenance of production equipment.

9   The TQMEX model

Introduction

As explained earlier, **TQM focuses on the needs of customers**. In order to fully understand TQM we need to understand how all elements of an organisation work towards the ultimate goal – customer satisfaction.

Ho (1999) devised his TQMEX model to indicate the relationship between quality management and other aspects of operations management. The model demonstrates how contemporary **approaches** to quality may be **integrated** to achieve a **philosophy of quality** throughout the organisation.

Ho's TQMEX model

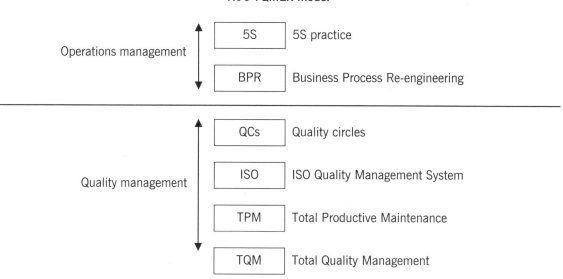

We covered **Business Process Re-engineering** (BPR) previously in relation to developments in the finance function. You should refer back to your notes on this because BPR is traditionally associated with operations management and you may be examined on it in this context too.

Exam alert

BPR could be examined together with process mapping – redesigning a process requires an understanding of the process that may best be obtained from a process map.

Section summary

Ho's **TQMEX model** indicates the relationship between quality management and other aspects of operations management.

10 Service quality

Introduction

Many of the models and techniques that we have already studied can be applied to the **service industry**. We have already seen how **SERVQUAL** can be used to measure quality in service organisations by reference to customer expectations. Therefore, managing these expectations and the actual service provided are key to service quality.

KEY TERM

SERVICE QUALITY is the totality of features and characteristics of that service which bears on its ability to meet stated or implied needs.

Service organisations have a different nature to those that manufacture goods. For example:

(a) Goods have a physical presence, whereas **services are intangible** and **consumed immediately** (ie they cannot be stored).

(b) Delivery of goods is a separate process to production and purchase and does not involve the customer. In service industries, **delivery is part of the service** and customers may be involved in it.

(c) The manufacture of goods does not usually involve **face to face contact** with the customer. In service industries, there usually is face to face contact. This means that the social skills of the person providing the service will be evaluated by the customer when deciding on the overall quality of the service.

(d) Manufacturing organisations are usually machine intensive. Service industries are usually **labour intensive**.

10.1 Dimensions of service quality

Service quality has a number of dimensions.

(a) **Technical quality** of the service encounter (ie what is received by the customer). Was the meal edible? Was the train on time? Were the shelves fully stocked? Problems of this sort must be addressed by improving the processes of production and delivery.

(b) **Functional quality** of the service encounter (ie how the service is provided). This relates to the psychological interaction between the buyer and seller and is typically perceived in a very subjective way.

　　(i) **Relationships between employees**. For example, do these relationships appear to be professional? Do they chat to each other while serving the customer? Does each appear to know their role in the team and the function of their colleagues?

　　(ii) **Appearance and personality of service personnel**. For instance, do they seem interested in the customer and the customer's needs? Are they smartly presented? Do they convey a positive image?

　　(iii) **Service-mindedness of the personnel**. For example, do they appear to understand and identify with the needs of the customer? Do they convey competence? Do they show willingness to help?

　　(iv) **Accessibility of the service to the customer**. Do the service personnel explain the service in language which the customer can understand?

　　(v) **Approachability of service personnel**. For instance, do the service personnel appear alert, interested or welcoming? Or are they daydreaming, yawning or looking at their watches?

10.2 Role of customer

For many service operations, the **customer** represents both the input and the output of a transformation process, eg a patient visiting a dentist.

10.3 Satisfaction as a measure

Service quality therefore focuses on the extent of success achieved in creating a **transformed customer**. This can be answered in terms of customer satisfaction. Johnston and Clark (2001) state that customer satisfaction levels may be 'represented on a continuum from (extreme) delight to (extreme) dissatisfaction'.

10.4 Customer expectations

Going back to the beginning of the transformation process, the **input is a customer with certain expectations**. The organisation delivers a service that is intended to meet those customer expectations. This overall process is depicted as follows.

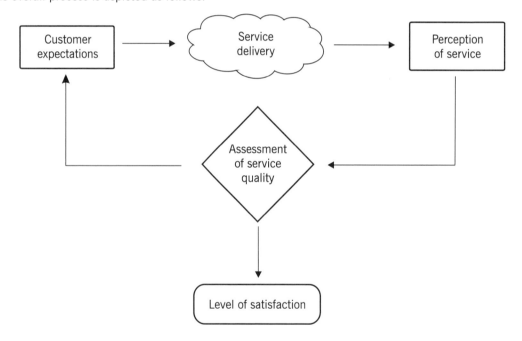

10.4.1 Influencing customer expectations

A prerequisite to being able to manage customers' expectations or designing services to meet expectations is to accurately identify and understand them.

A customer's preconceived expectations are likely to influence a **customer's assessment of service quality** – eg a guest at an expensive hotel is likely to expect a high level of attentiveness from the hotel staff.

Various authors have tried to identify **generic factors** that determine a customer's assessment of service quality. The following is a useful list of 18 **service quality factors**. (Johnston and Clark, 2001)

Access	Comfort	Friendliness
Aesthetics	Commitment	Functionality
Attentiveness	Communication	Integrity
Availability	Competence	Reliability
Care	Courtesy	Responsiveness
Cleanliness	Flexibility	Security

The following diagram and table explain some **major factors** that shape customer expectations.

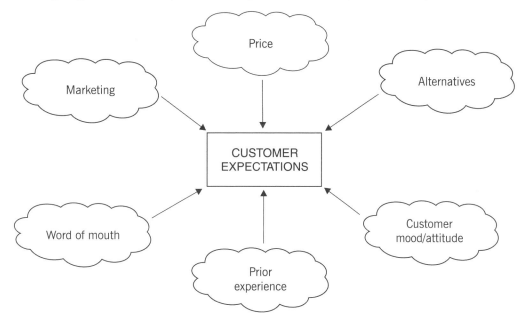

Factor	Example
Marketing	Claims may be difficult to deliver, eg an optician advertises that no appointments are required, but a client has to actually wait 50 minutes for an eye test.
Price	Customer expectations usually increase as price increases, eg if a hair salon charges high prices, clients expect a good cut and styling.
Alternatives	A good past experience at one service provider is likely to set the standard next time for an alternative service provider, eg a tasty meal at one burger chain is likely to engender expectations of a similar dining experience when visiting another outlet.
Word of mouth	Often this is the most influential source for setting up customer expectations.
Previous experience	This helps the customer develop a clearer view of what to expect. This adds to the challenge faced by the service provider but on the other hand also helps to moderate consumers' expectations, eg experience of travelling with a certain rail service may inject a certain sense of reality into what a passenger can expect.
Customer's mood and attitude	It is inevitable that a customer's mood and attitude is likely to influence their expectations, eg a guest at a restaurant who has received some good news (got a promotion or passed an exam etc) is more likely to be tolerant of slow service.

There are various ways in which service quality factors may be **classified**.

Classifications	Comment
Hygiene factors	These are very much baseline factors. If not present they will tend to dissatisfy a customer, eg a hotel guest will expect proper security but it is unlikely to delight.
Enhancing factors	These may partially delight but will not be a source of dissatisfaction if absent, eg a hotel guest is likely to really appreciate friendly staff but might not be dissatisfied if they are not all that cheerful.
Critical factors	These have the potential to delight as well as dissatisfy, eg a hotel guest will expect staff responsiveness.
Neutral factors	These usually have little impact on satisfaction, eg a hotel guest may be delighted if a hotel is aesthetically pleasing with nice wallpaper, smart fittings etc, but may well not miss them if not present.

Question 7.2	Service quality factors

Learning outcome D2(ix)

You have recently been appointed to manage an underground rail system for a major international city.

Required

Classify the 18 service quality factors (from the previous section) in terms of the four key categories:
Hygiene factors, **Critical factors**, **Neutral factors** and **Enhancing factors**.   **(8 marks)**

10.5 Perception of service

In product operations there is a physical output which is relatively easy to measure in terms of quality. With service operations, the expression 'perception is reality' applies. Differences arise between the **service delivered** and the **customers' perception of quality** because people filter what they see and experience.

Exam alert

The concepts of quality, quality assurance and quality management are now well established in the business world. Quality has proved highly popular as a topic for examination questions in the past, and can be expected to feature prominently in the future.

Section summary

Service quality is the totality of features and characteristics of that service which bears on its ability to meet stated or implied needs.

Chapter Summary

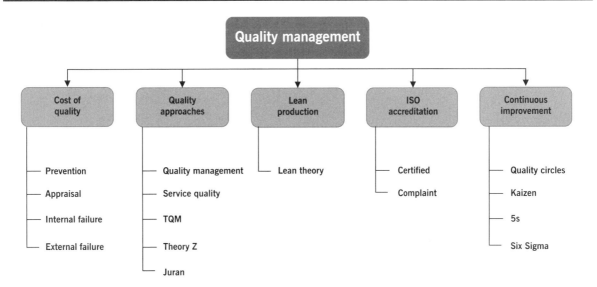

Quick Quiz

1   List five principles of TQM.

    1   ....

    2   ....

    3   ....

    4   ....

    5   ....

2   Which of the following is not one of the 5Ss?

    A   Structurise
    B   Systemise
    C   Simplify
    D   Self-discipline

3   An ISO 9000 compliant organisation:

    A   Has its processes independently checked and verified as meeting the ISO requirements
    B   Has self-certified the fact that its processes meet the ISO requirements
    C   Aims to meet the ISO requirements
    D   Meets ISO 9000 requirements at least 90% of the time

4   Which of the following is not a critical service quality factor?

    A   Responsiveness
    B   Integrity
    C   Communication
    D   Competence

5   Who devised the TQMEX model?

    A   Kaplan and Norton
    B   Deming
    C   Ouchi
    D   Ho

Answers to Quick Quiz

1   Any five from the following: prevention, right first time, eliminate waste, continuous improvement, everybody's concern, participation and teamwork.

2   C   The other elements are sanitise and standardise.

3   B   An ISO-compliant organisation self-certifies the fact that its processes meet the ISO requirements. ISO-certified or -registered organisations have their claims independently verified.

4   B   Integrity is a hygiene factor.

5   D   Ho devised the TQMEX model.

Answers to Questions

7.1 TQM and consistency

When producing a product or service, consistency means using the same standard of resources and employing the same methods and procedures (processes). Consistency in processes should result in consistently high-quality output and a consistently satisfied customer.

7.2 Service quality factors

Hygiene factors	Critical factors	Neutral factors	Enhancing factors
Access	Responsiveness	Comfort	Attentiveness
Availability	Communication	Aesthetics	Care
Functionality	Competence		Cleanliness
Integrity			Commitment
Reliability			Friendliness
Security			Courtesy
			Flexibility

Now try these questions from the Practice Question Bank	Number
	31, 32, 33, 34, 35

MANAGING CAPACITY AND INVENTORY

 In this final chapter on operations management, we turn our attention to strategies for **balancing capacity with demand** and the **management of inventory**.

Capacity management is concerned with the organisation's ability to meet the demand for its products or services. Capacity is a limiting factor on how much an organisation can produce, and how much it can earn.

Today's business environment demands **speed** and **efficiency** in the delivery of products and services. This changing nature of business has implications for **inventory management**.

The **just-in-time** philosophy, covered in the final section of this chapter, is one approach that minimises holding costs while allowing timely production and delivery of products and services.

8

Topic list	Learning outcomes	Syllabus references	Ability required
1 Capacity management	D2(a)	D2(viii)	application
2 Balancing capacity and demand	D2(a)	D2(viii)	application
3 Capacity planning	D2(a)	D2(iv), D2(viii)	application
4 Capacity control	D2(a), D2(b)	D2(viii), D2(ix)	application
5 Inventory management	D2(a)	D2(viii)	application
6 Just-in-time (JIT)	D2(a)	D2(viii)	application
7 Production processes and technology	D2(a)	D2(v), D2(vi), D2(vii)	application

Chapter Overview

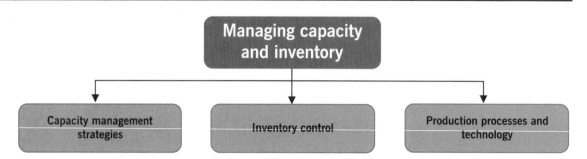

1   Capacity management

Introduction

Capacity is a measure of what an operation is able to produce within a specified period of time. Capacity management aims to maximise the returns an organisation achieves on the assets and systems it utilises.

KEY TERM

CAPACITY has been defined as the maximum level of value-added activity over a period of time that can be achieved by a process or production unit under normal working conditions.

Overcapacity or undercapacity can be detrimental to the business activities of an organisation.

1.1 Overcapacity

Overcapacity means that **resources** available for production are **not fully utilised**.

(a)   Resources are underutilised and return on assets is lower than it could be. If an attempt is made to increase selling prices to improve the return, products and services may become expensive relative to competitors.

(b)   In the service industry it could send out the wrong messages to customers, eg a restaurant that is not full may give the impression that the food is not good.

1.2 Undercapacity

Undercapacity means **more production is being demanded than is able to be produced**.

(a)   If the organisation is unable to satisfy customer demand, it is missing out on profits from the products or services the market was ready to buy. Also, the customer is likely to acquire the product or service from a rival organisation and the customer may be lost.

(b)   In the service industry, undercapacity may result in slower or less comfortable service, reducing customer satisfaction and customer retention.

Capacity planning aims to **balance capacity** with the **demand** for the product or service.

Section summary

Overcapacity means resources available for production are not fully utilised.

Undercapacity means more production is being demanded than is able to be produced.

2   Balancing capacity and demand

Introduction

One important operations management task within an organisation is **balancing** the amount it is able to produce (**capacity**) with the amount it is able to sell (**demand**).

2.1 Dealing with uncertainty

Uncertainties in capacity could be caused by a number of factors, for example the shortage or a delay in the supply of a resource.

Uncertainties in demand are often due to the unpredictable nature of customers and potential customers.

Dealing with uncertainty requires a flexibility in **planning and control**.

Dependent demand is demand that **is predictable** because it is based on a factor that is known. For example, an organisation providing school meals can predict the demand for its meals because the size of each school population is known.

Dependent demand occurs often in manufacturing, where the demand for raw materials and components can be predicted from the demand for the main product. **Materials requirement planning (MRP)** is a form of **dependent demand planning and control**. However, many organisations and/or operations within organisations aren't able to predict demand as easily. They have to make capacity decisions based on **experience** and **judgement** about the **likely** level of **demand**.

Fast turnaround time is important for airlines because by minimising time on the ground an airline can maximise the productivity of its planes in the air (ie maximise capacity).

To help airlines achieve the benefits of a fast turnaround time, the Airbus A320 family aircraft has the following features:

- Larger passenger doors
- Wider aisles
- Larger overhead storage compartments
- Convenient access to underfloor baggage holds
- Wider outward-opening cargo doors

2.2 Planning and control activities

There are **four planning and control activities** associated with balancing capacity and demand:

(a) Loading
(b) Sequencing
(c) Scheduling
(d) Monitoring and controlling

2.2.1 Loading

Loading is the **amount of work allocated to an operating unit**. The term was first applied to the allocation of work to a machine or group of machines, but is applicable to any operating unit (eg a hair salon).

2.2.2 Sequencing

Decisions have to be taken when work comes in about **the order in which different jobs will be done** or different orders fulfilled. **The sequencing of operations** could be on the basis of any of the following:

(a) Customer priority
(b) Due date
(c) Last in first out
(d) First in first out
(e) Longest operation time first
(f) Shortest operation time first

The preferred sequencing criteria should be the one that **optimises operational performance** in terms of:

(a)   Dependability of delivery (ie meeting the due dates promised to customers)
(b)   Speed of delivery (ie minimising the amount of time that jobs spend in the process)
(c)   Cost
(d)   Minimising idle time in work centres (which is an aspect of cost)
(e)   Minimising inventory levels (which is another aspect of cost)

2.2.3 Scheduling

Once work has been sequenced, it might be necessary to prepare **a detailed timetable** specifying the time that jobs should be started and when they should end.

Formal schedules are only needed when detailed planning is necessary to make sure that **customer demand can be met**. In operations where demand is unpredictable, scheduling is impracticable and the operation must simply **react to orders as they arrive**, for example petrol stations.

For an operation that processes a large number of jobs, there is a risk that with poor scheduling **bottlenecks** will occur in different parts of the operation at different times.

2.2.4 Monitoring and controlling

Having loaded, sequenced and scheduled the work, management must monitor the operation to make sure that the **work is proceeding as planned**. If a deviation from the plan is shown, corrective measures may be required so that the work can be rescheduled.

The terms 'push control' and 'pull control' refer to when control action is taken to manage the flow of work. With **push control**, production and inventory levels are forecasted and the focus is on pushing work through each stage of the process, regardless of whether the next stage is ready to receive it.

With **pull control**, the focus is on each stage of the process calling for work to be delivered from the previous process when it is needed. The work is not delivered from the previous process until it is needed. With pull control, there should be less inventory in the system.

Section summary

There are **four planning and control activities** associated with balancing capacity and demand: **loading**, **sequencing**, **scheduling** and **monitoring and controlling**.

3   Capacity planning

Introduction

Capacity planning aims to balance the **capacity** of an operation with the **demand** from customers. The objective is to maximise both **profits** and **customer satisfaction**.

3.1 Purpose of capacity planning and control

Planning and controlling capacity involves:

(a)   Planning the **normal capacity** of the operation
(b)   Reacting to **changes** in demand

Long-term **strategic decisions** have to be made about what the capacity of an operation should be, and investment decisions taken to achieve the planned capacity.

Capacity planning in the short and medium term has several implications for operational performance.

Implication	Comment
Cost	Costs are affected by planned capacity. When the capacity of an operation exceeds demand, there will be underutilised resources and costs will be higher than if capacity were more closely matched to demand.
Revenue	On the other hand, revenues could also be affected by the capacity of an operation. If demand exceeds the capacity of an operation to meet it, revenues will be forgone that could otherwise have been earned.
Quality	The quality of an operation could be affected by capacity planning. For example, if an operation varies its capacity by using part-time or temporary staff, the quality of the product or service might be impaired.
Speed of response to demand	The speed of response to demand can be improved either by building up finished goods inventories (which has a cost) or by providing sufficient capacity to avoid customers having to queue or to wait (which also has a cost).
Dependability of supply	The closer an operation works to its capacity limit, the less easily it will be able to cope with unexpected disruptions to the workflow. Supply will therefore be less dependable.
Flexibility	The flexibility of an operation, and in particular its ability to vary the volume of output it can produce, will be improved by having surplus capacity. An operation working at or close to its capacity limit is much less flexible.

3.2 Measuring demand and capacity

3.2.1 Forecasting demand

In most organisations, the **sales and marketing department** is responsible for forecasting demand. However, demand forecasts are relevant to operations management and capacity planning.

(a) For operations management purposes, demand forecasts should be expressed in terms of units rather than sales revenue. For example, for a manufacturing operation it is more relevant to express demand in terms of labour hours or machine hours.

(b) Forecasts should be as **accurate** as possible because capacity will be planned on the basis of the forecasts.

(c) Forecasts of demand should give some indication of the degree of uncertainty. Where possible, the **variation** in demand should be **assessed statistically**, perhaps on the basis of demand patterns from the past.

3.2.2 Surveys and analysis

The following methods can be used to help forecast demand:

(a) **Expert opinion polls** provide subjective demand information based on the views of product experts.

(b) **Delphi technique** is a form of expert opinion poll where the experts are repeatedly questioned on similar topics and provided with feedback on answers to previous questions until there is a consensus among the experts.

(c) **Customer surveys** based on all customers or just a sample can be used to judge their future demand.

(d) **Statistical analysis** (such as time-series or regression analysis) can be used to estimate future demand from past actual data. Time-series analysis provides trends over time and identifies seasonal variations.

Regression analysis plots demand against time and a straight line of best fit can be used to predict future demand. This method is most appropriate where there is a strong correlation between demand and time.

3.2.3 Measuring capacity

Measuring capacity is not a straightforward task, except for standardised and repetitive operations. When an operation produces a range of different products or services, measuring capacity in terms of output produced is difficult because there isn't a standard measure of output.

Capacity might therefore be measured in terms of either **input resources available** or **output produced**.

Operation	Capacity measure in terms of input resources	Capacity measure in terms of output produced
Football club	Ground capacity Squad size Number of matches	Number of paying spectators
Doctors' surgery	Number of doctors Number of surgery hours	Number of patients treated
Department store	Shelf space or volume, or floor area	Number of customers through the checkouts
Air travel	Number of seats available on a route	Number of passengers carried on the route each week

Where output is non-standard, any capacity measurement based on output will have to use an **average** measure. For example, a doctors' surgery might measure its capacity in terms of being able to treat 400 patients each week; this might be based on the assumption that an average time for treating each patient is ten minutes. In practice, some patients will need more than ten minutes and some less.

Often, one or more parts of an operation will work at their capacity limit. The parts of an operation that work at their capacity limit are the **capacity constraints for the entire operation**. Capacity constraints limit the total output achievable. They can cause bottlenecks in the workflow and result in unsatisfied demand. For example, if visitors to an out of town shopping centre all use the centre's car park and the car park is limited to 1,000 spaces, the number of car parking spaces is a capacity constraint for the centre.

3.3 Planning for capacity

There are different ways of **planning for capacity**:

- A level capacity plan
- A chase demand plan
- A demand management plan
- A mix of the above three types of plan

3.3.1 Level capacity plan

A **level capacity plan** is a plan to maintain **activity at a constant level** over the planning period and to ignore fluctuations in forecast demand. Staffing and other resource levels are kept constant.

In a manufacturing operation, when demand is lower than capacity the operation will produce goods for inventory.

In a service operation there will be idle resources when demand is low, and delays and probably lower service quality when demand is high.

3.3.2 Chase demand plan

This plan is the opposite of a level capacity plan – it aims to **match capacity** to forecast **fluctuations in demand**.

To achieve this, **resources must be flexible**. For example, staff numbers might have to be variable and staff might be required to work overtime or extra shifts. Variations in equipment levels might also be necessary, perhaps by means of short-term rental arrangements.

Project-based teams and **virtual organisations** may help provide the flexibility needed to implement a chase demand plan.

3.3.3 Demand management planning

Some organisations attempt to **stabilise demand** and then plan capacity accordingly.

The aim of **demand management planning** is to reduce peak demand by switching it to the off-peak periods.

The most obvious way of managing demand is through **price discrimination**. Examples include:

(a) Offering low off-peak fares on trains to encourage some customers to switch their travelling time
(b) Off-peak telephone charges
(c) Off-peak holiday prices to build up demand out of the holiday season

Producers can also use **advertising** and other **marketing** tools to attempt to **stabilise demand**.

3.3.4 Mixed plans

In practice, capacity planning is often a **mixture** of level capacity planning, chase demand planning and demand management planning.

3.3.5 Yield management

In operations with a fairly fixed short-term and medium-term capacity, such as hotels, restaurants, theatres and airlines, an objective could be to achieve as much revenue as possible from the available fixed resources.

A **yield management approach** is particularly well suited to an operation where:

(a) Capacity is fairly fixed in the short to medium term
(b) The market can be segmented, to allow some price discrimination
(c) The service cannot be sold in advance
(d) The marginal cost of making an additional sale is low

Yield management techniques have been evident in airline operations, where the techniques used include:

(a) **Price discounting**. When demand is expected to be low, an airline might sell a block of tickets at a very cheap price.

(b) **Varying the capacity of different types of service**. In an airline operation, this could mean switching the space in an aircraft from first class or business seats to economy class, or vice versa.

(c) **Overbooking**. An airline will expect a percentage of its customers who have booked in advance to fail to arrive for their flight. Airlines therefore tend to book more passengers onto a flight than they have seats. If more passengers arrive than there are seats, some passengers will be offered inducements to take a later flight, or will be upgraded to first class or business class travel.

3.4 Other methods of managing capacity

The use of **flexible manufacturing systems (FMSs), queuing theory** and **forecasting** can also be used to manage capacity.

3.4.1 Flexible manufacturing systems (FMSs)

FMSs use **automated computer systems** to produce output **quickly** in response to **specific customer orders**. For example, print on demand services are operated by some printing organisations. Books or other publications are stored by the printer and copies are produced in response to customer orders.

These systems enable production to **switch quickly** between orders of **small batches** of output. This provides a **responsive, customer-focused** service. However, they may be **less efficient** than production systems which focus on a single product, as these benefit from economies of scale and specialisation.

3.4.2 Queuing theory

Queuing theory seeks to **balance customer waiting** (or queuing) **time** and **idle service capacity** through mathematical modelling. The theory states that **customer satisfaction** and **throughput increases** if a **single queue** is used rather than several shorter queues. This is because the frustration of being in a 'slow queue' is removed. The theory can be applied in **many situations**, such as some shops, hospitals, banks and airport check-ins, but has a number of other uses (such as in call centres).

Benefits of applying **queuing theory** include the ability to give customers an **estimated waiting time**, plan peaks and dips in demand to ensure **staffing levels are appropriate**, manage demand through **appointment systems** and use queuing theory data as **benchmarks** to compare performance.

3.4.3 Forecasting

Forecasting systems seek to **match production** with **customer demand** by anticipating the latter. These systems rely on **accurate customer information** and **past demand data**, which is not always available. The organisation must also **understand demand** and its **processes** well enough to match the two.

Section summary

There are four main ways of **planning for capacity**: **level capacity** plans, **chase demand** plans, **demand management** plans and a **mix of the other three** types of plan.

CASE STUDY

Balancing capacity and demand

One of the biggest challenges electronics companies are facing in 2010 is lengthening component lead times. After a year of slow sales, just as demand is picking up, lead times are stretching out.

The problem is that component suppliers are unwilling to increase capacity or inventory until recovery is clearly underway. Given the economic uncertainties that still exist, it is hard to blame component manufacturers for being reluctant to take a leap of faith and increase inventories and/or capacity.

At the same time, electronics manufacturers are seeing revenues drop, not because of order cancellations but because of an inability to get materials. What can these companies do?

At this point, the best business strategy is to address the current situation both reactively and proactively.

The reactive strategy should focus on bringing quality components in as quickly as possible in the given current market conditions. While creative sourcing may be required, reactive measures should continue to support customer-approved vendor list integrity and avoid questionable sources of supply.

The proactive strategy focuses on longer-term solutions that help address a market that could have extended lead times for several more quarters and prevent excess inventory liability. Proactive strategy steps should include:

• Working with customers to develop extended forecasts so that orders can be placed with sufficient lead time.

• Working with the customer to expand the approved vendor list, where possible to increase sourcing options on critical components.

- Careful monitoring of total company inventories of critical components. Companies should have ERP systems and component numbering practices which allow real-time visibility into inventory by customer and inventory across the company.

- Careful monitoring of lead-time trends and pricing.

Strong supply chain relationships will help.

The good news is that lengthening lead times are often indicative of a recovering market.

Adapted from an article:

Susan Mucha, www.emtworldwide.com, March 2010

4 Capacity control

Introduction

Capacity control involves **reacting** to actual demand and influences on actual capacity as they arise.

4.1 Materials requirements planning (MRP I)

Materials requirements planning (MRP I) is a technique for deciding the volume and timing of materials in manufacturing conditions where there is dependent demand. MRP I is not appropriate if sales cannot be forecasted.

The purpose of an MRP I system is to:

(a)   Calculate the **quantity** of materials required, for each type of material
(b)   Determine **when** they will be required

The **materials requirements** are calculated from:

(a)   Known future orders, ie firm orders already received from customers
(b)   A forecast of other future orders that, with a reasonable degree of confidence, will be received

The quantities of each type of materials required for the product or service will be defined in its **bill of materials**. Estimates of firm and likely demand can therefore be converted into a **materials requirements schedule**.

MRP I enables manufacturing organisations to determine **when to order material** by working back from when they will be required for production, and allowing the necessary lead time for production or for purchasing from the external supplier.

There are **numerous benefits** to an organisation which uses an **MRP I system**. For example, it can reduce its stock levels while being able to meet orders, the system can identify and warn of production problems such as bottlenecks, and it can assist with just-in-time (JIT) management by forging close relationships with suppliers.

4.2 Manufacturing resource planning (MRP II)

Manufacturing resource planning, or MRP II, evolved out of **MRP I**. It is a plan for **planning and monitoring** all the **resources** of a **manufacturing company**: manufacturing, marketing, finance and engineering.

MRP II is a computerised system that incorporates a **single database** used by many different areas of the organisation. The engineering department, manufacturing function and finance function will all be using the same version of the bill of materials. All functions work from a **common set of data**.

MRP II is a sophisticated system that enables **optimal inventory control** based on the matching of supply and demand.

Features include:

- Production planning
- Capacity planning
- Forecasting
- Purchasing
- Order-entry
- Operations control
- Financial analysis

Brown (2001) believes **possible benefits** include:

- Reduced stock-outs – better customer service
- Reduced inventory holding costs
- Improved plant/facilities utilisation
- Reliable order fulfilment times
- Reduced 'crisis management' time

However, MRP II implementations are not always successful. Some potential **drawbacks** are illustrated in the following case study.

CASE STUDY

A family-owned building construction company builds residential and commercial buildings. At any time, the company is working on about 12 projects.

The operations department is organised around project managers, each responsible for between two and four projects at any time, and a foreman for each site. Full-time employees are organised into work groups of two, three or four individuals, and each work group has a specialist skill. The company also uses subcontractors for many aspects of building work.

The company has recently installed an MRP II system.

One of the projects it is working on is the construction of a new residential estate of 50 houses. The houses on the estate will be of three different designs. Each design differs in terms of size, layout, window sizes, roof tile design, electricity supply features, water supply and central heating, furnishings and kitchen fittings. House buyers also have the option to pay for extra items, such as additional or more expensive bathroom fittings.

Project managers and site foremen have complained about the MRP II system. They identified the following issues.

(1)   The system generates a lot of figures, often using complex formulae (algorithms) to estimate the required quantities and timing of materials. The figures are produced by production planning staff, but a large number of people need to be kept informed – the foremen, project managers, possible subcontractors and possibly also specialist work teams. This is bureaucratic.

(2)   The material requirements are estimated by a computer system of the production planning section. The final users of the information – and the materials – have no sense of ownership of the figures. The figures, having been computer-produced, will be difficult to check. Project managers and foremen etc will probably have no incentive to check the figures to see whether they appear to make sense.

(3)   Small hold-ups or difficulties in the building work can have a significant effect on materials requirements. For example, bad weather could hold up production. Whenever scheduling has to be

changed, there will be a new materials requirements schedule, and this new information will have to be distributed to all the people affected. This will add to the problems of information overload.

(4)   MRP II methods work reasonably well for standardised building, but are not easily applied to one-off construction work where materials requirements and scheduling have to be done on a one-off basis.

4.3 Optimised production technology (OPT)

Optimised production technology (OPT) is a computer-based method for scheduling production that focuses on the known capacity constraints (**bottlenecks**) of the operation.

It is used to:

(a)   Identify the capacity constraints in the system
(b)   Schedule production to these capacity constraints
(c)   Try to identify ways of overcoming the capacity constraint, so as to increase capacity
(d)   Having done that, identify the next capacity constraint and schedule production to this constraint

4.4 Enterprise resource planning (ERP)

Enterprise resource planning (ERP) developed out of MRP II. ERP performs a similar function but on a wider basis, integrating and using databases from all parts of the organisation.

ERP software attempts to integrate all departments and functions of an organisation in a computer system able to meet the needs of users from across the whole organisation.

An ERP system includes a number of integrated modules designed to support all the key activities of an enterprise. This includes managing the key elements of the supply chain such as production planning, purchasing, inventory control and customer service including order tracking.

ERP has been extended to the growing number of e-business applications, connecting to customers and supply chain members.

One of the most popular ERP systems has been the R/3 system supplied by **SAP**. The R/3 system integrates most of an organisation's business applications and contains sections for manufacturing and logistics, sales and distribution, financial accounting and human resource management.

ERP has been effective in some situations, for example where it has been implemented as a means of **rationalising and integrating systems** where mergers and acquisitions have led to an uncoordinated mix of systems. ERP also provides efficiencies in supply chain management through facilitating reduced lead times.

However, many ERP implementations **have failed to live up to expectations**, failing to deliver significant efficiency gains.

As they cover many areas of an organisation, ERP implementations are relatively expensive. They also carry significant 'hidden' costs through requiring organisations to change the way they operate. Some businesses have been restructured simply to fit the restrictions of the ERP software.

Question 8.1	Capacity management

Learning outcome D2(viii)

Identify the ways that service organisations differ from manufacturing organisations when considering capacity management.

(5 marks)

Section summary

MRP I, **MRP II**, **OPT** and **ERP** systems all include elements of capacity control.

5 Inventory management

Introduction

Inventories held in any organisation can generally be classified under four main headings:

- Raw materials
- Spare parts/consumables
- Work in progress
- Finished goods

For example, the raw materials of a furniture company would be wood and upholstery. Consumables would be items such as nails, screws and castors. Work in progress would be partly completed furniture. Finished goods would be tables, chairs, desks etc ready for sale. Not all organisations will have inventories of all four general categories.

Inventory control includes the functions of inventory ordering and purchasing, receiving goods into store, storing and issuing inventory and controlling the level of inventory.

5.1 Why hold inventories?

Brown (2001) identified the following reasons for holding inventory:

- **Protection** against supply problems
- To **meet unexpected increases** in demand
- To **improve delivery times** to customers
- To **allow bulk purchases** and associated **discounts**
- To **provide** a **buffer protecting against quality problems** in raw materials of newly finished goods
- To **improve reliability**
- To **smooth** out production when **demand fluctuates**

5.2 Controls

There should be controls over the following functions:

- The **ordering** of inventories
- The **purchase** of inventories
- The **receipt** of goods into store
- **Storage**
- The **issue** of inventory and maintenance of inventories at the most appropriate level

Inventory controls are **required** for a number of reasons:

(a) Holding costs of inventory may be expensive.
(b) Production will be disrupted if the company runs out of raw materials.
(c) If inventory with a short shelf life is not used or sold, its value may decline.
(d) If customer orders cannot be supplied immediately, customer satisfaction will suffer.

5.3 Importance of keeping inventory records

Proper records should be kept of the **physical procedures** for ordering and receiving a consignment of goods to ensure the following:

- That enough inventory is held
- That there is no duplication of ordering
- That quality is maintained

5.4 Storage of inventories

Storekeeping involves storing materials to achieve the following objectives:

- Speedy **issue** and **receipt** of goods
- Full **identification** of all goods at all times
- Correct **location** of all goods at all times
- **Protection** of goods from damage and deterioration
- Provision of **secure stores** to avoid pilferage, theft and fire
- **Efficient** use of storage space
- **Maintenance** of correct inventory levels
- Keeping correct and up to date **records** of receipts, issues and inventory levels

One of the objectives of storekeeping is to maintain **accurate records** of current inventory levels. This involves the accurate recording of inventory movements (issues from and receipts into stores).

5.5 Perpetual or continuous inventory

Continuous or **perpetual inventory** is the name for a system that involves recording every **receipt and issue** of inventory **as it occurs**. This means that there is a continuous record of the balance of each item of inventory.

When the inventory levels drop below a predetermined level, an order for a fixed amount is issued to replenish inventory.

5.6 Periodic inventory systems

These systems involve a check of inventory levels at **specific time intervals**. The checks may trigger an order for new inventory. The quantity ordered depends on the current inventory level.

5.7 ABC system

Under this system, items may be **classified as expensive, inexpensive or in a middle-cost range**. Because of the practical advantages of simplifying stores control procedures without incurring unnecessary high costs, it may be possible to segregate materials for selective stores control.

(a) Expensive and medium-cost materials are subject to careful stores control procedures to minimise cost.

(b) Inexpensive materials can be stored in large quantities because the cost savings from careful stores control do not justify the administrative effort required to implement the control.

This selective approach to stores control is sometimes called the **ABC method** whereby materials are classified A, B or C according to their **value**. A refers to **high** value inventory, B to **medium** and C to **low** value inventory. It is based on the **Pareto 80/20 rule** which suggests that 20% of the items are likely to account for 80% of the overall value.

5.8 Obsolescence and wastage

Obsolete inventories are those items which have become **out of date** and are **no longer required**. Obsolete items are disposed of and treated as an expense in the company's financial statements.

From the perspective of operations management, proper controls should be instituted to minimise the incidence of losses arising from obsolescence or wastage.

Slow-moving inventories are items which are likely to take a long time to be used up.

5.9 Holding costs

If stocks are too high, **holding costs** will be incurred unnecessarily. Such costs occur for a number of reasons.

(a)   **Costs of storage and stores operations**. Larger stocks require more storage space and possibly extra staff and equipment to control and handle them.

(b)   **Interest charges**. Holding inventory involves the tying up of capital (cash) on which interest must be paid.

(c)   **Insurance costs**. The larger the value of inventory held, the greater insurance premiums are likely to be.

(d)   **Risk of obsolescence**. The longer an inventory item is held, the greater the risk of obsolescence.

(e)   **Deterioration**. When materials in store deteriorate to the extent that they are unusable, they must be thrown away with the likelihood that disposal costs would be incurred.

5.10 Costs of obtaining inventories

If inventories are kept low, small quantities will have to be ordered more frequently, thereby increasing the following **ordering or procurement costs**:

(a)   **Clerical and administrative costs** associated with purchasing, accounting for and receiving goods

(b)   **Transport costs**

(c)   **Production run costs**, for stock which is manufactured internally rather than purchased from external sources

5.11 Running out of inventory (stock-outs)

An additional type of cost which may arise if inventories are kept too low is the type associated with **running out of inventories**:

- Lost contribution from lost sales
- Loss of future sales due to disgruntled customers
- Loss of customer goodwill
- Cost of production stoppages
- Labour frustration over stoppages
- Extra costs of urgent, small quantity, replenishment orders

5.12 Objective of inventory control

The overall objective of inventory control is, therefore, to **maintain inventory levels** so that the total of the following costs is minimised:

- Holding costs
- Ordering costs
- Stock-out costs

5.13 Inventory control levels and Economic Order Quantity (EOQ)

KEY POINT

Inventory control levels can be calculated in order to maintain inventory at the optimum level. The three critical control levels are **reorder level**, **minimum level** and **maximum level**. The **Economic Order Quantity (EOQ)** is the order quantity which minimises inventory costs.

Based on an analysis of past inventory usage and delivery times, a series of control levels can be calculated and used to maintain inventories at their **optimum level** (in other words, a level which minimises costs). These levels will determine 'when to order' and 'how many to order'.

(a) **Reorder level**. When inventories reach this level, an order should be placed to replenish stocks. The reorder level is determined by considering the rate of consumption and the lead time (lead time is the time between placing an order with a supplier and the stock becoming available for use).

(b) **Minimum level**. This is a warning level to draw management attention to the fact that inventories are approaching a dangerously low level and that outages are possible.

(c) **Maximum level**. This acts as a warning level to signal to management that stocks are reaching a potentially wasteful level.

(d) **Reorder quantity**. This is the quantity of inventory which is to be ordered when stock reaches the reorder level. If it is set so as to minimise the total costs associated with holding and ordering inventory, then it is known as the **EOQ**.

(e) **Average inventory**. The formula for the average inventory level assumes that inventory levels fluctuate evenly between the minimum (or safety) inventory level and the highest possible inventory level (the amount of inventory immediately after an order is received, ie safety inventory + reorder quantity).

Exam skills

You need to understand that holding inventories and ordering inventories involve costs and that these should be minimised and balanced against the risk of stock-outs.

Section summary

Continuous or **perpetual inventory** is the name for a system that involves recording every receipt and issue of inventory as it occurs.

These systems involve a check of inventory levels at **specific time intervals**.

Under the **ABC method of inventory control**, materials are classified A, B or C according to their **value**. **A** refers to **high** value inventory, **B to medium** and **C to low** value inventory. It is based on the Pareto 80/20 rule which suggests that 20% of the items are likely to account for 80% of the overall value.

If inventory levels are too high, **holding costs** will be incurred unnecessarily.

If inventories are kept low, small quantities will have to be ordered more frequently, thereby increasing **ordering or procurement costs**.

There are also **costs** involved in **running out of inventory** (stock-outs).

The overall **objective** of inventory control is to **maintain inventory levels** so that the total of holding, ordering and stock-out costs is **minimised**.

Inventory control levels can be calculated in order to maintain inventory at the optimum level. The three critical control levels are **reorder level**, **minimum level** and **maximum level**. The **Economic Order Quantity (EOQ)** is the order quantity which minimises inventory costs.

6   Just-in-time (JIT)

> ## Introduction
>
> JIT is an approach to operations based on the idea that goods and services should be produced **only when they are needed** – neither too early (so that inventories build up) nor too late (so that the customer has to wait). JIT is also known as 'stockless production' and may be used as part of a lean production process. In its extreme form, a JIT system seeks to hold **zero inventories**.

6.1 Operational requirements of JIT

JIT requires the following **characteristics** in operations:

(a)   **High quality**. Any errors in quality will reduce throughput and reduce the dependability of supply.

(b)   **Speed**. Throughput in the operation must be fast so that customer orders can be met through production rather than out of inventory.

(c)   **Reliability**. Production must be reliable and not subject to hold-ups.

(d)   **Flexibility**. To respond immediately to customer orders, production must be flexible and in small batch sizes (often a 'batch' of one).

(e)   **Lower costs**. As a consequence of high-quality production, and with a faster throughput and the elimination of errors, costs will be reduced.

Under JIT, if there is no immediate demand for output the operation should not produce goods.

It is important that organisations which run a JIT system develop **close relationships** with their **suppliers**. This is because they rely heavily on the quality of their goods and on their ability to deliver on time as required.

Advantages of developing such close relationships include:

(a)   **Location of suppliers** – Suppliers may locate close to the manufacturing plant. This reduces costs and delivery times.

(b)   **On-time delivery** – Close relationships should improve the reliability of suppliers to deliver on time.

(c)   **Quality of supplies** – The quality of goods supplied should improve as the supplier gets to know the requirements of the customer better. This means less need to inspect delivered goods, resulting in fewer production delays and better quality of output.

(d)   **Low inventory levels** – The combination of the three factors above should mean that the organisation can rely on small, frequent deliveries that match its production schedule.

6.2 The JIT philosophy

The **JIT philosophy** originated in Japan in the 1970s, with companies such as the car manufacturer Toyota.

6.2.1 Three key elements in the JIT philosophy

Element	Comment
Elimination of waste	Waste is defined as any activity that does not add value. Examples of waste identified by Toyota are: • **Overproduction**, ie producing more than is immediately needed by the next stage in the process. • **Waiting time**. Waiting time can be measured by labour efficiency and machine efficiency. • **Transport**. Moving items around a plant does not add value. Waste can be reduced by changing the layout of the factory floor so as to minimise the movement of materials. • **Waste in the process**. There could be waste in the process itself. Some activities might be carried out only because there are design defects in the product, or because of poor maintenance work. • **Inventory**. Inventory is wasteful. The target should be to eliminate all inventory by tackling the things that cause it to build up. • **Simplification of work**. An employee does not necessarily add value by working. Simplifying work is an important way of getting rid of waste in the system because it eliminates unnecessary actions. • **Defective goods** are quality waste. This is a significant cause of waste in many operations.
The involvement of all staff in the operation	JIT is a cultural issue, and its philosophy has to be embraced by everyone involved in the operation if it is to be applied successfully. Critics of JIT argue that management efforts to involve all staff can be patronising.
Continuous improvement	The goal is to meet demand immediately with perfect quality and no waste. In practice, this ideal is never achieved. However, the JIT philosophy is that an organisation should work towards the ideal, and continuous improvement is both possible and necessary. The Japanese term for continuous improvement is Kaizen.

6.2.2 Criticism of JIT

A **criticism of JIT**, in its extreme form, is that to have no inventory between any stages in the production process ignores the fact that some stages, by their very nature, could be less reliable than others. It could therefore be argued that some inventory should be held at these stages to provide a degree of protection to the rest of the operation.

6.3 JIT techniques

JIT is a **collection of management techniques**. Some of these relate to basic working practices.

(a)   **Work standards**. Work standards should be established and followed by everyone at all times.

(b)   **Flexibility in responsibilities**. The organisation should provide for the possibility of expanding the responsibilities of any individual to the extent of their capabilities. Grading structures and restrictive working practices should be eliminated as far as possible.

(c)   **Equality of all people working in the organisation**. Equality should exist and be visible. For example, there should be a single staff canteen.

(d) **Autonomy**. Authority should be delegated to the individuals directly responsible for the activities of the operation. Management should support people involved in production, not direct them.

(e) **Development of personnel**. Individual workers should be developed and trained.

(f) **Quality of working life**. The quality of working life should be improved through better work area facilities, job security and involvement of everyone in job-related decision making.

(g) **Creativity**. Employees should be encouraged to be creative in devising improvements to the way their work is done.

(h) **Use several small, simple production units**. Small machines can be moved around more easily, and so offer greater flexibility in a shop floor layout. The risk of making a bad and costly investment decision is reduced, because relatively simple small machines usually cost much less than sophisticated large machines.

(i) **Work floor layout and workflow**. Work can be laid out to promote the smooth flow of operations. Workflow is an important element in JIT, because the work needs to flow without interruption in order to avoid a build-up of inventory or unnecessary down-times.

(j) **Total productive maintenance (TPM)**. TPM seeks to eliminate unplanned breakdowns and the damage they cause to production and workflow. Staff operating on the production line are brought into the search for improvements in maintenance.

(k) **JIT purchasing**. With JIT purchasing, an organisation establishes a close relationship with trusted suppliers, and develops an arrangement with the supplier for being able to purchase materials only when they are needed for production. The supplier is required to have a flexible production system capable of responding immediately to purchase orders.

6.4 JIT planning and control

Holding inventories is one source of waste. Not having materials when they are needed is another. In other words, both having inventories in hand and having stock-outs is wasteful practice.

6.4.1 Kanban

Kanban is the Japanese word for **card** or **signal**. A kanban system controls the flow of materials between one stage in a process and the next. In its simple form, a card is used by an 'internal customer' as a signal to an 'internal supplier' that the customer now requires more parts or materials. The card will contain details of the parts or materials required.

The receipt of a card from an **internal customer** sets in motion the movement or production or supply of one unit of an item, or one standard container of the item.

6.5 JIT in service operations

The JIT philosophy can be applied to **service operations**. Whereas JIT in manufacturing seeks to eliminate inventories, JIT in service operations seeks to eliminate queues of customers.

Queues of customers are **wasteful** because:

(a) They waste customers' time
(b) Queues require space and this space does not add value
(c) Queuing lowers the customers' perception of the quality of the service

The application of JIT to a service operation calls for **multiskilling**, so that employees can be used more flexibly and moved from one type of work to another in response to workflow requirements.

A postal delivery service has delivery staff allocated to their own routes. However, there may be scenarios where, say, Route A is overloaded while Route B has a relatively small number of deliveries.

Rather than have items for Route A piling up at the sorting office, the person responsible for Route B could finish their route and then help out on Route A.

Teamwork and flexibility can be difficult to introduce because some people are more comfortable with clearly defined boundaries and responsibilities.

However, the customer is only interested in receiving a timely service.

Some service organisations use a **buffer operation** to minimise customer queuing or the likelihood of customer dissatisfaction during queuing.

For example, hairdressers often give clients a shampoo to reduce the impact of waiting for the stylist. Restaurants may have an area where guests can have a drink if no vacant tables are available immediately. Such facilities may even encourage guests to plan in a few drinks before dinner, thereby increasing the restaurant's revenues.

Question 8.2	Capacity management and JIT

Learning outcomes D2(viii)

Discuss why a level capacity strategy might be difficult for a firm wishing to adopt a just-in-time (JIT) philosophy.   **(5 marks)**

Section summary

Just-in-time is an approach to operations based on the idea that goods and services should be produced **only when they are needed**.

The key elements of JIT are **elimination of waste**, **the involvement of all staff in the operation** and **continuous improvement**.

Kanban is the Japanese word for **card** or **signal**. A kanban control system is a system for controlling the flow of materials between one stage in a process and the next.

JIT philosophy can be applied to **service operations**. Whereas JIT in manufacturing seeks to eliminate inventories, JIT in service operations seeks to **remove queues of customers**.

7 Production processes and technology

Introduction

Layout refers to how a workplace is physically arranged. **Flow** is the rate at which a product travels through a process. The modern production process takes advantage of a number of advances in **technology**.

We shall now consider how a **production process** or **workplace** can be optimised using **work study** and the impact on how it is laid out on the rate at which a product or service is created. There are a number of **technological advances** that can be used to increase the rate of product flow and efficiency of production.

7.1 Work study

Work study involves the examination of how production activities are carried out in order to seek efficiencies and improve the use of resources. It can be said to be based on the work of Taylor and his **scientific approach** to finding the '**one best way**' to do work. By organising work in the most efficient way employees become more productive and their salaries can be increased. Taylor believed that higher salaries increase employee motivation, so therefore the motivation of the workforce could be increased by improving work processes. The setting of performance standards of activities is also often an important part of work study.

A **work study process** often follows a set procedure, for example:

- **Select** the process for study and break it down into functions

- **Record** facts about the process

- **Review** the facts collected

- **Develop** a new process that makes more efficient use of resources (divide work between that of the managers, ie planning and supervision, and that of the workers, ie carrying out tasks)

- **Set** performance standards for new process

- **Implement** new method

- **Manage/maintain** new method, check that performance standards are being met (train workers and provide detailed work instructions)

Improvements to the use of resources might include:

- **Increased product throughput** due to less distance for materials to travel in the process
- **Increased quality** due to reduced number of steps in the process
- **Reduced labour costs** due to use of technology
- More **efficient use of materials** (more output for same input)
- **Reduced use of energy** such as electricity and heat

7.2 Layout and flow

Work study can be used to determine a process's **layout** and **flow**. Layout describes how the workplace or factory is **physically set up**, for example how people and machinery are positioned relative to each other. This has an impact on the **flow of materials** and products through the system and the rate at which completed products are produced.

7.2.1 Effect of layout on flow

The primary effect of layout is on the **distance** materials, people and information travel through the operation. **Long distances** increase throughput time and **reduce flow**. Therefore layouts are often designed to minimise distance travelled. A secondary effect is on **quality**. The more movements materials, people and information must flow through then the number of points where processes can go wrong increases. Therefore layouts often try to minimise the number of movements. A final consideration is the amount of **space** the layout takes up. Floor space has a **cost** attached to it and therefore small layouts are often preferred by businesses concerned about cost.

7.2.2 Types of layout

The following are **basic types of layout** that an organisation might adopt; however, in reality, the actual layout a particular business uses is likely to be a combination of one or more of them.

Fixed layout

In this layout the product being created remains in a fixed location and people, materials and other resources travel to it. This layout is often used when building large items of machinery such as planes and boats because it is easier or cheaper to move resources than the product.

Process layout

In this layout, products move between different processes depending on the work required. The processes are grouped together in clusters based on their function, and products flow through the processes using a variety of routes depending on their requirements. This layout is useful where the same process can be applied to a range of different products. It is a flexible approach but can become complex if product flows cross over or if products take irregular pathways. The diagram below illustrates how the production of different products can go through the same processes.

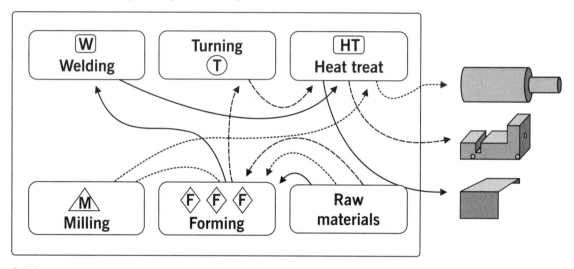

Cell layout

This layout type is also based on processes, but it attempts to reduce the complexity by using small clusters of cells that work on specific individual products. The rate that products flow through the process is determined by the needs of the customer. This layout requires the use of small, flexible machines that are of the right size to fit into a cell (a defined area where work takes place), rather than large, high-volume machines that produce single products. Rather than operate a single machine, workers in a cell layout are responsible for operating multiple pieces of equipment and, as a consequence, teams of workers become semi-autonomous. This form of layout increases the flexibility of an organisation to vary output to meet actual demand. The diagram below shows how the same process would be dealt with in a cell layout.

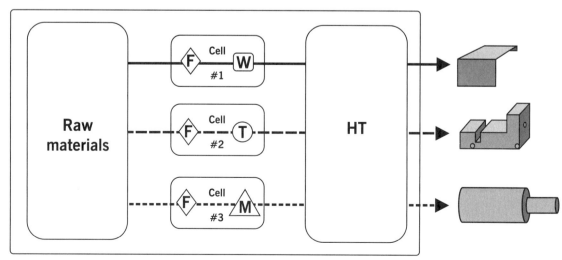

Product layout

The key feature of this layout is that resources are placed to maximise product flow. Each particular product or service will follow a path that is determined by its specific needs.

The order and location of resources are therefore determined by the product's processing requirements. Most traditional production lines in factories follow this layout.

7.3 Process technology

Technology has a role to play in **increasing the rate of flow** of a product and the **efficiency** of a process. Some examples include:

- **Computer Numerical Control** (CNC)
- **Robots**
- **Automated Guided Vehicles** (AGVs)
- **FMS**
- **Computer Integrated Manufacturing** – see Chapter 4
- **Decision Support Systems** – see Chapter 4
- **Expert systems** – see Chapter 4

7.3.1 Computer Numerical Control (CNC)

CNC is a system where the operations of a **machine tool** are controlled by a **computer program**. The program, rather than a human, determines the operation of the tool from inputs such as speed of material feed, speed and depth of cut, and other functions such as turning a spindle on or off, or applying heat to a process. These inputs are usually determined by converting a design produced by Computer Aided Design into numbers.

CNC is often used to operate lathes, drills, grinders, laser cutting and tube bending machines. CNC has also been applied to welding machines and electronic assembly of computer motherboards.

CNC allows **high speed** and **high accuracy** in manufacturing as well as being **flexible** (the program can be adapted to different processes). Human error is reduced and output is increased. However, such machines are **expensive**, may require a high degree of **maintenance** and require a **skilled programmer** to operate.

7.3.2 Robots

Robots have been used in manufacturing processes for some time and involve a **computer-controlled device**, such as a gripper or arm, to control a work process. Robots are commonly used in three ways.

Material-handling robots are used to transfer materials and products and to load or unload other machines. Such tasks are often quite simple, such as moving products from one conveyor to another. Others might be more complicated, such as stacking products in a particular way or feeding small objects into other machines.

Inspection robots can be used to ensure products meet certain quality standards. They are equipped with a sensor to determine whether the product is consistent with preset criteria.

Assembly robots are used to assemble sub-parts into a larger product. Certain assembly methods, such as tightening screws and nuts, are difficult for a robot to do due to a lack of dexterity, so they are most effectively used where parts are snapped together or other simple attachment methods are used.

7.3.3 Automated Guided Vehicles (AGVs)

AGVs are used to increase the speed and accuracy of transporting materials and products around a production system. They are autonomous and therefore require no human input other than developing their operational software. Some AGVs follow a **fixed path** and are useful for routine tasks, while others

have a form of artificial intelligence and can be told to **find their own route** to a particular location. These are useful for one-off tasks or roles where a number of destinations are possible.

7.3.4 FMS

We have already seen the use of **FMSs** in relation to capacity control. In terms of process control, an FMS is used to **synchronise** the operations of a number of **machine tools**. Each machine in the system processes a different part of the product and, because different products can be created from a range of standard parts, the system permits the production line to process more than one product type at a time.

This **flexibility** means that an FMS can **respond to changes** in product mix and production schedules as demand changes over time. The system can also deal with **new types of product** provided they can be created from the parts that the system is designed to process.

The use of FMSs is most appropriate when **demand** for the products is **low or medium** and is subject to **fluctuation** or where '**economies of scope**' make it economical to produce **small batches of a relatively wide range of products** using the same machines or production facilities. This is the opposite of traditional large-scale assembly lines with their emphasis on **economies of scale**. However, there is an enhanced cost involved with FMSs in order to benefit from the extra flexibility.

Section summary

The concepts of **layout** and **flow** are important in determining the most efficient and effective methods of production.

There are various forms of **process technology** that may increase the rate of flow and efficiency of a production process.

Chapter Summary

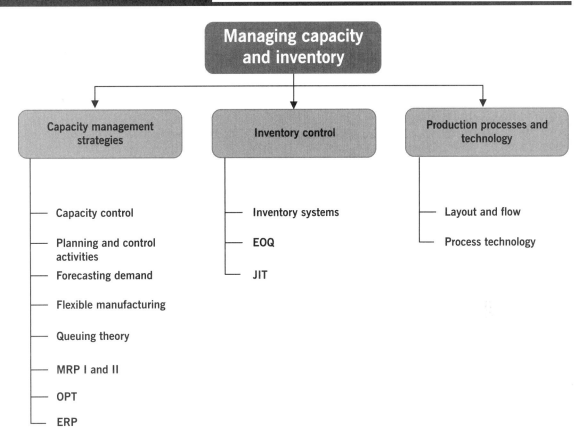

Managing capacity and inventory

- Capacity management strategies
  - Capacity control
  - Planning and control activities
  - Forecasting demand
  - Flexible manufacturing
  - Queuing theory
  - MRP I and II
  - OPT
  - ERP

- Inventory control
  - Inventory systems
  - EOQ
  - JIT

- Production processes and technology
  - Layout and flow
  - Process technology

Quick Quiz

1   An organisation is unable to produce enough output to fulfil demand. This is an example of:

      A   Overcapacity
      B   Undercapacity
      C   Demand-pull production
      D   Stock-outs

2   'A plan to maintain activity at a constant level over the planning period.' This statement defines:

      A   A chase demand plan
      B   A steady capacity plan
      C   A level capacity plan
      D   A demand management plan

3   Which inventory control level indicates that inventories are nearing a potentially wasteful level?

      A   Reorder level
      B   Minimum level
      C   Maximum level
      D   Economic Order Quantity

4   'A perpetual inventory system may be referred to as a continuous inventory system.'

      True   ☐

      False   ☐

5   The main feature of the Kanban system is that:

      A   Cards are used to signal that more items of inventory are required
      B   Stocks are ordered when they reach the minimum level
      C   Stock-outs are commonplace
      D   Holding costs are maximised

Answers to Quick Quiz

1　　B　　Undercapacity occurs where an organisation is unable to produce enough output to fulfil demand.

2　　C　　A level capacity plan seeks to maintain constant activity over a planning period.

3　　C　　The maximum level indicates that inventories are nearing a potentially wasteful level.

4　　True　A perpetual inventory system can also be referred to as a continuous inventory system.

5　　A　　The main feature of the Kanban system is that cards are used to signal that more items of inventory are required.

Answers to Questions

8.1 Capacity management

Service organisations differ from manufacturing organisations when considering capacity management in the following ways:

- **Production** and **consumption** occur at the same time. Inventories of services can't be built up in quieter times, which makes the balancing of capacity and demand more difficult.

- **Greater interaction**. The customer plays an active role in the delivery process. Customer service quality is integral to the customer experience.

- **Output** is **different each time**. Each customer service interaction is different in some way, eg different conversation, attitude. Achieving a consistently high level of output is more challenging.

- **Generally greater reliance on staff**. Service delivery depends on the people delivering the service. The 'mood' of staff on the front line shouldn't adversely impact on the customer experience.

- **Intangible output** makes **measuring** the **quality level** of output more difficult as there is no physical product to inspect. Obtaining feedback of customer satisfaction is important.

8.2 Capacity management and JIT

A **level capacity strategy** involves building up an inventory buffer to enable orders to be met from stores when demand exceeds capacity.

A **just-in-time (JIT)** approach involves producing goods when they are needed – eliminating the need to hold inventory.

The **build-up of inventory** required under a level capacity strategy contradicts the no-inventory approach required under JIT. Therefore, the two approaches are **incompatible**.

Under **JIT, production** is **driven** by **immediate demand**. The capacity management approach consistent with JIT is a **chase strategy** – which involves adjusting production levels to match demand. This would allow nil (or minimal) inventory, as required under JIT.

Now try these questions from the Practice Question Bank	**Number**
	36, 37, 38, 39, 40

MARKETING

Part E

THE MARKETING CONCEPT

In Part E of this Text we cover the **marketing** area of the syllabus.

We start this chapter with an explanation of marketing, the **marketing concept** and the **marketing environment** which organisations operate in.

The bulk of this, and the next, chapter concerns an organisation's **marketing activities**. We begin by looking at how marketing plans are **organised** and **managed** – and the role of marketing within an organisation.

The key activities that we are concerned with in this chapter are market research, segmentation, targeting and positioning – the **marketing strategy**.

Topic list	Learning outcomes	Syllabus references	Ability required
1 The marketing concept	E1(a)	E1(i)	application
2 The marketing environment	E1(a)	E1(ii)	application
3 Marketing and corporate strategy	E1(a)	E1(iii)	application
4 Marketing strategy	E2(a)	E2(i), E2(ii)	application

Chapter Overview

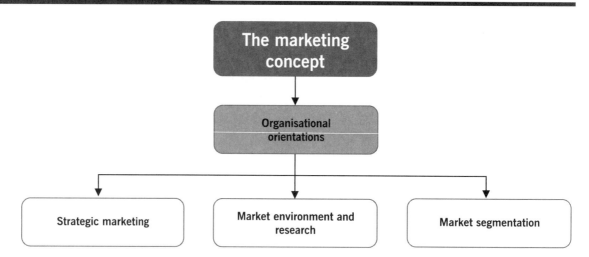

1 The marketing concept

Introduction

We begin our study of marketing by considering what marketing is and what adopting a marketing orientation means. We consider the **marketing concept** as a business philosophy.

Later in the chapter we look at marketing as a core element of an organisation's **corporate strategy** and the **processes** involved in creating a **marketing plan**.

1.1 What is marketing?

KEY TERM

MARKETING is the process of planning and executing the concepts of pricing, promotion and distribution of ideas, goods and services in order to create exchanges that satisfy individual and organisational objectives.

Another definition is given by the UK's **Chartered Institute of Marketing**: 'Marketing is the management process which identifies, anticipates and supplies customer requirements efficiently and profitably'.

This definition emphasises the **wide scope of marketing**, ranging from initial identification of customer needs by means of **research**, right through to eventual, **profitable satisfaction of those needs**. This definition is important because it stresses the importance of the customer and, more particularly, **customer satisfaction**.

Kotler, on the other hand, emphasised the importance of marketing as getting 'the **right product** or **service** to the customer, at the **right price**, at the **right time**'.

1.2 Products, goods and services: a note on terminology

A **product** is something that is offered to a market.

(a) Soap powder is an example of a **fast moving consumer good** (FMCG). It is a physical product that is bought often.

(b) **Durable goods** are purchased less often and tend to be more expensive than FMCGs. Televisions, cars and computers are examples of durable goods.

(c) A haircut is also a type of product – it is an example of a **service** product.

Broadly speaking, the word **product** can refer to physical **goods** or **services**. FMCGs and durable goods combined are sometimes referred to as **consumer goods**.

1.3 Strategic and tactical marketing

Marketing involves several types of activity and many types of decision. For many organisations, the products they provide are **fundamental** to their existence.

(a) **Strategic marketing** is tied in with corporate strategy, by identifying which products and markets the organisation wishes to operate in.

(b) **Tactical marketing** is focused more on the short term and on particular elements of the marketing mix.

Example: retail	
Strategic marketing	A fashion retailer decides to open in the capital city of a country it had not operated in before as it believes there are new, wealthy customers.
Tactical marketing	End of season sale to make way for new stock.

| Question 9.1 | Strategic and tactical marketing |

Learning outcome E1(i)

Distinguish between strategic and tactical marketing, and provide an example.   **(4 marks)**

1.4 Exchanges

The role of marketing is to **identify**, **anticipate** and **supply satisfactions** to **customers** in order to facilitate mutually beneficial exchanges.

Mutually beneficial exchanges

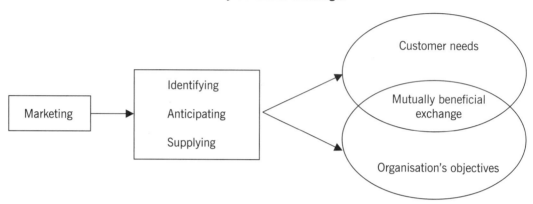

1.5 The marketing concept and a marketing orientation

The **marketing concept** and **marketing orientation** are two interrelated terms. The definitions that follow are from Brassington and Pettit (2000).

Marketing concept	Marketing orientation
A philosophy of business, permeating the whole organisation, that holds that the key to organisational success is meeting customers' needs more effectively and more closely than competitors.	An approach to business that centres its activities on satisfying the needs and wants of its customers.
= a belief system	= actual practices

1.6 The marketing concept

The **marketing concept** is a belief system. A belief system can be incorporated into the culture of the organisation. Culture involves beliefs and patterns of behaviour.

The organisation as a whole can claim to be '**customer orientated**'. Many organisations refer to customer satisfaction in their statements of corporate purpose (mission statements). But official claims to be customer orientated are often just claims with little basis in fact.

As part of becoming properly 'customer orientated', organisations need to **seek out gaps in the market** where the organisation or its competitors fail to meet customer demand. They should then produce appropriate products.

1.6.1 The marketing concept in practice

Even though the marketing concept, with its attempt to match goods to consumer needs, is widely accepted, most organisations will still require salespeople. The sales team's effort will be more successful if products and services meet market needs.

A **market-led approach** will make what is on sale more appealing to customers. Salespeople will be able to devote a greater proportion of their time to more productive activities such as developing leads, providing better customer service and identifying changes in customer requirements.

All good **sales presentations** focus **on the benefits that customers will receive** from the company's product or service.

1.7 Marketing orientation (or market orientation) and other orientations

The marketing concept and marketing orientation are often compared to other '**orientations**' which are briefly described below.

1.7.1 Production orientation

Under a **production orientation**, management believe that success is achieved through producing goods or services of optimum quality as cost efficiently as possible. The major task of management is to pursue improved production and distribution efficiency.

It assumes that customers will want to buy products that have been produced efficiently.

The comparison between a **marketing orientation** built around the **customer** and an orientation built around **production** is illustrated in the following diagram.

Comparison of marketing orientation with production orientation

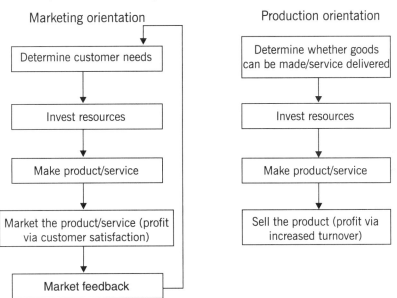

Perhaps the most well-known example of **production orientation** is the **Model T Ford**, one of the earliest motor cars to be produced for the mass market. Henry Ford famously said that Ford's customers could have the (mass-produced) Model T in any colour, so long as it was black.

1.7.2 Sales orientation

Under a sales orientation, the tendency is to make the product and then **actively** and perhaps aggressively **sell it**. Underlying this philosophy is a belief that a good sales force can sell just about anything to anybody.

Selling is preoccupied with the seller's need to convert their product into **cash**. **Marketing** is concerned with **satisfying the needs of the customer** by means of the product and the whole cluster of things associated with creating, delivering and finally consuming it.

1.7.3 Product orientation

Product-orientated organisations focus on **product development**, for example the introduction of new product features. This approach is based on the belief that a more advanced product or one with more features will be perceived as superior.

1.8 The potential impact of a marketing orientation

The marketing concept suggests that companies should focus on customer needs. The organisation needs to interpret customer needs and then produce products and services that meet them at a price that customers accept. Do this and, in theory at least, minimal sales effort will be needed.

CASE STUDY

Customers of banking services generally have expectations that their accounts will be updated efficiently and effectively, over a period of time, so that they have access to funds. They may also have other needs.

(a)   **Traditional 'Western' banking**

Banks like to offer other products to their customers, so that a customer with a current account may also open a savings account. The bank is able to use the money to lend, at higher interest rates, to other customers, thereby earning a profit. Competition between banks is often based on interest rates.

(b)   **'Islamic' banking**

The classic banking model is held by some Muslims to contradict certain tenets of Islam (such as the payment of interest). Many banks are now able to structure lending transactions in a fashion that is acceptable to Islam.

In both cases (a) and (b) the bank is providing a service and, over the long term, engaging in a relationship with its customers.

Question 9.2	Product and production orientation

Learning outcome E1(i)

Compare and contrast product-orientated organisations and production-orientated organisations.

(4 marks)

1.9 Push vs pull marketing

Traditionally, marketing activities focus on **pushing** goods out to resellers and consumers. Product promotion is by the final seller in the value chain.

A **'pull' approach**, on the other hand, aims to produce a product that consumer demand will **pull** into retail outlets. Product promotion is shared between the manufacturer and final seller.

1.10 The marketing concept: summary

To conclude, **marketing has three dimensions**:

(a)   It is a **culture**. The marketing concept is to focus on consumer needs.

(b)   It involves **strategy**. A company must select the markets it intends to sell to and the products or services it will sell. These selections are strategic decisions.

(c)   It involves **tactics**. Marketing tactics can be considered as the 7Ps of the marketing mix.

Exam skills

The syllabus refers to the marketing concept as a business philosophy. Therefore, you may be tested on whether you understand that 'marketing' means more than the traditional view of 'advertising' and 'public relations'.

Section summary

Marketing is the process of planning and executing the concepts of pricing, promotion and distribution of ideas, goods and services in order to create exchanges that satisfy individual and organisational objectives.

The **marketing concept** is a business philosophy which attempts to **match goods to consumer needs**.

A **production orientation** may be defined as the management view that success is achieved through producing goods or services of optimum quality and cost.

Under a **sales orientation**, the tendency is to make the product and then actively and aggressively sell it.

Product-orientated organisations focus on product development.

2 The marketing environment

Introduction

All organisations **exist in**, **interact with** and are **influenced by factors** in their **environment**. It is important for organisations to **identify** and **monitor** these factors as they often have a direct effect on the performance of the business.

The marketing environment consists of three levels.

The **macro environment** includes all factors that can influence the organisation, such as the PESTEL factors explained in the next section. The macro environment is generally out of the organisation's control.

The **micro environment** is comprised of factors specifically related to the organisation, such as the organisation's customers and suppliers. The organisation can have some influence over these factors.

The **internal environment** refers to factors within the organisation, such as its assets, employees and finance. These factors are able to be controlled by the organisation.

2.1 PESTEL factors

Factors in the environment that influence marketing can be classified using the PESTEL framework, as shown below.

PESTEL factors					
Political	Economic	Social/Cultural	Technological	Ecological	Legal

These factors influence the organisation in many ways. However, in marketing, we are particularly interested in how they impact on **markets** and **customers**.

Environment and markets

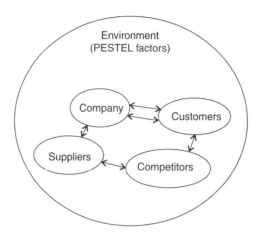

For example, **political factors** may influence the market for financial services by encouraging customers to take out certain types of investment. **Economic factors** may influence customers' buying power. The following table shows the type of impact on customers.

Factor	Impact on customers
Political factors • Changes in government and/or changes in government policy • Political instability could lead to warfare or civil unrest	This can affect consumers' confidence in the future, their spending power or their rights. Clearly this fundamentally affects normal business. Government policy could give consumers more rights in relation to business.
Economic factors These include overall rate of economic growth, inflation, interest rates, exchange rates, and consumers' propensity to save.	Ultimately, this determines consumers' effective demand for products and services. Uncertainty about the future may lead to more saving and less spending. General prosperity may lead to more spending on luxury items.
Social/cultural factors Demography relates to the composition of the population, where people live, and social classification. Culture relates to people's values and beliefs. There may be many subgroups (subcultures) within a culture. Johnson and Scholes suggest the following social and cultural factors should be considered: • Population demographics • Distribution of income between parts of the country and target markets • Social classes and mobility between them • Lifestyle trends and social values • The level of consumerism in society • Levels of education, basic to degree or beyond	Demographic factors suggest the size and purchasing power of customer groups. Some products may indicate high status. Culture has significant consequences for the acceptability of marketing communications messages, attitudes to products (eg alcoholic drinks), attitudes towards purchasing, and so on.

Factor	Impact on customers
Technological factors • New products • New processes • New working methods •. New communication methods • New ways of distribution	Companies may be able to change the products or services they offer, but they can also communicate in different ways. Customers may have different attitudes to innovation, some preferring to stay with tried and tested products or patterns of behaviour.
Ecological factors • Long-term trends in the global physical environment, such as climate change • Natural climatic impacts, such as flooding and earthquakes • As well as considering the physical environment, we should consider customers' attitudes to it, as a developing cultural factor with an influence on political decision making.	The effect on customers is twofold. Changing attitudes enable businesses to satisfy new needs with new products, for example organic vegetables. Natural disasters are a business opportunity for insurance companies, but also those supplying aid and construction companies.
Legal factors • The law affects ways of doing business. • Specific laws exist for particular areas of economic activity.	• Do legislation and judicial decisions increase the customer's rights? • Particular classes of customer may be protected in some cases (eg funeral services). • Are customers increasingly willing and able to take legal action?

Exam skills

Exam questions may test the environment an organisation operates in. The PESTEL factors would be relevant in this case.

2.2 SWOT analysis

Another method of environmental analysis looks at an organisation's internal **strengths** and **weaknesses** as well as external **opportunities** and **threats**. This is known as **SWOT** analysis.

2.2.1 Internal appraisal: strengths and weaknesses

An **internal appraisal** will identify:

(a)   The areas of the organisation that have **strengths** that should be exploited by suitable strategies
(b)   The areas of the organisation that have **weaknesses** which need strategies to improve them

The strengths and weaknesses analysis is intended to shape the organisation's approach to the external world. For instance, the identification of shortcomings in products could lead to a programme of product development.

2.2.2 External appraisal: opportunities and threats

The **external appraisal** identifies **opportunities** that can be exploited by the organisation's strengths and also anticipates environmental **threats** against which the company must protect itself.

Opportunities

(a) What opportunities exist in the business environment?
(b) What is their inherent profit-making potential?
(c) Can the organisation exploit the worthwhile opportunities?
(d) What is the comparative capability profile of competitors?
(e) What is the company's comparative performance potential in this field of opportunity?

Threats

(a) What threats might arise to the company or its business environment?
(b) How will competitors be affected?
(c) How will the company be affected?

2.2.3 Using a SWOT analysis

The SWOT analysis can be used in one of two ways:

(a) The organisation can develop **resource-based strategies** which enable the organisation to extend the use of its strengths. This is common in retailing, for example, as supermarket chains extend their own brands from food to other areas.

(b) The business can develop **positioning-based strategies** – in other words, identifying what opportunities are available and what the firm has to do to exploit them.

Section summary

An organisation's **marketing environment** can be analysed into **political**, **economic**, **social**, **technological**, **ecological** and **legal factors** (PESTEL).

3 Marketing and corporate strategy

Introduction

In this section we look at how an organisation develops and implements a **marketing plan**. The process begins by considering what the overall **corporate strategy** is – the marketing plan is driven by the overall corporate strategy.

Later in the chapter we explain the **structure of a marketing plan**.

3.1 Corporate and marketing strategies

The process of corporate planning and the relationship with marketing strategy is shown in the following table.

	Corporate	Marketing
Set objectives	For the organisation as a whole: eg increase profits by X%	For products and market: eg increase market share by X%; increase turnover.
Internal appraisal (strengths and weaknesses)	Review the effectiveness of the different aspects of the organisation	Conduct a marketing audit. A review of marketing activities. Does the organisation have a marketing orientation?

	Corporate	Marketing
External appraisal (opportunities and threats)	Review political, economic, social, technological, ecological factors impacting on the whole organisation	Review environmental factors as they affect customers, products and markets
Gaps	There may be a gap between desired objectives and forecast objectives. How should the gap be closed?	The company may be doing less well in particular markets than it ought to. Marketing will be focused on growth.
Strategy	Develop strategies to fill the gap: eg diversifying, entering new markets	A marketing strategy is a plan to achieve the organisation's objectives by specifying: • Resources to be allocated to marketing • How those resources should be used In the context of applying the marketing concept, a marketing strategy would: • Identify target markets and customer needs in those markets • Plan products which will satisfy the needs of those markets • Organise marketing resources, so as to match products with customers
Implementation	Implementation is delegated to departments of the business	The plans must be put into action, eg advertising space must be bought.
Control	Results are reviewed and the planning process starts again	Has the organisation achieved its market share objectives?

3.2 The marketing plan

The **marketing plan** must be **consistent** with the **corporate strategy**. It might take the following form (based on Kotler).

Section	Content
The executive summary	This is the finalised planning document with a summary of the main goals and recommendations in the plan.
Situation analysis	This consists of a SWOT analysis and forecasts.
Objectives and goals	What the organisation is hoping to achieve, or needs to achieve, perhaps in terms of market share or 'bottom line' profits and returns. Objectives should be SMART (Specific, Measurable, Achievable, Realistic and Time-bound).
Marketing strategy	This considers the selection of target markets, the marketing mix and marketing expenditure levels, as described in the preceding table.
Strategic marketing plan	• Three to five or more years long • Defines scope of product and market activities • Aims to match the activities of the organisation to its distinctive competences

Section	Content
Tactical marketing plan	• One-year time horizon • Generally based on existing products and markets • Concerned with marketing mix issues

Action plan	This sets out how the strategies are to be achieved.
	
	• Marketing mix strategy
	   – Product – People
	   – Price – Processes
	   – Place (distribution) – Physical evidence
	   – Promotion (advertising etc)
	
	• The mix strategy may vary for each segment.

Budgets	These are developed from the action programme.
Controls	These will be set up to monitor the progress of the plan and the budget.

To summarise, the following diagram shows how **marketing planning** fits into the corporate plan.

Marketing and corporate planning

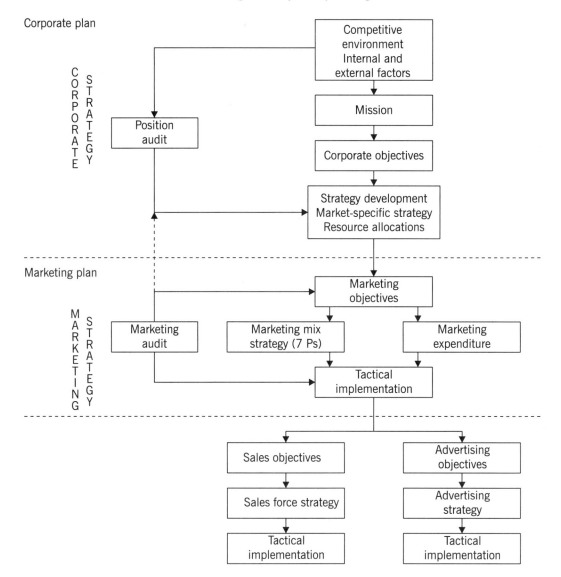

Section summary

An organisation's **marketing plan** is **driven by** and must therefore be **consistent** with its **corporate strategy**.

4 Marketing strategy

Introduction

In this section we look at **marketing strategy** – in other words, how the organisation decides which markets to attack and how to position itself within each market. The **key activities** in this process are **market research**, **market segmentation**, **targeting** and **positioning**.

Market research is the initial stage in which the organisation obtains data about its customers and their needs.

A **market segment** is a group of customers with similar characteristics who can be **targeted** with the same **marketing mix**. Segmentation bases can include **objective classifications** (eg age) as well as more **subjective approaches** such as lifestyle and attitudes.

Having analysed the **attractiveness of a segment**, the organisation chooses one or more **target markets**.

Market positioning is the act of designing the company's offer and image so that it occupies a **distinct** and **valued place** in the **target** customer's mind.

4.1 Market research

KEY TERM

MARKET RESEARCH is the process of gathering, recording, analysing and reporting data and information relating to the company's market, customers and competitors.

Typically, market research is used to determine the **characteristics of markets**, suggest **opportunities for products** and **selling approaches** and to suggest **segments**.

The research can relate to:

(a) **Existing products** and services
(b) **New products** and services

4.1.1 A market research plan

Market research plans can be analysed into **five steps**.

Defining the problem

Example

- Explaining a fall in sales
- Investigating potential demand for a new product
- Investigating attitudes to the brand
- Investigating what matters most to consumers

Developing the hypotheses to be tested, and the purpose of the research

Example

In some studies, the researchers have a particular question they want to test. The purpose of some research may be to see if it is worth doing further research.

STEP 3 Collecting data

Example

A variety of approaches are used, such as surveys and questionnaires.

 STEP 4 Analyse and interpret the data

Example

The type of analysis depends on the type of research. Not all research is quantitative with statistical validity. The emphasis on statistical assumptions is important – statistics can be misunderstood and misused.

 STEP 5 Report the findings

Example

The results of the research are written up and presented in a report to the client.

4.1.2 Quantitative vs qualitative data

KEY POINTS

Quantitative data enables measurement. The purpose is to measure the response of a sample of consumers, on the assumption that measurable conclusions can be drawn from it. An example could be a survey of structured questionnaires sent out to a sample of a population.

Qualitative data is not measurable, but it is useful to get people to say what they feel and think, as opposed to giving relatively simple answers to unstructured questions.

4.1.3 Secondary vs primary data

KEY POINT

Secondary data may be generated by sources internal or external to the organisation. It is termed secondary because its intended use is not the specific research the organisation is using it for. Secondary data is usually gathered before primary data as it is often cheaper to collect and is used to guide the primary research. It is not normally sufficient for research purposes by itself.

Secondary data	
Source	**Uses**
Internal • From existing information systems • Accounting data • Customer databases • Data produced by other departments (eg complaints) **External** • Published statistics from government, professional/ trade bodies • Review of journals • Research already collected by market research agencies can be purchased, eg Nielsen Index on grocery chains and random surveys	• Before primary research to give guidance • Instead of expensive primary research – some questions may already be answered • Some information can only be acquired via secondary data • Where primary research is not possible

Primary data may be collected from sources internal or external to the organisation and may be qualitative or quantitative in nature. Primary data is collected for a specific research purpose.

Primary data	
Data collection method	**Comment**
Questionnaires, such as the following. • Post surveys • Telephone • In street, via market researchers • Over the internet • At home • In hotels • In shops	A number of precise questions requiring precise responses. Ensuring questions are free of ambiguity is absolutely vital. Survey must be relevant to the data required. Questionnaires often move from the general to the specific. The interviewer always has to locate suitable respondents. A danger with postal questionnaires is that the response is self-selected.
Experiment	The researcher may set up artificial surroundings or may test a product in real surroundings (eg asking software purchasers to try out Beta versions of certain packages).
Observation	People can be observed using a product.
Unstructured interviews	There is no structure to what is effectively a conversation but the interviewer may have a checklist of topics to be covered.
Depth interviews	The aim is to explore attitudes and motives for behaviour that may not be conscious. If conducted properly, respondents can be encouraged to say what they feel.
Projective techniques	People often say that they will act in a different way than they actually behave. Researchers have borrowed methods from psychologists, and seek to uncover unconscious motives. Examples include: • Inkblot tests ('What images do you see in this inkblot?') • Word association • Thematic apperception tests ('What is going on in this picture?')
Focus groups	Focus groups usually consist of eight to ten respondents and an interviewer taking the role of group moderator. The group moderator introduces topics for discussion and intervenes as necessary to encourage respondents or to direct discussions if they threaten to wander too far off the point. The moderator will also need to control any powerful personalities and prevent them from dominating the group.

4.2 Forecasting demand

Forecasting demand for new products can be difficult. A **forecast** could be developed based on a range of information and mathematical techniques. Possible types of data and information are explained below.

4.2.1 Current demand

An estimate of demand as it would be 'today' could involve considering a number of factors, such as:

- Total market potential
- Area market potential (geographical)
- Total industry sales
- Relative market shares

4.2.2 Forecasting future demand

Preparing a sales (income) or demand forecast usually involves five stages:

 Prepare a **macroeconomic forecast** – what will happen to overall economic activity in the relevant economies in which a product is to be sold.

 Prepare an **industry sales forecast** – what will happen to overall sales in an industry based on the issues that influence the macroeconomic forecast.

 Prepare a **company sales forecast** – based on what management expect to happen to the company's market share.

 Prepare a **demand forecast** – based on three types of information:

- What customers are currently doing in the market (industry sales data, company sales data)

- Customer intentions in relation to buying products (survey of buyers' intentions, market tests, sales force opinions, expert opinions)

- What customers have done in the past in the market (past-sales analysis)

 Prepare an **income forecast** – based on the information created in Steps 1–4. Income is dependent on forecasted demand and prices.

4.2.3 Survey of buyers' intentions

There are many market research agencies that undertake surveys of **customer intentions** and sell this information on. The value of a customer intention survey increases when there is a relatively small number of customers, the cost of reaching them is small, and they have clear intentions.

4.2.4 Market tests

Instead of simply asking customers about their intentions, marketers may conduct **market tests**. Tests may be particularly useful when **finalising product design**. Alternative designs may be evaluated, with different features.

4.2.5 Sales force opinions

Another option is to use opinions from members of the **sales force** to forecast sales. This may be difficult if the product is new, although salespeople may be able to get a feel for the market by talking with clients and potential clients.

Unfortunately, **salespeople may try to forecast low sales** if these forecasts will form the basis of their future sales targets. On the other hand, **marketing executives** may provide **overoptimistic forecasts** to help gain approval for the project or motivate the sales force.

4.2.6 Expert opinions

Expert opinion studies are widely used for forecasting marketing problems. For example, forecasts may be obtained from **industry experts**, **distributors** or **consultancies**. Sometimes independent forecasts from more than one expert source may be combined to produce what should be a more realistic forecast.

4.2.7 Past-sales analysis

Many businesses use past sales as a starting point for future sales forecasts. Figures may then be processed through a model (for example a spreadsheet) that aims to take into account various factors, such as:

- Trends: are sales growing, remaining steady ('flat-lining') or in decline?
- Seasonal or cyclical factors that occur in a regular pattern
- Likely competitor activity
- Sales and marketing campaigns

4.2.8 Sales potential

The amount of sales a product can achieve is known as **sales potential**. Factors influencing sales potential include:

- How '**essential**' the product is to consumers
- The **overall size** of the **market**
- The **level of competition** in the market
- Whether consumers may **delay purchasing** the product (non-essential luxury items)
- **Price** – high prices may restrict the market
- **Promotional expenditure** – investment in promotion may broaden the market

4.3 Market segmentation

A **market** is not a single homogeneous group of customers wanting an identical product. Markets consist of **potential buyers** with **different needs** and **different buying behaviour**.

KEY TERM

MARKET SEGMENTATION may be defined as the subdividing of a market into distinct and increasingly homogeneous subgroups of customers, where any subgroup can conceivably be selected as a target market to be met with a distinct marketing mix.

Although the total market consists of widely different groups of consumers, each group consists of people (or organisations) with **common needs and preferences**, who perhaps react to 'market stimuli' in much the same way. Each market segment can become a **target market for an organisation**, and would require a unique marketing mix if the organisation is to exploit it successfully. The organisation can then **position its offer** to account for the roles of each segment.

4.3.1 The bases for segmentation

There are many different **bases for segmentation**. One basis will not be appropriate in every market, and sometimes two or more bases might be valid at the same time. One **segmentation variable** might be 'superior' to another in a hierarchy of variables.

Simple segmentation could be on one of the bases below.

- Demographic (geographical area, age, gender, family life cycle stage – see below)

- Situational and end use (products being bought at different times or for different uses such as for work or leisure)

- Level of income

- Occupation

- Education

- Religion

- Ethnicity

- Nationality

- Socioeconomic (social class – A Upper middle class, B Middle class, C1 Lower middle class, C2 Working class, D subsistence)

- Buyer behaviour (buying for a particular occasion, how frequently an individual makes a purchase and how loyal a customer they are)

- Psychological (lifestyle – see below)

Demographical segmentation considers a number of factors such as gender and stage in family life cycle. For example, individuals and families may be categorised as **bachelor**, **newly married couple**, **full nest (i, ii and iii)** and **empty nest (i and ii)**.

Bachelors (unmarried males) are considered to be the most financially well-off and may be frequent purchasers of cars, holidays and expensive kitchen equipment.

Newly married couples still have some disposable income but their priorities change.

The **full nest** category describes most families. Those in the full nest category are often the least financially well-off as much of the family income is spent on housing and raising children. Categories ii and iii describe families becoming better off as the children age and perhaps both partners work. As incomes rise, the products purchased become less practical and more luxury.

The final category of **empty nest** describes two possible situations in later life. Those in the empty nest i category have a good level of income and can spend on expensive goods and holidays. Empty nest ii describes people with very little disposable income, for example those living on just the state pension and struggling to get by. Purchases are limited to necessities such as food and medicines.

Geo-demographic segmentation combines demographics and geography to provide segmentation at a highly localised level.

Lifestyle segmentation deals with the **person** as opposed to the product and attempts to discover the particular lifestyle patterns of customers. Lifestyle refers to 'distinctive ways of living adopted by particular communities or subsections of society'. It involves combining a number of behavioural factors such as motivation, personality and culture.

One simple example generalises **lifestyle** in terms of **four categories**, as follows.

Lifestyle categories	
Upwardly mobile, ambitious	These individuals seek a better and more affluent lifestyle, principally through better paid and more interesting work, and a higher material standard of living. A customer with such a lifestyle will be prepared to try new products.
Traditional and sociable	Here, compliance and conformity to group norms bring social approval and reassurance to the individual. Purchasing patterns will therefore be 'conformist'.
Security and status seeking	This group stresses 'safety' and 'ego-defensive' needs. This lifestyle links status, income and security. It encourages the purchase of strong and well-known products and brands, and emphasises those products and services which confer status and make life as secure and predictable as possible. Products that are well established and familiar inspire more confidence than new products, which will be resisted.
Hedonistic preference	This lifestyle places emphasis on 'enjoying life now' and the immediate satisfaction of wants and needs. Little thought is given to the future.

4.3.2 Segment validity

A market segment will only **be valid if it is worth designing and developing a unique marketing mix** for it.

A general rule suggested by Kotler is that a valid segment must be **substantial**, **measurable** and **accessible**. The following questions are commonly asked to decide whether or not the segment can be used for developing marketing plans.

Criteria	Comment
Can the segment be measured?	It might be possible to conceive a market segment, but it is not necessarily easy to measure it. For example, with a segment based on people with a conservative outlook to life, can conservatism of outlook be measured by market research?
Is the segment big enough?	There has to be a large enough potential market to be profitable.
Can the segment be reached?	There has to be a way of getting to the potential customers via the organisation's promotion and distribution channels.
Do segments respond differently?	If two or more segments are identified by planners, but each segment responds in the same way to a marketing mix, the segments are effectively one and the same. Consequently there is no point in distinguishing them from each other.
Can the segment be reached profitably?	Do the identified customer needs cost less to satisfy than the revenue they earn?
Is the segment suitably stable?	The stability of the segment is important if the organisation is to commit huge production and marketing resources to serve it. The organisation does not want the segment to 'disappear' next year. Of course, this may not matter in some industries.

4.3.3 Segment attractiveness

A segment might be valid and potentially profitable, but is it potentially **attractive**? Segments which are most attractive will be those whose needs can be met by building on the company's strengths and where forecasts for demand, sales profitability and **growth** are favourable.

4.3.4 Industrial segmentation

Industrial and commercial customers may also be **segmented**. Typical bases used for **industrial segmentation** include:

- Location – geographical area

- Ordering characteristics – such as frequency of orders and average order size

- Company characteristics – type of business, the market they operate in, and their size

- Expectations – what benefit does the company expect to get out of the product? Ie reliability, quality, serviceability, support and safety

4.3.5 Benefits of market segmentation

The organisation may be able to identify **new marketing opportunities** because it will have a better understanding of customer needs in each segment, with the possibility of spotting further subgroups.

Specialists can be used for each of the organisation's major segments. For example, small business counsellors can be employed by banks to deal effectively with small organisations. A computer consultancy can have specialist sales staff for, say, shops, manufacturers, service industries and local government authorities. This builds competences and establishes effective marketing systems.

The **total marketing budget** can be allocated proportionately to each segment and the likely return from each segment. This optimises return on investment.

The organisation can **make small adjustments** to the product and service offerings and to the promotional aspects for each segment. This again promotes efficient use of resources.

The organisation can try to **dominate particular segments**, therefore gaining competitive advantage. Advantages created may function synergistically, promoting improved competitive ability – in other words, the outcome is more than the sum of its parts.

The **product range** can more closely reflect differences in customer needs. Marketing relies on responsiveness to the consumer. When this is improved, benefits can flow.

| Question 9.3 | Market segmentation |

Learning outcome E2(ii)

Identify five benefits that a company may obtain through market segmentation.   **(5 marks)**

4.4 Competitor analysis

It is important for the organisation to consider any **competitors** before entering a market. Potential target markets should be researched and competitors identified. Further research into the competitors should be undertaken, for example to find out their **strategies** and how they apply the **marketing mix**. This will prevent the business from entering a market where the competition is too strong.

4.5 Target markets

Limited resources, competition and large markets make it ineffective and inappropriate for companies to sell to the entire market – that is, every market segment. For the sake of efficiency they must select target markets. A **target market** is a market or segment selected for special attention by an organisation (possibly served with a distinct marketing mix). The management of a company may choose one of the following policy options.

Marketing strategy	Comment	Alignment to competitive strategy
Mass (or undifferentiated) marketing	This policy is to produce a single product and hope to get as many customers as possible to buy it – segmentation is ignored entirely.	The mass (or undifferentiated) marketing approach can be pursued by cost leaders or companies pursuing a differentiation strategy with a single market.
Concentrated marketing	The company attempts to produce the ideal product for a single segment of the market (for example, Rolls-Royce cars). The disadvantage of concentrated marketing is the business risk of relying on a single segment of a single market.	Concentrated marketing is effectively a focus strategy, whether by cost or differentiation.
Differentiated marketing	The company markets several product versions, each aimed at a different market segment. The disadvantage of differentiated marketing is the additional costs of marketing and production. When the costs of further differentiation of the market exceed the benefits from further segmentation and target marketing, an organisation is said to have 'overdifferentiated'.	Differentiated marketing is effectively a multi-focus strategy, with a company pursuing different opportunities in different segments.

4.6 Positioning

Market position refers to how customers perceive a brand or product relative to other brands or products. When positioning their products and services, most organisations want to achieve a clear, unique and positive position, such as the cheapest supermarket or highest-quality vehicle manufacturer.

(a)   Many products are, in fact, very similar, and the key issue is to make them distinct in the customer's mind.

(b)   Few products occupy a market space on their own. Inevitably they will be positioned in relation to competing products and companies.

(c)   People remember 'number 1', so the product should be positioned as 'number 1' in relation to a positioning variable.

    (i)   Attributes (eg size)
    (ii)   Benefits (eg convenience)
    (iii)   Use/application (ease of use; accessibility)
    (iv)   User (the sort of person the product is meant to appeal to)
    (v)   Product category (consciously differentiated from competition)
    (vi)   Image
    (vii)   Quality/price (premium price)

4.7 Developments in market segmentation and product positioning

Approaches to **market segmentation** and **product positioning** are continually changing. Here are a few developments in recent years.

Development	Comment
There is a growing awareness that consumers should be segmented according to the purpose of the segmentation.	For example, the same customers of a retail bank can be segmented by their account profile, for the purpose of product cross-selling, by their attitudes to risk taking for the purpose of delivering advertising messages and by socioeconomic type for the purpose of selecting a marketing medium.
There is growing interest in customer database analysis and the idea of 'letting the data speak for itself'.	Customer information on a database is analysed in order to identify segments or patterns of behaviour. This technique, known as 'data mining', is likely to increase in significance as e-commerce grows in popularity.
There is growing emphasis on segmentation by 'soft' data.	Consumer attitudes and needs and lifestyles (as distinct from 'hard data' such as age, lifestyle and socioeconomic grouping).
There is a growing use of sub-segmentation or 'hybrid segmentation' methods.	Consumers within a particular segment can be subdivided into different segments, and each sub-segment is targeted in a different way.
Computer models are used.	These will discover suitable additions to a product line that will appeal to a separately distinguished market segment.

4.8 The Ansoff matrix

Ansoff (1987) devised a matrix showing **possible strategies for products and markets**.

Ansoff's competitive strategies (Ansoff matrix)

Products

		Existing	New
Markets	**Existing**	Market Penetration 1	Product Development 4
	New	Market Development 2	Diversification 16

The numbers in the quadrants are an approximate indication of the **risk** attached to each strategy. Diversification is the riskiest.

(a) **Market penetration** involves increasing sales of the **existing products in existing markets**.

(b) **Market development** entails **expansion into new markets using existing products**.

(c) **Product development** involves the redesign or repositioning of existing products or the introduction of completely new ones in order to appeal to existing markets.

(d) **Diversification** involves producing new products for new markets. It is much more risky than the other three because the organisation is moving into areas in which it has little or no experience.

Question 9.4	Marketing strategy

Learning outcome E2(ii)

Identify and explain Ansoff's possible strategies for products and markets as shown in his matrix.

(4 marks)

4.9 Porter's potential strategies

Porter identified four potential positioning strategies.

	Low cost	High cost
Broad target	Cost leadership	Differentiation
Narrow target	Cost focus	Differentiation focus

You should already understand the terms **cost leadership** and **differentiation**. Porter suggests that these strategies can be applied in a broad or narrow range of the market.

4.10 Perceptual mapping

Perceptual mapping involves using customer perceptions of brands to map out how the market is currently serviced. Any gaps in the market could be used by an organisation to deploy new products or reposition existing ones.

Two **critical success factors** (such as price and quality) are identified and the current market is mapped.

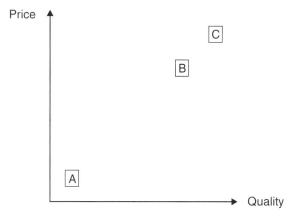

A, B and C are products in the market. Product A is a budget model, B is a high-quality model and C is a bespoke model.

The gap between A and B suggests a gap in the market for a low- to mid-range product in terms of price and quality.

Section summary

Market research is used to determine the **characteristics of markets**, to suggest **opportunities for products** and **selling approaches** and to **suggest segments**.

Market research information can help **forecast future sales levels**.

Market segmentation involves subdividing a market into distinct and increasingly homogeneous subgroups of customers which may be selected as a **target market** to be met with a distinct marketing mix.

Market position refers to how customers perceive a brand or product relative to other brands or products.

Market penetration involves increasing sales of **existing products in existing markets**.

Market development entails expansion into **new markets** with **existing products**.

Product development involves the redesign or repositioning of existing products or the introduction of completely new ones in order to appeal to existing markets.

Diversification involves producing **new products** for **new markets**.

Chapter Summary

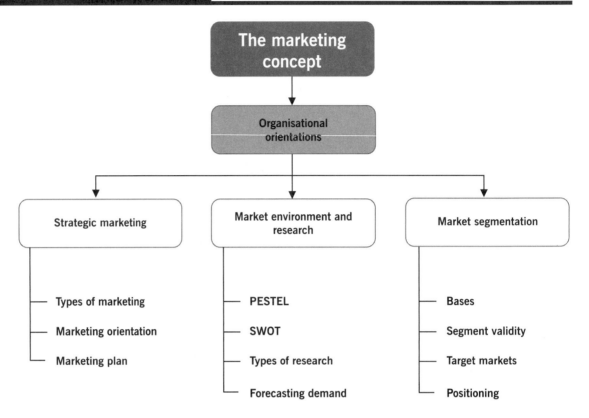

The marketing concept

Organisational orientations

Strategic marketing
- Types of marketing
- Marketing orientation
- Marketing plan

Market environment and research
- PESTEL
- SWOT
- Types of research
- Forecasting demand

Market segmentation
- Bases
- Segment validity
- Target markets
- Positioning

Quick Quiz

1   Which type of marketing involves identifying the products and markets the organisation wishes to operate in?

    A   Mass marketing
    B   Target marketing
    C   Strategic marketing
    D   Tactical marketing

2   Which of the following factors may be useful when forecasting demand?

    A   Area market potential
    B   Total industry sales
    C   Relative market share
    D   All of the above

3   According to Ansoff, which approach should be taken when introducing a new product to an existing market?

    A   Market development
    B   Product development
    C   Market penetration
    D   Diversification

4   List five possible bases for market segmentation.

    1   ....
    2   ....
    3   ....
    4   ....
    5   ....

5   Which of the following is an example of data mining?

    A   Analysing customer information held in a database to identify behavioural patterns
    B   Setting up a database to store customer sales records
    C   Storing and recording customer surveys in a database
    D   Statistical analysis of macroeconomic data

Answers to Quick Quiz

1   C   Strategic marketing involves identifying the products and markets the organisation wishes to operate in.

2   D   All may help forecast demand.

3   B   According to Ansoff, product development should be undertaken when introducing new products into an existing market. This means making sure the product will be acceptable to the market.

4   Geographical area, age, gender, income level, occupation – others may be equally valid.

5   A   Data mining involves analysing a database to identify new information such as behavioural patterns of customers.

Answers to Questions

9.1 Strategic and tactical marketing

Strategic marketing covers long-term decisions such as which market to operate in.
Example: a retailer decides to set up an outlet in a new country.

Tactical marketing covers short-term decisions relating to the marketing mix.
Example: a retailer decides to cut prices to clear space for new stock.

9.2 Product and production orientation

Product-orientated organisations focus on product development, particularly product features.

Production-orientated organisations focus on production efficiency and minimising costs.

Both production- and product-orientated organisations place little emphasis on market research or customer needs – and producing products takes precedence over identifying customers.

9.3 Market segmentation

The table below contains some examples of benefits. You may have thought of others.

Benefit	Brief explanation
Better satisfaction of customer needs	One approach will not satisfy all customers.
Revenue growth	Segmentation means that more customers may be attracted by, and pay more for, what is on offer, in preference to competing products.
Customer retention	By targeting customers, their needs are more likely to be met, leading to repeat purchase.
Targeted communications	Segmentation enables clear communications as people in the target audience share common needs.
Innovation	By identifying un-met needs, companies can innovate to satisfy them.

9.4 Marketing strategy

Ansoff's matrix shows possible strategies for products and markets.

Market penetration – increasing sales of existing products in existing markets

Market development – expansion into new markets using existing products

Product development – changing existing products or introducing new ones into existing markets

Diversification – both new products and new markets

Now try this question from the Practice Question Bank

Number

41, 42, 43, 44, 45

MARKETING TECHNIQUES

 Once an organisation has formed its overall marketing strategy, work can begin on an **action plan** which consists of the **marketing activities** required for the strategy to be successful.

The **key activities** are centred around the traditional **4Ps** of the marketing mix (for **products**) and the **7Ps** of the extended marketing mix (for **services**). The different mixes are required due to the differing nature of products and services.

Once the action plan has been developed, the organisation's **message needs to be communicated**. This can be achieved in a myriad of ways, the choice of which depends on whether a consumer or another business is the subject of the marketing campaign.

Topic list	Learning outcomes	Syllabus references	Ability required
1 Marketing action plans	E1(b), E2(a), E2(b)	E1(v), E2(iv), E2(v), E2(vi), E2(xiv), E2(xvi), E2(xvii)	application
2 Branding	E2(b)	E2(xv)	application
3 Marketing communications	E2(a), E2(b)	E2(iii), E2(iv), E2(viii), E2(x), E2(xi), E2(xii), E2(xiii), E2(xiv), E2(xviii)	application

Chapter Overview

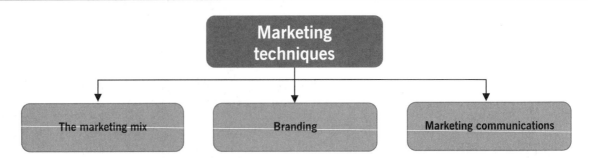

1 Marketing action plans

Introduction

Once an organisation has determined which market segments to attack and which strategies it should use, the next stage in the marketing plan is to develop an **action plan**.

Action plans are usually based around what is known as the **marketing mix**. Kotler and Keller (2006) define the marketing mix as 'the set of controllable variables and their levels that the firm uses to influence the target market'.

These variables should be **carefully considered** as each will directly affect the success or failure of the marketing effort.

1.1 The marketing mix

Most of us have experience of being marketed 'to' in a variety of ways. In developed countries and, increasingly, in developing ones, people are subjected to a variety of different marketing activities.

Media and public spaces are full of advertisements such as posters, TV ads, pop-up ads on websites, even text messages on mobile phones. In marketing terminology these are known as **promotions** (or marketing communications).

Many of these messages aim to persuade people that they need to have certain **products** or services and to purchase them. **People** are trained to produce and deliver these products or services to **places** where we can buy them. Sophisticated **processes** might be involved in production and managing the sale. Delivery is also designed and managed.

For a service (which by its nature is intangible), sometimes we require **physical evidence** that the service is to be provided – for example, a letter or guarantee for building work or testimonials or references to reassure potential customers. The **price** we pay is not arbitrary – it has been thought through. Phrases such as 'that was good value for money' suggest that price and value are important in buying decisions.

In the paragraphs above, seven words or phrases beginning with 'p' have been emboldened. These form what is known as the **extended marketing mix**. Traditionally, the marketing mix was the **'four Ps'** (**product**, **price**, **place**, **promotion**). **Three extra 'Ps'** have been added to describe the issues in **service industries** (eg for a restaurant: **people** – waiters, **processes** – the cooking process, **place** – the physical environment of the restaurant).

The extended marketing mix: the 7Ps	
The traditional marketing mix (4Ps)	**You can add ... (3Ps)**
Product	People (the 'fifth P')
Price	Processes
Place (distribution)	Physical evidence
Promotion	

1.2 Product

KEY TERM

A **PRODUCT** (goods or services) is anything that satisfies a need or want. It is not a 'thing' with 'features' but a package of benefits.

From the organisation's point of view the **product element** of the marketing mix is what is being sold, whether it be widgets, power stations, haircuts, holidays or financial advice. From the customer's point of view, a **product is a solution to a problem or a package of benefits**. Many products might satisfy the same customer need.

On what **basis** might a **customer choose a product**?

(a) **Customer value** is the customer's estimate of how far a product or service goes towards satisfying their need(s).

(b) Every product has a price, and so the customer makes a **trade-off** between the **expenditure** and **the value offered**.

(c) According to Kotler a customer must feel that they get a **better deal** from buying an item than by any of the alternatives.

1.2.1 Product classification

KEY POINTS

Products can be classified as **consumer goods or industrial goods**. Consumer goods are sold directly to the person who will ultimately use them. Industrial goods are used in the production of other products.

Consumer goods can be classified as follows.

Convenience goods	Weekly groceries are a typical example. There is a further distinction between **staple goods** (eg bread and potatoes) and **impulse buys**, like the bar of chocolate found at the supermarket checkout. **Brand awareness** is extremely important in this sector.
Shopping goods	These are the more durable items that you buy, like furniture and washing machines. This sort of purchase is usually only made after a good deal of advance planning and shopping around.
Speciality goods	These are items like jewellery or expensive items of clothing.
Unsought goods	These are goods that the customer did not realise they needed! Typical examples are new and sometimes 'gimmicky' products, such as 'wardrobe organisers' or fire-resistant car polish.

Industrial goods can be classified as follows.

- **Installations**, eg major items of plant and machinery like a factory assembly line
- **Accessories**, such as PCs
- **Raw materials**, for example plastic, metal, wood, foodstuffs and chemicals
- **Components**, eg the Lucas headlights on Ford cars, the Intel microchip in most PCs
- **Supplies**, such as office stationery and cleaning materials

1.2.2 Product levels

It is useful for marketers to think of a product, and its attributes, at different levels.

Product attributes

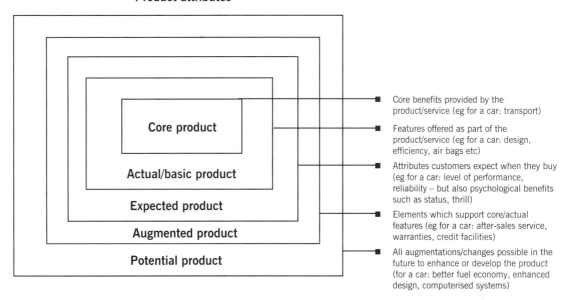

KEY POINTS

The **core/generic product** is those benefits that all the products in the category would have – all cars, for example, provide transport.

The **augmented product** is the core product plus extra benefits that differentiate it from other products in the category. These might include warranty, delivery, installation, after-sales support.

Many products are marketed at the **augmented product** level – the total package of the customer's experience of purchasing and consuming the product/service is relevant. The **expected product** level is also important, because of the potential for customers to be dissatisfied (by disappointed expectations) or delighted (by exceeding expectations). The **potential product** is important in providing the marketing organisation with future avenues to develop the product (and marketing message) in order to stay competitive and 'fresh' in the market. **Product issues** in the marketing mix will include such factors as **design** (size, shape), **after-sales service** (if necessary), **features**, **packaging**, **quality** and **reliability**.

1.2.3 Product range

KEY POINT

A company's **product range** (or product portfolio, assortment or mix) is all the product lines and items that the company offers for sale.

A company's **product range** can be described in the following terms.

Characteristic	Defined by:
Product item	A specific product, such as a chocolate bar or pair of trainers; businesses usually sell multiple product items
Product line	A set of similar items that the organisation produces, for example different flavours of crisp
Width/Breadth	Number of product lines: eg cosmetics, haircare, toiletries and health products
Depth	Average number of items per product line: eg cosmetics including moisturiser, cleanser, toner, lipstick, eyeshadow
Consistency	Closeness of relationships in product range for the benefit of users and production/distribution processes

1.2.4 Managing the product range

There are benefits to be gained from using a systematic approach to the management of the product range. It can be **reduced** (eg by discontinuing a product) or **extended** by:

(a)   Introducing variations in models or style (eg a paint manufacturer introducing different colours, types and pot sizes)

(b)   Differentiating the quality of products offered at different price levels (eg 'premium' paints and 'value' paints)

(c)   Developing associated items (eg a paint roller and brushes, paint trays, colour charts)

(d)   Developing new products with little technical or marketing relationship to the existing range (eg wallpaper and DIY accessories – or something completely different)

Managing the product range also raises **broad issues** such as:

(a)   What role a product should play in the range. ('Flagship' brand? Profit provider? Niche filler? New market tester/developer? Old faithful, retaining customer loyalty?) The roles of products in the mix should create a balanced range, with sufficient **cash-generating** products to support **cash-using** (declining or new/market-developing) products.

(b)   How resources should be allocated between products.

(c)   What should be expected from each product.

(d)   How far products should be integrated within the brand image and be recognisable as part of the brand family.

Marketing is not an exact science and there is no definitive approach or technique which can determine how resources should be shared across the product range. There are, however, techniques which can aid decision making. Ultimately the burden of the decision is a management responsibility and requires judgement, but tools such as the **BCG matrix** and the **product life cycle** can help the decision-making process.

1.2.5 The BCG matrix

KEY POINT

The **BCG matrix** classifies products or brands on the basis of their market share and according to the rate of growth in the market as a whole, as a way of assessing their role in the product range.

Relative market share

		High	Low
Market growth rate	**High**	Star	Question mark (or Problem child)
	Low	Cash cow	Dog

On the basis of this classification, each product may fall into one of four broad categories.

(a) **Question mark** (or problem child): A small market share in a high-growth industry.

The generic product is clearly popular, but customer support for the particular brand is limited. A small market share implies that competitors are in a strong position and that if the product is to be successful it will require substantial funds, and a new marketing mix. If the market looks good and the product is viable, then the company should consider a 'build' strategy to increase market share by increasing the resources available for that product to permit more active marketing. If the future looks less promising, then the company should consider withdrawing the product. Which strategy is chosen will depend on the strength of competitors, availability of funding and other relevant factors.

(b) **Star**: A high market share in a high-growth industry.

The star has potential for generating significant earnings, currently and in the future. At this stage it may still require substantial marketing expenditure as part of a 'maintain' strategy, but this is probably regarded as a good investment for the future.

(c) **Cash cow**: A high market share in a mature slow-growth market.

Typically, a well-established product with a high degree of consumer loyalty. Product development costs are typically low and the marketing campaign is well established. The cash cow will normally make a substantial contribution to overall profitability. The appropriate strategy will vary according to the precise position of the cash cow. If market growth is reasonably strong then a 'holding' strategy will be appropriate. However, if growth and/or share are weakening, then a 'harvesting' strategy may be more sensible by cutting back on marketing expenditure to maximise short-term profit.

(d) **Dog**: A low market share in a low-growth market.

Like the cash cow, this is a well-established product, but one which is apparently losing consumer support and may have cost disadvantages. The usual strategy would be to consider divestment, unless the cash flow position is strong, in which case the product would be harvested in the short term, prior to deletion from the product range.

1.2.6 Product development

The following stages are often followed in the **development of a product** or **service**.

Stage 1   **Customer needs**
            The product is designed to fulfil particular customer needs (such as quality, price and design).

Stage 2   **Screening**
            The concept should be considered carefully to ensure it meets certain criteria such as profitability or taking market share.

Stage 3   **Design**
            The design process can be in different forms such as building an electronic or physical prototype. Value engineering procedures may be followed to ensure all components add value.

Stage 4   **Time-to-market**
            This is the time a product or service takes to get to the marketplace. A short time span is desirable to reduce cost and to get ahead of the competition.

Stage 5   **Testing**
            The product or service should be tested to check that it works, that it meets the needs of the customer and that the customer likes it.

1.2.7 The product life cycle

KEY POINT

The classic pattern of a **product life cycle (PLC)** is in **four stages**: an **introduction** to the market, a **growth**, **market maturity** and then **decline**. However, products can be rejuvenated so that their life cycle continues.

The priorities for performance objectives will change as a product goes through the phases of its life cycle.

(a)   **Introduction stage**. The product or service offers something new to customers. There are unlikely to be any competing products, but heavy advertising costs may be incurred to raise customer awareness. Design changes may be required as customer needs become better understood. A business needs to establish an operational capability that allows it to be flexible and capable of adapting and changing.

(b)   **Growth stage**. The volume of demand for the product increases, and there are likely to be more competitors in the market. Product features may become important between different suppliers. The main objective for the operations function could be to keep up with the growing demand. Speed of response to customer orders and reliability of supply could also be significant. Quality standards will have to be maintained or improved in response to the growing competition, and cost and price are likely to be much more significant.

(c)   **Market maturity**. Demand levels off. Some early competitors are likely to have left the market, which might now be shared by a small number of organisations. Product design will be largely standardised, although organisations might try to develop new varieties of the product to extend its life cycle. Organisations in the market are likely to compete on price and/or value for money (product differentiation). To remain competitive, it will be important to achieve low costs through productivity improvements, while still providing reliability of supply.

(d)   **Decline stage**. Total demand declines and competitors will start to withdraw from the market. There will nevertheless be excess capacity in the industry, and the remaining organisations will compete on price. Cost targets will remain the key operational objective. The company may also decide to stop making and selling the product, and to focus its energies instead on another developing/growing product.

Some writers refer to an additional phase between market growth and market maturity. Often at this time some of the weaker players in the market (initially attracted by market growth) are 'shaken out' of the market by the stronger organisations. This is referred to as a '**shakeout**'.

The Product Life Cycle

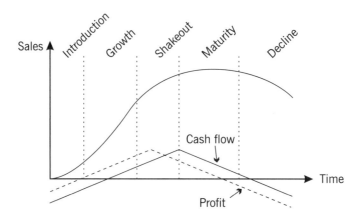

1.3 Place

Place deals with how the **product is distributed**, and how it reaches its customers.

(a) **Channel**. Where are products sold? Supermarkets, corner shops? Which outlets will be chosen? **Zero level distribution** is where the organisation sells directly to the customer. In **one level distribution**, the organisation sells to the retailer, who sells to the customer. **Two level distribution** involves the organisation selling to a wholesaler who in turn sells to the retailer.

(b) **Logistics**. The location of warehouses and efficiency of the distribution system is also important. A customer might have to wait a long time if the warehouse is far away. Arguably, the **speed of delivery** is an important issue in **place**.

An organisation can distribute the product itself (**direct distribution**) or distribute it through intermediary organisations such as **retailers**.

1.4 Promotion

Many of the practical activities of the marketing department are related to **promotion**. Promotion is the element of the mix over which the marketing department generally has most control. A useful mnemonic is AIDA which summarises the aims of promotion:

- Arouse **Attention**
- Generate **Interest**
- Inspire **Desire**
- Initiate **Action** (ie buy the product)

Promotion in the marketing mix includes all **marketing communications** which let the public know of the product or service:

- Advertising (newspapers, billboards, TV, radio, direct mail, internet)
- Sales promotion (discounts, coupons, special displays in particular stores)
- Direct selling by sales personnel
- Public relations

Lancaster and Withey (2005) identified the following elements of successful advertising. It must be:

- **Well planned** and **executed**
- **Effective** as a method of communication
- Part of an **overall effective promotional mix**
- **Aligned** with the overall **values** and **mission** of the **company**

1.4.1 The range of promotional tools

KEY TERMS

ABOVE-THE-LINE campaigning is advertising placed in paid-for media, such as the press, radio, TV, cinema and outdoor sites. The 'line' is one in an advertising agency's accounts, above which are shown its earnings on a commission basis, from the buying of media space for clients.

BELOW-THE-LINE promotion involves product-integral and negotiated sales incentives, such as packaging, merchandising, and on-pack discounts and competitions.

In recent years the range of **promotional tools** has continued to grow. The variety of media that can be used for **above-the-line** campaigns has expanded, both in the printed advertising field and in the broadcast field. There are literally thousands of publications aimed at different target groups. In the broadcast field the number of television stations steadily increases through satellite, cable and digital television and the number of commercial radio stations has also grown considerably.

The traditional emphasis on heavy mass above-the-line advertising has given way to more highly targeted campaigns. Below-the-line, and even what Fill (2002) terms '**through-the-line**' promotion, is now far more common. The following quote is from Fill.

'The shift is from an **intervention-based approach** to marketing communications (one based on seeking the attention of a customer who might not necessarily be interested), towards **permission-based communications** (where the focus is upon communications with members of an audience who have already expressed an interest in a particular offering).'

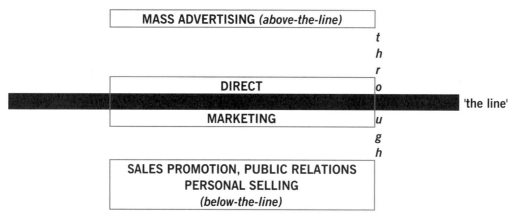

Digital marketing is challenging these approaches. It describes the use of electronic devices such as tablets, PCs, mobile phones and games consoles to communicate with the customer. Communication methods include the internet, apps, emails and social networks.

There are two types of digital marketing:

(a) **Pull digital marketing**

The individual seeks the marketing effort, for example through web searches or streaming media. The aim is to pull viewers in and turn them into customers.

(b) **Push digital marketing**

The individual is sent the marketing message directly, for example by seeing an online advert on another website or being sent an email or text message without requesting it. The aim is to advertise the organisation to as many people as possible and turn a reasonable percentage of recipients into customers.

1.4.2 The product life cycle (PLC) and promotional strategy

Each of the stages of the **PLC**, from introduction to decline, have different strategic requirements from their promotional activities.

Promotional Activities	Introduction	Growth	Maturity	Decline
Strategic focus	Strong push then pull for awareness	Pull to differentiate	Pull and push to sustain loyalty and exposure through reassurance	Some pull to remind core users
Public relations	✗		✗	
Advertising	✗	✗	✗	
Direct marketing		✗	✗	✗
Personal selling	✗	✗	✗	✗
Sales promotion	✗		✗	

The table above sets out the **strategic focus for each phase** and the main promotional activities to be considered.

What the table does not show is the way the promotional tools are used to support a push as opposed to pull approach. One particular benefit of the PLC is that it is possible to overlay the various stages of the process of **diffusion**. Through this it is possible to identify the **different types of buyer** involved with the product at each stage and through this fine-tune the appropriate message and media.

1.4.3 Introduction

For consumer brands this phase is critical, as the primary need is to **secure trade acceptance** (and hence shelf space) and then build **public (target audience) awareness**. Sunny Delight was developed by Procter & Gamble in consultation with multiple major grocers. When the product was launched, the multiples accepted the brand as it had been developed partly to their specification on price, ingredient and packaging/size.

1.4.4 Growth

During growth, promotional activity is used competitively to **build market share**. Customers are normally willing to buy, having been made aware, but their problem becomes one of **brand choice**. Marketing communications should therefore be used to **differentiate and clearly position** the product such that it represents significant value for the customer.

1.4.5 Maturity

Once the rapid growth in a market starts to ease, the period of maturity commences. The primary characteristic of this stage is that there is little or no growth. The battle therefore is to **retain customer loyalty**. To do this, sales promotions are often used to encourage trial by non-users and to reward current users.

1.4.6 Decline

As sales start to decline it is normal practice to withdraw a great deal of promotion support. **Direct marketing** and a little well-targeted advertising to **remind** and **reassure** brand loyalists is the most commonly used.

1.4.7 Co-ordinating promotional tools

Promotion aims to **influence customers** favourably towards an organisation's products or services. It is necessary to co-ordinate all the promotional elements to achieve the maximum influence on the customer. This can involve trial and error, and market research to establish the effectiveness of various combinations of promotional tools (the **promotion mix**). The aim is optimal **effectiveness**, **economy** and **efficiency** of the promotional tools.

1.5 Price

There are three main types of influence on **price setting**: **costs**, **competition** and **customers** (the **3Cs**). Other aspects of the **pricing mix** include factors such as any **bulk purchase discounts given**, **credit offered** and **methods of payment**.

1.5.1 Costs

In practice, cost is the most important influence on price. Many organisations base price on simple **cost-plus** rules. In other words, costs are estimated and then a profit margin is added in order to set the price. This method is fairly easy to apply and ensures that costs are covered. A common example occurs with the use of **mark-up** pricing. This is used by retailers and involves a fixed margin being added to the buying-in price of goods for resale.

Because the cost-plus approach leads to price stability, with price changing only being used to reflect cost changes, it can lead to a marketing strategy which is **reactive** rather than **proactive**. In addition, there is very limited consideration of **demand** in cost-based pricing strategies. From a marketing perspective, cost-based pricing may lead to **missed opportunities** as little or no account is taken, particularly in the short run, of the price consumers are **willing** to pay for the brand, which may actually be higher than the cost-based price.

Economies of scale and the **experience curve** will also have an effect on cost. Large organisations that can buy materials in bulk can achieve lower average costs than smaller organisations (economies of scale). Businesses that have a vast experience of producing a product can also produce at a lower cost because they have learnt the best way of working through past experience.

1.5.2 Competition

In some markets, **going-rate pricing**, **(**where some form of average level of price is used) has become the norm. For example, in the case of a high level of branding in the market, there may be standard price differentials between brands.

In some market structures **price competition may be avoided by informal agreement** leading to concentration on non-price competition – the markets for cigarettes and petrol are examples of this.

1.5.3 Customers

Rather than cost or competition as the prime determinants of price, an organisation may base pricing strategy on the **intensity** and **elasticity** of demand. **Strong demand may lead to a high price, and a weak demand to a low price** – much depends on the ability of the organisation to segment the market price in terms of elasticity. In other words, **price** is determined by what **customers** are **willing to pay**.

For products or services with a typical downward-sloping demand curve, fewer purchasers will buy at a **higher price**. If a supplier can identify those purchasers still willing to pay the higher price, the supplier could benefit by charging them a higher price. This is called **price discrimination** or **differential pricing**.

In practice, **measurement of price elasticity** and **implementing differential pricing** can be **very difficult**. There are a number of bases on which discriminating prices can be set.

(a) **By market segment**. A cross-channel ferry company would market its services at different prices in England, Belgium and France, for example. Services such as cinemas and hairdressers are often available at lower prices to old-age pensioners and juveniles.

(b) **By product version**. Many car models have 'add-on' extras which enable one brand to appeal to a wider cross-section of customers. Final price need not reflect the cost price of the add-on extras directly. Usually the top of the range model would carry a price much in excess of the cost of provision of the extras, as a prestige appeal.

(c) **By place**. Theatre seats are usually sold according to their location so that patrons pay different prices for the same performance according to the seat type they occupy.

(d) **By time**. This is perhaps the most popular type of price discrimination.

Price sensitivity will vary amongst purchasers. **Those who can pass on the cost of purchases will be least sensitive** and will respond more to other elements of the marketing mix.

Pricing research is notoriously difficult, especially if respondents try to give a rational rather than their 'real' response. As the respondent is not actually faced with the situation they may give a hypothetical answer that is not going to be translated into actual purchasing behaviour. Nevertheless, pricing research is increasingly common as organisations struggle to assess the perceived value customers attribute to a brand to provide an input to their pricing decisions.

1.5.4 Competitors' actions and reactions

An organisation, in setting prices, **sends out signals to rivals**. **These rivals are likely to react** in some way. In some industries (such as petrol retailing) pricing moves in unison; in others, price changes by one supplier may initiate a price war, with each supplier undercutting the others.

In established industries dominated by a few major organisations, it is generally accepted that a **price initiative by one organisation** will be countered by a **price reaction** by competitors. Here, prices tend to be fairly stable, unless pushed upwards by inflation or strong growth in demand.

In the event that a **rival cuts prices** expecting to increase market share, an organisation has several options.

(a)   It will **maintain its existing prices** if the expectation is that only a small market share would be lost, so that it is more profitable to keep prices at their existing level. Eventually, the rival organisation may drop out of the market or be forced to raise its prices.

(b)   It may **maintain its prices** but respond with a **non-price counter-attack**. This is a more positive response, because the organisation will be securing or justifying its current prices.

(c)   It may **reduce its prices**. This should protect the organisation's market share at the expense of profitability. The main beneficiary from the price reduction will be the consumer.

(d)   It may **raise its prices** and respond with a **non-price counter-attack**. The extra revenue from the higher prices might be used to finance promotion on product changes. A price increase would be based on a campaign to emphasise the quality difference between the organisation's own product and the rival's product.

1.5.5 Perceived quality pricing

In the absence of other information, some customers tend to **judge quality by price**. Therefore a price change may send signals to customers concerning the quality of the product. A rise in price may be taken to indicate improvements in quality; a reduction in price may signal reduced quality.

1.5.6 New product pricing

Most pricing decisions for existing products relate to price changes. Such changes have a **reference point** from which to move (the existing price). But **when a new product is introduced for the first time there may be no such reference point** and therefore pricing decisions will be difficult to make.

In some cases, **intermediate customer pricing** may be used. This involves the setting of a recommended retail price to assist the reseller in setting their own price.

1.5.7 Multiple products

Most organisations market not just one product but a **range of products**. These products are commonly interrelated, perhaps being complements or substitutes. The pricing strategy is likely to focus on the **profit** from the **whole range** rather than that on each single product – for example, the use of **loss leaders**. A very low price for one product is intended to make consumers buy other products in the range which carry higher profit margins.

1.6 Price-setting strategies

After considering the issues above, the following **price-setting strategies** can be developed.

1.6.1 Market penetration

The organisation **sets a relatively low price** for the product or service in order to **stimulate growth of the market and/or to obtain a large share** of it. This strategy is appropriate under three conditions:

- Unit costs will fall with increased output (economies of scale) and experience (experience curve).
- The market is price sensitive and relatively low prices will attract additional sales.
- Low prices will discourage new competitors.

1.6.2 Market skimming

The organisation **sets a high initial price for a new product in order to take advantage of those buyers who are ready to pay a much higher price for it**. A typical strategy would be initially to set a premium price and then gradually to reduce the price to attract more price-sensitive segments of the market.

This strategy is appropriate under three conditions:

- There is insufficient production capacity and competitors cannot increase their capacity.
- Some buyers are relatively insensitive to high prices.
- High price is perceived as high quality.

1.6.3 Early cash recovery

The organisation **aims to recover the investment in a new product or service as quickly as possible** to achieve a minimum payback period. The price is set to facilitate this objective.

This objective tends to be used in three circumstances:

- The business is high risk.
- Rapid changes in fashion or technology are expected.
- The innovator is short of cash.

1.6.4 Product line promotion

The organisation **focuses on profit from the range of products** which the organisation produces **rather than to treat each product as a separate entity**.

This strategy looks at the whole range from two points of view:

- The interaction of the marketing mix
- Monitoring returns to ensure that net contribution is worthwhile

1.6.5 Cost-plus pricing

The organisation sets its price by **marking up its unit costs** by a certain percentage or fixed amount.

1.6.6 Target pricing

The organisation selects the price that gives a **specified rate of return** for a given output.

1.6.7 Price discrimination/selective pricing

The organisation **sets different prices** for **the same product** when it is **sold in different markets**.

Three sub-categories have evolved:

(a) **Category**

The product is cosmetically modified to justify a price differential. For example, a 'budget' version of a product is modified into a 'premium' version. **Premium pricing** is the term given where rich customers are targeted with a high-price, differentiated product.

(b)   **Consumer group**

The price differential is justified by **targeting different consumer groups** – for example, OAP and student prices. They are often used by leisure facilities such as leisure centres and galleries.

(c)   **Peak**

The **price** is **set in accordance** with **demand**. For example, the price of a train ticket is often more expensive in the morning when most people travel to work. Alternatively, a lower price can be set during quiet periods to stimulate demand. This is also known as a **variable pricing policy**.

The danger is that price cuts to one buyer may be used as a **negotiating lever** by another buyer. This can be countered in three ways:

(a)   Buyers can be split into clearly defined segments, such as overseas and home, or students' concessionary fares.

(b)   Own branding, where packaging is changed for that of a supermarket, is a variation on this.

(c)   Bulk-buying discounts and aggregated rebate schemes can favour large buyers.

1.6.8 Going rate/competitive prices

The organisation tries to **keep in line with the industry norm for prices**. This is also known as **competitive pricing** where prices are set with reference to competitors' pricing.

1.6.9 Price leadership/predatory pricing

In some markets a **price leader** (often a large corporation) emerges. A price leader dominates price levels for a class of products; increases or decreases by the price leader are followed by the market. The price-dominant organisation may lead without moving at all. The price leader generally has a large market share and will usually be an efficient producer with a reputation for technical competence.

The **role of price leader** is based on a track record of having initiated price moves that have been accepted by both competitors and customers. Any dramatic changes in industry competition (a new entrant, or changes in the board room) may endanger the price leadership role.

Predatory pricing is a similar strategy but the reason for setting a low price is to damage the competition.

1.6.10 Quantum pricing

The organisation sets prices up to a psychological level but not beyond it. For example, a product's price is set at 99p, not £1.

1.7 Services and service marketing

Services have a different nature to goods and therefore the **marketing of services** presents a number of different challenges. As a consequence, particular marketing practices have been developed.

KEY TERM

SERVICES include:

'... those separately identifiable but intangible activities that provide want-satisfaction, and that are not, of necessity, tied to, or inextricable from, the sale of a product or another service. To produce a service may or may not require the use of tangible goods or assets. However, where such use is required, there is no transfer of title (permanent ownership) to these tangible goods.'   (Cowell, 1995)

'... any activity of benefit that one party can offer to another that is essentially intangible and does not result in the ownership of anything. Its production may or may not be tied to a physical product.' (Kotler *et al*, 2002)

The following **characteristics of services distinguish them from goods** and have marketing implications.

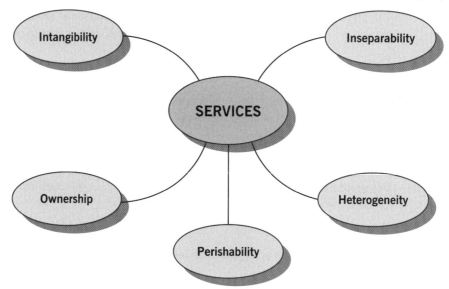

1.7.1 Intangibility

'Intangibility' refers to the **lack of substance** which is involved with service delivery. Unlike goods, there are no substantial material or physical aspects to a service – no taste, feel, visible presence and so on. This creates difficulties and can inhibit the desire to consume a service, since customers are not sure what they will receive.

Marketers and consumers need to try to overcome this problem. The marketer wishes to make the choice of the product 'safer' and make the consumer feel more comfortable about paying for something they do not then own and which has no physical form.

Dealing with intangibility may involve the following:

(a) **Increasing the level of tangibility**. Use physical or conceptual representations/illustrations to make the customer feel more confident as to what it is that the service is delivering.

(b) **Focusing the attention of the customer on the principal benefits of consumption**. Communicating the benefits of purchasing the service so that the customer visualises its use. Promotion and sales material could provide images or records of previous customers' experience.

(c) **Differentiating the service and reputation-building**. Enhancing perceptions of customer service and customer value by offering excellence in the delivery of the service. This reputation can be attached to brands, which must then be managed to secure and enhance their market position (for example, the Virgin brand).

1.7.2 Inseparability

Services often cannot be separated off from the provider, for example having dental treatment or taking a journey. Neither exists until they are actually being experienced/consumed by the person who has bought them. The 'creation' of many services is simultaneous with consumption, where the service is:

- Made available ⎫
- Produced ⎬ all at the same time
- Sold ⎪
- Consumed ⎭

Provision of the service may not be separable from the person or personality of the seller. Consequently, increasing importance is attached to the need to **instil values of quality and reliability** and to generate a **service ethic** in customer-facing staff.

This points up the need for excellence and customer orientation and the need to invest in high-quality people and high-quality training.

1.7.3 Heterogeneity (lack of 'sameness' or consistency)

Many services face the problem of **maintaining consistency** in the standard of output. Variability of quality occurs because of the large number of variables involved. The quality of the service may depend heavily on who it is that delivers the service. For example, booking a holiday using standard procedures may well be quite different on a quiet winter afternoon and on a hectic spring weekend, and may well vary according to the person dealing with your case.

In terms of **marketing policy**, heterogeneity highlights the need to develop and maintain processes for:

- Consistency of quality control, with clear and objective quality measures
- Consistency of customer service and customer care, standardising as far as possible
- Effective staff selection, training and motivation in customer care
- Monitoring service levels and customer perceptions of service delivery

1.7.4 Perishability

Services cannot be stored – they are innately perishable. Seats on a bus or the services of a doctor exist only for periods of time. If they are not consumed, they 'perish'. They cannot be used later. They cannot be 'produced' in advance, to allow for peaks in demand.

This presents specific marketing problems. Meeting customer needs depends on staff being available as and when they are needed. This must be balanced against the need for an organisation to minimise unnecessary expenditure on staff wages. **Anticipating and responding to levels of demand** is, therefore, a key planning priority.

Policies must seek to **smooth out fluctuations** in supply/demand relationship, or allow for contingencies. Examples include:

- Using price variations to encourage off-peak demand (eg on travel services)

- Using promotions to stimulate off-peak demand (eg free mobile calls between certain hours)

- Using flexible staffing methods to cover fluctuations in demand (eg part-time and temporary working, outsourcing to call centres)

1.7.5 Ownership

Services do not result in the transfer of property. The purchase of a service only gives the customer access to or the right to use a facility, not ownership. This may lessen the perceived customer value of a service – particularly if the benefit does not accrue until some time in the future (like a pension, or a voucher for future use).

There are **two basic approaches** to addressing this problem:

(a) **Promote the advantages of non-ownership**. This can be done by emphasising the benefits of paid-for maintenance, or a periodic upgrading of the product.

(b) **Make available a tangible symbol or representation of ownership** such as a certificate, voucher, merchandise item or simple receipt. This can come to embody the benefits enjoyed.

Railways and airlines

In the UK, in the 19th century, railway passengers could buy tickets for first, second and third classes. Now they buy first and 'standard' classes. The UK was a society heavily stratified by wealth, and so offering three classes of tickets would seem a natural way of targeting a market segmented by wealth.

In India today, there are first, second and third classes (with permutations based on air conditioned compartments, sleepers etc). In China there exist 'hard' and 'soft' classes.

Airlines offer a useful contrast. Segmentation is partly based on purpose of visit and time of booking. Business class was directed to people travelling on business expense accounts (who would travel economy on their own account). Some airlines offer 'premium' economy seats to those who want more legroom. The 'low-cost' airlines flying in the US and Europe designed for the 'no-frills' consumer are increasingly frequented by business travellers for short-haul trips.

1.8 The extended marketing mix

As a consequence of the **differences** between **goods** and **services**, the **service marketing mix** developed. The intangible nature of services makes these extra three Ps particularly important (people, processes and physical evidence).

1.8.1 People

The role of employees in the marketing mix is particularly important in **service marketing** because of the **inseparability** of the service from the service provider. Front-line staff must be selected, trained and motivated with particular attention to customer care and public relations.

In the case of some services, the **physical presence** of people performing the service is a vital aspect of customer satisfaction. The staff involved are performing or producing a service, selling the service and also liaising with the customer to promote the service, gather information and respond to customer needs.

1.8.2 Processes

Efficient **processes** can become a marketing advantage in their own right. If an airline, for example, develops a sophisticated ticketing system, it can offer shorter waits at check-in or wider choice of flights through allied airlines. Efficient order processing not only increases customer satisfaction, but cuts down on the time it takes the organisation to complete a sale.

Issues to be considered include the following:

- Policies, particularly with regard to ethical dealings (a key issue for many consumers)
- Procedures, for efficiency and standardisation
- Automation and computerisation of processes
- Queuing and waiting times
- Information gathering, processing and communication times
- Capacity management, matching supply to demand in a timely and cost-effective way
- Accessibility of facilities, premises, personnel and services

Such issues are particularly important in service marketing. This is because the range of factors and people involved make it **difficult to standardise** the service offered. Quality in particular specifications will vary with the circumstances and individuals. This creates a need for **process planning** to ensure efficient work.

1.8.3 Physical evidence

As we saw earlier, services are **intangible** – there is no physical substance to them. This often means that the customer has no **evidence of ownership**. This may make it difficult for consumers to compare the qualities of service provision and reduce the incentive to consume.

Issues of **intangibility** and **ownership** can be tackled by making available **a physical symbol** or representation of the service and the benefits it confers. For example, tickets and programmes relating to entertainment and certificates of attainment in training are symbolic of the service received and provide a history of past positive experiences.

Physical evidence of service may also be incorporated into the **design** and **specification of the service environment** by designing premises to reflect the quality and type of service. Such environmental factors include finishing, decor, colour scheme, noise levels, background music, fragrance and general ambience.

Question 10.1	The extended marketing mix

Learning outcome E1(v)

Briefly explain the nature of services and the three additional Ps relevant to services marketing. **(5 marks)**

Section summary

Traditionally, the **marketing mix** was the **'four Ps'** (**product, price, place, promotion**). The **three extra 'Ps'** have been added to describe additional issues relevant to **service industries** (**people, process, physical evidence**), giving an extended marketing mix of seven Ps.

---

2 Branding

Introduction

A **brand** is a name, term, sign, symbol or design intended to identify the product of a seller and to differentiate it from those of competitors. It is a key element of marketing and corporate strategy as it generates revenue and therefore has a value.

KEY POINTS

Branding is a very general term covering brand names, designs, trademarks, symbols, jingles and the like. A **brand name** refers strictly to letters, words or groups of words which can be spoken. A **brand image** distinguishes a company's product from competing products in the eyes of the user.

Brand equity is the premium customers are prepared to pay for the branded product compared to a non-branded product.

Brand management is the development of a long-term strategy to keep the brand in customers' minds at all times.

Branding might be discussed under any of the **four Ps**. For instance, part of the branding of a Rolls-Royce is the unmistakeable design of the product, or you might buy a 'cheaper brand' of washing-up liquid if you are concerned about price. Consumers often use brands to make **statements** about themselves (especially in relation to cars and clothes) and brand names also help guide **product choice** (strong brands are seen as safe to buy).

A good brand is an **important asset** for a business as it can be a reason for consumers choosing its products or services rather than a competitor's. Although brands are **intangible**, they can have a **high value**, allow an organisation to charge higher prices and therefore have a positive impact on share price.

A strong **brand identity** may begin with a distinctive name, such as 'Kleenex' or 'Ariel', but extends to a range of visual features which should assist in stimulating demand for the particular product. The additional features include **typography**, **colour**, **package design** and **slogans**. Also important are **distinctive features** associated with the product that make it recognisable (such as the Nike 'swoosh'). **Consistency of the product** is also an essential element of a strong brand. For example, it is important to McDonald's that the same type of burger is identical wherever in the world it is purchased.

2.1 Objectives of branding

The **key benefit of branding** is product differentiation and recognition. Products may be branded for a number of reasons.

(a) It aids **product differentiation**, conveying a lot of information very quickly and concisely. This helps customers readily to identify the goods or services and thereby helps create customer loyalty to the brand. It is therefore a means of increasing or maintaining sales.

(b) It maximises the impact of **advertising** for product identification and recognition. The more similar a product (whether an industrial good or consumer good) is to competing goods, the more branding is necessary to create a separate product identity.

(c) Branding leads to a **readier acceptance** of a manufacturer's goods by wholesalers and retailers.

(d) It reduces the importance of **price differentials** between goods.

(e) It supports **market segmentation**, since different brands of similar products may be developed to meet specific needs of categories of user.

(f) It supports **brand extension** or **stretching**. Other products can be introduced into the brand range to 'piggy back' off the articles already known to the customer (but ill-will as well as goodwill for one product in a branded range will be transferred to all other products in the range).

(g) It **eases the task of personal selling** by enhancing product recognition.

The **relevance of branding** does not apply equally to all products. The cost of intensive brand advertising to project a brand image nationally may not be justified.

The decision as to whether a brand name should be given to a **range of products** or whether products should be branded **individually** depends on quality factors.

(a) If the brand name is associated with quality, all goods in the range must be of that standard.

(b) If a company produces different quality (and price) goods for different market segments, it would be unwise and confusing to give the same brand name to the higher- and the lower-quality goods.

2.2 Brand management

Once a brand has been developed, it is important that it is **effectively managed** so that its value is protected. A **brand's value** is based on customer loyalty, awareness of the name, the quality it stands for, and other factors such as celebrity associations and patents and trademarks. These are the factors that brand management should focus on.

In addition, a **customer's experience** of a brand is critical in maintaining their relationship with a brand (so brand management also needs to consider this). The following factors may reduce the value of a brand:

• Expiry of a patent so that **generic versions** of the same product can be made by competitors
• Poor-quality, **illegal versions** of branded products
• Any **adverse publicity** for the brand
• The use of **exclusive brands** on **low-quality goods**

The **benefits of good brand management** are essentially the benefits of a good brand. These include increased profitability, ownership of a valuable asset, being able to differentiate products and charge higher prices, to connect with customers and create loyalty and to get the best out of other marketing exercises.

2.3 Branding strategies

Kotler identified five broad **branding strategies – line extension**, **brand extension**, **multi-branding**, **new brands** and **co-brands**.

2.3.1 Line extension

This is where a **brand** is applied to a **variant of a product** within the same product category. It is often used by car manufacturers when they produce variants within the same class of car.

2.3.2 Brand extension

This is the introduction of new flavours, sizes etc to a brand, to capitalise on existing brand loyalty. Examples are the introduction of Persil washing-up liquid (Persil used to be a washing powder for clothes) and Mars ice cream (Mars made its name as a chocolate bar).

New additions to the **product range** are beneficial for two main reasons:

* They require a lower level of marketing investment (part of the 'image' already being known).

* The extension of the brand presents less risk to consumers who might be worried about trying something new.

2.3.3 Multi-branding

This is the introduction of a **number of brands** that all satisfy **very similar product characteristics**. This can be used where there is little or no brand loyalty, in order to pick up buyers who are constantly changing brands.

The best example is washing detergents. The two major producers, Unilever and Procter & Gamble, have created a barrier to fresh competition as a new company would have to launch several brands at once in order to compete.

Family branding uses the power of the **brand name** to assist all products in a range. This strategy is being used more and more by **large companies**, such as Heinz. In part it is a response to retailers' own-label (family branded) goods. It is also an attempt to consolidate expensive television advertising behind one message rather than fragmenting it across the promotion of individual items.

2.3.4 New brands

Where a **new product** or **market** is created, an organisation may decide to create a new brand rather than use one of its existing brands. One reason for this could be to avoid risking its existing brand's reputation. Another reason could be that none of its existing brands are compatible with the new product or market.

For example, when Whitbread PLC entered the hotel market (in the UK) it created the Premier Inn brand.

2.3.5 Co-brands

Co-branding is where two separate but compatible brands are used to support each other. For example, Nike developed running shoes that are compatible with Apple's iPod.

2.4 Brand value

Brands are often a source of **competitive advantage**. Products with strong brands often sell themselves and can command **high prices** when compared to competitor products. Therefore, a value can be attributed to them.

The following are **three approaches to valuing a brand**:

- Market approach
- Cost approach
- Income approach

2.4.1 The market approach

This approach generates a value on the basis of **market transactions**. A common method used in this form of valuation is known as **relief from royalty**. This reflects the fact that owners of brands have use of the brand for free, whereas they could generate an income by licensing it. This income stream, or royalty rate, is derived by reference to royalty or licence agreements for similar assets and can be used to generate a value.

2.4.2 The cost approach

This approach is based on the **costs incurred to build the brand** – for example, costs involved in registering trademarks and promotional activities. However, it is not the most accurate method of valuation because the cost of building the brand is usually unrelated to its ability to generate revenue.

2.4.3 The income approach

This approach is based on **net present values**. The brand's expected future earnings, or cash flows, can be used to calculate the overall **economic benefit** that it will generate over its life. This benefit is **reduced** by all **expenditure** relating to **brand awareness** (such as advertising) that will be incurred over its life to calculate a net income figure. This income figure is then **discounted** at an interest rate that an investor would expect as a return based on the brand's **risk profile** and **characteristics**. This final value is the value of the brand.

Question 10.2   Branding

Learning outcome E2(xv)

Define what a 'brand' is and briefly explain three methods by which an organisation may value its brand.

(5 marks)

Section summary

Branding is a very general term covering brand names, designs, trademarks, symbols, jingles and the like. A **brand name** refers strictly to letters, words or groups of words which can be spoken. A **brand image** distinguishes a company's product from competing products in the eyes of the user.

The key **benefit of branding** is **product differentiation** and **recognition**.

There are **three approaches to valuing a brand – market, cost** and **income**.

3 Marketing communications

Introduction

Once an organisation has decided on its marketing plan, it needs to put it into practice. This means **communicating its message** to the market and customers. There is a growing range of methods that it can employ for this purpose, which we will now look at.

When conducting a **marketing campaign**, there is a range of possible communication methods and channels the campaign could utilise. The most popular methods are shown below.

Promotional tools

3.1 The promotion mix

The **promotion mix** consists of the blend of promotional tools that are considered appropriate for a specific marketing campaign.

These tools represent the deployment of deliberate and intentional methods calculated to bring about a **favourable response in the customer's behaviour**. Approaches to promotion may be grouped in three general categories:

- **Mass media** – the whole market segment is targeted with the same communication

- **Personal and interactive** – two-way communication between a salesperson and potential customer

- **Personal and direct** – one-way communication from the seller to the potential customer, usually by letter or email

The diagram represents the most obvious **promotion methods**, though other parts of the marketing mix, including the product itself, pricing, policy and distribution channels, are also important.

Choosing the **correct tools** for a particular promotions task is not easy. The process is still very much an art, though it is becoming more scientific because of the access to consumer and media databases. Computer systems may be utilised to match consumer characteristics with promotional tools.

In reality, an experienced marketing manager may be able to reach **sensible conclusions** almost intuitively based on what has been successful in the past and on knowledge of both customers and competitors.

3.2 Consumer and business to business markets

The comment above about experience of a particular market can be generalised in the case of the two broad categories of consumer and business to business markets.

KEY POINTS

Consumer markets (or business to consumer markets) are categorised as consisting of mass audiences which are cost-effectively accessible by television or national newspaper advertising. Supermarkets allow customers to serve themselves and there is little or no personal selling.

Business to business markets (B2B), by contrast, involve a great deal of personal selling at different levels in the organisation. The needs of individual companies are different and therefore mass advertising would be most wasteful. Building on these generalised comments it is possible to present the mix of appropriate tools in the following diagram.

Variation of promotion tools with type of market

3.3 Integrated marketing communications

It is necessary to integrate all the promotional elements to achieve the maximum influence on the customer. **Integrated marketing communications** represent all the elements of an organisation's marketing mix that favourably influence its customers or clients. It goes beyond the right choice of promotion tools to the correct choice of marketing mix. This is illustrated in the diagram below.

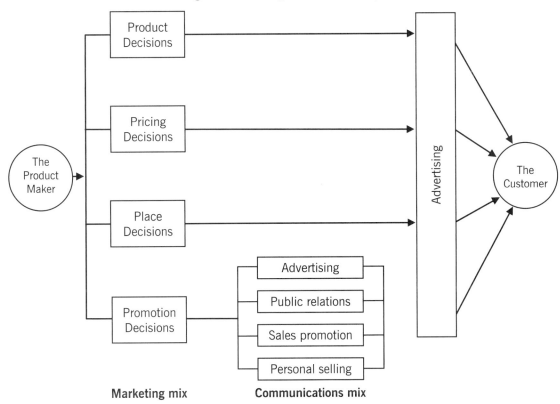

The integrated marketing communication process

Marketing mix   **Communications mix**

3.4 Types of marketing

The following **types of marketing** can be applied by an organisation:

- Consumer marketing (the 4Ps)
- Services marketing (the 3Ps of the extended marketing mix)
- Direct/indirect marketing
- Guerrilla marketing
- Viral marketing
- Interactive marketing
- Experiential marketing
- E-marketing
- Relationship marketing
- Postmodern marketing

3.5 Direct marketing

KEY TERM

The Institute of Direct Marketing in the UK defines DIRECT MARKETING as 'The planned recording, analysis and tracking of customer behaviour to develop relational marketing strategies'. It is worth noting some further key words and phrases associated with direct marketing:

(a) **Response**. Direct marketing is about getting people to respond to invitations and offers.

(b) **Interactive**. The process is two-way involving the supplier and the customer.

(c) **Relationship**. Direct marketing is in many instances an ongoing process of communicating and selling again and again to the same customer.

(d) **Recording and analysis**. Response data is collected and analysed so that the most cost-effective procedures may be arrived at.

(e) **Strategy**. Direct marketing should be seen as part of a comprehensive plan stemming from clearly formulated objectives.

Because direct marketing **removes all channel intermediaries** apart from the advertising and delivery mediums, it is known as a '**zero level channel**'. There are no other parties between the seller and the customer.

Direct marketing encompasses a wide range of media and distribution opportunities, such as:

- Television
- Radio
- Direct mail

- Inserts (eg in newspapers)
- Telemarketing
- The internet

CASE STUDY

Direct Line, the insurance company, turned the motor insurance industry on its head through its ability to bypass the traditional brokers and offer the average consumer not only a cheaper form of insurance, but a high degree of service.

The power of the computer and the internet has transformed the processes by which marketers relate to their customers. Improvements in database software mean the smallest of operations are able to benefit from the information era.

3.5.1 Telemarketing

One form of direct marketing is telemarketing. Telemarketing is a quick, accurate and flexible tool for gathering, maintaining and helping to exploit relevant up to date information about customers and prospects.

KEY TERM

TELEMARKETING is the planned and controlled use of the telephone for sales and marketing opportunities.

Characteristics of telemarketing

(a) **Targeted**. The message is appropriately tailored to the recipient.

(b) **Personal**. Telemarketers can determine and respond immediately to the specific needs of individuals, building long-term personal and profitable relationships.

(c) **Interactive**. Since the dialogue is live, the conversation can be guided to achieve the desired results; the representative is in control.

(d) **Immediate**. Every outbound call achieves an immediate result, even if it is a wrong number or 'not interested'. Customers can be given 24-hour constant access to the company (for inbound calls).

(e) **Flexible**. Conversations can be tailored spontaneously as the representative responds to the contact's needs. Campaign variables can be tested quickly, and changes made while the campaign is in progress.

Possible disadvantages of telemarketing

Telemarketing can be **costly**. There are few economies of scale, and in some situations techniques such as direct mail may be more cost effective.

If poorly handled, telemarketing may be interpreted as **intrusive**. This may alienate potential customers.

3.6 Indirect marketing

KEY TERM

INDIRECT MARKETING is the marketing of products as a consequence of another activity or action.

With indirect marketing the organisation does not push products or services onto customers. Instead it performs a number of related activities that arouse interest in the product or service.

Examples include posting blogs on the internet and publishing articles. A common example is food magazines including 'advertising features' in the form of recipes which use a particular producer's products.

Another form of indirect marketing is **'word of mouth'** advertising. This involves customers who have had positive experiences with the organisation recommending the organisation to their family and friends.

Recent developments in indirect marketing have been **guerrilla** and **viral marketing**.

3.7 Guerrilla marketing

Guerrilla marketing involves taking people by **surprise** and **'creating a buzz'** in **unexpected places**. It relies more on the use of **imagination** than on large sums of money.

The term guerrilla marketing was created by Jay Conrad Levinson in the 1980s. Levinson encouraged marketers to devise their own ideas, utilising their contacts and the organisations' products and services as sources of inspiration.

3.7.1 Principles of guerrilla marketing

Levinson identified the following **principles of guerrilla marketing**:

- It is specifically geared for small organisations and entrepreneurs.

- It should be based on psychology rather than experience, judgement and guesswork.

- It should be based on time, energy and imagination rather than money.

- Organisations should be judged on profit, not sales.

- Marketers should focus on the number of new relationships created in each time period.

- Organisations should focus on creating a standard of excellence in their products and services rather than diversifying.

- Organisations should focus on increasing the numbers of customer referrals as well as the number and size of transactions, rather than just aiming to attract new customers.

- Organisations should co-operate with competitors.

- A combination of marketing methods should be used in a guerrilla marketing campaign.

- The campaign should make use of technology.

CASE STUDY

Guerrilla marketing

More extreme attempts at guerrilla marketing can be risky.

In an effort to promote an online gaming site, a Canadian man leapt into an Olympic pool at the 2004 Games in Athens. He was convicted of trespassing and creating a disturbance and sentenced to months in a Greek prison, but eventually released with a fine of just a few hundred dollars.

In the US (Boston) in 2007, a number of flashing electronic signs designed to promote the television programme Aqua Teen Hunger Force were planted around the city. Unfortunately these were mistakenly identified as explosive devices, causing huge disruption.

However, even examples of guerrilla marketing 'gone wrong' may actually be considered a success by some, as they can generate more publicity than campaigns that 'go well'.

3.8 Viral marketing

KEY POINT

Viral marketing involves the use of **pre-existing social networks** to spread brand awareness or other marketing objectives. This form of marketing is termed 'viral' because the life of the marketing message is comparable to the self-replication and spread of biological and computer viruses. The **viral campaign** is successful when a customer receives the marketing message, copies it, and sends it to their friends or posts it on **social networking sites** such as Twitter and Facebook.

3.8.1 Forms of viral marketing

Examples of viral marketing include:

- Video clips (including those taken on mobile phones)
- Novelty, quirky computer games (usually created using 'Flash')
- E-books
- Text messages
- Music
- Mobile phone ringtones

Viral marketing messages will eventually run out of steam as people who receive the message fail to pass it on. They can be effective, though, even with a relatively short life span.

Individuals who pass on viral marketing are said to have a **high 'Social Networking Potential'**. These people tend to use social networks for much of their time and like to become involved in spreading messages. It is the goal of viral marketers to identify these individuals and design messages that have a high probability of being passed on by them.

3.8.2 The six principles of viral marketing

Dr Ralph F Wilson describes **six principles of an effective viral marketing strategy**:

(a) Provide free products or services – free items attract attention.

(b) The form of the message must be easy to pass on.

(c) The transmission method must be scalable from small to large very quickly to aid the spread of the message.

(d) The message must exploit common motivations and behaviours. Greed, love, success and the need to look 'cool' can provide motivation to spread the message.

(e) Use existing communication networks. People have lists of contacts on their email and social networking sites – getting the message in the right place means it will multiply very quickly.

(f) Take advantage of other people's resources – for example getting banner ads and links onto other websites.

3.8.3 Examples of viral marketing

Four recent examples of viral marketing are:

(a) 'Will it blend?' – a series of video clips where various items were blended in a Blendtec blender.

(b) The Cadbury Dairy Milk Gorilla advert which was made popular on YouTube and Facebook.

(c) The movie 'Cloverfield' where Myspace pages were created for the characters and websites created for fictional companies mentioned in the film.

(d) 'Compare the meerkat.com', a website created as part of a viral marketing campaign for 'Compare the Market.com'. It was featured in a national TV advertising campaign.

3.9 Interactive marketing

KEY POINT

According to Deighton (1996), 'interactive marketing is the ability to address the customer, remember what the customer says and address the customer again in a way that illustrates that we remember what the customer has told us'.

E-commerce has made interactive marketing easier as customer information can be 'remembered' in databases and electronic communications with the customer occur very quickly through the internet.

An organisation which makes good use of interactive marketing is **Amazon.com**. Customers can set preferences and the site records their past transactions. In future visits they are presented with possible purchases based on this information.

3.10 Experiential marketing

KEY POINT

Experiential marketing involves providing an experience that creates an emotional connection between a person and a brand, product or idea.

Experiential marketing encourages potential customers to engage with the personality of the brand **through experiencing it**. It is a combination of in-store promotion techniques and field marketing. It aims not only to sell more products in the short term, but also to encourage customers and potential customers to engage with the personality of the brand.

Experiential marketing is seen as an effective way of connecting with customers, as the emotional connection encourages brand loyalty.

CASE STUDY

In Australia, Absolut Vodka launched a brand called 'Cut' using experiential marketing – combining public relations, point of sale, online and event marketing. Absolut leased two bars in Sydney and Melbourne, and put on DJ sets, band concerts and photo exhibitions in these spaces.

Visitors to the Absolut Cut bars got a free bottle of Cut, and consumers were given a chance to contribute their photos to the exhibits, generating what Absolut hoped would be a viral element to the campaign. The campaign flew in the face of traditional ways to launch a brand. Instead of using mass marketing to blanket the millions in order to reach the few, Absolut chose to target the few to eventually reach the masses.

Question 10.3	Guerrilla and viral marketing

Learning outcome E2(xiii)

Briefly explain the concepts of guerrilla and viral marketing, providing an example of each.   **(4 marks)**

3.11 Digital marketing, e-marketing and social media marketing

Most companies of any size now have a **website** and promotion via the internet is known as **e-marketing**. A website is a **collection of screens** providing information in text and graphic form, any of which can be viewed simply by clicking the appropriate button, word or image on the screen.

Digital marketing is the use of electronic devices (such as PCs, smartphones, tablets, digital TVs, games consoles) to engage with customers. It can be through websites, email, apps and social networks.

Gaining internet traffic or publicity through the use of social network sites such as Facebook and Twitter is known as **social media marketing**. Being able to get the attention of millions of social media users through a very simple online presence is highly attractive to most businesses. It can be an effective way of

obtaining customer feedback and dealing with issues quickly when they arise. It is a particularly effective method of reaching a younger target audience.

3.11.1 Successful websites

To be successful, the **website** should do the following:

(a) **Attract visitors** – good quality, up to date content, easy to navigate, fast to download and quick response times

(b) **Enable participation** – interactive content, and suitable facilities to allow for transactions

(c) **Encourage return visits** – design the site to target the needs of particular segments, offer free services and added-value facilities

(d) **Allow for two-way information sharing** – personalisation reflecting visitor preferences, direct marketing and information retrieval provide visitors with the information they are seeking

(e) **Integrate with back-office systems** – systems must be in place to process orders and dispatch products that have been generated by the website

(f) **Security** – protect visitors' and customers' privacy and security

3.11.2 Benefits of an effective website

Seven benefits of an effective website and how they are generated are shown in the following table.

Benefit	How generated
Market size	Internet-based organisations have a global market and opportunities to develop new methods of distributing their products
Loyalty	Website offers and features
Productivity	Better management of the supply chain
Reputation	Opportunity to offer real customer benefits (such as free information) and develop intimate relationships with customers
Costs	Generally lower than for retail outlets
Communication	Allows quick responses to queries
Convenient	Easy customer access from home or work
Opportunity	Smaller organisations can compete globally with large, established ones
Information	Customer information can be stored and used in marketing. Opportunity for enhanced market segmentation

3.11.3 Potential problems with websites

The main **risks** associated with running a website are with security issues, such as **viruses** or **hackers** damaging the website and perhaps accessing any linked systems. Online payment facilities may make the organisation more susceptible to **credit card fraud**. There is also the risk of the site failing due to **hardware** or **software issues** and potential damage to the organisation's reputation if **confidential customer information** is lost.

Set-up and running costs for a state of the art website can be high, especially with **search engine optimisation** being required to ensure the website appears high up in the search rankings.

3.11.4 Website promotion

To encourage people to **visit** a website and then to **return** at a later date, two promotional tools have become popular. These tools are **banner advertising** and email **promotion**.

3.11.5 Banner advertising

Companies such as YouTube make money by **selling advertising space**. The more popular a site is in terms of visitor numbers, the higher the charges will be to advertise on the site.

Banner adverts are a source of revenue for the websites they appear on. **Affiliate schemes** and **pay-per-click advertising** pay the host site a small fee for every visitor they attract or if they make a subsequent purchase.

Search engines such as **Google** make money in a similar way, but organisations can also pay them a fee to display an advert whenever **key words** are entered into the search box. For example, if you search for 'accountant', results will include paid-for listings – ie an advertisement.

Advertisers may get visitors to **register their interest** in the product when they are on the site so that they can be **directly targeted** in future. At the very least advertisers know exactly how many people have viewed their message and how many were interested enough in it to click on it to find out more.

3.11.6 Email marketing

Email is cheap, relatively easily targeted and can be sent to large numbers of people quickly. It is therefore of great interest to marketers, but there is increasing concern at the prevalence of 'junk' email.

There are various **uses of email for marketing purposes**:

- To advertise a product/service, usually with a link to a website
- To update a subscriber to a product/service with useful information
- To confirm an order
- To invite users to write in or to respond to a helpline

Unsolicited email is probably more intrusive than traditional 'junk mail', though less so than the telephone. However, poor use of email can upset large numbers of people.

3.12 Relationship marketing

The aim of **relationship marketing** is to maximise **customer retention** and satisfaction through two-way communication, rather than to directly increase sales through traditional promotion. Therefore, it recognises the long-term value of building customer relationships through dialogue, rather than to bombard the customer with advertising and promotional messages.

The methods businesses should use to develop **customer relationships** will depend on the nature of the business and available technology. However, some basic principles can be applied:

- Make the most of every customer interaction
- Ensure offers and promotions are relevant to customers
- Value customers and treat them with respect
- Listen to customer comments and complaints
- Act on customer comments and complaints
- Reward customers for loyalty

The internet and mobile phones have created **new communication channels** that businesses can exploit. Interactive marketing is a form of relationship marketing.

3.13 Postmodern marketing

Postmodern marketing is a relatively recent marketing development that is attributed to academic Stephen Brown. It recognises that traditional, broad marketing theory and generalisations may no longer apply. Instead, the focus of marketing should be on giving the **customer an experience** that is **customised** to them and to ensure they receive marketing messages in a form that they prefer.

A key principle is that marketing that is aimed at the world as a whole, generated by a marketer and aimed at many customers should be replaced with a **multidimensional approach** where a marketer communicates with individual customers.

For example, **new media** such as tablets and mobile phones can be used to generate an **interactive** or **immersive experience** rather than something that is static, such as a magazine advert or radio commercial. This approach is more **flexible** than the traditional approach because it is usually controlled electronically online and can be updated at any time. The use of **customer-generated material** is encouraged rather than a single 'brand' message communicated by the business.

This method of marketing encourages flexibility, and enables the organisation to be **nimble**, **reactive** and to **shift position** to align with customers.

3.14 Big Data analytics and marketing

Many of the **marketing developments** discussed in this chapter will generate **large volumes of data**. For example, visitor data from the company's website, responses from online advertising and emails, relationship management software and tablet and phone apps and social networks will all collect information, often without the user being aware of it. This data can be put to a number of uses by a marketing team.

3.14.1 Forecasting demand

Big Data from sources such as website traffic, online trends, customer feedback, promotions and microeconomic factors specific to the business's industry can be processed and an **accurate model of future demand** can be generated (also known as demand sensing). Such analysing uses data correlations alongside other known demand trends to predict **customer demand responses** to new products and marketing campaigns and this information can be fed into the sales forecast. The information will also be passed on to the operations so that the supply side of the business can be balanced with the demand.

3.14.2 Identifying customer preferences

A key benefit of Big Data is the ability to understand the **preferences** and **desires of each customer**. Consumers are increasingly happy to share information about themselves with a business, but only if they trust the organisation first. Once this trust is built, data will come from the customer because they see the benefit of a more personal experience that is created. This saves the customer time in finding what they want (because the website knows the products they are interested in) and more relevant promotions can be created (see below).

Sources of information on customer preferences include **past transactions**, **website data cookies**, responses to **emails** and **online promotions** and **adverts**, and data contained about them on **social networks**. This data about a specific person can also be combined with more general **demographic data** and **trends** to generate predictions about the products the customer might be interested in but no preference has yet been determined through the available data.

3.14.3 Customer experience

Once customer preferences are identified, marketers can use Big Data to **create unique customer experiences** from hard data and evidence instead of relying on intuition and estimates that are applied to all customers.

Therefore, the days of marketing departments working on hunches and simple analytics are over. Marketers can now design **online product pages** around the customer concerned that introduce the **most relevant** and **desirable offers** and **promotions** to the customer at the most **appropriate time**. The online interface can be optimised and even customised to each particular customer so that the whole shopping process becomes as **friction-free** as possible. This is all possible because the information from Big Data allows the system to know what mix of promotions will work best for each customer.

3.14.4 Monitoring transactions

Many years ago the only place to buy goods was at a local shop. Then, as **technology developed**, goods became available to purchase by mail order and over the telephone. In more recent times, goods can now also be bought over the internet, on mobile phones and tablets, and on other devices such as TVs and games consoles.

Each method of purchasing goods is known as a **channel** and therefore, in current times, customer transactions are said to be '**multi-channel**'. Customers expect a simple and consistent experience whenever and however they choose to transact with an organisation.

Big Data has a role to play in **monitoring customer transactions** to ensure the customer experience is consistent. This is usually achieved by creating a **customer account** that contains **basic information** about the customer (such as name, address, email, phone number and past transactions) and tapping into this when the customer transacts with the company. For online and app transactions this is achieved by requiring the customer to **log into their account**, but for telephone and face to face transactions this is more difficult. However, the use of **loyalty cards** and requesting **email addresses** can be used to link the customer to their account.

By **linking transactions** to the **customer account**, the business can monitor all of a **customer's activity** and expand its knowledge about them – for example, when they are most likely to visit a shop and how much will they spend. The customer benefits because having their **purchase history** in one place means that returning goods or making complaints is easier and it demonstrates loyalty to the brand.

Section summary

Once the organisation has decided on its **marketing plan**, it needs to get its message out to the market and its customers.

Common forms of **marketing communication** include:

- Consumer marketing (the 4Ps)
- Services marketing (the 7Ps of the extended marketing mix)
- Direct marketing
- Indirect marketing
- Guerrilla marketing
- Viral marketing
- Interactive marketing
- E-marketing
- Relationship marketing
- Postmodern marketing

Big Data has an important role to play in modern marketing.

Exam alert

'New' forms of marketing such as e-marketing and viral marketing are topical. CIMA are keen for their exams to be topical and up to date, so these topics could be examined regularly.

Chapter Summary

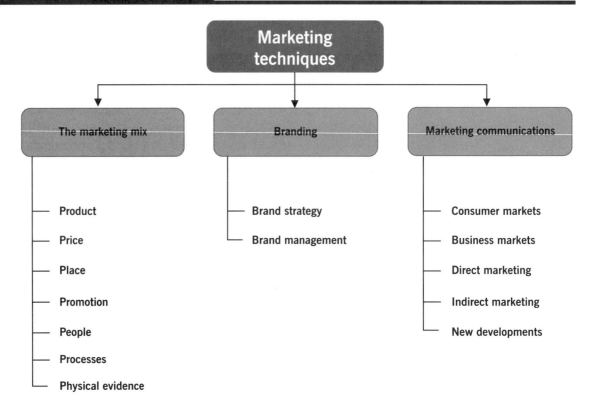

Quick Quiz

1   Which of the following is included in the additional 3Ps of the extended marketing mix?

    A   Processes
    B   Product
    C   Promotion
    D   Price

2   Which of the following stages comes immediately after 'introduction' in the product life cycle?

    A   Growth
    B   Market maturity
    C   Market penetration
    D   Decline

3   Which branding strategy uses the power of the brand name to assist all products in a range?

    A   Brand expansion
    B   Multi-branding
    C   Family branding
    D   Corporate branding

4   In the context of marketing, which type of marketing is referred to as B2B marketing?

    A   Business to brand
    B   Brand to brand
    C   Business to business
    D   Buyer to business

5   State four attributes of a successful website.

    1   ....

    2   ....

    3   ....

    4   ....

Answers to Quick Quiz

1   A   Processes is one of the 3Ps of the marketing mix extended to services.

2   A   Growth follows the introduction stage as demand for the product increases.

3   C   Family branding uses the power of the brand name to assist all products in a range.

4   C   In the context of marketing, B2B means business to business marketing.

5   Four possible attributes include:

   1   Attract visitors
   2   Enable participation
   3   Encourage return visits
   4   Allow for two-way information sharing

Answers to Questions

10.1 The extended marketing mix

Services have a **different nature** to traditional products. In particular, they have the following characteristics that products do not. They have no physical form, are inseparable from the provider and may lack consistency as a different member of staff may provide them each time. Additionally, they cannot be stored and usually do not result in the transfer of property.

The **three additional elements of the extended marketing mix** are:

People – services are provided by members of staff who are inseparable from the service

Process – services involve a process, for example a hair cut may involve waiting to be served, a hair wash, styling, colouring and hair drying.

Physical evidence – as services are intangible, some physical item should be provided to give the customer evidence of ownership.

10.2 Branding

A **brand** is a name, term, sign, symbol or design intended to identify the product of a seller and to differentiate it from those of competitors.

There are three main methods of valuing a brand:

The market approach

This approach generates a value on the basis of **market transactions**. A common method used is known as **relief from royalty**. A potential income stream is calculated on the basis of what the owner of the brand could generate by licensing it to third parties and it is the value of this income stream which is used to calculate the brand's value.

The cost approach

Under this approach, the value of the brand is based on the **amount of costs incurred in building it**. However, it is not the most accurate method of valuation because the cost of building the brand is usually unrelated to its ability to generate revenue.

The income approach

This approach is based on the brand's **expected future earnings**, or cash flows – ie the amount of cash it is expected to generate less the costs of building it. The net income figure is then **discounted** at an interest rate that an investor would expect as a return based on the brand's **risk profile** and **characteristics**. This final value is the value of the brand.

10.3 Guerrilla and viral marketing

Guerrilla marketing

Guerrilla marketing is an unconventional method of marketing and involves taking people by **surprise** and 'creating a buzz' in **unexpected places**.

Example: Surprising store customers with 'for today only sales' to which they are given very little notice.

Viral marketing

Viral marketing involves the use of **pre-existing social networks** to spread brand awareness or other marketing objectives.

Example: Video clips posted on websites such as YouTube

Now try this question from the Practice Question Bank	**Number**
	46, 47, 48, 49, 50

DEVELOPMENTS IN MARKETING

 In this chapter we conclude our study of marketing by considering several 'standalone' areas.

Consumer behaviour and the purchasing process is an important consideration for marketers since understanding how consumers think and act will help them to fine-tune their marketing activities.

Not-for-profit organisations have different requirements of marketing than those for whom profit maximisation is key. There is a distinct **charity marketing mix** which is important for you to understand.

Internal marketing is about training and motivating employees to support the organisation's external marketing activities. **Employee 'buy-in'** is often critical to the success of the marketing effort – especially in service organisations.

Finally, we turn our attention to the increasingly important issue of **social marketing** and **corporate social responsibility**. Society now expects organisations to have a wider responsibility than earning profit for shareholders.

Topic list	Learning outcomes	Syllabus references	Ability required
1 Consumer behaviour	E1(b), E2(a)	E1(vi), E2(iii)	application
2 Marketing in not-for-profit organisations	E1(a), E2(a)	E1(iv), E2(ix)	application
3 Internal marketing	E2(a)	E2(iii), E2(vii)	application
4 Corporate social responsibility and social marketing	E1(b), E2(b)	E1(vii), E1(viii) E2(xix)	application

Chapter Overview

1 Consumer behaviour

Introduction

Marketing aims to produce mutually beneficial **exchanges** between **customer** and **supplier**. However, 'the customer' in a transaction can involve a number of different roles.

1.1 The customer

The table below sets out the **different roles** 'the customer' may have in a transaction.

'Customer'		Household example: a family pet animal needing vaccination	Business example: ordering of office stationery
Buyer	The person who selects a product or service	A veterinary surgeon, on the pet owner's behalf, recommends and orders a vaccine.	The office manager may order stationery for other departments.
Payer	The person who finances the purchase	The pet owner pays for the vaccination – or perhaps an insurance company pays in the end.	The payer is the company, via the accounts department.
User	Receives the benefit of the product or service	The pet receives the benefit of the vaccination (but the owner receives emotional benefits too, perhaps).	Users are those with access to the stationery.

The value of this distinction is that it enables **marketing efforts** and **activities** to be correctly **focused** on the people involved in the transaction. For example, an office supplies company would direct most of its marketing efforts to the office manager buying the stationery. The approach to the accounts department would be slightly different – a relationship might have to be built up to ensure speedy payment.

1.2 Buyer behaviour

Buyer behaviour describes the **activities** and **decision processes** relating to buying. Treating buying behaviour as a process enables us to distinguish between the **different buying roles** that customers sometimes assume. Typically, marketers make a distinction between:

- Consumers as buyers
- Organisations as buyers

1.3 Consumer buying behaviour

There are three main theories of consumer behaviour:

- The **cognitive paradigm** sees a purchase as the outcome of a rational decision-making process.
- The **learned behaviour** theory emphasises the importance of past purchases.
- The **habitual decision-making** theory emphasises habit and brand loyalty.

1.3.1 A consumer decision-making model

Lancaster and Withey (2003) identified five steps in consumer decision making.

	Element	Comment
STEP ①	**Need/problem recognition**	The customer recognises a need or a problem to solve. This is a motive to search for a solution.
STEP ②	**Pre-purchase/information search**	Marketers can provide product information, tailored to need. The customer might come up with alternatives.
STEP ③	**Evaluation of alternatives**	Marketers can make products available for evaluation and provide comparative information about competing products. The important thing, though, is to get the product onto the shortlist of options.
STEP ④	**The purchase decision**	Selection and purchase
STEP ⑤	**Post-purchase evaluation**	Experience 'feeds back' to the beginning of the process, providing positive or negative reinforcement of the purchase decision. If the consumer is dissatisfied, they will be back at the problem recognition stage again. If the consumer is satisfied, the next decision process for the product may be cut short and they may skip straight to the decision, on the basis of loyalty.

Such a model provides a useful descriptive **framework** for marketers.

Question 11.1	Consumer buying

Learning outcome E1(vi)

Briefly explain the five stages of the consumer buying process. **(5 marks)**

1.4 Influences on consumer buying

Some of the main influences on consumer buying are shown in the following diagram (based on Lancaster and Withey).

Influences on buyers

```
                                    ┌─────────────────┐
                                    │ Personal factors │
                                    │ Age and life cycle│   ┌─────────────────┐
                                    │      stage       │   │  Psychological  │
                                    │   Occupation     │   │     factors     │
┌─────────────┐   ┌─────────────┐   │    Economic      │   │   Motivation    │
│Social factors│  │Cultural factors│ │  circumstances   │   │    Learning     │
│Reference groups│ │   Cultural   │  │ Lifestyle and    │   │   Perception    │
│   Family     │  │  Sub-culture │  │  personality     │   │ Beliefs and     │
│Roles and status│ │ Social class │  └─────────────────┘   │   attitudes     │
└─────────────┘   └─────────────┘                          └─────────────────┘
```

```
                        ┌─────────────┐
                        │    Buyer    │
                        └─────────────┘
```

1.4.1 Social factors

Social factors relate to the social groupings a consumer belongs to or aspires to, and trends in society which influence buying patterns. The learning of gender-related, consumer and occupational roles are examples of socialisation.

A **reference group** is an actual or imaginary group that influences an individual's evaluations, aspirations or behaviour.

Reference groups influence a buying decision by making the individual **aware** of a product or brand, allowing them to **compare** their attitude with that of the group, encouraging the individual to **adopt an attitude consistent** with the group, and then **reinforcing and legitimising** the individual's decision to conform.

Social interaction theory states that an individual's buying decision can be influenced by what they think others in society are doing. For example, trends towards people buying ethical products may be a consequence of individuals perceiving that purchasing such goods is expected by society.

A 'role' is the sum or 'system' of expectations which other people have of an individual. For example, a male may consider himself to be a **father** and **husband**, a good **neighbour**, an active member of the **local community**, a **supporter** of his sports club, an amateur **golfer** and perhaps a **tradesman** or a **professional**.

Families differ in many ways, not only in broad issues of socioeconomic status but in buyer behaviour and consumption patterns.

1.4.2 Cultural factors

Culture comprises the **values**, **attitudes** and **beliefs** in the pattern of life adopted by people, that help them integrate and communicate as members of society. Culture comprises cultural artefacts, lifestyles, and so on. For example, alcohol consumption is part of the culture of many countries in Western Europe, whereas it is frowned on in Muslim and some other countries.

1.4.3 Personal factors

'**Personal' factors** include such things as **age**, **stage of family** and **life cycle**, **occupation**, **economic circumstances** and **lifestyle**.

Individuals will buy different types of product depending on their **age**. This is particularly relevant to such products as clothes, furniture and recreation.

The **family life cycle** is used in the West to model purchase behaviour patterns. For example, couples in the early stages of their marriage before having children will have different needs and consumption patterns from those, say, after their children have left home. In the UK, where house purchase is the norm, this has particular implications for sellers of financial services.

A person's **occupation** will influence consumption, and the task for marketers is to identify the occupational groups that have an above-average interest in their products and services.

Buying patterns are also heavily influenced by an individual's **economic circumstances**. An individual's economic circumstances consist of:

- Spendable income: its level, stability and time pattern
- Savings and assets, including the percentage that is liquid
- Borrowing power
- Attitude towards spending versus saving

A **lifestyle** is an individual's way of living as identified by their activities, interests and opinions. Marketers will search for relationships between their products and lifestyle groups. There are many different lifestyle classifications.

1.4.4 Psychological factors

The process of buyer behaviour is also influenced by **four psychological factors**:

- Motivation
- Perception
- Learning
- Beliefs and attitudes

Motivation is an inner state that energises, activates or moves, that directs or channels.

(a) Maslow's (1954) theory of motivation seeks to explain why people are driven by particular needs at particular times. Maslow argues that human needs are arranged in a **hierarchy** comprising, in their order of importance: physiological needs, safety needs, social needs, esteem needs and self-actualisation needs.

(b) Herzberg (1968) developed a 'two-factor theory' of motivation that distinguishes between **factors that cause dissatisfaction and factors that cause satisfaction**. The task for the marketer is, therefore, to avoid 'dissatisfiers' such as poor after-sales service, as these things will not sell the product but may well unsell it. In addition, the marketer should identify the major satisfiers or motivators of purchase and make sure that they are supplied to the customer.

Perception is the process whereby people select, organise and interpret sensory stimuli into a meaningful and coherent picture. The way consumers view an object (for example, their mental picture of a brand or the traits they attribute to a brand) may vary according to their past experience, expectation, needs, interests, attitudes and beliefs.

Learning concerns the process whereby an individual's behaviour changes as a result of their experience.

A **belief** is a descriptive thought that a person holds about something. Beliefs are important to marketers as the **brand beliefs** that people have about products make up the brand images of those products.

An **attitude** describes a person's enduring favourable or unfavourable cognitive evaluations, emotional feelings and action tendencies towards some object or idea. **Attitudes** lead people to behave in a fairly **consistent** way towards similar objects. Attitudes tend to settle into a consistent pattern – to change one attitude may entail major changes to other attitudes.

1.4.5 Rational consumer behaviour

Buying behaviour of consumers can be analysed by considering the following four factors:

(a) **Frequency**

Frequent purchases (such as washing powder) do not need a high level of attention from the consumer because the price is low and they have made similar purchases many times in the past.

(b) **Relevance**

Important decisions (such as expensive ones) or decisions made when purchasing a product for the first time require a high degree of attention from the consumer. This is because the consumer wants to reduce the risk of making the wrong choice and will therefore spend time gathering and processing information.

(c) **Influence**

Some consumers are more prone than others to being influenced by their friends, family and society.

(d) **Freedom**

Some decisions can be made voluntarily and others involuntarily. For example, having to use a petrol station because you have run out of fuel, rather than your usual filling station, is an example of an involuntary decision. Buying books and music would be a voluntary choice.

CASE STUDY

Children as consumers

What do you call a consumer who wants to buy everything you have, doesn't care what it costs and is less than five feet tall? A marketer's dream? Nope. You call them kids. (*AdRelevance Intelligence Report*, 2000)

Children are bombarded by brand messages almost from birth, including counting books for preschoolers that use M&Ms or Cheerios, exposure to brightly coloured and appealing branded packaging in the supermarket, movie and toy tie-ins in fast-food restaurants, product placement in movies, advertisements on television and the internet, and pitches from entertainment and sports stars in a range of media. In fact, it's almost impossible to escape marketing messages. No wonder, then, that children as young as two are starting to recognise logos and request specific brands as soon as they begin to speak.

Children are a prime target for marketers. Not only do children today have more disposable income at younger ages, but they have significant influence over family purchases. YTV's 2002 Tween Report estimated that Canadian children aged 9 to 14 spend $1.9 billion and influence $20 billion in family purchases per year. Marketing experts call it 'pester power', or the 'nag factor' – the ability to get kids to nag their parents to buy a specific product or take them to a specific restaurant. After all, if your child asks you for the latest toy 37 times a day for a week, the odds are that you'll eventually give in and buy it.

As a result, there is now a whole segment of the marketing industry devoted to figuring out how to sell things to kids.

Professionals who work with children are becoming increasingly concerned about this onslaught. In 2003, the Canadian Paediatric Society issued a position statement on the impact of media on children and youth that raised several concerns about advertising.

In 2004, a coalition of Canadian health groups led by the Centre for Science in the Public Interest called for a ban on advertising aimed at children 13 or younger. Quebec has already banned print and broadcast advertising aimed at children under 13, although children certainly see advertising from other sources as well.

Many activists consider food advertising to be a leading cause of the increase in overweight children. A report released in December 2005 by the Institute of Medicine, Food Marketing to Children and Youth: Threat or Opportunity?, observed that in the US alone, over $11 billion dollars a year is spent on marketing food and beverages to children. And the food advertised to children is generally less than nutritious: most of it is highly processed, rich in saturated fat, salt and sugar, and poor in nutrients like fibre, vitamins, calcium and iron.

http://television-vs-children.blogspot.com/2008/11/target-market-children-as-consumers.html,
19 November 2008

1.5 Organisations as buyers

KEY POINT

Organisations are viewed as more **rational** than individuals. The buying decision-making process is likely to be formal. **Organisational (or industrial) buying** is the process organisations use to establish the need to purchase products and services and how these products and services are selected and purchased.

As we saw earlier, **transactions between organisations** are referred to as **business to business** or **B2B**, whereas transactions involving an **organisation and a consumer** are sometimes referred to as **business to consumer** or **B2C**.

When considering **organisational markets**, the following factors should be taken into account:

(a)   Organisational markets normally comprise **fewer buyers**, with a few buyers responsible for the majority of sales.

(b)   Because of this smaller customer base and the importance and power of larger customers, there is generally a **close relationship between buyer and seller**.

(c) **Demand** for industrial goods is ultimately derived from the demand for consumer goods. In addition, the total demand for many industrial products is **inelastic** – in other words, it is not affected much by price changes.

(d) Size of orders, quality and service level agreements can make B2B transactions **complex** technically.

(e) Businesses have greater **purchasing power** than consumers and can afford higher-value items. Due to this, business customers have a higher financial value than consumers.

(f) The purchase decision is usually made by **consensus** in an organisational setting, rather than being the responsibility of one person.

1.5.1 Process of organisational buying behaviour

A typical **organisational buying process** is summarised in the following table.

Stage in behaviour	Comment
Stage 1. **Recognise the problem**	The stimulus may come from within or outside the organisation.
Stage 2. **Develop product specifications or service requirements to solve the problem**	People participating in the buying decision assess the problem or need and determine what will be required to resolve or satisfy it. This may take the form of detailed specifications.
Stage 3. **Search for products and suppliers**	The third stage of the process is similar to that of information search, utilising trade shows, trade publications, supplier catalogues, and soliciting proposals from known suppliers. This should result in a list of several alternative products.
Stage 4. **Evaluate products relative to specifications**	These are evaluated in order to ascertain whether they meet the product specifications developed in the second stage. Suppliers may also be evaluated according to criteria such as price, service and ability to deliver.
Stage 5. **Select and order the most appropriate product**	The most appropriate product and supplier is then selected. In some cases an organisational buyer may select a number of suppliers in order to reduce the possibility of disruption caused by strikes, shortages or bankruptcy of suppliers. The order will then be made, often with specific details regarding terms, credit arrangements, delivery dates and technical assistance or after-sales service.
Stage 6. **Evaluate the product and supplier performance**	The product and supplier will then be evaluated by comparing with specifications regarding product quality and so on, and the performance of the supplier over the terms of the contract for the sale.

1.5.2 The decision making unit (DMU) in the organisation

A major difference between consumer and organisational buying behaviour is the fact that **organisational purchase decisions are rarely made by a single individual**. Normally, purchasing decisions are made by a number of people from different functional areas, possibly at different levels within the organisation.

Groups within the DMU	
Initiators	Initiate the buying process and help define purchase specifications
Influencers	Help define the specification and also provide an input into the process of evaluating the available alternatives
Deciders	Have the responsibility for deciding on product requirements and suppliers
Approvers	Authorise the proposals of deciders and buyers
Buyers	Have the formal authority for the selection of suppliers and negotiating purchase terms
Gatekeepers	By controlling the flow of information, may be able to stop sellers from reaching individuals within the buying centre
Users	The end user, or operator, of the items purchased

The **size**, **structure** and **formality of the decision making unit (DMU)** will vary depending on the specific situation. Key considerations include:

- **Who** are the principal participants in the buying process?

- In what areas do they exert the **greatest influence**?

- What is their **level of influence**?

- What **evaluative criteria** do each of the participants make use of and how **professional** is the buying process?

- To what extent is **buying centralised** in large organisations?

The **people** involved in the buying process must be convinced that the purchase will be safe for them – for example, there was an advertising slogan to the effect that 'nobody gets sacked for buying IBM'.

1.5.3 Selection criteria

The issue of precisely how **organisational buyers** make the **purchase decision**, in terms of the selection criteria determining the choice of supplier, has been the subject of various pieces of research.

Important **selection criteria** could be as follows:

- Delivery capability
- Quality
- Price
- Repair and after-sales service
- Technical capability
- Performance history
- Production facilities
- Help and advice
- Control systems
- Reputation

- Financial position
- Attitude towards the buyer
- Compliance with bidding procedures
- Training support
- Communications on the progress of the order
- Management and organisation
- Packaging
- Moral/legal issues
- Location
- Labour relations

1.5.4 Business to government marketing

Business to government marketing (B2G) is a form of B2B marketing but, rather than dealing with another business, the organisation deals with a government department or other public service, for example a pharmaceutical company that supplies the National Health Service in the UK.

The key difference between B2G and B2B marketing is that contracts for the Government are usually determined by a **tendering process** and the **contract** is often for a **longer** duration and for a substantially **greater amount** of value than B2B contracts.

This puts the Government in a strong position to choose the most cost-effective suppliers. Also, some government **contracts** are **predetermined** and suppliers are expected to fulfil strict contractual requirements for a set price.

Successful organisations may receive a **lower profit margin**, but the length of the contract and greater security provided by having the Government as a customer should make up for this.

Section summary

In **consumer marketing**, the **customer** may combine **a number of roles** – for example **buyer**, **payer** and **user**.

The **influences on a consumer's purchasing decision** may be classified as **social**, **cultural**, **personal and psychological**.

Business to business marketing reflects the more complex and **formal organisational buying process**.

2 Marketing in not-for-profit organisations

Introduction

Increasingly, public sector and charitable organisations are adopting a more commercial approach to their operations, including the use of marketing techniques.

2.1 Charity and not-for-profit marketing

Marketing has a lot to offer charities and not-for-profit organisations, for example in terms of **marketing research** and a clear understanding of **segmentation**, **targeting** and **positioning**.

Marketing techniques are now recognised as just as appropriate in not-for-profit (NFP) organisations as in a commercial environment. The tasks of setting objectives, developing strategies, devising appropriate marketing mixes and implementing controls are just as relevant for charities and NFP organisations.

Public sector organisations may use marketing tools to encourage competitive tendering to provide government services. Almost all organisations need to compete with other employers to recruit employees.

Many NFP organisations have introduced initiatives to raise money, such as hospitals selling paramedical services to local industry, and universities developing commercial centres to sell research and consultancy skills.

2.1.1 What are public sector organisations 'exchanging'?

Lancaster and Withey (2006) identified typical exchanges between public sector organisations and their 'customers'. For example, a university provides education, qualifications and the prospect of career advancement in return for time and fees. A local government council provides local services and contributes to the lifestyle of residents in return for taxation payments and perhaps votes.

There are many other possible examples; the key point is that even though we are talking about public sector bodies an exchange is taking place, and therefore there is likely to be a role for marketing.

2.2 Characteristics of charity and not-for-profit (NFP) marketing

Dibb *et al* suggests NFP organisations need to consider their **marketing objectives**, **target markets**, **marketing mixes** and how they will **control** marketing activities.

(a)   **Objectives** will not be based on profit achievement but rather on achieving a particular response from target markets. The organisation will need to be open and honest in showing how it has managed its budget and allocated funds raised. Efficiency and effectiveness are particularly important in the use of taxpayer funds or donations.

(b)   **Target marketing** will involve identifying a number of different audiences. Bruce (2005) identifies three **types of customers for charities**.

     (i)   **Beneficiaries** include not only those who receive tangible support, but also those who benefit from lobbying and publicity.

     (ii)   **Supporters** provide money, time and skill. Voluntary workers form an important group of supporters. Those who choose to buy from charities are supporters, as are those who advocate their causes.

     (iii)   **Regulators** include both formal bodies, such as the Charities Commission and local authorities, and less formal groups such as residents' associations.

The groups that NFPs' marketing activities try to reach can be classified as contributors (for example of time), customers (for example clients, patients, students) and volunteers.

(c)   Charities and NFP organisations often deal more with services than products. In this sense the **extended marketing mix** that includes people, processes and physical evidence is important.

     (i)   **Appearance** should be businesslike rather than appearing extravagant.

     (ii)   **Process** is increasingly important – for example, the use of direct debit to pay council tax or donations reduces administration costs.

     (iii)   **People**, whether employed or volunteers, must offer good service and be caring in their dealings with clients.

     (iv)   **Distribution channels** are often shorter with fewer intermediaries than in the profit-making sector. Wholesalers and distributors available to business organisations do not exist in most non-business contexts.

     (v)   **Promotion** for charities often includes personal selling with street-corner and door to door collections. Advertising is becoming increasingly important for large charities. Direct marketing is growing due to the ease of developing databases. Sponsorship (online), competitions and special events are also widely used.

     (vi)   **Pricing**. Value for money is important. Opportunity cost, where an individual is persuaded of the value of donating time or funds, is often relevant.

(d)   **Control** aims to ensure progress is proceeding as planned. For example, a charity would compare donations and expenditure to budget. To control NFP marketing activities, managers must specify what factors need to be monitored and permissible variance levels. Relevant measures could include number of employees, number of volunteers (charities), number of 'customers' served and satisfaction levels.

2.2.1 Public sector organisations

Public sector organisations are increasingly being run on a more commercial basis and therefore management of them is becoming involved in marketing decisions. Much of this is in regards to obtaining information about those using social services. For example, the elderly may be asked what their needs are so that social services can help look after them in the community. In this context, 'marketing decisions' relate to what services to provide, where to provide them and how to provide them. Private sector

consultancies may be used to carry out the research if there is insufficient expertise available in the public sector.

2.2.2 Non-governmental organisations (NGOs)

Non-governmental organisations (NGOs) are private sector, voluntary organisations that contribute to, or participate in, education, training or other humanitarian, progressive or watchdog activities. Some NGOs are accredited by the UN.

Important NGOs include the International Committee of the Red Cross, International Organization for Standardisation, Amnesty International and the World Wildlife Fund.

NGOs use marketing to find a position for themselves in the market, gain supporters, establish client and donor needs and communicate with stakeholders.

2.3 The charity marketing mix

The following four elements of the **marketing mix** are particularly relevant to **charities** (product, price, processes and place). The mix adopted must suit the charity's overall philosophy.

2.3.1 Product

A charity's **product** is essentially the **cause** it supports and the **help** it provides – for example, cancer research aims to reduce the suffering and improve the prospects of future cancer patients. It is important to communicate what work the charity does and what donations are used for.

When a supporter provides money to a charity, the idea of what the money will be used for is their source of satisfaction, knowing they have helped others or furthered a particular cause.

2.3.2 Price

Price is very important to larger charities since sales of goods and services provide their largest single source of income. Proper cost accounting techniques must be applied where appropriate.

2.3.3 Processes

Since supporters are crucial to a charity's income and beneficiaries are the reason why it exists, **processes** must be as customer friendly as possible. This is certainly an area where philosophy is important.

2.3.4 Place

If charities distribute physical goods this can present challenges – for example, providing disaster relief overseas.

On the other hand, charities that distribute funds to the poor, for instance, or to pay for medical research, may have very short and easily managed distribution chains. Donations for many charities are increasingly being made online.

Section summary

Charities and **not-for-profit organisations** are increasingly utilising marketing tools and techniques, particularly in relation to **segmentation**, **targeting** and **positioning**.

Charities are **similar** in some respects to **service organisations** and the extended marketing mix is particularly relevant to them.

The **charity marketing mix** adopted must suit the charity's overall philosophy.

3   Internal marketing

Introduction

In this section we shall study what internal marketing is and its importance in motivating employees to support the marketing effort of the organisation.

KEY POINT

Internal marketing has been well summarised by Peck *et al*:

> *'Internal marketing is concerned with creating, developing and maintaining an **internal service culture and orientation**, which in turn assists and supports the organisation in the achievement of its goals. ...*
>
> *'The basic premise behind the development of internal marketing is the acknowledgement of the **impact of employee behaviour and attitudes** on the relationship between staff and external customers. The skills and customer orientation of these employees are, therefore, critical to the customers' perception of the organisation and their future loyalty to the organisation.'*

In other words, it is through internal marketing that all **employees** can develop an **understanding of how their tasks**, and the way they perform them, **create** and **deliver customer value** and **build relationships**.

CASE STUDY

LL Bean (US catalogue retailer)

To inspire its employees to practise the marketing concept, LL Bean has for decades displayed posters around its office that proclaim the following:

> *'What is a customer? A customer is the most important person ever in this company, in person or by mail. A customer is not dependent on us, we are dependent on him. A customer is not an interruption of our work, he is the purpose of it. We are not doing a favour by serving him, he is doing us a favour by giving us the opportunity to do so. A customer is not someone to argue or match wits with, nobody ever won an argument with a customer. A customer is a person who brings us his wants; it is our job to handle them profitably to him and to ourselves.'*

3.1   Implementing internal marketing

Peck *et al* identified several **interrelated activities** thought critical **in implementing internal marketing**.

- **Organisational design**: eg drawing key employees together in cross-functional customer service or quality teams

- **Regular staff surveys**: assessing the internal service culture and attitudes

- **Internal customer segmentation**: adapting the internal marketing mix to different employee groups

- **Personal development and training**: focused on core competencies for internal marketing

- **Empowerment and involvement**: enabling staff, within defined parameters, to use their discretion to deliver better service to customers

- **Recognition and rewards**: based on employees' contribution to service excellence

- **Internal communications**: ensuring information flows to support cross-functional co-ordination, and all-employee awareness of their role and contribution to service

- **Performance measures**: evaluating each individual's contribution to marketing objectives

- **Building supportive working relationships**: creating a climate of consideration, trust and support, within which internal communications and service delivery can be encouraged and improved

3.2 The internal marketing mix

Jobber directly relates the elements of the **marketing mix** to internal customers as follows.

Product	The **marketing plan** and strategies that are being proposed to employees or other functions, together with the values, attitudes and actions needed to make the plan successful (eg marketing budgets, extra staff).
Price	What internal customers are being asked to **pay or sacrifice** as a result of accepting the marketing plan (eg lost resources, lower status, new ways of working or harder work).
Promotion (or communications)	The communications **media and messages** used to inform, persuade and gain the support of internal customers for the marketing plan. The message and language will have to be adapted to the needs, concerns and understanding of the target audience (eg eliminating marketing jargon).
Place	How the product (plan) and communications are **delivered** to internal customers: eg via meetings, committees, seminars and informal conversations. This may be direct or via intermediaries (eg consultants).

3.3 Segmenting the internal market

The **internal marketing mix** (like the external marketing mix) will need to be adapted to the needs and drivers of the target audience. The internal market can (like the external market) be **segmented** to allow targeting to the distinctive needs of each group. **Two methods of segmentation** have been suggested.

3.3.1 Jobber's method of segmentation

Jobber (2007) suggests segmentation of internal customers into:

- **Supporters**: those who are likely to gain from the change or plan, or are already committed to it
- **Neutrals**: those who are likely to experience both gains and losses from the change or plan
- **Opposers**: those who are likely to lose from the change or plan, or are traditional opponents

The **product** (plan) and **price** may have to be **modified** to **gain acceptance** from opponents. Place decisions will be used to reach each group most effectively (eg high-involvement approaches such as consultation meetings for supporters and neutrals). Promotional objectives will also differ according to the target group, because of their different positions on issues.

3.3.2 Christopher et al's method of segmentation

Christopher *et al* (2002) suggest an alternative way of segmenting internal customers, according to **how close they are to external customers**:

(a) **Contactors** have frequent or regular customer contact and are typically heavily involved with conventional marketing activities (eg sales or customer service roles).

   They need to be well versed in the organisation's marketing strategies and trained, prepared and motivated to service customers on a day to day basis in a responsive manner.

(b) **Modifiers** are not directly involved with conventional marketing activities, but still have frequent contact with customers (eg receptionists, switchboard, the credit department). These people need a clear view of the organisation's marketing strategy and the importance of being responsive to customers' needs.

(c) **Influencers** are involved with the traditional elements of marketing, but have little or no direct customer contact (eg in product development or market research). Companies must ensure that these people develop a sense of customer responsiveness, as they influence the total value offering to the customer.

(d)   **Isolateds** are support functions that have neither direct customer contact nor marketing input – but whose activities nevertheless affect the organisation's performance (eg HR and IT). Such staff need to be sensitive to the needs of **internal** customers as well as their role in the chain that delivers value to customers. Gummesson uses the term 'part-time marketers' to describe such employees.

3.4 The importance of internal customer communications

Information and **communication** are the foundation of all organisational activity. From a marketing point of view, internal communications may be particularly important in the following areas.

Employer branding	The **organisation's image**, mediated by communication, creates an employer brand: the organisation's image or identity as an employer in the market in which it competes for quality labour.
	Recruitment communications (job ads, application handling, interviews and so on) are public relations and marketing exercises. They must reflect the organisation's values and make an attractive offering to potential employees.
Employee communication and involvement	In many countries, there are **legal requirements** for communication and consultation with employees on matters that affect them.
	The sharing of marketing information encourages employees to **identify with the organisation**, its products/services and its customers and other stakeholders: the marketing function effectively 'sells' quality – and customer-focused values.
	Information sharing also supports **task performance** (keeping employees informed about new products and marketing plans, and equipping them to make a competent contribution) and **decision making** (eg by supplying market information or customer feedback to managers in other departments).
	Internal communications (eg through meetings, presentations, newsletters, intranet sites or suggestion schemes) can be used to improve **information flow** in all directions through the organisation. This may be particularly helpful where it encourages information and ideas sharing between management and front-line customer-facing staff, and between different organisational functions.
Employee relations	Armstrong (2000) describes the aims of employee relations as:
	• Building **stable and co-operative relationships** with employees
	• Achieving **commitment** through employee involvement and communications
	• Developing **mutuality**: a common interest in achieving the organisation's goals through the development of a culture of shared values
	Co-operative employee relations depend on direct and open communication with employees, and giving employees a voice on matters that concern them (including customer care and corporate social responsibility).

3.5 Challenges for internal communication

Jones and Cheeseman (2005) argue that it is growing more **difficult** for organisations to maintain communication with staff, while other pressures contribute to increasing staff diversity and isolation – making such communications even more **necessary** for integration and involvement. Some of the challenges they identify include:

(a) **Flatter management structures**, meaning that managers have more people reporting to them (a wider 'span of control')

(b) **Downsizing**, creating workload pressures that may hinder communication and networking

(c) A trend towards **teleworking** and **'virtual' organisations**, so that staff may be geographically remote from the office, manager and each other

(d) **Globalisation**, creating increasingly diverse workforces and culturally distinctive units within the organisation, which pose barriers to 'mass' communication

CASE STUDY

Jobber (2007) cites the example of software giant **Microsoft**.

'It is very easy for senior management to decide upon a set of values that represent a company's ethos, but much harder to engage employees' attention. This was the problem Microsoft faced when trying to communicate its identity as a company internally. It expressed its company values in terms of six attributes: passion, respect, accountability, integrity, self-criticism and eagerness.

Its internal marketing strategy was to ensure this ethos was communicated to employees in three stages. First, there was a campaign across the UK to generate positive feelings about the project. Second, a series of road-shows was held around the firm's UK offices to discuss the core values in depth. Third, a compulsory education programme was launched to ensure all staff understood the proposition.

The creative element of the programme was centred on the well-known David Brent character from the BBC series The Office. Actor Ricky Gervais, who played this character, became involved and a special 15-minute video in the style of the programme was filmed, adding humour to the project and raising its appeal to staff.

The result was that the project achieved high recognition levels for the main message of the campaign among employees, national press coverage and an award for the best internal marketing campaign from the magazine Marketing.'

3.6 Tools of internal communication

A variety of communication tools are used in **formal internal communications**, including: company brochures and newsletters, intranets, video presentations (often web-based), team meetings, personal presentations, conferences, one to one interviews, negotiating and consultative meetings (eg with employee representatives), letters, email and web-based 'meetings'.

Let's consider some of these in more detail.

3.6.1 Email for internal communication

You should already be aware of the use of email for marketing purposes. We now consider the use of email for internal communication.

The **advantages of email** for internal communication include:

(a) Messages can be sent and received very **quickly**.

(b) Email is cheap.

(c) A '**hard copy**' may be printed if required.

(d) Messages can be sent worldwide at any time: email is **24/7**, regardless of time zones and office hours.

(e) The user can **attach complex documents** (spreadsheets, graphics, photos) where added data or impact are required.

(f) Email message **management software** (such as Microsoft Outlook) enables the sending of messages to multiple recipients, integration with an 'address book' (database of contacts), corporate stationery options and facilities for mail organisation and filing.

3.6.2 Intranet

An **intranet** is an **internal, mini version of the internet**, using a combination of networked computers and web technology.

'Inter' means 'between' and 'intra' means 'within'. This may be a useful reminder. The **internet** is used to disseminate and exchange information among the public at large, and between organisations. An **intranet** is used to disseminate and exchange information within an organisation; only employees are able to access this information.

The **corporate intranet** may be used for:

(a) **Performance data**: linked to sales, inventory, job progress and other database and reporting systems, enabling employees to process and analyse data to fulfil their work objectives

(b) **Employment information**: online policy and procedures manuals (health and safety, equal opportunity, disciplinary rules, customer service values and so on), training and induction material, internal contacts for help and information

(c) **Employee support/information**: advice on first aid, healthy working at computer terminals, training courses offered and so on

(d) **Notice boards**: for the posting of messages to and from employees: notice of meetings, events, trade union activities and so on

(e) **Departmental home pages**: information and news about each department's personnel and activities, to aid cross-functional understanding

(f) **Bulletins or newsletters**: details of product launches and marketing campaigns, staff moves, changes in company policy – or whatever might be communicated through the print equivalent, plus links to relevant pages for details

(g) **Email facilities**: for the exchange of messages and reports between employees in different locations

(h) **Upward communication**: suggestion schemes, feedback questionnaires, employee attitude surveys

(i) **Individual personnel files**: to which employees can download their training materials, references, certificates, appraisals, goal plans and so on

Benefits of intranets include the following:

(a)   **Cost savings** from the elimination of storage, printing and distribution of documents that can instead be exchanged electronically or made available online.

(b)   **More frequent use** made of online documents than printed reference resources (eg procedures manuals) and more flexible and efficient searching and updating of data.

(c)   **Wider access to corporate information**. This facilitates multi-directional communication and co-ordination (particularly for multi-site working). It is also a mechanism of internal marketing and corporate culture.

(d)   **Virtual team working**. The term 'virtual team' has been coined to describe how technology can link people in structures which simulate the dynamics of team working (sense of belonging, joint goals, information sharing and collaboration) despite the geographical dispersion of team members in different locations or constantly on the move.

3.6.3 Team meetings

Meetings play an important part in the life of any organisation.

(a)   **Formal discussions** are used for information exchange, problem solving and decision making – for example, negotiations with suppliers, meetings to give or receive product/idea presentations or 'pitches', and employee interviews.

(b)   **Informal discussions** may be called regularly, or on an ad hoc basis, for communication and consultation on matters of interest or concern – for example, informal briefings and marketing or project team meetings.

Despite the relative inconvenience (compared to group emails, say) of gathering people together in a physical location, team meetings are an **excellent tool of internal communication** and marketing.

Face to face discussion is particularly **effective in exchanging information** and **developing relationships**.

Information exchange	Developing relationships
Encourages **ideas generation**: participants encouraging and prompting each other	Brainstorming meeting for promotion planning or **customer care** improvement
Encourages **problem solving** and **conflict resolution**: allows exchange, supportive communication and sensitivity to personal factors	**Customer complaint handling**, or team conflict resolution
Improves **decision making**: adds different viewpoints and information in real time	Team meetings to **decide plans** or **allocate roles and tasks**
Facilitates **persuasion**: use of personal charisma, logic, sensitivity to feedback	**Sales negotiations**, pitching ideas to internal customers, promoting service values
Encourages **co-operation**: information sharing and all-member participation	**Cross-functional team meetings**, briefings, project meetings
Shows the **human face** of an organisation and encourages identification with it	**Personal internal/external customer service**, internal marketing

3.6.4 The grapevine

In addition to formal attempts by the organisation to communicate with its employees, there **are informal communication channels** such as the '**grapevine**' – for example friends, colleagues and contacts developing internal networks, sharing news, information and gossip. This is a fast and effective way of transmitting information; unfortunately, it is often **inaccurate**, **subjective** and **difficult for management to control**.

Question 11.2   Internal marketing

Learning outcome E2(vii)

Briefly explain four benefits that an intranet will bring an organisation in terms of its internal marketing.

(4 marks)

Section summary

Internal marketing enables employees to develop an understanding of how their role delivers customer value and builds relationships.

The internal market can be segmented according to the roles employees play in relation to the customer.

Internal marketing has **implications** for **employer branding**, **employee communication** and **employee relations**.

Key communication tools used in internal marketing include email, intranets, team meetings and personal/informal communication.

4   Corporate social responsibility and social marketing

Introduction

Marketing techniques may be applied to encourage consumption of products which are **potentially damaging** to the health and wellbeing of the individual and society. Examples include tobacco, alcohol, cars, detergents and even electronic goods such as computers.

There may be conflict between what is profitable for a business organisation and the interests of the customer, or of society.

Many organisations and businesses now accept **responsibility** for **their actions**, rather than simply setting out to provide consumer satisfaction and maximise profits.

KEY TERM

CORPORATE SOCIAL RESPONSIBILITY involves an organisation accepting that it is part of society and, as such, is accountable to society for the consequences of its actions. Socially responsible firms believe that they have an obligation to maximise the positive impact they have on their stakeholders.

4.1 Social responsibility, ethics and the law

Social responsibility is closely related to ethics. However, ethics is just one aspect of social responsibility – ethics also concerns **personal moral principles** and **values**. **Business ethics** is similar to personal ethics, but relates to principles and standards that govern the behaviour of a business organisation. Ethical business decisions are ones that 'feel right' and may be judged as being 'right' or 'wrong' in the eyes of those outside the organisation.

Ethics is concerned with **judgements of society** that have no enforceable impact on an organisation. On the other hand, **laws** are rules that can actually be **upheld in court**. Behaviour which is not subject to legal penalties may still be unethical and socially irresponsible.

We can **classify marketing decisions** according to ethics and legality in four different ways:

- **Ethical and legal** (eg printing on recycled paper)
- **Unethical and legal** (eg targeting young adults in an 'alcopops' advertising campaign)
- **Ethical but illegal** (eg publishing stolen but revealing documents about mis-selling)
- **Unethical and illegal** (eg passing off cheap imitation goods as designer brands)

4.1.1 Benefits of being socially responsible

The following are benefits to an organisation of acting in a socially responsible manner:

(a) **Positive publicity**

Making changes to business practices in advance of legislation enforcing them will show the business in a positive light.

(b) **Cost reduction**

Many social responsibility policies (such as reducing waste and recycling) can actually save a business money.

(c) **Unique selling point (USP)**

Being socially responsible is a way of standing out from the competition and giving products a USP.

(d) **Increased revenue**

Volume of sales may increase as well as the price consumers are prepared to pay. Both benefits can significantly increase company revenue.

4.1.2 Corporate citizenship in practice

Companies have devised a number of different **definitions or approaches to corporate citizenship**.

CASE STUDY

Abbott Laboratories

Global citizenship reflects how a company advances its business objectives, engages its stakeholders, implements its policies, applies its social investment and philanthropy, and exercises its influence to make productive contributions to society.

At Abbott, global citizenship also means thoughtfully balancing financial, environmental and social responsibilities with providing quality healthcare worldwide. Our programmes include public education; environment, health and safety; and access to healthcare. These efforts reflect an engagement and partnership with stakeholders in the pursuit of sustainable solutions to challenges facing the global community.

AT&T

For AT&T, corporate citizenship means caring about the communities it is involved with, keeping the environment healthy, making AT&T a safe and rewarding place to work and behaving ethically in all its business dealings.

Coca-Cola

Responsible corporate citizenship is at the heart of The Coca-Cola Promise, which is based on four core values:

- **Marketplace**. We will adhere to the highest ethical standards, knowing that the quality of our products, the integrity of our brands and the dedication of our people build trust and strengthen relationships. We will serve the people who enjoy our brands through innovation, superb customer service, and respect for the unique customs and cultures in the communities where we do business.

- **Workplace**. We will treat each other with dignity, fairness and respect. We will foster an inclusive environment that encourages all employees to develop and perform to their fullest potential, consistent with a commitment to human rights in our workplace. The Coca-Cola workplace will be a place where everyone's ideas and contributions are valued, and where responsibility and accountability are encouraged and rewarded.

- **Environment**. We will conduct our business in ways that protect and preserve the environment. We will integrate principles of environmental stewardship and sustainable development into our business decisions and processes.

- **Community**. We will contribute our time, expertise and resources to help develop sustainable communities in partnership with local leaders. We will seek to improve the quality of life through locally relevant initiatives wherever we do business.

Texas Instruments

Beyond the bottom line, the worth of a corporation is reflected in its impact in the community. At TI, our philosophy is simple and dates back to our founding fathers. Giving back to the communities where we operate makes them better places to live and work, in turn making them better places to do business. TI takes its commitment seriously and actively participates in community involvement through three ways – philanthropy, civic leadership and public policy, and grass roots efforts.

4.2 Ethical marketing

Ethical issues usually revolve around **safety**, **quality** and **value** and frequently arise from failure to provide adequate information to the customer.

Ethical issues relating to the product or service may range from **omission of uncomfortable facts** in product literature to **deliberate deception**.

A particularly serious problem is when **an unsafe product is supplied**, requiring **product recall**.

Ethical considerations are also relevant to **promotional practices**. Advertising and personal selling are areas in which there may be temptation to exaggerate, slant, conceal, distort and falsify information.

Many people think that persuading people to buy something they don't really want is intrinsically unethical, especially if '**hard sell**' tactics are used.

The **targeting of children** in marketing campaigns has also attracted criticism – potentially damaging an organisation's reputation and brand.

Also relevant to this area is the issue of **inducements**. It is widely accepted that a small gift such as a mouse mat or a diary is a useful way of keeping a supplier's name in front of an industrial purchaser. However, most people would condemn the payment of substantial gifts as a way of encouraging use of a particular supplier. But where does the dividing line lie between these two extremes?

Some **important considerations** that an ethical organisation may make include:

- Whether its advertising is fair, balanced and truthful.

- Who does it sell to – who is the marketing aimed at?

- Is the business acting honestly and responsibly when communicating with customers?

- Competition within the market. Is the business operating with competitors as a cartel?

- Are its products appropriate, safe and environmentally friendly?

- How does it deal with unhappy customers?

- Does it consider customers' privacy and security when holding data on them?

- Does it exploit anyone, for example in its advertising or pricing strategies? How does it deal with vulnerable people?

- Are employees considered? Some may be uncomfortable acting in an unethical way.

Summary of benefits to socially responsible and ethical organisations
Competitive advantage: Being socially responsible may be a USP and offer the organisation an opportunity to create a distinct identity for itself and its products.
Greater revenue: Socially responsible organisations can often charge a premium for their products.
Reduced costs: Some costs may be reduced if an organisation adopts socially responsible practices – for example, recycling may reduce costs of sending waste to landfill.
Positive publicity: Introducing changes voluntarily, before any regulations come into force, will reflect favourably on the organisation.

CASE STUDY

Banks accused of mis-selling risky investments to the elderly

Banks and wealth advisers are preying on vulnerable elderly people, with commission-driven staff encouraging customers in their 70s or 80s to move large sums of money from savings accounts into equities.

Many elderly people do not understand the implications of their new investments and end up losing tens of thousands of pounds when they thought their capital was secure.

Emma Parker of the Financial Ombudsman Service (FOS) says: 'We receive thousands of complaints from elderly people who believe that they have been mis-sold a long-term investment product. Increasingly, the complaints are about bank or building society branch staff.'

With today's complex financial products, some pensioners believe they are receiving advice when they are merely hearing a sales pitch. Since April the FOS has received 1,809 investment complaints from consumers aged 65 or older. The elderly now account for 22% of all investment complaints, compared with 19% last year.

(*The Times*, 15 August 2009)

CASE STUDY

Toyota car recall hits US, Europe and China

Toyota has announced the recall of vehicles in the US, Europe and China over concerns about accelerator pedals getting stuck on floor mats.

The firm has announced plans to recall 1.1 million more cars in the US a day after saying it was suspending sales of eight popular US models.

According to an application to China's quality control office, it wants to recall 75,552 RAV4 vehicles there. The cars in question were manufactured between 19 March 2009 and 25 January 2010 in Tianjin, according to a notice on the website of the General Administration of Quality Supervision, Inspection and Quarantine of the People's Republic of China.

The specifics of the recall in Europe have yet to be decided – the carmaker was trying to establish how many European models shared the parts used in the cars recalled in the US.

Last week, Toyota recalled 2.3 million cars in the US with faulty pedals. It has now recalled almost 8 million cars in the US in the past 4 months. Last November, it recalled 4.2 million cars because of worries over pedals getting lodged under floor mats.

'Toyota's remedy plan is to modify or replace the accelerator pedals on the subject vehicles to address the risk of floor mat entrapment,' the company said.

The latest recall affects five models in the US: the 2008–2010 Highlander and the 2009–2010 Corolla, Venza, Matrix and Pontiac Vibe.

Toyota shares fell a further 3.9% in Japan, after dropping 4.3% on Wednesday, as concerns about the impact of the recalls on the carmaker's financial health and reputation gripped investors.

Separately, Ford said it would be suspending production of a van made and sold in China that has an accelerator pedal made by the same firm at the centre of Toyota's investigations.

However, Ford said it had only been using the pedal in the Transit Classic model since December, with only 1,663 vehicles produced.

www.bbc.co.uk, 28 January 2010

4.3 Marketing sustainability

As business organisations are increasingly making sustainability part of their **corporate strategy**, there is an important role for marketing to play to make the most of a business's sustainable credentials. The role of marketing in relation to sustainability might include:

- **Identifying the impact** of the organisation on the environment and generating solutions where the organisation and society might benefit

- **Ensuring sustainability** is **part** of all business processes

- **Generating a genuine role** for the organisation to fulfil in terms of being sustainable and benefiting society

- **Generating organisational** and **brand values** relating to sustainability

- **Developing new ideas** for business processes, products and services that are truly sustainable

- **Consistently getting sustainability messages across** in all communications

4.4 Social marketing

KEY TERM

SOCIAL MARKETING is the application of marketing techniques to achieve non-commercial goals, for example to encourage behaviour that benefits the environment and to encourage good health.

Governments may attempt to use social marketing to encourage consumption of **merit goods** and discourage consumption of **demerit goods**.

Merit goods are goods or services provided free for the **benefit of society** by the Government, for example education and healthcare.

Demerit goods are those considered by the Government to be **unhealthy or damaging to society**. Examples are alcohol, cigarettes and gambling.

For example, a social marketing campaign could encourage people to stop smoking, drive safely, eat healthily or practise safe sex.

Exam skills

You should remember that 'social marketing' and 'social media marketing' are two very different things, so you need to read questions carefully to make sure your answer is appropriate!

4.5 Social media

KEY TERM

SOCIAL MEDIA was defined by Kaplan and Haenlein (2010) as internet-based applications that build on the ideological and technological foundations of Web 2.0, and that allow the creation and exchange of user-generated content.

4.5.1 Types of social media

Kaplan and Haenlein (2010) provide the following examples of social media:

- **Blogs** (Wordpress)
- **Micro-blogging** (Twitter)

- **Social networking sites** (Facebook)
- **Virtual social worlds** (Second Life)
- **Collaborative projects** (Wikipedia)
- **Content communities** (YouTube)
- **Virtual game worlds** (World of Warcraft)

Some businesses communicate internally and externally using **Instant Messaging** (IM). This allows interconnected users to exchange text messages and files. IM can also be used for **'live' customer service** provision. Organisations such as Microsoft (Office Communicator) and BlackBerry (BlackBerry Messenger) offer free messaging tools. The use of social media such as **Facebook** and **LinkedIn** is becoming very significant in corporate promotional strategies. As well as being used by employees as alternatives to the telephone or email, social networking sites give businesses a fantastic opportunity to widen their circle of contacts.

Using Facebook, for example, a small business can target an **audience of thousands** without much effort or advertising. With a good company profile and little in terms of costs, a new market opens up, as do the opportunities to do business.

Employees' behaviour on social networking sites can cause organisations problems. The headlines seem to confirm employers' prejudices: 'Twitter costs businesses £1.4bn' and 'Facebook scandal – 233 million hours lost monthly as employees waste time on social networking'. Even the BBC in the UK advertises its Facebook presence with 'Say goodbye to worktime boredom'.

4.5.2 Effect of social media on the organisation

Kaplan identified a number of potential business uses for social media:

(a) **Marketing research**

The use of social media by customers may provide a business with a wealth of information, such as a person's sex, age and online habits, that can be used for marketing purposes.

(b) **Communication**

The company can use social media to communicate directly with the customer, such as through Facebook posts. Sales promotions and new products can be advertised quickly and at a low cost. There is also the opportunity for the customer to communicate directly with the company – for example by creating their own content and sharing with the company. In addition, positive or negative word of mouth may be spread faster, and to a wider audience, than through traditional means. Therefore there is a risk of a company's official marketing campaign being undermined by customers posting negative feedback about the organisation through social media.

(c) **Sales promotions and discounts**

With social media being increasingly consumed through mobile devices such as phones and tablets, there is an opportunity to use a person's location to target specified offers and promotions. For example, the O2 Priority app allows users to find special offers in their local area.

(d) **Relationship development and loyalty programmes**

A key purpose of marketing is to generate repeat business, and social media has an important role to play. Loyalty programmes can be created that encourage repeat business such as an app for a coffee shop that rewards a customer with a free drink after a number of visits to a particular location.

4.5.3 Four I's of Social Media

Kaplan developed the Four I's of Social Media as advice to businesses on how best to communicate with customers:

- **Individualise** – activities should take a customer's interests and preferences into account
- **Involve** – engaging conversations should be used to involve the customer in the interaction
- **Integrate** – activities should be integrated into a customer's life so they do not become a nuisance
- **Initiate** – customer-generated content should be encouraged

Exam skills

Exam questions on corporate social responsibility, social marketing and social media may focus on definitions and basic principles.

Section summary

Corporate social responsibility involves an organisation accepting that it is part of society and, as such, is **accountable to society** for the consequences of its actions.

Unethical marketing practices are ultimately likely to **damage** an organisation's reputation and brand – and ultimately sales.

Social marketing is the application of marketing techniques to achieve **non-commercial goals**, for example to encourage behaviour that benefits the environment or encourages good health.

Chapter Summary

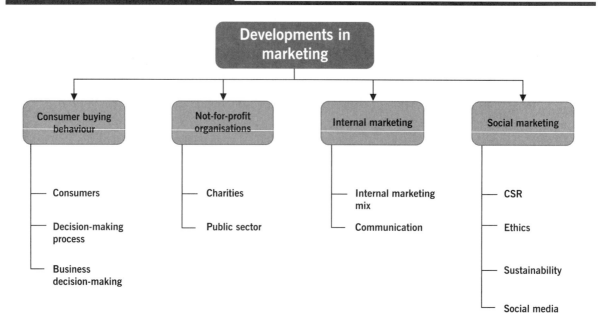

Quick Quiz

1   Which type of customer is described as 'the person who selects a product or service'?

    A   The payer
    B   The user
    C   The consumer
    D   The buyer

2   Which group within an organisation's decision-making unit initiates the buying process and helps define purchase specifications?

    A   Initiators
    B   Influencers
    C   Deciders
    D   Gatekeepers

3   Which of the following is not a type of customer of a charity?

    A   Beneficiaries
    B   Supporters
    C   Regulators
    D   Lobbyists

4   Briefly describe the purpose of internal marketing.

5   According to Caroll and Buchholtz (2000), what are the four main layers of corporate social responsibility?

    A   Charitable, ethical, economic and philanthropic
    B   Economic, legal, ethical and philanthropic
    C   Legal, charitable, ethical and economic
    D   Social, economic, ethical and legal

Answers to Quick Quiz

1   D   The buyer selects the product or service.

2   A   Initiators are the group within an organisation's decision-making unit that initiates the buying process and helps define purchase specifications.

3   D   Lobbyists are not a type of charity customer.

           Beneficiaries are those who receive tangible support from the charity and who benefit from lobbying and publicity.

           Supporters are those who provide the charity with money, time and skill.

           Regulators include formal bodies, such as the Charities Commission, and less formal groups such as residents' associations.

4   'Internal marketing is concerned with creating, developing and maintaining an internal service culture and orientation, which in turn assists and supports the organisation in the achievement of its goals.'

5   B   According to Caroll and Buchholtz (2000), the four main layers of corporate social responsibility are economic, legal, ethical and philanthropic (this revises what you studied in Chapter 2).

Answer to Questions

11.1 Consumer buying

The **five stages in the consumer buying process** are:

Stage 1: Need/problem recognition

The customer recognises a need or a problem to solve. There is a motive to search for a solution.

Stage 2: Pre-purchase/information search

The customer searches for information they can use to base their decision on.

Stage 3: Evaluation of alternatives

The customer evaluates the various options they have generated.

Stage 4: The purchase decision

The purchase decision is made and the product or service selected based on how it meets their needs and other factors such as cost.

Stage 5: Post-purchase evaluation

The customer evaluates their purchase. If they are dissatisfied, they will be back at the problem recognition stage again. If they are satisfied, the next decision process for the product may be cut short and they may skip straight to the decision, on the basis of loyalty.

11.2 Internal marketing

Four benefits that an intranet will bring an organisation in relation to its internal marketing are:

Cost savings

Intranets eliminate the need to store, print and distribute documents of internal marketing. Instead they can be exchanged electronically or be made available online.

Efficiency

It is often quicker, easier and generally more efficient to search for and update material which is stored electronically.

Distribution

Intranets facilitate multi-directional communication and co-ordination. This means information can be distributed quickly to a number of sites in many countries.

Virtual team working

Employees may work in isolated locations but still be part of a team. Intranets promote virtual teams by providing a central source of information and corporate culture that enables such individuals to feel part of the organisation.

Now try this question from the Practice Question Bank	Number
	51, 52, 53, 54, 55

MANAGING HUMAN RESOURCES

Part F

HUMAN RESOURCE MANAGEMENT

 In this chapter we examine the subject of **human resource management (HRM)** and, by way of introduction, we note that HRM is different from traditional personnel management.

HRM takes a **strategic** approach to an organisation's recruitment, training and appraisal systems. **Personnel management** is concerned with the **low-level detail** of day to day management.

However, we will focus most of our attention on a number of human resource theories which aim to get the maximum output from employees. In particular we will focus our attention on the factors which contribute to employee motivation.

Later in the chapter we shall consider recent developments in terms of how organisations are structured and the effect this has had on working arrangements for employees.

Before concluding with a look at **ethical issues**, we revisit HRM from a strategic perspective by looking at how organisations develop an HR plan.

Topic list	Learning outcomes	Syllabus references	Ability required
1 Human resource management	F1(a)	F1(i)	comprehension
2 Human resource management theories	F1(a)	F1(i), F1(ii), F1(iii)	comprehension
3 Employee motivation: Remuneration	F1(b), F2(a)	F1(vii), F2(v)	application
4 Employee motivation: Other factors	F2(a), F2(b)	F2(v), F2(vii)	application
5 HR management in different types of organisation	F1(a)	F1(iv)	comprehension
6 Working arrangements	F2(a)	F2(v)	application
7 The HR plan	F2(b)	F2(viii), F2(ix)	application
8 CIMA's Ethical Guidelines	F2(b)	F2(x)	application

Chapter Overview

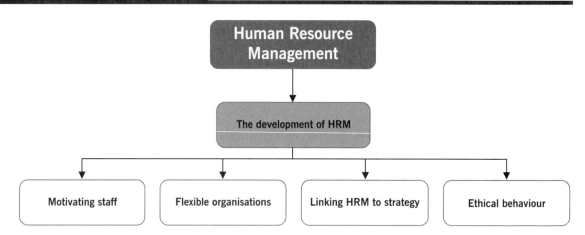

1 Human resource management

Introduction

In this chapter we look at what **human resource management** is, the **theories** behind it and how it contributes to the **success of an organisation**. We also consider the importance of **ethics** to organisations and its relevance to the line manager.

1.1 What is human resource management?

KEY TERMS

HUMAN RESOURCE MANAGEMENT (HRM) is the process of evaluating an organisation's human resource needs, finding people to fill those needs, and getting the best work from each employee by providing the right incentives and job environment. It has the overall aim of helping an organisation achieve its goals.

PERSONNEL MANAGEMENT deals with day to day issues such as hiring and firing and industrial relations in general. Unlike HRM, it does not play a strategic role in an organisation.

1.2 The objectives of human resource management (HRM)

It is possible to identify **four main objectives of HRM**:

(a) To **develop an effective human component** for the organisation which will respond effectively to change

(b) To **obtain and develop the human resources** required by the organisation and to **use** and **motivate** them **effectively**

(c) To **create and maintain a co-operative climate** of relationships within the organisation and to this end to perform a 'firefighting' role dealing with disputes as they arise

(d) To meet the organisation's **social and legal responsibilities** relating to the human resource

1.3 Why is HRM important?

Effective HRM and employee development are strategically necessary as they contribute to the success of the organisation. Particular benefits of HRM are:

(a) **Increased productivity**. Developing employee skills might make employees more productive.

(b) **Enhanced group learning**. Employees work more and more in multiskilled teams. Each employee has to be competent at several tasks. Some employees have to be trained to work together (ie in team working skills).

(c) **Reduced staff turnover**. Training and developing staff often reduces turnover rates. This increases the effectiveness of operations and profitability as staff become more experienced.

(d) **Encouragement of initiative**. Organisations can gain significant advantage from encouraging and exploiting the present and potential abilities of the people within them.

1.4 HRM

KEY POINT

> **Human resource management (HRM)** is based on the assumption that the management and deployment of staff is a key **strategic factor** in an organisation's competitive performance. HRM requires top management involvement and the **promotion** of **culture** and **values** so that employees' commitment, as opposed merely to their consent, is obtained.

HRM reflects a **wider, more modern view** than **traditional personnel management** which is primarily concerned with managing day to day operations.

The table below identifies other differences in approach.

Issue	Personnel	HRM
Employees	Viewed as a cost	View as assets
Employee motivation	Payment/coercion	Consent/involvement
Management concern	Operational (eg fire underperforming staff)	Operational and strategic (eg fill vacancy and meet future needs of organisation)
Manager role	Negotiator/transactional	Facilitator/transformational leadership

There are two types of HRM – hard and soft. **Hard HRM** views employees as a resource just like tools and equipment. Hard HRM suggests that empowerment of employees should not be encouraged and human resources (HR) effort should be limited to recruiting and retaining staff. **Soft HRM** views employees as the organisation's most important asset and as a source of competitive advantage. HR effort should be high, with staff being empowered and competitive rates of pay offered (performance should be rewarded).

1.4.1 Armstrong

Armstrong (2003) defined HRM as 'a strategic approach to the acquisition, motivation, development and management of the organisation's human resources'.

1.4.2 Bratton and Gold

Bratton and Gold (1999) gave a more detailed definition. 'HRM emphasises that employees are crucial to achieving sustainable competitive advantage, that human resources practices need to be integrated with the corporate strategy, and that human resource specialists help organisational controllers to meet both efficiency and equity objectives.'

A precise interpretation of HRM centres on the following notions:

(a)   The **personnel function** has become centrally concerned with issues of broader relevance to the business and its objectives, such as change management, the introduction of technology, and the implications of falling birth rates and skill shortages for the resourcing of the business.

(b)   HRM should be **integrated with strategic planning** – that is, with management at the broadest and highest level. The objectives of the HR function should be directly related to achieving the organisation's goals for growth, competitive gain and improvement of 'bottom line' performance.

(c)   HRM managers should be **professionals**.

1.4.3 Tyson and Fell

S Tyson and A Fell (*Evaluating the Personnel Function*) suggest **four major roles** for HRM which illustrate the shift in emphasis to the strategic viewpoint:

(a)   To represent the organisation's **central value system** (or culture)
(b)   To **maintain the boundaries of the organisation** (its identity and the flow of people in and out of it)

(c)   To provide **stability and continuity** (through planned succession, flexibility and so on)

(d)   To adapt the organisation to **change**

Some companies will have a **separate HR function** with staff authority over other departments. Smaller companies may not be able to afford the luxury of such a function.

HRM is therefore a **set of activities** that may or may not have a separate department to manage it.

Exam alert

You may be tested on the role of an 'HR' division.

Question 12.1	Human resource management

Learning outcome F1(i)

Briefly explain how human resource management contributes to the success of an organisation.

(2 marks)

1.5 The human resource cycle

A common approach to viewing HR is as a **six-stage cycle**:

(1)   **Recruitment**
(2)   **Selection**
(3)   **Induction**
(4)   **Appraisal, training and development**
(5)   **Motivation and retention**
(6)   **Termination**

Another relatively simple model that provides a framework for explaining the nature and significance of HRM is the human resource cycle (Devanna, 1984). The model is shown below.

Human resource cycle

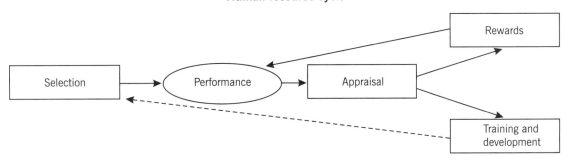

Selection is important to ensure the organisation obtains people with the qualities and skills required.

Appraisal enables targets to be set that contribute to the achievement of the overall strategic objectives of the organisation. It also identifies skills and performance gaps, and provides information relevant to reward levels.

Training and development ensure skills remain up to date, relevant, and comparable with the best in the industry.

The **reward system** should motivate and ensure valued staff are retained.

Performance depends on each of the four components and how they are co-ordinated.

1.6 The Guest model of HRM

David Guest (1997) developed a model to show the relationship between an organisation's HRM strategy and HRM activities.

Guest's six components					
① **HRM** strategy	② **HRM** practices	③ **HRM** outcomes	④ **Behavioural** outcomes	⑤ **Performance** outcomes	⑥ **Financial** outcomes
Differentiation (innovation)	Selection Training	Commitment Quality	Effort Motivation	**High:** Productivity	Profits Return on investment
Focus (quality)	Appraisal Rewards	Flexibility	Co-operation Involvement	Quality Innovation	
Cost (cost reduction)	Job redesign Involvement Status and security		Organisational citizenship	**Low:** Absenteeism Employee turnover Conflict Customer complaints	

The model proposes that HRM practices should aim to result in **high staff commitment** and **high-quality, flexible employees**. Achieving these three HRM outcomes will facilitate the achievement of the behavioural, performance and financial outcomes shown in the table.

1.7 Limitations of HRM models

Models of HRM practices (such as Devanna's and Guest's) tend to **underestimate** the influence of external **opportunities** or **threats** and internal **strengths** and **weaknesses**.

KEY POINTS

External factors such as **competition, technology, political/legal factors, economic factors** and **social/cultural factors** will all impact on HRM.

Internal factors such as the **organisational structure** and **culture** will also impact on HRM.

In addition, the way people are managed often depends on the approach favoured by their **line manager**. Some managers favour the 'hard' or rational approach – others believe in a 'softer' approach that emphasises individual and organisational development.

Cultural, **economic** and **legal traditions** within a country will also shape HR policies. For example, in **Japan** and the **US** there is little state intervention in business and therefore organisations are free to form their own practices. However, in former communist states such as **China** and some **Eastern European** countries, there remains a relatively high degree of state intervention.

1.8 HR and knowledge workers

Economies are increasingly moving from manufacturing to service provision. As a result, staff are becoming **knowledge workers** and this has the following implications for HR.

As professionals, workers should be given a **good degree of autonomy** and **flexibility** to do their jobs and there should be good prospects for **career progression** available for those who contribute high-quality information on a consistent basis. **Appraisal** and **reward systems** should be aligned with the goal of **providing quality information**.

Employees should be **recruited for their knowledge,** not just their ability to physically do something. Once developed, **knowledge should be retained** within the organisation, so policies such as filling vacancies from within and providing career paths are important. HR policies should also promote the **sharing of**

knowledge by utilising team working and job rotation. Training, development and appraisal plans should seek the **attainment** and **development of knowledge**, possibly by encouraging employees to take ownership of their own training and development. Finally, **reward systems** should make use of performance-related pay and profit-sharing schemes to motivate employees to perform at their best.

1.9 High-performance work arrangements

High-performance work arrangements (practices to achieve high employee performance) are dependent on the skills, ideas, commitment and intelligence of employees for their success. To achieve this it is important that employees participate in job design, enrichment and rotation (see later). There should be open and honest communication between people at all levels, and everyone should be empowered and listened to. It is also important for the employer to compromise and negotiate with employees.

Section summary

Human resource management (HRM) involves evaluating an organisation's human resource needs, finding people to fill those needs, and getting the best work from each employee by providing the right incentives and job environment.

HRM contributes to the success of an organisation through increased productivity, enhanced group learning, reduced staff turnover and encouragement of initiative.

HRM is important at each stage in the **human resource cycle**.

There are a number of **factors** both **internal** and **external** to the organisation which **limit the success** of any HRM policy.

2 Human resource management theories

Introduction

In this section we look at some of the most **significant theories** related to the management of people. Exam questions may require you to spot them in a scenario or you may be asked to explain them directly.

HRM theories often relate to three interlinked aspects: **ability**, **opportunity** and **motivation**. Many theorists believe that individual employee performance is a multiplicative function of ability and motivation and that the environment also determines the level of performance.

2.1 Ability

Ability refers to the **skill**, **knowledge** and **capability** required of employees in order to fulfil the objectives of the organisation.

2.1.1 Taylor: scientific management

One of the first theorists to discover the link between employee ability and the objectives of the organisation was Frederick W Taylor who pioneered the **scientific management** movement. He argued that management should be based on 'well-recognised, clearly defined and fixed principles, instead of depending on more or less hazy ideas'.

Taylor was an engineer and mostly concerned with **engineering** management. His aim was increased **efficiency** in production; that is, increased productivity. His methods were later applied to many other types of work.

2.1.2 Principles of scientific management

The **principles of scientific management** are outlined below.

(a) **The development of a true science of work**. 'All knowledge which had hitherto been kept in the heads of workmen should be gathered and recorded by **management**. Every single subject, large and small, becomes the question for scientific investigation, for reduction to law.'

(b) **The scientific selection and progressive development of workers**. Workers should be carefully trained and given jobs to which they are best suited.

(c) **The bringing together of the science and the scientifically selected and trained men**. The application of techniques to decide what should be done and how, using workers who are both properly trained and willing to maximise output, should result in maximum productivity.

(d) **The constant and intimate co-operation between management and workers**. 'The relations between employers and men form without question the most important part of this art.' There is much that is relevant today in this approach and the pursuit of productivity is still a major preoccupation for management at all levels.

2.1.3 Examples of scientific management

The following are **examples of scientific management** in practice.

(a) **Work study techniques** established the 'one best way' to do any job. No discretion was allowed to the worker. Subsequently, Henry Ford's approach to mass production broke each job down into its smallest and simplest component parts; these single elements became the newly designed job.

(b) **Planning the work and doing the work were separated**. Workers did what they were told – they did not have any control over how they completed a task.

(c) **Workers were paid incentives** on the basis of acceptance of the new methods and output norms as the new methods greatly increased productivity and profits.

(d) All aspects of the work environment were **tightly controlled** in order to attain maximum productivity.

CASE STUDY

It is useful to consider an application of Taylor's principles. In testimony to the House of Representatives Committee in 1912, Taylor used as an example the application of scientific management methods to shovelling work at the Bethlehem Steel Works.

(a) Facts were first gathered by management as to the number of shovel loads handled by each man each day, with particular attention paid to the relationship between weight of the average shovel load and the total load shifted per day. From these facts, management was able to decide on the ideal shovel size for each type of material handled in order to optimise the speed of shovelling work done.

(b) By organising work a day in advance, it was possible to minimise the idle time and the moving of men from one place in the shovelling yard to another.

(c) Workers were paid for accepting the new methods and 'norms' and received 60% higher wages than those given to similar workers in other companies in the area.

(d) Workers were carefully selected and trained in the art of shovelling properly; anyone consistently falling below the required norms was given special teaching to improve performance.

(e) 'The new way is to teach and help your men as you would a brother; to try to teach him the best way and to show him the easiest way to do his work.'

(f) At the Bethlehem Steel Works, Taylor said, the costs of implementing this method were more than repaid by the benefits. The labour force required fell from 500 men to 140 men for the same work.

2.2 Opportunity

Employees work within an **environment** that is provided by their employer. This environment must be **appropriate** if employees are to be given the opportunity to **perform** their role at their **maximum**.

2.2.1 Weber: bureaucracy, rational form

In the 1940's Max Weber, a German sociologist, developed a theory of **bureaucracy**. Under bureaucracy, authority is bestowed by dividing an organisation into jurisdictional areas (production, marketing, sales and so on), each with specified duties. Authority to carry them out is given to the officials in charge, and rules and regulations are established in order to ensure their achievement. Managers get things done because their orders are accepted as legitimate and justified. Weber suggested that organisations naturally evolved towards this **rational** form.

2.2.2 Lawrence and Lorsch: Contingency theory

KEY POINT

Contingency theory is a concept based on the idea that the organisation's structure and management approach must be tailored to the situation. There is no one best way to manage.

One form of contingency theory was developed by Lawrence and Lorsch (1967). They concluded that organisations in a **stable environment** are more effective if they have more detailed procedures and a more centralised decision-making process, while organisations in an **unstable environment** should have decentralisation, employee participation, and less emphasis on rules and procedures to be effective.

2.3 Motivation

KEY POINT

Motivation is an **employee's desire to perform their role**. It is often linked to the outcome and any reward.

It is in an organisation's interests to know the reasons or **motives** behind **people's behaviour**. Motivation influences employee productivity and their quality of work. By understanding what motivates their staff, an organisation is better equipped to provide an environment that maximises employee performance. We now outline some of the main theories of motivation.

2.3.1 Taylor: maximising prosperity

In the late 19th and early 20th centuries, Taylor established four principles to achieve the **maximum prosperity** for employers and employees.

(a)   **Science** should be used to **determine fair pay** for a **day's work**.

(b)   **Scientific methods** should be used in the **recruitment** and **selection** of staff who should be developed to ensure they are capable of **meeting output** and **quality targets**.

(c)   '**Mental revolution**'. Staff should be encouraged to fulfil their potential.

(d)   There should be **constant** and **intimate co-operation** between **management** and **staff**.

Taylor appreciated how productivity would improve if staff were specialised and equipped with the **knowledge** and **skills** required to perform their role. Jobs should be broken down into functions that would each be performed by an individual. However, this view resulted in overstaffing in some organisations as a relatively large number of middle managers controlled the other workers.

Taylor also held the view that as **workers were rational** they would be **motivated** by the **highest remuneration** that was possible.

2.3.2 Mayo, Schein: human relations

In the 1930s, a critical perception of scientific management emerged. Elton Mayo pioneered a (then) new approach called **human relations**. This concentrated mainly on the concept of Schein's 'Social man' where **people are motivated by 'social' or 'belonging' needs**, which are satisfied by the social relationships they form at work.

Attention shifted towards people's **higher psychological needs** for **growth**, **challenge**, **responsibility** and **self-fulfilment**. Herzberg suggested that only these things could positively motivate employees to improved performance.

The human relations approaches contributed an important awareness of the influence of the **human factor** at work on organisational performance.

(a)   Most theorists offer **guidelines** to enable practising managers to satisfy and motivate employees and so (theoretically) to obtain improved productivity.

(b)   However, as far as the practising manager is concerned there is still **no simple link between job satisfaction** and **productivity** or the achievement of **organisational goals**.

2.3.3 Maslow's hierarchy of needs

KEY TERM

HIERARCHY OF NEEDS: a ranked structure of behavioural stimuli within the individual which explain motivation. It is an example of a **content theory** of motivation. Such theories ask '**what**' things motivate people and assumes that there is one best way to motivate everyone.

Apart from 'biogenic needs' or 'drives'; that is, biological determinants of behaviour activated by deprivation, there are **psychogenic needs** – emotional or psychological needs. The American psychologist Abraham Maslow argued that man has seven innate needs, and put forward certain propositions about the motivating power of these needs.

He described two **higher order** needs:

(a)   The need for **freedom of inquiry and expression**: for social conditions permitting free speech and encouraging justice, fairness and honesty.

(b)   The need for **knowledge and understanding**: to gain and order knowledge of the environment, to explore, learn, experiment. These are essential prerequisites for the satisfaction of the remainder.

The other five needs can be arranged in a 'hierarchy of relative pre-potency'. Each level of need is **dominant until satisfied** – only then does the next level of need become a motivating factor. A need which has been satisfied no longer motivates an individual's behaviour. The need for self-actualisation can never be satisfied.

In terms of rewards for work, physiological needs may be met by basic pay, safety needs by a pension scheme, social needs by team nights out, esteem needs by promotion and pay increases, and self-actualisation by challenge and achievement.

There are **various problems** associated with **Maslow's theory**:

(a) **Empirical verification** for the hierarchy is hard to come by. Physiological and safety needs are not always uppermost in the determination of human behaviour.

(b) **Research** does not bear out the proposition that needs become less powerful as they are satisfied, except at the very primitive level of primary needs like hunger and thirst.

(c) It is **difficult to predict** behaviour using the hierarchy: the theory is too vague.

(d) **Application** of the theory in work contexts presents various difficulties. For example, the role of money or pay is problematic, since it arguably represents other rewards like status, recognition or independence.

(e) The **ethnocentricity** of Maslow's hierarchy has also been noted – it does seem broadly applicable to Western English-speaking cultures, but it is less relevant elsewhere.

2.3.4 Herzberg's two-factor content theory

The American psychologist Frederick Herzberg interviewed 203 Pittsburgh engineers and accountants. The subjects were asked to recall **events which had made them feel good about their work, and others which made them feel bad about it**. Analysis revealed that the factors which created satisfaction were different from those which created dissatisfaction.

Herzberg identified two groups of work-related factors which caused satisfaction and dissatisfaction respectively. He called these factors **motivators** and **hygiene factors**.

KEY TERMS

MOTIVATORS produced satisfaction when present and were capable of motivating the individual.

HYGIENE FACTORS (or MAINTENANCE FACTORS) could not give satisfaction or provide motivation when present. Their absence, however, caused dissatisfaction.

In his book *Work and the Nature of Man*, Herzberg distinguished between **hygiene factors** and **motivator factors**, based on what he saw as two separate 'need systems' of individuals.

(a) There is a **need to avoid unpleasantness**. This need is satisfied at work by hygiene factors. Hygiene satisfactions are short-lived; individuals come back for more, in the nature of drug addicts.

(b) There is a **need for personal growth**, which is satisfied by motivator factors and not by hygiene factors.

A lack of motivators at work will encourage employees to focus on poor hygiene (real or imagined) and to demand more pay, for example. Some individuals do not seek personal growth; these are 'hygiene seekers' who may be able to be satisfied by hygiene factors.

KEY POINTS

Hygiene factors are essentially **preventative**. They prevent or **minimise dissatisfaction** but do not give satisfaction, in the same way that sanitation minimises threats to health but does not give 'good' health. They are called 'maintenance' factors because they have to be continually renewed to avoid dissatisfaction.

Motivator factors create job satisfaction and are effective in motivating an individual to superior performance and effort. These factors give the individual a sense of self-fulfilment or personal growth.

The following table contains examples of **hygiene** and **motivation factors**.

Hygiene factors	Motivation factors
Company policy and administration	Advancement
Salary	Gaining recognition
Quality of supervision	Responsibility
Interpersonal relationships	Challenge
Working conditions	Achievement
Job security	Growth in role
Status (may also be a motivation factor)	Autonomy

Herzberg suggested that if there is sufficient **challenge**, **scope** and **interest** in the job, there will be a lasting **increase in satisfaction**, the employee will work well and productivity will be above normal levels.

The extent to which a job must be challenging or creative to a motivator-seeker will depend on each individual's ability and their tolerance for **delayed success**.

2.3.5 Adams: equity theory

Equity theory deals with **issues of fairness** – in other words, that people seek a fair return for their efforts, not necessarily the maximum reward.

Adams makes these suggestions:

(a) People compare what they receive with what others receive, for a perceived level of effort.
(b) Inequity exists if another person gets more for a given level of input.
(c) People get more upset the more inequity there is.
(d) The more upset someone is, the harder they will work to restore 'equity'.

Equity theory was backed up in the laboratory but is **hard to apply** in the real world.

2.3.6 McGregor's Theory X and Theory Y

KEY TERM

THEORY X AND THEORY Y: Two contrasting managerial approaches to motivation described by Douglas McGregor.

McGregor categorises **managers' assumptions** into two types:

(a) **Theory X. Most people dislike work and responsibility and will avoid both if possible.** Therefore, most people must be coerced, controlled, and threatened with punishment to get them to make an adequate effort towards the achievement of the organisation's objectives.

(b) **Theory Y. Individuals want to satisfy their needs through work and wish to make a contribution towards goals that they have helped to establish.** Therefore managers who take a Theory Y approach seek to allow their staff to follow their own path and satisfy their own needs.

When deciding which approach to take, the following issues are important:

(i) **Strict controls** and **close supervision** may be a source of **conflict**.

(ii) **Self-motivation** and **commitment** may be more **effective** and **less confrontational**.

(iii) **Treating individuals** in a **Theory X manner** may **prevent** the use of **initiative** and **encourage** doing the **minimum required**.

(iv) **Theory X is ineffective** when managing individuals who are **not financially motivated** or who are **not afraid of punishment**.

2.3.7 Vroom: expectancy theory

The **expectancy theory** of motivation is a **process theory**. Such theories ask '**how**' people are motivated and are based on the assumptions of cognitive psychology that human beings are rational and are aware of their goals and behaviour.

In 1964 Victor Vroom, an American psychologist, worked out a formula by which human motivation could actually be assessed and measured based on an **expectancy theory** of work motivation. Vroom suggested that the strength of an individual's motivation is the product of two factors.

(a)   The **strength of their preference for a certain outcome**. Vroom called this **valence**. It may be represented as a positive or negative number, or zero – since outcomes may be desired, avoided or considered with indifference.

(b)   The individual's **expectation that the outcome will result from a certain behaviour**. *Vroom* called this **subjective probability** – it is the individual's 'expectation' and depends on their perception of the probable relationship between behaviour and outcome. As a probability, it may be represented by any number between 0 (no chance) and 1 (certainty). It is also called **expectancy**.

In its simplest form, the **expectancy equation** therefore looks like this.

Force or strength of motivation to do something	=	Valence ie strength of their preference for a certain outcome	×	Expectation that behaviour will result in desired outcome

Expectancy theories suggest the following **steps** to improve **employee motivation**.

 Determine what an **individual values**.

 Identify the desired **managerial behaviour**.

 Set performance levels which are **perceived** to be **achievable**.

 Determine methods to **link managerial behaviour** to **individual performance**.

 Ensure adequate rewards are in place to **encourage performance**.

 Ensure the reward system is **fair** and **equitable**.

2.3.8 Schein: common behavioural traits

Schein identified **four groups of 'man'** with common behavioural traits.

(a)   **Rational economic man**

This group is motivated by the maximisation of economic gain and by following their own self-interest.

(b) **Social man**

Performance of this group is improved by raising morale through socialisation at work. Rather than acting as a controller, managers should be seen as facilitators.

(c) **Self-actualising man**

This group is motivated through self-fulfilment. In terms of work they are motivated by challenge and responsibility.

(d) **Complex man**

Motivation is based on a 'psychological contract' between employers and employees. Each has their own expectations of the 'contract' and motivation depends on their fulfilment.

2.3.9 Goal-setting theory

Goal-setting theory suggests that **goals** can motivate.

(a) Challenging goals, providing they have been accepted, lead to better performance than easy goals.
(b) The best goals are specific as they focus people's attention.
(c) Knowledge of results is essential.

Goal theory has the most **empirical support** of any motivation theory, but there are some limits to how it applies.

(a) Research has concentrated on quantity, not quality, of output.

(b) At work, people pursue several goals consecutively; achieving one may mean neglecting another. This is particularly a problem for organisations where trade-offs have to be made.

2.3.10 Mullins's classifications of motivation

According to Mullins (2005), **motivation** is 'the driving force within individuals by which they attempt to achieve some goal in order to fulfil some need or expectation'. Mullins also identified **three classifications** for understanding motivation.

Classification	Examples
Economic reward	Pay and benefits
Intrinsic satisfaction	Enjoyment of the job and personal development
Social relationships	Team working and forming friendships with colleagues

Question 12.2	Theory X and Theory Y

Learning outcome F2(v)

Douglas McGregor suggested that managers have one of two views or theories about subordinates.

View 1. Individuals want to satisfy their needs through work and wish to make a contribution to the goals they have helped to establish.

View 2. Most people dislike work and responsibility, and so have to be coerced, controlled and threatened with punishment to get them to do their job adequately.

Which of the following statements is correct?

A   View 1 is called Theory X and view 2 is called Theory Y, and McGregor suggested that the most effective managers hold view 1.

B   View 1 is called Theory Y and view 2 is called Theory X, and McGregor suggested that the most effective managers hold view 2.

C   View 1 is called Theory X and view 2 is called Theory Y, and McGregor suggested that the most effective managers hold view 2.

D   View 1 is called Theory Y and view 2 is called Theory X, and McGregor suggested that the view held by the most effective managers depends on the circumstances. **(2 marks)**

2.4 Psychological contracts

A **psychological contract** exists between individuals in an organisation and the organisation itself. Handy suggested that they are based on what **each party wants** and what they are **prepared to give for it**.

(a)   The **individual** expects to derive certain benefits from membership of the organisation (such as pay, status, career progression) and is prepared to offer their labour and expend a certain amount of effort in return.

(b)   The **organisation** expects the individual to fulfil certain requirements (for example to work hard and meet its expectations) and is prepared to offer certain rewards (such as pay, benefits and continued employment) in return.

Three types of **psychological contract** can be identified:

(a)   **Coercive contract**. This is a contract in which the individual considers that they are being forced to contribute their efforts and energies involuntarily, and that the rewards they receive in return are inadequate compensation.

(b)   **Calculative contract**. This is a contract, accepted **voluntarily** by the individual, in which they expect to do their job in exchange for a readily identifiable set of rewards. With such psychological contracts, motivation can only be increased if the rewards to the individual are improved.

If the organisation attempts to demand greater efforts without increasing the rewards, the psychological contract will revert to a coercive one, and motivation may become negative.

(c)   **Co-operative contract**. This is a contract in which the individual identifies themselves with the organisation and its goals, so that they actively seek to contribute further to the achievement of those goals. Motivation comes out of success at work, a sense of achievement and self-fulfilment.

The individual will probably want to share in the planning and control decisions which affect their work, and **co-operative contracts are therefore likely to occur where employees participate in decision making**.

Motivation happens when the psychological contract, within which the individual's motivation calculus operates for new decisions, is viewed in the same way by the organisation and by the individual, and when both parties are able to fulfil their side of the bargain. The individual agrees to work, or work well, in return for whatever rewards or satisfactions are understood as the terms of the 'contract'.

Psychological contracts are particularly relevant when considering **staff turnover and retention rates**. Employees are more likely to stay and be loyal to an organisation where they perceive themselves to have a co-operative contract rather than a coercive one.

Section summary

The success of any **HRM policy** can be measured by the **contribution of the employees** to the success of the organisation.

There are a number of **HRM theories** which relate to **ability**, **opportunity** and **motivation**.

Psychological contracts are the expectations that the employee and employer have of each other.

3 Employee motivation: Remuneration

Introduction

Pay is part of the reward system, and can be a **motivator** in certain circumstances. However, this depends on the value individuals ascribe to pay and the way in which incentive schemes are implemented. Pay is usually considered a hygiene factor.

Employees need an income to live and most probably have two basic concerns – to earn **enough** money and that their pay should be **fair**. This can be assessed in two ways.

(a) **Equity** – a fair rate for the job

(b) **Relativity**, or fair differentials; that is, justified differences between the pay of different individuals

3.1 Payment systems

Armstrong and Murlis (1998) suggested that payments to employees have two elements.

- **Pay** with scope to reward **progression** and **promotion**
- **Benefits** such as pensions, company cars and medical insurance

3.1.1 Organisational aims for payment systems

At the **organisational (strategic) level**, payment systems have the following goals.

- Aid **recruitment**
- **Retain** employees
- **Reward** employees for performance

3.1.2 Managerial aims for payment systems

At the **managerial level**, payment systems are used to:

- Attract and retain staff of a suitable quality
- Reward and motivate employees fairly and consistently
- Further the organisation's objectives by providing competitive rewards
- Encourage performance and progression through development
- Recognise non-performance factors such as skill and competence
- Ensure salary costs are controlled

3.2 Pay structures

Common types of **pay structure** include:

(a) **Graded**. A pay range is attached to particular levels of job grades.

(b) **Broad-banded structures**. These usually encompass the whole workforce from the clerk to the senior manager. The range of pay in this structure is typically higher than in graded structures.

(c) **Individual**. Pay is allocated to individuals rather than 'bands'. It is used for senior management positions and avoids the problem of over/underpayment which can result from grading.

(d) **Job family structures**. Jobs in specific functions such as accounts and HR are grouped into families. The jobs differ in terms of skill levels or responsibility (such as Accounts Technician and Management Accountant) and pay is determined accordingly.

(e) **Pay** or **profession/maturity curves**. These recognise that in certain roles, pay must be progressive to allocate pay fairly – especially where knowledge or experience is key to the role.

(f)   **Spot rates**. These allocate a rate of pay for a specific job often linked to the market price.

(g)   **Rate for age**. This allocates a rate of pay or pay bracket for employees based on age.

(h)   **Pay spines**. These are often used by government organisations where it is important for pay to be relative across a range of roles. They are a series of incremental points from the lowest- to the highest-paid jobs. Pay scales for specific jobs are superimposed onto the spine to ensure pay is relative.

(i)   **Manual worker pay structures**. These recognise the difference in status between those who work in manual roles against those in other parts of the organisation. Real differentials are incorporated that reflect differences in skill and responsibility but otherwise are similar to other pay structures.

(j)   **Integrated structures**. These incorporate one grading system for all employees except senior management. They are often used where employees were paid historically under separate agreements.

The assumption behind most payment systems is that **money is the prime motivating factor**. As Herzberg, among others, suggested, however, it is more likely to be a cause of dissatisfaction.

Herzberg himself admitted that pay is the most important of all the hygiene factors. Goldthorpe, Lockwood *et al*, in their *Affluent Worker* study of the Luton car industry, suggested that workers may have a purely **instrumental** orientation to work – deriving satisfaction not from the work itself but from the rewards obtainable with the money earned by working. The Luton workers experienced their work as routine and dead-end, but had made a rational decision to enter employment which offered high monetary reward rather than intrinsic interest.

As **expectancy theory** indicates, pay is only likely to motivate a worker to improved performance if there is a clear and consistent link between performance and monetary reward and if monetary reward is valued. **Salary structures** do not always allow enough leeway to reward individual performance in a job (since fairness usually dictates a rate for the job itself, in relation to others). **Incentive schemes**, however, are often used to re-establish the link between effort and reward.

3.3 Pay differentials

Pay differentials are often key to **determining salaries for employees**. To calculate pay differentials, an organisation should refer to market rates for the roles and decide a policy of how its pay levels will reflect the market rate. The following methods may be used in determining pay rates.

3.3.1 Points-factor evaluation scheme

 Evaluate the roles and calculate evaluation job scores based on the level or category of employee.

 Plot job scores on a scatter diagram and draw a line of 'best fit'.

 Plot the upper, median and lower market pay rates from the available information.

 Plot a desired pay policy line based on the market data.

 Decide on the overall shape of the pay structure based on the pay policy.

Define pay ranges for each level taking into account flexibility for pay progression.

3.3.2 Ranking/market method

 Rank the existing jobs and plot actual pay rates to show current pay policy.

 Plot market data and derive a 'best fit' policy.

 Decide on a pay range policy and plot upper and lower pay rates using the 'best fit' policy as the mid-range.

 Develop a grade structure and pay rates for each grade.

3.4 Incentive schemes

The purpose of incentive schemes is to **improve performance by linking it to reward**. It is believed that performance incentives take effect in several ways.

(a) Staff members' effort and attention are **directed to where they are most needed** – performance.

(b) **Commitment and motivation are enhanced**. This is particularly important when there are cultural obstacles to improvement.

(c) **Achievement** can be rewarded separately from **effort**, with advantages for the recruitment and retention of high-quality employees.

A further advantage is that **labour costs are linked to organisational performance**.

Schemes may be based on **individual performance** or on **group performance**. It is difficult to apply schemes to **knowledge workers** because of the difficulty in determining performance levels. Performance can only be judged subjectively rather than objectively in terms of output.

Individual schemes are common when the work is essentially individualistic and the output of a single person is easy to specify and measure. However, much work is performed by **teams** and it is impossible to identify each person's output. Such work calls for a **group incentive scheme**.

The **main problem with team incentive payments** is that there is unlikely to be a single consistent standard of effort or achievement within the group. Inevitably there will be those who perform better than others and they are likely to be aggrieved if all group members are rewarded equally.

The ultimate group incentive scheme is the **organisation-wide scheme**, in which all employees are rewarded in accordance with overall performance, usually as measured by profit. This tends to be very popular in good times and the cause of disappointment and resentment when the business is doing badly. The value of such schemes is questionable.

There are **three main types of incentive scheme**:

* Performance-related pay (PRP)
* Bonus schemes
* Profit sharing

3.4.1 Performance-related pay (PRP)

The most common individual PRP scheme for wage earners is straight **piecework**: payment of a fixed amount per unit produced, or operation completed.

For managerial and other salaried jobs, however, a form of **management by objectives** will probably be applied. The SMART criteria (Specific, Measureable, Achievable, Realistic and Time-bound) should be applied.

(a) **Key results** will be identified and specified, for which merit awards (on top of basic salary) will be paid.

(b) There will be a **clear model for evaluating performance** and knowing when, or if, targets have been reached and payments earned.

(c) The **exact conditions and amounts of awards** can be made clear to the employee, to avoid uncertainty and later resentment.

For service and other departments, a PRP scheme may involve bonuses for **achievement of key results**, or points schemes where points are awarded for performance on various criteria (efficiency, cost savings, quality of service and so on). Certain points totals (or the highest points total in the unit, if a competitive system is used) win cash or other awards.

However, Otley (1987) discovered that employees become **demotivated** if they fail to meet targets, resulting in a high degree of performance reduction.

3.4.2 Bonus schemes

Bonus schemes are supplementary to basic salary, and have been found to be popular with entrepreneurial types, usually in marketing and sales. Bonuses are both incentives and rewards.

Group incentive schemes typically offer a bonus for a group (equally, or proportionately to the earnings or status of individuals) which achieves or exceeds specified targets. Typically, bonuses would be calculated monthly on the basis of improvements in output per man per hour against standard, or value added to the cost of raw materials and parts by the production process.

Value-added schemes work on the basis that improvements in productivity increase value added, and the benefit can be shared between employers and employees on an agreed formula. So if sales revenue increases and labour costs stay the same, or sales revenue remains constant but labour costs decrease, the balance becomes available. There has been an increase in such schemes in recent years.

3.4.3 Profit-sharing schemes and employee shareholders

Profit-sharing schemes offer employees (or selected groups of them) bonuses, perhaps in the form of shares in the company, related directly to profits. The formula for determining the amounts may vary, but in recent years a straightforward distribution of a percentage of profits above a given target has given way to a value-added related concept.

Profit sharing is in general based on the belief that **all employees can contribute to profitability**, and that that contribution should be recognised. If it is, the argument runs, the effects may include profit-consciousness and motivation in employees and commitment to the future prosperity of the organisation.

The actual **incentive value** and effect on productivity may be wasted if the scheme is badly designed.

(a) A **perceivably significant sum** should be made available to employees – once shareholders have received appropriate return on their investment – say, 10% of basic pay.

(b) There should be a clear, and not overly delayed, **link between performance and reward**. Profit shares should be distributed as frequently as possible – consistent with the need for reliable information on profit forecasts and targets and the need to amass a significant pool for distribution.

(c) The scheme should only be introduced if **profit forecasts** indicate a reasonable chance of achieving the target. Profit sharing is welcome when profits are high, but the potential for disappointment is great.

(d) The greatest effect on **productivity** arising from the scheme may arise from its use as a focal point for discussion with employees, about the relationship between their performance and results, and areas and targets for improvement. Management must be seen to be committed to the principle.

Exam alert

Exam questions may test the difficulties of designing and operating a reward scheme for performance.

3.4.4 Difficulties associated with incentive schemes

Incentive schemes have the following potential difficulties:

(a) **Increased earnings simply may not be an incentive** to some individuals. An individual who already enjoys a good income may be more concerned with increasing their leisure time, for example.

(b) **Workers are unlikely to be in complete control of results**. External factors, such as the general economic climate, interest rates and exchange rates, may play a part in **profitability** in particular. In these cases, the relationship between an individual's efforts and their reward may be indistinct.

(c) Greater **specialisation in production processes** means that particular employees cannot be specifically credited with the success of particular products. This may lead to frustration amongst employees who think their own profitable work is being adversely affected by inefficiencies elsewhere in the organisation.

(d) Even if employees are motivated by money, the effects may not be altogether desirable. An **instrumental orientation may encourage self-interested performance** at the expense of teamwork. It may encourage attention to output at the expense of quality, and the lowering of standards and targets (in order to make bonuses more accessible).

(e) It is often all too easy to **manipulate the rules of the incentive scheme**, especially where there are allowances for waiting time, when production is held up by factors beyond the control of the people concerned. Special allowances, guaranteed earnings and changes in methods also undermine incentive schemes.

(f) **Poorly designed schemes** can produce labour cost increases out of proportion to output improvements.

All such schemes are based on the principle that people are willing to work harder to obtain more money. However, the work of Elton Mayo and Tom Lupton has shown that there are **several constraints** which prevent most people from seeking to maximise their earnings.

(a) Workers are capable of influencing the timings and control systems used by management.

(b) Workers remain suspicious that if they achieve high levels of output and earnings then management will alter the basis of the incentive rates to reduce future earnings. Work groups therefore tend to restrict output to a level that they feel is fair and safe.

(c) Generally, the workers conform to a group output norm. The need to have the approval of their fellow workers by conforming to that norm is more important than the money urge.

In the *Affluent Worker* study referred to above, Goldthorpe and Lockwood recognised that people do not, by and large, seek to maximise their earnings. Instead, a person will work as hard as necessary to earn

the money they want – but not past the point at which the deprivations demanded of them (in terms of long hours or dangerous or antisocial conditions) are greater than they feel are worthwhile.

3.4.5 Total reward schemes

KEY TERM

A TOTAL REWARD SCHEME (or package) is a bundle of cash and non-cash motivators offered to staff.

Total reward schemes recognise that individuals are all different and may not all be motivated by money. The fact that an individual can supplement their remuneration package may in itself be an attraction for prospective employees.

Carrington (2004) identified the drivers for the development of the total reward package. The key driver was the skills shortage in the 1990s that caused '**talent wars**' where organisations had to **attract staff** in a more **competitive manner**. Around the same time, many organisations were **developing** a **vision** and **culture** – these schemes helped further this development.

Flexible benefits are another method of rewarding staff. Certain incentives have become more or less popular over time and Prickett (2006) identified which are growing, static and declining in popularity.

Growing	Static	Declining
Bicycles	Personal shopping and dry cleaning (city firms mainly)	Golden parachutes
Childcare	Shopping vouchers	Bonus schemes
Computers	Health and dental insurance	Share schemes
Flexible pension schemes (tax efficient)	Gym membership	Final salary pension schemes

Examples of other **non-cash benefits** that may be offered include:

- **Training**

- **Flexible working hours**

- **Working at home**

- **Career progression**

- The **pursuit** of **green** or **ethical policies** by the company (may be an attraction to individuals with strong views on these issues)

Carrington (2004) identified a number of **advantages** of such schemes. In particular they make a **positive statement** about the culture of the organisation, the **creation** of a **more inclusive** rather than a 'them and us' attitude and **improved recruitment** and retention as a result of **employer branding**.

Other **advantages** and **disadvantages** of **total reward schemes** include:

Advantages	Disadvantages
Attracts potential employees	It might have no effect
Improves employee motivation	It might cause organisational stagnation as employees may not push themselves for further reward
	It ignores employee welfare
	Employees may prefer to have cash only

3.4.6 Motivation and incentives

Gratton (2004) concluded that although money is important as a staff motivator, its importance is often overestimated. She found that money often signified **status** between employees, and that this was sometimes more important than purchasing power.

She also emphasised the importance of people being **involved** in decisions and procedures that affected them. This was an important source of motivation.

Section summary

In many circumstances **pay can be a motivator** for employees.

There are many **methods of determining the pay** of employees.

Schemes that **link reward** to **employee performance** include **profit-related pay, bonus schemes** and **profit sharing**.

Total reward schemes offer employees bundles of benefits from which they can pick and choose what they want.

4 Employee motivation: Other factors

Introduction

Frustration, conflict, feelings of failure and **low prospects** tend to show themselves in such effects as **high labour turnover, absenteeism** or **preoccupation with financial rewards** (in compensation for lack of other satisfactions). These can be as self-defeating for the organisation as they are unhealthy for the individual.

However, there are a great many other **work** and **non-work variables** in the equation. A happy workforce will not necessarily make the organisation profitable (if the market is unfavourable). They will not necessarily be more productive (if the task itself is badly designed or resources scarce) nor even more highly motivated.

Therefore, to ensure that employee performance benefits the organisation, organisations should take into account all factors that influence employee motivation.

4.1 Job redesign, rotation, enlargement and enrichment

Job redesign, rotation, enlargement and **enrichment** can all be used to improve the motivation of employees by introducing changes to their work.

(a) **Job redesign** aims to improve performance through increasing the understanding and motivation of employees. Job redesign also aims to ensure that an individual's job suits them in terms of what motivates them and their need for personal growth and development.

(b) **Job rotation** allows for a little variety by moving a person from one task to another. Employees often do this spontaneously. Job rotation permits the development of extra **skills**, but does not develop **depth of skill**.

(c) **Job enlargement** increases the **width** of the job by adding extra, usually related, tasks. It is not particularly popular with workers, many of whom prefer undemanding jobs that allow them to chat and daydream.

(d) **Job enrichment** increase the **depth** of responsibility by adding elements of **planning** and **control** to the job, therefore increasing its meaning and challenge. The worker achieves greater autonomy and growth in the role.

4.2 Job characteristics model

Hackman and Oldham developed the **job characteristics model** that sets out the links between employee motivation, satisfaction and performance (including personal growth) and the characteristics of their job or role.

Hackman and Oldham's **motivating potential score (MPS)** is an attempt to measure a job's potential to produce motivation and satisfaction. The MPS is computed from scores in questionnaires designed to diagnose the extent to which the job displays **five core characteristics**.

(a)   **Skill variety**: the breadth of job activities and skills required

(b)   **Task identity**: whether the job is a whole piece of work with a visible outcome

(c)   **Task significance**: the impact of the job on other people

(d)   **Autonomy**: the degree of freedom allowed in planning and executing the work

(e)   **Feedback**: the amount of information provided about the worker's job performance

Hackman and Oldham suggest that the first three characteristics above contribute to the '**experienced meaningfulness of the work**' and this is borne out by empirical research. The extent to which a job's autonomy and feedback, as measured by Hackman and Oldham, contribute to job satisfaction is less clear-cut.

Exam alert

Exam questions may test the motivational impact of changes proposed by management.

Section summary

There are a number of methods of **improving an employee's experience of work** and their **motivation**. These include **job redesign, rotation, enlargement** and **enrichment**.

5 HR management in different types of organisation

Introduction

Some organisations have found a need to **develop new ways of working**. This has been brought about partly by the changing nature of business and the evolvement of different types and forms of organisations.

5.1 Project-based teams

There is a general trend in organisation structures (particularly in service organisations) away from traditional hierarchies towards **flatter structures** with reporting lines that **cross functional boundaries**. Instead of traditional departments, some organisations operate using multiskilled employees organised into various work teams based around factors such as customer groups and particular projects.

This has implications for the HR plan and policies. For example, if a general pool of multiskilled employees is required, **recruitment policy** should reflect that fact – rather than recruiting large numbers of specialists. Extensive training programmes are also likely to be required. The **advantages and disadvantages of project-based organisations** can be summarised as follows.

Advantages	Disadvantages
Greater flexibility of: • **People**. Employees develop an attitude geared to accepting change. • **Workflow and decision making**. Direct contact between staff encourages problem solving and big-picture thinking. • **Tasks and structure**. The organisational structure may be readily amended, where projects are completed.	**Dual authority** threatens a conflict between functional managers and product/project area managers.
Interdisciplinary co-operation and a mixing of skills and expertise, along with improved communication and co-ordination.	An individual with two or more bosses may suffer stress from **conflicting demands or ambiguous roles**.
Motivation and employee development: providing employees with greater participation in planning and control decisions.	**Cost**: product management posts are added, more consultation is required eg meetings.
Market awareness: the organisation tends to become more customer/quality focused.	**Slower decision making**.
Horizontal workflow: Reduced bureaucracy.	Possible **lack of accountability**.

5.2 The 'new organisation'

Some recent trends (identified by writers such as Blyton and Peters) have emerged from the focus on **flexibility** as a key organisational value.

(a) **Flat structures**. The flattening of hierarchies does away with levels of organisation which lengthened lines of communication and decision making and encouraged ever-increasing specialisation. Flat structures are more responsive, because there is a more direct relationship between the organisation's strategic centre and the operational units serving the customer.

(b) **'Horizontal structures'**. What Peters *(Liberation Management)* calls 'going horizontal' is a recognition that functional versatility (through multi-functional project teams and multiskilling, for example) is the key to flexibility. In the words (quoted by Peters) of a Motorola executive: 'The traditional job descriptions were barriers. We needed an organisation soft enough between the organisational disciplines so that ... people would run freely across functional barriers or organisational barriers with the common goal of getting the job done, rather than just making certain that their specific part of the job was completed.'

(c) **'Chunked' and 'unglued' structures**. So far, this has meant team working and decentralisation, or empowerment, creating smaller and more flexible units within the overall structure. Charles Handy's **'shamrock organisation'** (with a three-leafed structure of professional core, contractual fringe and flexible part-time labour) is gaining ground as a workable model for a leaner and more flexible workforce, within a controlled framework.

(d) **Output-focused structures**. The key to all the above trends is the focus on results, and on the customer, instead of internal processes and functions for their own sake. A **project management** orientation and structure, for example, is being applied to the supply of services within the organisation (to internal customers) as well as to the external market, in order to facilitate listening and responding to customer demands.

(e) **'Jobless' structures**. The employee becomes not a jobholder but the vendor of a portfolio of demonstrated outputs and competences (Bridges). This is a concrete expression of the concept of **employability**, which says that a person needs to have a portfolio of skills which are valuable on the open labour market. Employees need to be mobile, moving between organisations rather than settling in to a particular job.

5.3 Virtual organisations

As we have seen previously, developments in technology have enabled the creation of **virtual teams** and even **virtual organisations**.

These have enabled organisations to:

(a) **Outsource** areas of organisational activity to other organisations and freelance workers (even 'off-shore' in countries where skilled labour is cheaper) without losing control or co-ordination.

(b) **Organise 'territorially'** without the overhead costs of local offices, and without the difficulties of supervision, communication and control. Dispersed centres are linked to a 'virtual office' by communications technology and can share data freely.

(c) **Centralise** shared functions and services (such as data storage and retrieval, technical support and secretarial services) without the disadvantages of 'geographical' centralisation, and with the advantages of decentralised authority. Databases and communication (eg via email) create genuine interactive sharing of, and access to, common data.

(d) **Adopt flexible cross-functional and multiskilled working**, by making expertise available across the organisation. A 'virtual team' co-opts the best people for the task – regardless of location.

Section summary

Organisations may adopt **new structures** or develop their own. Recent trends in organisational structure include **project-based teams, flat structures, horizontal structures, chunked** and **unglued structures, output-focused structures** and **'jobless' structures**. Some have even become **virtual organisations**.

6 Working arrangements

Introduction

The ways in which people are **allowed** and **encouraged to work** will **affect their motivation** and performance. For example, allowing employees flexibility in when they complete their weekly hours (flexitime) may allow them to deal with domestic issues when they arise, meaning the time they actually spend working is more productive.

6.1 Attitudes and values

Working methods and arrangements cover much more than the nuts and bolts of hours and pay. For example, modern management theorists emphasise values such as the following:

(a) **Multiskilling**. Multiskilled teams involve individuals who are able to perform a variety of team tasks, as required. This enables tasks to be performed more flexibly, using labour more efficiently.

(b) **Flexibility**. Flexibility is about being able to respond and adapt quickly to rapidly changing customer demands, or to other changes such as technological change and different working methods. This has created the following:

     (i) Smaller, **multiskilled**, temporary structures, such as project and task-force teams.

     (ii) Multi-functional units, facilitating communication and co-ordination across departmental boundaries. This is sometimes referred to as a **matrix structure**, since an employee may report both to a line manager **and** to a project or product manager.

     (iii) **Flexible deployment** of the labour resource, for example through part-time and temporary working, outsourcing, flexitime and so on.

(c) **Empowerment**. Empowerment is based on the idea that those who are actually doing a job are best positioned to make decisions relating to how the work is done.

It involves giving employees the freedom to take responsibility for their goals and actions and may release hidden resources (creativity, initiative, leadership, innovation) which would otherwise remain inaccessible. People are allowed to use their own judgement.

The extent to which these values are incorporated into an organisation's **HR plan and policies** will depend on the type of organisation, the role of the employees and the philosophy of top management.

6.2 Flexible working arrangements

When establishing policies and procedures on **flexible work arrangements**, organisations seek to provide employees with a means to achieve a **balance between professional and personal responsibilities** in a manner that benefits both the employee and the employer.

A **well-structured policy** should be developed that provides a **clear understanding** of the expectations and responsibilities of all parties involved in the flexible work arrangement, and ensures that the same criteria for making decisions on flexible work arrangements are applied to all employees.

KEY POINT

The key to **successful flexible work arrangements** is to tailor the arrangement to the particular needs of the individual and the organisation. When considering which flexible work arrangements to offer employees, organisations should consider the arrangement's practicality, fairness, and flexibility within the environment of the organisation.

Typical flexible work arrangements include:

(a) **Flexitime**. Flexitime is an arrangement where employees work the standard number of hours in a workday (or in some arrangements within a work week), but are given some flexibility as to when they work these hours. Most organisations establish 'core working hours', meaning there are certain hours during the day in which it is mandatory for the employee to be at the workplace. For example, an employee on flexitime may have to work 7.5 hours per day, but be able to start their day any time between 7 and 10am and finish between 3 and 6pm.

(b) **Compressed week**. A compressed week is an arrangement where an employee works the standard number of hours in a one- or two-week period, but compresses those hours into fewer work days (therefore working longer hours on the days the employee is at work). For example, in a 40-hour work week an employee on a compressed work week may work four 10-hour days in a week with one day off, or nine 9-hour days with one day off every two weeks.

(c) **Job sharing**. Job sharing is an arrangement where two employees share one position. There are many combinations of work hours that are used for job sharing. For example, one employee might work Monday to Wednesday and the other employee Thursday and Friday, or one employee might work mornings and the other afternoons.

(d) **Part-time/Reduced hours**. Part-time or reduced hours are arrangements where an employee works less than the standard work week hours (and are paid only for those hours).

(e) **Telecommuting or homeworking**. Telecommuting is an arrangement where an employee works either part or all of the week from a location other than the standard place of work (office). Typically employees in such an arrangement work from their homes. For example, an employee may work three days a week at the office and two days a week from home.

(f) **Shift working**. Shift patterns, outside of regular working hours, may be used to add flexibility in relation to the time of day people work.

Organisations introducing flexible working should compile a formal **flexible work agreement** to be completed and signed by the employer and the employee. The agreement should include the specific details of the arrangement.

Often there is an **unreasonable requirement** that individuals who work a compressed work week should be required to be available or on-call on their day off or, on the other hand, the probably reasonable expectation that employees with the right to work at home should come into work for a meeting held on their work at home day. These issues should be covered by the flexible work arrangement agreement.

6.2.1 Flexibility in organisations

Three types of flexibility organisations look to achieve in the context of HRM are numerical flexibility, financial flexibility and task flexibility.

(a)   **Numerical flexibility** can be achieved through the use of temporary workers – both contractors and agency staff. Atkinson (1984) distinguished between 'core employees' (high status, job security) and 'periphery workers' on temporary or flexible-hour contracts.

(b)   **Financial flexibility** is achieved through variable systems of reward (eg performance-related pay).

(c)   **Task flexibility** (sometimes referred to as functional flexibility) involves having employees able to undertake a wider range of tasks. Introducing task flexibility could involve employees undertaking a wider range of tasks at the same 'level' (horizontally) or undertaking tasks previously carried out by employees at higher or lower levels (vertically).

Exam alert

Exam questions may test how an organisation could achieve workforce flexibility.

Advantages	Disadvantages
The **potential benefits to the employer** are: <ul><li>Increased employee motivation and productivity</li><li>Increased employee commitment to the organisation</li><li>The ability to attract high-performing individuals</li><li>Reduced absenteeism and staff turnover</li></ul>	Possible **disadvantages to the employer** include: <ul><li>Increased difficulty co-ordinating work</li><li>Loss of direct control</li><li>Dilution of the organisation's culture as employees see less of each other</li></ul>
The potential **benefits to the employee** are: <ul><li>Reduction in stress due to conflicting personal and professional priorities</li><li>Increased job satisfaction, energy and creativity</li><li>Reduced cost of commuting</li><li>Wider choice of housing as employees can live further from work</li><li>Ease of balancing work/life commitments</li><li>Privacy</li></ul>	Potential **disadvantages to employee** include: <ul><li>Loss of the distinction between home and office life</li><li>Increased possibility of being distracted from work tasks</li><li>Lack of space at home for office equipment</li><li>Lack of facilities such as IT equipment</li><li>Increased utility bills as the employee is at home more often</li><li>Lack of social contact with other employees</li></ul>

6.2.2 Flexible HR systems and e-HR

Organisations are increasingly moving towards electronically based HR processes and systems, sometimes referred to as **e-HR**. Enterprise-wide systems usually include tools to manage and administer employees.

Section summary

Organisations are increasingly offering **flexible working schemes** for employees.

7 The HR plan

Introduction

HR planning should be based on the **organisation's strategic planning processes**, with relation to analysis of the labour market, forecasting of the external supply and internal demand for labour, job analysis and plan implementation.

KEY TERM

PLANNING: '(the) establishment of objectives, and the formulation, evaluation and selection of the policies, strategies, tactics and action required to achieve them'

7.1 HR planning

HR planning concerns the acquisition, utilisation, improvement and return of an enterprise's human resources. HR planning may sometimes be referred to as 'workforce planning' or 'workforce strategy'. HR planning deals with:

- Budgeting and cost control
- Recruitment
- Retention (company loyalty, to retain skills and reduce staff turnover)
- Downsizing (reducing staff numbers)
- Training and retraining to enhance the skills base
- Dealing with changing circumstances

The process of human resources planning

> **1. STRATEGIC ANALYSIS**
> - Of the environment
> - Of the organisation's manpower strengths and weaknesses, opportunities and threats
> - Of the organisation's use of employees
> - Of the organisation's objectives

↓

> **2. FORECASTING**
> - Of internal demand and supply
> - Of external supply

↓

> **3. JOB ANALYSIS**
> - Investigating the task performed in each job
> - Identifying the skills required

↓

> **4. RECRUITMENT AND TRAINING**
> - Recruiting and selecting required staff
> - Training and developing existing staff

7.2 Strategic analysis

The current and future position should constantly be kept under review.

(a)   **The environment**. Population and education trends, policies on the employment of women and on pension ages and trends generally in the employment market must be monitored.

(b)   The organisation's HR **strengths, weaknesses, opportunities and threats** need to be analysed so as to identify skills and competence gaps and the level of innovation. Threats may involve competitors 'poaching' staff.

(c)   **HR utilisation**. An assessment should be made of how effectively the organisation is currently utilising its staff.

(d)   **Objectives**. Core and subsidiary corporate objectives should be analysed to identify the manpower implications. New products, technology, 'culture' and structure will all make demands on staff.

Timescales are very important. An immediate gap may prompt instant recruitment while long-term corporate objectives allow planned staff development, providing them with the skills required.

Human resources are hard to predict and control.

(a)   **Demand**. Environmental factors (eg the economy) create uncertainties in the demand for labour.

(b)   **Supply**. Factors such as education and the demands of competitors for labour create uncertainties in the supply of labour.

(c)   **Goals**. Employees have their own personal goals, and make their own decisions about whether to undertake further training. When large numbers of individuals are involved, the pattern of behaviour which emerges in response to any change in strategy may be hard to predict.

(d)   **Constraints**. Legislation as well as social and ethical values constrain the ways in which human resources are used, controlled, replaced and paid.

7.3 Forecasting

Estimating demand. Planning future HR needs requires accurate forecasts of turnover and productivity (eg if fewer staff are required for the same output). The demand can be estimated from:

- New venture details
- New markets (need new staff)
- New products/services
- New technology (new skills)

- Divestments
- Organisational restructuring (eg relocation)
- Cost reduction plans

Estimating supply

(a)   **Current workers**. **A stocks and flows analysis** will define the **internal labour market**. It describes not just aggregate quantities, but movements in and out of certain grades, by occupation and grade and according to length and service. This can be used in **modelling**.

(b)   The **external labour market**. Labour **market research** does four things:

(i)   It measures potential employees' awareness of the organisation.
(ii)   It discerns attitudes of potential employees towards the organisation.
(iii)   It suggests possible segments for advertising purposes.
(iv)   It provides analysis of population trends for long-term forecasting.

A **position survey** compares demand and supply. Differences in the numbers required/available, their grade, skills or location can be removed by applying an integrated manpower strategy.

7.4 Closing the gap between demand and supply: the HR plan

At the business unit level, the **HR plan** will arise out of the strategic HR plan.

(a) The **work required to be done** will largely result **from the business plan**. Production management might determine **how** the work will be done. If, for example, the company is introducing new machinery, then the HR requirements (eg training, possible redundancy, safety measures) need to be considered.

(b) **The skills base** includes technical skills, interpersonal skills and management skills. The need for **technical** and **management** skills are obvious enough. **Interpersonal skills** are important, as they deal with the service offered to customers and affect teamwork.

The HR plan is prepared on the basis of **staffing requirements** and the implications for productivity and costs. It should include **budgets**, **targets** and **standards**, and should also allocate responsibilities for **implementation** and **control** (reporting, monitoring achievement against plan).

The HR plan can be broken down into **subsidiary plans** as shown in the following table.

Plan	Comment
Recruitment plan	Numbers; types of people; when required; recruitment programme
Training plan	Numbers of trainees required and/or existing staff needing training; training programme
Redevelopment plan	Programmes for transferring, retraining employees
Productivity plan	Programmes for improving productivity, or reducing manpower costs; setting productivity targets
Redundancy plan	Where and when redundancies are to occur; policies for selection and declaration of redundancies; redevelopment, retraining or relocation of redundant employees; policy on redundancy payments, union consultation etc
Retention plan	Actions to reduce avoidable labour wastage

7.5 Tactical plans

Tactical plans can then be made, within this integrated framework, to cover all aspects of the HRM task.

- Pay and productivity bargaining
- Physical conditions of employment
- Management and technical development and career development
- Organisation and job specifications
- Recruitment and redundancies
- Training and retraining
- Staffing costs

7.6 Staffing shortages or surpluses

Shortages or surpluses of labour which emerge in the process of formulating the position survey must be dealt with.

(a) Dealing with a **shortage**

    (i) Internal transfers and promotions, training etc

    (ii) External recruitment

    (iii) Reducing labour turnover, by reviewing possible causes

    (iv) Overtime

    (v) New equipment and training to improve productivity so reducing the need for more people

(b)   Dealing with a **surplus**

    (i)   Allowing employee numbers to reduce through natural wastage
    (ii)   Restricting recruitment
    (iii)   Introduce part-time working for previously full-time employees
    (iv)   Redundancies – as a last resort, and with careful planning

Exam alert

Exam questions may test the main issues and stages in devising a HR plan.

7.7 Stages in human resource planning

Laurie Mullins (2002) devised a model of the different elements involved in HRM planning.

Stages in human resource planning

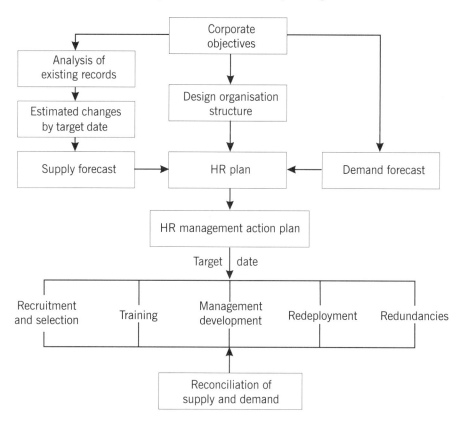

7.8 Control over the HR plan

Once the HR plan has been established, regular **control reports** should be produced.

(a)   Actual numbers recruited, leaving and promoted should be compared with planned numbers. Action may be required to correct any imbalance – depending on the cause.

(b)   Actual pay, conditions of employment and training should be compared with assumptions in the HR plan. Do divergences explain any excessive staff turnover?

(c)   Periodically, the HR plan itself should be reviewed and brought up to date.

Question 12.3   Employee enthusiasm/commitment

Learning outcome F2(v)

Enthusiastic and committed employees ensure business success. Do you agree?   **(4 marks)**

Section summary

HR plans identify the needs of the organisation in terms of **numbers of staff** and their **skills** and **compare** this with the **resources that the organisation currently** has. A **plan** is formed to **close the gap** between the two.

---

8 CIMA's Ethical Guidelines

Introduction

Ethics refers to a code of **moral principles** that people follow with respect to what is right or wrong. Ethical principles are not necessarily enforced by law, although the law incorporates moral judgements (eg theft is wrong ethically, and is also punishable legally). In relation to HR, companies have to follow **legal standards**, or else they may be subject to legal action. Employees are expected to act ethically and **CIMA's Ethical Guidelines** provide an ethical code for CIMA members to follow.

8.1 CIMA's Ethical Guidelines

All CIMA members and registered students are subject to **CIMA's Ethical Guidelines**.

These **guidelines** make it clear that individuals must:

- Observe the highest standards of conduct and integrity
- Uphold the good standing and reputation of the profession
- Refrain from any conduct which might discredit the profession

In particular, members should pay attention to the **fundamental principles** given in the Introduction and the discussion of objectivity and the resolution of ethical conflicts that appear in Part A. Despite being aimed at accountants, these guidelines are also **equally relevant** to **any employee** or **manager** within an organisation and are discussed briefly below.

Ethical behaviour and CIMA's Ethical Guidelines are core to the CIMA qualification and feature in many of the syllabuses.

CIMA's Ethical Guidelines are examinable. You should download a copy from the CIMA website (www.cimaglobal.com).

8.1.1 Fundamental principles

The **fundamental principles of CIMA's Ethical Guidelines** are:

(a)   **Integrity**. This is more than not telling lies – professional accountants must not be party to anything which is deceptive or misleading. You should be straightforward, honest and truthful in all professional and business relationships.

(b)   **Objectivity**. This is founded on fairness and avoiding all forms of bias, prejudice and partiality.

(c)   **Professional competence and due care**. Individuals must ensure they remain up to date with current developments and are technically competent. Those working under your authority must also have the appropriate training and supervision.

(d)   **Confidentiality**. Employers and clients are entitled to expect that confidential information will not be revealed without specific permission or unless there is a legal or professional right or duty to do so.

(e)   **Professional behaviour**. Accountants should behave in such a way as to protect the reputation of the professional and the professional body, and comply with relevant laws and regulations.

8.1.2 Ethical conflicts

Resolution of **ethical conflicts** is also covered by CIMA's guidance. The possibility of such conflicts arising is discussed. Potentially difficult situations include:

*   Pressure from an overbearing supervisor
*   Pressure from a friend or relation
*   Divided loyalties

A CIMA member or student should act responsibly, honour any legal contract of employment and conform to employment legislation. When dealing with an **ethical dilemma**, an individual should consider:

*   Whether more information or evidence is required

*   Whether there is an internal system in place for dealing with ethical concerns

*   Whether it is necessary or important to pass the matter up the organisation's hierarchy (including the audit committee)

*   Whether to obtain professional advice or consult CIMA

In cases where the CIMA member/student is encouraged or required to act illegally, resignation may be the only option (if discussion fails to resolve the situation).

Question 12.4	Principles

Learning outcome F2(x)

For each of CIMA's fundamental principles, give an example of a situation where someone would be acting unethically.   **(5 marks)**

Section summary

Ethics are **moral principles** that people follow with respect to what is right or wrong.

All CIMA members and registered students are subject to **CIMA's Ethical Guidelines**. These guidelines are also relevant to other employees.

Chapter Summary

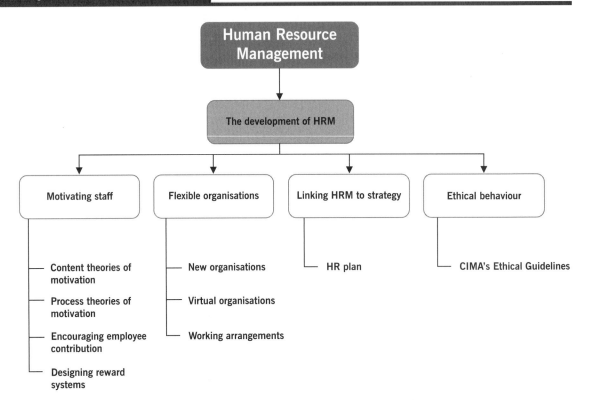

Quick Quiz

1   What are the objectives of human resource management?

2   Who developed a version of contingency theory?

    A   Mayo and Schein

    B   Weber

    C   Lawrence and Lorsch

    D   Taylor

3   In terms of HRM, what is a coercive psychological contract?

    A   A contract in which the individual considers that they are being forced to contribute their efforts and energies involuntarily

    B   A contract, accepted voluntarily by the individual, in which they expect to do their job in exchange for a readily identifiable set of rewards

    C   A contract in which the individual identifies themselves with the organisation and its goals, so that they actively seek to contribute further to the achievement of those goals

    D   A contract in which the individual is made to believe their working conditions will be better than they actually are

4   Which of the following is the correct formula as stated in Victor Vroom's expectancy theory?

    A $F = V \times E$

    B $V = E + F$

    C $E = V \times F$

    D $F = V / E$

5   Which one of CIMA's fundamental principles is based on fairness and avoiding all forms of bias, prejudice and partiality?

    A   Integrity

    B   Objectivity

    C   Confidentiality

    D   Professional behaviour

Answers to Quick Quiz

1 The objectives of HR management include:

- To develop an effective human component for the organisation which will respond effectively to change

- To obtain and develop the human resources required by the organisation and to use and motivate them effectively

- To create and maintain a co-operative climate of relationships within the organisation

- To deal with employment disputes as they arise

- To meet the organisation's social and legal responsibilities relating to the human resource

2 C Lawrence and Lorsch developed a form of contingency theory.

3 A A coercive psychological contract is one in which the individual considers that they are being forced to contribute their efforts and energies involuntarily.

4 A Force = Valance × Expectation is the formula in Victor Vroom's expectancy theory.

5 B Objectivity is based on fairness and avoiding all forms of bias, prejudice and partiality.

Answers to Questions

12.1 Human resource management

Human resource management concerns the strategic decisions organisations take in order to get the maximum contribution from their workforce. The main benefit is increased productivity, but others include reduced staff turnover, enhanced learning and the encouragement of employees to use their initiative.

12.2 Theory X and Theory Y

D The more effective view of managers depends on the circumstances of the work. If a manager is in charge of a large number of people doing repetitive, routine work, a Theory X approach is likely to be more effective. At other times, a Theory Y approach will be more effective, for example in dealing with subordinates who are managers or professionals.

12.3 Employee enthusiasm/commitment

Although enthusiastic and committed employees are often the driving force behind business success, they do not guarantee or ensure success.

(a) No matter how good, loyal, committed and enthusiastic the people are, if the basic commercial strategy is wrong, the company will fail.

(b) A strong culture of enthusiasm for all initiatives can inhibit people who have genuine valid concerns from voicing these – which may lead to expensive mistakes.

12.4 Principles

There is a huge range of possible answers. Here are some examples, and you probably thought of others.

- Integrity – handing over work to a colleague that you know contains errors
- Objectivity – allowing personal feelings to cloud your judgement
- Professional competence and due care – taking on work you are not qualified to do
- Confidentiality – leaving sensitive or confidential information where anyone can look at it
- Professional behaviour – cheating in professional exams

Now try these questions from the Practice Question Bank	Number
	56, 57, 58, 59, 60

HUMAN RESOURCE PRACTICES

 In this final chapter we shall concentrate on **good HR practice** at each stage of the employment process – from recruitment to dismissal. We shall also consider **legal and ethical issues** at each stage where relevant.

Employee development is key to maintaining the workforce's skills and providing a source of future managers for the organisation. **Appraisal** plays a major role in employee development as this is very often where training needs and future potential are discovered.

Topic list	Learning outcomes	Syllabus references	Ability required
1 Good human resource (HR) practice	F1(a), F1(b), F2(a), F2(b)	F1(i), F1(iv), F1(vii), F2(i), F2(ii), F2(vi), F2(vii)	application
2 Human resource development	F1(b), F2(a)	F1(v), F1(vi), F2(iii)	application
3 Appraisal	F1(b), F2(a), F2(b)	F1(i), F2(v), F2(vi)	application

Chapter Overview

1 Good human resource (HR) practice

Introduction

It is important that **effective human resource management** policies and procedures are followed if maximum employee performance is to be achieved.

Good practice at the **recruitment** and **selection stages** help ensure the most suitable candidates become employees. **Training and development policies** provide employees with skills and experience that enable them to progress through the organisation, providing them with the motivation to stay and the organisation with a **flexible workforce** that can meet its future needs.

1.1 Recruitment and selection

KEY TERMS

RECRUITMENT is concerned with finding applicants: going out into the labour market, communicating opportunities and information, and generating interest.

SELECTION consists of procedures to choose the successful candidate from among those made available by the recruitment effort.

A systematic approach to recruitment and selection should be followed.

 Detailed personnel **planning**.

 Job analysis, so that for any given job there are two things:

    (a)   A statement of the component tasks, duties, objectives and standards (**a job description**)

    (b)   A definition of the kind of person needed to perform the job (**a person specification**)

 Identify and **agree vacancies**, by way of the personnel plan (if vacancies are created by demand for new labour) or requisitions for replacement staff by a department which has 'lost' a current jobholder. Do vacancies need to be filled? Can the work be done by an existing member of staff? Could a cheaper part-time worker be used instead?

 Evaluation of the **sources of labour**, again by way of the personnel plan, which should outline personnel supply and availability, at macro and micro levels. Internal and external sources, and media for reaching both, will be considered.

 Review of applications, assessing the relative merits of broadly suitable candidates.

 Notifying applicants of the results of the selection process.

 Preparing employment contracts, induction, training programmes and so on.

1.2 The recruitment process

The recruitment process begins by determining the nature of the vacancies and ends with the shortlisting of candidates for selection.

1.2.1 Step 1: Job analysis

KEY TERM

JOB ANALYSIS is 'the process of collecting, analysing and setting out information about the content of jobs in order to provide the basis for a job description and data for recruitment, training, job evaluation and performance management. Job analysis concentrates on what jobholders are expected to do.'

(Armstrong)

The management of the organisation needs to analyse the sort of work needed to be done in order to **recruit effectively**. The **type of information** needed is outlined below.

Type of information	Comments
Purpose of the job	This might seem obvious. As an accountant, you will be expected to analyse, prepare or provide financial information, but this has to be set in the context of the organisation as a whole.
Content of the job	The tasks you are expected to do. If the purpose of the job is to ensure, for example, that people get paid on time, the tasks involved include many activities related to payroll.
Accountabilities	These are the results for which you are responsible. In practice they might be phrased in the same way as a description of a task.
Performance criteria	These are the criteria which measure how good you are at the job. These are largely task related.
Responsibility	This denotes the importance of the job. For example, a person running a department and taking decisions involving large amounts of money is more responsible that someone who only does what they are told.
Organisational factors	Who does the jobholder report to directly (line manager)?
Developmental factors	Likely promotion paths, if any, career prospects and so forth. Some jobs are 'dead-end' if they lead nowhere.
Environmental factors	Working conditions, security and safety issues, equipment and so on.

1.2.2 Step 2: Job design

A current approach to job design is the development and outlining of **competences** within a **competency framework**.

KEY TERMS

A person's COMPETENCE is 'a capacity that leads to behaviour that meets the job demands within the parameters of the organisational environment and that, in turn, brings about desired results'. (Boyzatis)

Some take this further and suggest that a competence embodies the ability to **transfer** skills and knowledge to new situations within the occupational area.

COMPETENCY FRAMEWORKS are a formal method of grouping, analysing and defining competences that are expected of those employed by an organisation.

They are used to take an **organisation's strategic needs** for different types of worker into account when developing job and person specifications. They help to ensure that a business's employee pool reflects its **culture and values** as well as having an appropriate mix of **skills and behaviours** to build diversity and talent within its workforce.

Competency frameworks should be periodically **re-evaluated** against the needs of the organisation, in terms of the nature of jobs and the changing requirements of roles, in order for them to remain relevant to the business.

Different types of competences

(a)   **Behavioural/personal** competences are underlying personal characteristics and behaviour required for successful performance – for example, 'ability to relate well to others'. Most jobs require people to be good communicators.

(b)   **Work-based/occupational competences** are 'expectations of workplace performance and the outputs and standards people in specific roles are expected to obtain'. This approach is used in NVQ systems. They cover what people have to do to achieve the results of the job. For example, a competence for a Chartered Management Accountant might be to 'produce financial and other statements and report to management'.

(c)   **Generic competences** can apply to all people in an occupation.

Some competences for managers are shown in the following table.

Competence area	Competence	
Intellectual	• Strategic perspective • Analytical judgement • Planning and organising	
Interpersonal	• Managing staff • Persuasiveness • Assertiveness and decisiveness	• Interpersonal sensitivity • Oral communication
Adaptability	• Flexibility • Coping with change	
Results	• Initiative • Motivation to achievement • Business sense	

These competences can be elaborated by identifying **positive** and **negative** indicators.

According to Mintzberg, the parameters of job design include:

(a)   **Job specialisation**

   (i)   **How many different tasks** are contained in the jobs and how broad and narrow are these tasks? **The task may be determined by operations management**. Until recently there has been a trend towards narrow specialisation, reinforced, perhaps, by demarcations laid down by trade unions. On the production line, a worker did the same task all the time. Modern techniques, however, require workers to be **multiskilled**.

   (ii)   **To what extent does the worker have control over the work?** At one extreme ('Scientific Management') the worker has little control over the work. At the other extreme (eg an electrician) the worker controls the task.

(b)   **Regulation of behaviour**. Co-ordination requires that organisations formalise behaviour so as to predict and control it.

(c)   **Training** in **skills** and indoctrination in **organisational values**.

Belbin (1997) described a way of **tailoring job design** to delayered, team-based structures and flexible working systems.

(a)   Flattened delayered hierarchies lead to greater flexibility but also to uncertainty and sometimes to a **loss of control**.

(b)   Old hierarchies tended to be **clearer** in establishing responsibilities.

1.2.3 Step 3: Job description and person specification

A JOB DESCRIPTION sets out the purpose of the job, where it fits into the organisation structure, the context of the job, the accountabilities of the job and the main tasks the holder carries out.

There are **four main purposes of a job description**.

Purpose	Comment
Organisational	Defines the job's place in the organisational structure
Recruitment	Provides information for identifying the sort of person needed (person specification)
Legal	Provides the basis for a contract of employment
Performance	Performance objectives can be set around the job description

The main **contents of a job description** include:

(a) **Job title** (eg Assistant Financial Controller); this indicates the function/department in which the job is performed, and the level of job within that function.

(b) The **location** of the job within the organisation structure (division, department and section)

(c) The job title of the person to whom **the jobholder is responsible** (eg the Assistant Financial Controller reports to the Financial Controller); in other words, the person's immediate boss

(d) The job title(s) of the person(s) **responsible to the jobholder** and the number of staff directly supervised

(e) Responsibility and authority level for **budgets** and **expenditure**

(f) A brief description of the **overall purpose** of the role

(g) Principal accountabilities or **main tasks**, ideally listed in order of importance

(h) **Skills** required to perform the job, including technical skills and physical skills and capabilities

(i) Typical working patterns or **hours of work** (eg 9 to 5), including any part-time or job-share options

Very detailed job descriptions are perhaps most suited for roles where the work is largely repetitive and predictable. In other situations, a prescriptive job description could cause problems, with employees perhaps wanting to adhere strictly to it rather than responding **flexibly** to task or organisational requirements.

Increasingly, job descriptions are being written in terms of the **outputs and performance levels** expected. Some organisations are moving towards **accountability profiles** in which outputs and performance are identified explicitly.

An alternative to job descriptions is **role definitions**. A **role** is a part played by people in meeting their objectives by working competently and flexibly within the context of the organisation's objectives, structures and processes.

Another trend is increased use of **person specifications**. These focus on the skills and qualities required by the person who will fill the role.

Possible areas the specification may cover include:

- Personal skills
- Qualifications
- Motivation
- Personality and disposition
- Innate ability (aptitude)
- Intelligence

Alec Rodgers devised a framework for the recruitment process that identifies seven points which can be used to identify the type of person required by a particular position. It can be remembered using the mnemonic **BADPIGS**.

Point	Examples
Background/Circumstances	Location, car owner
Attainments	Qualifications, career achievements
Disposition	Calm, independent
Physical make-up	Strength, appearance, health
Interests	Mechanical, people-related
General Intelligence	Average, above average
Special attributes	Manual dexterity, mental sharpness

Fraser devised a similar framework which is known as the **Five Point Plan**.

Point	Description
Flexibility and adjustment	Ability to deal with stress, get on with others and emotional stability
Impact on other people	Communication skills, personality and appearance
Required qualifications	Experience, education and training
Motivation	Achievement, progression and determination
Innate abilities	Aptitude, comprehension, intelligence

1.2.4 Step 4: Advertising job vacancies

After a job description and a personnel specification have been prepared, the organisation should **advertise** the job vacancy (**internally** or **externally**, or both).

The job description and personnel specification can be used as **guidelines** for the wording of any advertisement.

The **choice of advertising medium** will depend on **cost, frequency**, the frequency with which the organisation wants to advertise the job vacancy and its **suitability** to the target audience.

A range of **options** are available when advertising a position.

- In-house magazines
- Professional journals
- National newspapers
- Local newspapers
- Local radio
- Job centres

- Recruitment agencies
- Schools careers officers
- University careers officers
- Careers/job fairs
- Open days
- The internet

Employment agencies may be used to ease the effort involved in both recruitment and selection. More junior posts can often be filled from among an agency's pool of registered candidates. Recruitment and selection of more senior staff may be outsourced to **executive search agencies** which will manage the whole process. This may include preparing the job definition and person specification, advertising and word of mouth communication, and the initial interview process. One or two candidates will then be presented for assessment.

1.2.5 Step 5: Initial screening

The final process in the recruitment phase (before moving on to 'Selection') is the initial screening of candidates, usually by reviewing curriculum vitaes (CVs) and selecting some candidates for interview.

1.3 Selection

Selection involves a filtering process by reviewing application forms, interviewing and testing. A **variety of techniques** may be used in selection, and those chosen in a particular circumstance must be:

- **Reliable** – generate consistent results
- **Valid** – accurately predict performance of employees
- **Fair** – non-discriminating
- **Cost effective** – the benefits of obtaining good-quality staff must justify the costs of selecting them

An **ineffective selection process** may result in the:

- Employment of unsuitable applicants
- Rejection of suitable applicants

Both errors may be costly to put right.

1.3.1 Application forms

Job advertisements usually ask for a CV (résumé) or require an application form to be completed. The CV is more usual in applications for executive posts, except in the public sector. Application forms are usual for jobs below executive level, and at all levels in the public sector.

The application form should therefore help those making the selection to **sift through the applicants**, and to reject some at once so as to avoid the time and costs of unnecessary interviews. It should therefore:

(a) **Obtain relevant information** about the applicant which can be compared with the requirements of the job

(b) **Give applicants the opportunity to write about themselves**, such as their career ambitions and why they want the job

1.3.2 The interview: preparation

Aims of the interview

- Finding the best person for the job, through direct assessment
- Giving the applicant the chance to learn about the business

In **preparation for the interview**, the interviewer should study three things:

(a) The **job description** (and specification if separate), to review the major demands of the job
(b) The **personnel specification**, to make an assessment of the applicant's character and qualifications
(c) The **application form**, to decide on questions or question areas for each applicant

1.3.3 The interview: conduct

The following factors should be taken into account.

(a) The **layout** of the room and the number of interviewers should be planned carefully.

(b) The **manner** of the interviewers, their tone of voice, and the way their early questions are phrased can all be significant in establishing the tone of the interview.

(c) **Questions** should be put **carefully**. The interviewers should not be trying to confuse the candidate, but should be trying to obtain the information they need.

(d) The **candidate should be encouraged** to **talk**.

(e) The **candidate** should be **given** the **opportunity** to **ask questions**.

1.3.4 Types of job interview

There are a number of different types of interview:

(a)   **Individual interview**. A one to one discussion between the candidate and the interviewer face to face.

(b)   **Problem-solving interview**. Similar to an individual interview but the candidate is set a hypothetical problem to solve.

(c)   **Tandem interview**. Two interviewers per candidate.

(d)   **Panel interview**. A group of interviewers interview the candidate together.

(e)   **Stress interview**. Another type of face to face interview where the candidate is put under pressure by an aggressive interviewer.

(f)   **Succession/sequential interviews**. An alternative to a panel interview where the candidate faces a number of individual interviews with different people within the organisation.

(g)   **Group interview**. Similar to a problem-solving interview but with a number of candidates who must solve the problem together.

1.3.5 Limitations of interviews

All the different types of interview have advantages and disadvantages. For example, an individual interview is more likely to allow a rapport to build, but is also more subject to bias and therefore possibly less reliable. Also, involving more than one interviewer could result in differing opinions, making it difficult to reach a decision.

Some general limitations of interviews are:

(a)   **Unreliable assessments**. Interviewers may disagree. A suitable candidate might be rejected or an unsuitable candidate offered a job.

(b)   **They fail to provide accurate predictions** of how a person will perform in the job. Research has shown this time and again.

(c)   The **interviewers are likely to make errors** of judgement even when they agree about a candidate.

    (i)   A **halo effect**: a **general** judgement based on a **single** attribute.

    (ii)   **Contagious bias**. Interviewers might change the behaviour of the applicant through the wording of questions or non-verbal clues.

    (iii)   Interviewers sometimes **stereotype** candidates on the basis of insufficient evidence, eg on the basis of dress, hair style, accent of voice.

    (iv)   **Incorrect assessment** of qualitative factors such as motivation, honesty and integrity. Abstract qualities are very difficult to assess.

    (v)   **Logical error**. An interviewer might draw conclusions about a candidate without logical justification.

Interviewers should be **trained** to conduct and assess interviews.

Question 13.1   Interviews

Learning outcome F2(i)

Some courses offer tuition in interview technique to candidates looking for jobs. Do you think this means interviews are likely to be less reliable as a means of candidate selection?   **(2 marks)**

1.3.6 Testing of candidates

Tests are used to **supplement interviews** or select applicants for interview. The following types of test may be used.

(a) **Psychological tests and personality tests**. An individual may be required to answer a long series of questions or score a variety of statements which indicate basic attitude profiles. The best-known personality test is the Cattell P16 PF (Personality Factors), covering 16 aspects of personality. An occupational personality questionnaire is another example. It helps to identify an individual's preferred behavioural style at work, and therefore how well they might fit into a work environment and cope with different job requirements.

(b) **Cognitive tests** relate to thinking processes. These include **intelligence tests** which measure the applicant's general intellectual ability (eg IQ tests) and **aptitude tests**. Aptitude tests aim to provide information about the candidate's abilities in different areas (eg tests in mathematics, general knowledge, typing, reasoning, persuasion). Hogan Business Reasoning Inventory is an exam that measures verbal reasoning and numeracy.

(c) **Proficiency tests** are perhaps the most closely related to an assessor's objectives, because they measure ability to do the **work involved**.

(d) **Psychometric tests** contain features of all the above. They are selection tests that seek to **quantify** psychological dimensions of job applicants, for example intelligence, personality and motivation. Candidates might be required to answer a list of questions. Those answers are then marked and the candidate is given a score.

(e) **Medical tests** can be used to eliminate candidates with health problems where these are deemed an appropriate barrier to employment (such as with airline pilots and roles in the armed forces).

CASE STUDY

The Myers–Briggs Type Indicator is used to categorise people as to whether they are introvert/extrovert, objective/intuitive, logical/emotional, decisive/hesitant, and so forth. These tests may be used:

(a) In the initial selection of new recruits

(b) In the allocation of new entrants to different branches of work

(c) As part of the process of transfer or promotion

1.3.7 Advantages and disadvantages of tests

Tests have the following advantages and disadvantages.

Advantages	Disadvantages
A test can be a sensitive measuring instrument.	They may oversimplify complex issues.
Tests are standardised, so that all candidates are assessed by the same yardstick.	They are culturally specific. Many tests for managers were developed in the US. The cultures in other countries may differ.
Tests always measure the same thing (eg IQ).	Results should only be used to support other selection methods.

1.3.8 Group selection methods

Group selection methods might be used by an organisation as the final stage of a selection process for management jobs. They are not generally used for lower-level staff due to their cost. They consist of a series of tests, interviews and group situations over a period of two days or so, involving a small number (eg six to eight) of candidates for a job. After an introductory chat to make the candidates feel at home, they will be given one or two tests, one or two individual interviews, and several group situations in which the candidates are invited to discuss problems together and arrive at solutions as a management team.

Advantages and disadvantages of group selection methods include:

Advantages	Disadvantages
Selectors have more time to study the candidates.	Time and cost.
They test interpersonal skills.	The lack of experience of interviewers/selectors.
They reveal more about the candidates' personalities.	Candidates might behave atypically in a contrived situation.
They are suitable for selection of potential managers.	

1.3.9 Assessment centres

A relatively recent development in the attempt to ensure good recruitment and selection decisions are made is the **assessment centre approach**.

An assessment centre may or may not be a particular permanent location – the term refers more to the process of selection rather than to any specific building. The approach involves the candidate's **behaviour being observed and judged** by more than one assessor, using specifically developed **simulations**. This approach is generally used for senior positions, as it is time consuming (in terms of combined people hours) and therefore relatively expensive.

Trained assessors observe and **evaluate candidates** on their managerial qualities while candidates are performing a variety of situational exercises. Video is frequently used to help the assessors gather information. **Assessment centre exercises** are intended to measure dimensions such as:

- Planning and organising skills
- Leadership
- Analytical skills
- Problem solving

- Decision making
- Creativity
- Sociability and sensitivity
- Delegation

Assessor opinions are pooled and ratings discussed with fellow assessors. The exercises should allow **key job success behaviours** to be directly observed and measured.

Examples of **exercises** include:

- Simulations
- Group discussions
- Presentations
- Self-appraisal
- Business games

- Speeches
- Role play tasks
- Peer rating
- Questionnaires
- Written tests

1.3.10 Are assessment centres effective?

Assessment centres are most often used as part of a **selection process**, but may also be used to identify training and development needs or to enhance skills (through simulations).

Studies reveal that if assessment techniques are robust, targeted, well designed and properly implemented, the assessment centre approach produces **reliable outcomes** when compared to single-method approaches such as interviews and questionnaires.

However, the approach can be costly and will only produce good results if the assessors have the required skills to make **meaningful judgements** based on the behaviour of candidates. For example, assessors should be able to organise their behavioural observations by job-related dimensions.

1.3.11 References

It is common to obtain **references** from the successful candidate's previous employers and other people the candidate is acquainted with.

A reference enables an employer to check the **basic accuracy** of the candidate's CV – but often only this because many previous employers will only provide factual information (for example the person's job title, duties, period of employment, salary and attendance record). General opinions about the person could be asked for, but are unlikely to be provided because they are subjective and may leave the previous employer open to a complaint of providing false or unfair information.

1.3.12 Job offers and negotiation

A job represents an **economic exchange**. The employer obtains the **services of the employee**, who receives **benefits** such as pay and paid holiday in return. Employees may also seek **job satisfaction**, **security of employment** and **personal development**.

Job offers must be in writing and contain details such as the job title, pay and benefits, place of work, contractual hours, notice period and other conditions of employment. **Negotiation** often follows the job offer as both parties look to reach agreement over various aspects of the contract.

It is important that both employer and employee feel that the exchange they have contracted is a **fair** one. If they do not, their relationship will be strained from the outset. An employee who feels undervalued will seek alternative employment. An employer who feels exploited will seek to cut pay, benefits and number employed at every opportunity.

1.3.13 Realistic job previews (RJPs)

One method (suggested by Herriot) sometimes used to ensure both parties 'know what they are letting themselves in for' is a **realistic job preview (RJP)**.

This usually involves a **prospective employee** spending some time **'shadowing' an existing employee** in a similar role.

RJPs have been found to **lower expectations** about the job and the organisation – sometimes resulting in **candidates withdrawing** from contention. Candidates that do complete an RJP and accept the role are more likely to be **committed** to the job and the organisation.

1.4 Induction

All new staff should go through a proper process of **induction**. The context of induction programmes may vary, depending on the role being undertaken, but it is unlikely that anyone can make a satisfactory start without at least some basic orientation. Induction may be carried out by the **recruit's supervisor**, by a **departmental trainer** or **mentor**, by **HR staff** or by a **combination** of all three. Very often, induction is preceded by **pre-employment communications** where joining instructions, conditions of employment and relevant literature about the company are sent to the new employee before their first day.

1.4.1 Induction elements

An **induction programme** typically would include the following elements.

(a)   A **welcome**.

(b)   **Introductions** to immediate colleagues, other colleagues and supervisor.

(c)   Explanation of the **nature of the job**: a written job description will make this process easier. Some detailed technical matters may be identified as suitable for deferment to a later date.

(d)   **Safety** rules and procedures.

(e)   **Terms and conditions of employment**: a booklet is often provided giving full details, but essential matters such as hours of work, authorisation of absence and overtime, and any important legal obligations should be explained in full.

(f) Orientation to the wider **mission** of the department and the organisation. This is particularly important in organisations that provide services, because of the importance of **staff attitude and motivation** in the provision of high-quality service.

(g) Explanation of any systems of continuing **training**, **coaching** or **mentoring**. Many recruits are expected (and indeed, themselves expect) to undertake significant amounts of training. Rules relating to attendance, qualification and failure to progress must be explained.

Induction should enable the **newcomer** to make a **quick start** as a productive member of staff. It also gives the recruit and the organisation a chance to become acquainted. From the point of view of the organisation this can be helpful in such matters as deciding **how best to make use** of the **recruit's particular set of abilities** and competences and how to deal with any problems. The recruit benefits by obtaining **a fuller picture of the new work environment**.

1.4.2 'Dialogic learning'

One element of induction emphasised by Harrison (1992) is integrating recruits into how the organisation operates, including the **overall culture**, **beliefs** and **mission**. Harrison referred to this as 'dialogic learning'.

1.5 Legal and ethical issues

We now consider some of the **ethical** and **legal issues** relevant to organisations in general, with a particular emphasis on issues related to human resource management. The legal issues covered are done so from a practical standpoint, rather than covering the precise legal position and legal penalties.

1.5.1 Issues relevant to employee recruitment and selection

From an **ethical standpoint**, employee selection should be made on the basis of **who can best perform the role** on offer. Other issues such as a candidate's sex, race/ethnicity, religion or sexual orientation are irrelevant so should not play a part in the decision. Practical steps that can be taken in the **employee recruitment process** include the following.

(a) **Advertising**

    (i) Any wording that suggests preference for a particular group should be avoided.

    (ii) Employers must not indicate or imply any 'intention to discriminate'.

    (iii) Recruitment literature should state that the organisation is an Equal Opportunities employer, and actions should back this up.

    (iv) The placing of advertisements only where the readership is predominantly of one race or sex could be construed as indirect discrimination.

(b) **Recruitment agencies**. Instructions to an agency should not suggest any preference.

(c) **Application forms**. These should avoid questions which are not work related (such as domestic details) or which only one or some groups are asked to complete.

(d) **Interviews**. Any non work related question should be asked of all subjects, if at all, and even then, some types of question may be construed as discriminatory. Interviewers should not, for example, ask only women about plans to have a family or care of dependants.

(e) **Selection tests**. These must be wholly relevant, and should not favour any particular group.

(f) **Records**. Reasons for non-selection, and interview notes, should be recorded.

1.5.2 Issues relating to disciplinary procedures and dismissal

The grounds and procedures for **dismissing an employee** should be stated clearly in the organisation's disciplinary procedures policy. Except for instances of exceptional misconduct, dismissal should be the final step in the disciplinary process.

Many minor cases of poor performance or misconduct are best dealt with by **informal advice, coaching or counselling**. If the problem persists, it may be decided that **formal disciplinary action** is needed. Disciplinary action is usually thought of as consecutive stages, reflecting a progressive response.

(a)   **First warning**. A first warning could be oral or written depending on the seriousness of the case.

    (i)   An **oral warning** should include the reason for issuing it, notice that it constitutes the first step of the disciplinary procedure and details of the right of appeal. A note of the warning should be kept on file but disregarded after a specified period, such as six months.

    (ii)   A **first written warning** is appropriate in more serious cases. It should inform the worker of the improvement required and state that a final written warning may be considered if there is no satisfactory improvement. A copy of the first written warning should be kept on file but disregarded after a specified period, such as 12 months.

(b)   **Final written warning**. If an earlier warning is still current and there is no satisfactory improvement, a final written warning may be appropriate.

1.5.3 Disciplinary sanctions

The final stage in the disciplinary process is the imposition of sanctions.

(a)   **Suspension without pay**

    This course of action would be next in order if the employee has committed repeated offences and previous steps did not result in sufficient improvement. In the UK, suspension without pay is only available if it is provided for in the contract of employment.

(b)   **Dismissal**

    Dismissal is **termination of employment** by the employer. **Termination** of an employee's **employment contract** must be done in a way which follows **correct procedures**, otherwise a claim for unfair dismissal may follow.

Acceptable reasons for dismissal (UK example)	
Conduct	• Unacceptable conduct continuing after warnings/counselling
Capability	• The employee is not capable of the role (after appropriate guidance, training etc)
Breach of statutory duty	• If continuing the employment relationship would mean the employer breaching a statutory duty
Other 'substantial reason'	• Dishonesty • Loss of trust
Redundancy	• Cessation of business • Relocation of business • Cessation of work employed for

Dismissal is a drastic form of disciplinary action, and should be reserved for the most **serious offences**. For the organisation it involves waste of a labour resource, the expense of training a new employee, and disruption caused by changing the make-up of the work team.

Employers should take care at all times to avoid instances of **constructive dismissal**. This occurs where the employee feels that they have been mistreated in a way that causes them to resign. It may happen if the employer decides to reduce an employee's salary or make their working conditions unbearable. If an employment tribunal feels that an employee has been constructively dismissed then the employer will be liable to pay compensation.

1.5.4 Unfair dismissal

In many countries some reasons are classed **automatically** as grounds for **unfair dismissal**. The main grounds applicable in the UK are set out below.

- Dismissal on grounds of race, sex or disability discrimination
- Pregnancy or other maternity-related grounds
- Due to a request for flexible working practices
- Trade union membership or activities
- Taking steps to avert danger to health and safety at work
- Seeking to enforce rights relating to the national minimum wage
- Refusing or opting out of Sunday working (in the retail sector)

1.5.5 Redundancy

True redundancy arises when **the role an employee performs is no longer required**, perhaps due to restructuring or different working methods. Some (unethical) organisations use redundancy as an excuse to terminate the employment of employees who are no longer wanted, but who could not justifiably be dismissed on disciplinary grounds.

Organisations should have **policies governing redundancy**. These tend to cover areas such as pre-redundancy **consultation** and post-redundancy **support**. Selecting which employees will be made redundant must be fair and in accordance with established policies.

In the UK, the legal position is that an employee dismissed on the grounds of **redundancy** (that is, that their position is no longer required) may claim remedies for unfair dismissal if in fact the position was not actually redundant.

Alternatives to enforced redundancies could include:

- Reduced overtime
- Recruitment limits (or a 'freeze')
- Enforced retirement (of those over retirement age)
- Voluntary early retirement (of those close to retirement age)
- Shorter hours
- Job shares (eg two employees working shorter hours)
- Voluntary redundancy

Redundancy is likely to be an **unpleasant experience**. Even if a generous redundancy payment is made, this is unlikely to provide the means to support previous expenditure levels for very long.

Managers also need to ensure **remaining employees** remain **motivated**, and **morale** is as **high** as can be expected in the circumstances.

1.5.6 Relationship management in disciplinary situations

Even if the manager uses sensitivity and judgement, imposing disciplinary action tends to generate **resentment**. The challenge is to apply the necessary disciplinary action as constructively as possible.

(a) **Immediacy**. This means that after noticing the offence, the manager proceeds to take disciplinary action as speedily as possible. On the other hand, care must be taken to avoid hasty decisions and on the spot emotions which might lead to unwarranted actions.

(b) **Advance warning**. Employees should know in advance what is expected of them and what the rules and regulations are.

(c) **Consistency**. Disciplinary action must be applied consistently. Any penalties should be connected with the act and not based on the personality involved. No grudges should be borne.

(d) **Privacy**. As a general rule, disciplinary action should be taken in private, to avoid the spread of conflict and the humiliation or martyrdom of the employee concerned.

Your knowledge of good HR practice, especially in regard to disciplinary proceedings, will be used again when studying for Paper E2.

Section summary

Good human resource practice should be followed in **all aspects** of human resource management, such as recruitment, selection and dismissal.

There are a number of **legal issues** that should also be considered when **recruiting** and **dismissing** employees.

2 Human resource development

Introduction

Resourcing an organisation is about building and maintaining its **skills and knowledge base**.

KEY TERMS

HUMAN RESOURCE DEVELOPMENT is the process of extending personal abilities and qualities by means of education, training and other learning experiences.

DEVELOPMENT is 'the growth or realisation of a person's ability and potential through the provision of learning and educational experiences'.

TRAINING is 'the planned and systematic modification of behaviour through learning events, programmes and instruction which enable individuals to achieve the level of knowledge, skills and competence to carry out their work effectively'. (Armstrong, *Handbook of Personnel Management Practice*)

The **overall purpose of employee and management development** includes:

- **Ensuring** the organisation meets current and future performance objectives
- **Continuous improvement** of the performance of individuals and teams
- **Maximising people's** potential for growth (and promotion)

2.1 Training and development strategy

Organisations often have a **training and development strategy**, based on the overall strategy for the business.

Identify the skills and competences needed by the **business plan**.

Draw up the **development strategy** to show how training and development activities will assist in meeting the targets of the corporate plan.

Implement the training and development strategy.

This approach produces **training** with the **right qualities**.

- Relevance
- Problem based (ie corrects a real lack of skills)
- Action oriented
- Performance related

2.2 Effective learning programmes

The following **principles** are key to **effective learning programmes**:

Principle	Explanation
Participants	Must have the ability, skills, knowledge and motivation to learn.
Overview	An overview of what is to be learnt should be provided before focusing on specific tasks.
Feedback	Participants should receive accurate and timely feedback on their progress.
Rewards	Progress should be rewarded by positive reinforcement such as praise or tangible items such as certificates.
Active involvement	Successful learning involves taking part rather than listening or reading.
Learning curve	Training must reflect the fact that some skills are picked up quickly whereas some will take time to develop. Progress is not always at the same pace.
Job specific	Training should be as realistic as possible to the job concerned to minimise problems of applying the new skill or knowledge.

2.3 Training and the organisation

The **benefits for the organisation** of training and development programmes are outlined in the following table.

Benefit	Comment
Minimise the learning costs of obtaining the skills the organisation needs	Training and development programmes ensure staff, and the organisation as a whole, have the skills required to deliver the **business strategy**.
Lower costs and **increased productivity**	Some people suggest that higher levels of training explain the **higher productivity** of German as opposed to many UK manufacturers.
Fewer accidents, and better health and safety	**EU health and safety directives** require a certain level of training. Employees can take employers to court if accidents occur or if unhealthy work practices persist.
Less need for detailed supervision	If people are trained they can get on with the job, and managers can concentrate on other things. Training is an aspect of **empowerment**.
Flexibility	Training ensures that people have the **variety** of skills needed – multiskilling is only possible if people are properly trained.
Recruitment and succession planning	Training and development **attracts new recruits** and ensures that the organisation has a **supply of suitable managerial** and technical staff to take over when people retire.
Change management	Training helps organisations **manage change** by letting people know why the change is happening and giving them the skills to cope with it.

Benefit	Comment
Corporate culture	Training programmes can be used to build the corporate culture or to direct it in certain ways, by indicating that certain **values** are espoused.
	Training programmes can **build relationships** between staff and managers in different areas of the business.
Motivation	Training programmes can **increase commitment** to the organisation's goals.

2.4 Training and the employee

For the individual **employee**, the **benefits of training** and **development** are more clear-cut, and few refuse it if it is offered.

Benefit	Comment
Enhances portfolio of skills	Even if not specifically related to the current job, training can be useful in other contexts, and the employee becomes **more attractive** to employers and more **promotable**.
Psychological benefits	The trainee might feel reassured that **they are of continuing value** to the organisation.
Social benefit	People's **social needs** can be met by training courses – they can also develop networks of contacts.
The job	Training can help people do their job better, thereby increasing **job satisfaction**.

2.5 Possible shortcomings of training

Training is not always the answer to **performance-related problems**.

(a) It is irrelevant to problems caused by faulty organisation, layout, methods, equipment, employee selection and placement and so on.

(b) Cost, time, inconvenience, apathy and unrealistic expectations of training in the past may restrict its effectiveness.

(c) Limitations imposed by intelligence, poor motivation and the psychological restrictions of the learning process also restrict its effectiveness.

2.6 Training and development needs

In order to ensure that training meets the real needs of the organisation, large businesses adopt a **planned approach to training**. This has the following steps.

 Identify and define the organisation's training needs. It may be the case that recruitment might be a better solution to a problem than training.

 Define the learning required – in other words, specify the knowledge, skills or competences that have to be acquired. For technical training, this may include all finance department staff having to become conversant with a new accounting system.

 Define training objectives – what must be learned and what trainees must be able to do after the training exercise.

Plan training programmes – training and development can be planned in a number of ways, employing a number of techniques. It covers three things:

- Who provides the training

- Where the training takes place

- Divisions of responsibilities between trainers, line managers or team leaders and the individual personally

Implement the training.

Evaluate the training: has it been successful in achieving learning objectives?

Go back to Step 2 if more training is needed.

CASE STUDY

Training for quality

The British Standards for Quality Systems (BS EN ISO 9000) identifies training needs for those organisations registering for assessment, and also shows the importance of a systematic approach to ensure adequate control.

The training, both specific training to perform assigned tasks and general training to heighten quality awareness and to mould attitudes of all personnel in an organisation, is central to the achievement of quality.

The comprehensiveness of such training varies with the complexity of the organisation.

The following steps should be taken:

(1)   Identifying the way tasks and operations influence quality in total

(2)   Identifying individuals' training needs against those required for satisfactory performance of the task

(3)   Planning and carrying out appropriate specific training

(4)   Planning and organising general quality awareness programmes

(5)   Recording training and achievement in an easily retrievable form so that records can be updated and gaps in training can be readily identified

2.6.1 Training needs analysis

Training needs analysis covers three issues.

	Current state	Desired state
1	Organisation's current results	Desired results, standards
2	Existing knowledge and skill	Knowledge and skill needed
3	Individual performance	Required standards

The difference between the two columns is the **training gap**. Training programmes are designed to improve individual performance, thereby improving the performance of the organisation.

Training surveys combine information from a variety of sources to discern what the training needs of the organisation actually are.

(a) The **business strategy** at corporate level.

(b) **Appraisal and performance reviews**. The purpose of a performance management system is to improve performance, and training may be recommended as a remedy.

(c) **Attitude surveys** of employees, asking them what training they think they need.

(d) **Evaluation** of existing training programmes.

(e) **Job analysis**, which deals with three things:

    (i) Reported difficulties people have in meeting the skills requirement of the job
    (ii) Existing performance weaknesses that could be remedied by training
    (iii) Future changes in the job

The **job analysis** can be used to generate a **training specification** covering the knowledge needed for the job, the skills required to achieve the result, and attitudinal changes required.

2.7 Setting training objectives

An investigation into the gap between job or competence requirements and current performance or competence should be undertaken. If training would improve work performance, training **objectives** can then be defined. They should be clear, specific and related to observable, measurable targets.

- Behaviour – what the trainee should be able to do
- Standard – to what level of performance
- Environment – under what conditions (so that the performance level is realistic)

Example

'At the end of the course the trainee should be able to describe ... or identify ... or distinguish x from y ... or calculate ... or assemble ...' and so on. It is insufficient to define the objectives of training as 'to give trainees a grounding in ...' or 'to encourage trainees in a better appreciation of ...'; this offers no target achievement which can be quantifiably measured.

Training objectives link the identification of training needs with the content and methods of training.

Training needs	Learning objectives
To assemble clocks faster	The employee will be able to assemble each clock within 30 minutes.
To know more about the Data Protection Act	The employee will be able to answer four out of every five queries about the Data Protection Act without having to search for details.
To establish a better rapport with customers	The employee will immediately attend to a customer unless already engaged with another customer.
	The employee will greet each customer using the customer's name where known.
	The employee will apologise to every customer who has had to wait to be attended to.

Having identified training needs and objectives, the manager will have to decide on the best way to **approach training**; there are a number of types and techniques of training, which we will discuss below.

2.8 Incorporating training needs into an individual development programme

KEY TERMS

A PERSONAL DEVELOPMENT PLAN is a 'clear developmental action plan for an individual which incorporates a wide set of developmental opportunities including formal training'.

The purpose of a **personal development plan** will vary.

- Improving performance in the existing job
- Developing skills for future career moves within and outside the organisation

SKILLS: what the individual needs to be able to do if results are to be achieved. Skills are built up progressively by repeated training. They may be manual, intellectual or mental, perceptual or social.

Preparing a personal development plan involves these steps.

Analyse the current position. You could do a personal SWOT analysis. The supervisor can have an input into this by categorising the skills use of employees on a grid as follows, in a **skills analysis**. The aim is to incorporate employees' interests into their actual roles.

Performance

		High	Low
Liking of skills	High	Likes and does well	Likes but doesn't do well
	Low	Dislikes but does well	Dislikes and doesn't do well

Set goals to cover performance in the existing job, future changes in the current role, moving elsewhere in the organisations, developing specialist expertise. Naturally, such goals should have the characteristics as far as possible of **SMART objectives** (ie **S**pecific, **M**easurable, **A**chievable, **R**ealistic and **T**ime-bound).

Draw up action plan to achieve the goals.

2.9 Formal training

2.9.1 Formal training methods

Formal training methods include the following:

(a)   **Internal courses** run by the organisation's training department or other employees.

(b)   **External courses** (held either on- or off-site) run by an outside organisation.

(c)   There are a wide range of training course types.

(i)   **Day release**: The employee works in the organisation and on one day per week attends a local college or training centre for theoretical learning.

(ii)   **Distance learning, evening classes and correspondence courses**, which make demands on the individual's time outside work. This is commonly used, for example, by typists wishing to develop or 'refresh' shorthand skills.

(iii)   **Revision courses** for examinations of professional bodies.

(iv)   **Block release** courses which may involve four weeks at a college or training centre followed by a period back at work.

(v)   **Sandwich courses**, which usually involve six months at college then six months at work, in rotation, for two or three years.

(vi)   A **sponsored full-time course** at a university for one or two years.

(d)   **Techniques** used in training delivery might include:

(i)   Lectures

(ii)   Seminars, in which participation is encouraged

(iii)   Simulations

(e)   **Computer-based training** involves interactive training via PC. This could involve the use of CD-ROMs, DVDs or online delivery via the internet.

2.9.2 Methods used on courses

Common course training methods include the following:

(a)   **Lectures**. Lectures are suitable for large audiences and can be an efficient way of putting across information. However, lack of participation may lead to an audience's lack of interest and failure to understand.

(b)   **Discussions**. Discussions aim to impart information but allow much greater opportunity for audience participation. They are often suitable for groups of up to 20 people and can be a good means of maintaining interest.

(c)   **Exercises**. An exercise involves a particular task being undertaken with pre-set results following guidance laid down. They are a very active form of learning and are a good means of checking whether trainees have assimilated information.

(d)   **Role plays**. Trainees act out roles in a typical work situation. They are useful practice for face to face situations. However, they may embarrass and may not be taken seriously.

(e)   **Case studies**. Case studies identify causes and/or suggest solutions. They are a good means of exchanging ideas and thinking out solutions. However, trainees may see the case study as divorced from their real work experience.

2.9.3 Disadvantages of formal training

(a)   An individual will not benefit from formal training unless they **want to learn**. The individual's superior may need to provide encouragement in this respect.

(b)   If the **subject matter** of the training course does not **relate to an individual's job**, the learning will quickly be forgotten.

(c)   Individuals may not be able to **carry over** what they have learned to their own particular job.

2.10 On the job training

On the job training can include a wide range of activities. One **employee shadowing** another is one common method; being assigned a **'mentor'** is another.

Pedler (1986) pointed out that at **management level, learning** and **development** are often **accidental** or **unconscious**. Any activity that results in a manager being more willing or capable to control events has a developmental aspect to it.

More **specific or structured** on the **job training** schemes typically have the following characteristics:

(a)   The assignments should have a **specific purpose** from which the trainee can learn and gain experience.

(b)   The organisation must **tolerate any mistakes** which the trainee makes. Mistakes are an inevitable part of on the job learning.

(c)   The work should **not be too complex**.

Methods of on the job training include the following:

(a)   **Demonstration/instruction**: Show the trainee how to do the job and let them get on with it. It should combine **telling** a person what to do and **showing** them how, using appropriate media. The trainee imitates the instructor, and asks questions.

(b)   **Coaching**: The trainee is put under the guidance of an experienced employee who shows the trainee how to do the job. The coach should:

   (i)   Establish learning targets
   (ii)   Plan a systematic learning and development programme
   (iii)   Identify opportunities for broadening the trainee's knowledge and experience
   (iv)   Take into account the strengths and limitations of the trainee
   (v)   Exchange feedback

(c)   **Job rotation**: The trainee is given several jobs in succession, to gain experience of a wide range of activities.

(d)   **Temporary promotion**: An individual is promoted into their superior's position while the superior is absent.

(e)   **'Assistant to' positions**: A junior manager with good potential may be appointed as assistant to the managing director or another executive director.

(f)   **Action learning**: A group of managers are brought together to solve a real problem with the help of an adviser who explains the management process that actually happens.

(g)   **Committees**: Trainees might be included in the membership of committees in order to obtain an understanding of interdepartmental relationships.

(h)   **Project work**: Work on a project with other people can expose the trainee to other parts of the organisation.

2.10.1 Advantages and disadvantages of on the job training

Some advantages and disadvantages of on the job training are summarised below:

Advantages	Disadvantages
Training is provided that is **relevant** to the job being undertaken.	Training is **difficult** when **real customers** are being talked to – they may not take kindly to a person being trained when they are attempting to arrange insurance, for example.
Training is **'just-in-time'** – that is, specific queries are identified.	Where training is being carried out by a manager, they **may not have** the **appropriate training skills**.

2.11 Learning styles

Kolb and Honey and Mumford developed theories on how people learn.

2.11.1 The learning cycle (Kolb)

Kolb suggested that **formal classroom-type learning** is 'a specialist activity **cut off** from the real world and unrelated to one's life': a teacher or trainer directs the learning process on behalf of a **passive** learner.

Experiential learning, on the other hand, involves **doing** and puts the learners in an **active** problem-solving role.

Self-learning encourages learners to formulate and commit themselves to their own learning objectives.

The implication of Kolb's theory is that to be effective, learning must be **reinforced by experience**.

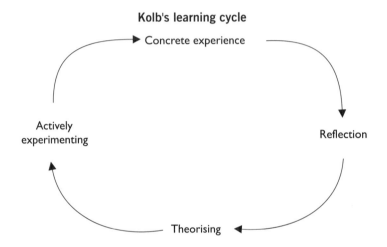

Kolb's learning cycle

2.11.2 Honey and Mumford's learning styles

Honey and Mumford identified four types of learning style:

(a)   **Theorist**

Theorists feel unhappy with subjective judgements and having to think laterally. They prefer certainty and process information logically.

(b)   **Reflector**

Reflectors are cautious by nature and are often shy or indecisive individuals. They prefer to think and absorb information before taking action and even see how others use the information before making their minds up.

(c)   **Pragmatist**

Pragmatists are open, practical people who like to experiment with ideas and theories. They are quick to adapt ideas they like but do not enjoy debates that are open-ended.

(d)   **Activist**

Activists are enthusiastic individuals who seek challenges and are open-minded. They are keen to become, without bias, fully involved in new experiences. Once the initial excitement dies down, however, they become disinterested with implementation and long-term input.

2.12 Training in different industries or sectors

Training and development activities vary in both approach and frequency/quantity across different sectors and employee groups.

Hendry (1995) attributes these differences to different types of labour markets and points out that service sectors tend to rely on retraining and training employees (an **internal** labour market).

Manufacturing industries have instead tended to rely on the apprenticeship system, which provides a more 'portable' qualification resulting in an **external**, occupational labour market.

2.13 Evaluating training

There are a number of ways of **validating** and **evaluating** a training scheme.

KEY TERMS

VALIDATION OF TRAINING means observing the results of the course and measuring whether the training objectives have been achieved.

EVALUATION OF TRAINING means comparing the actual costs of the scheme against the assessed benefits which are being obtained. If the costs exceed the benefits, the scheme will need to be redesigned or withdrawn.

(a) **Trainees' reactions to the experience**: course assessment sheets completed after training can ask trainees whether they thought the training programme was relevant to their work, and whether they found it useful.

(b) **Trainee learning**: measuring what the trainees have learned on the course by means of a test at the end of it. A further test can be taken some time after the course to see if the trainee has retained the knowledge learnt.

(c) **Changes in job behaviour following training**: this is relevant where the aim of the training was to learn a skill.

(d) **Organisational change as a result of training**: finding out whether the training has affected the work or behaviour of other employees not on the course.

(e) **Impact of training on the achievement of organisational goals**: seeing whether the training scheme has contributed to the achievement of the overall objectives of the organisation.

(f) **Trainer assessment**: the trainer can complete an assessment that identifies gaps in trainee knowledge or other deficiencies.

(g) **HR review**: human resources employees can conduct a critical review that evaluates the training using a range of information to see if the organisation's objectives for the training have been met.

2.13.1 Levels of evaluation

Kirkpatrick (1998) identified four levels at which **training can be evaluated**.

- **Reaction** – how the trainees act, enjoyment level
- **Learning** – has the knowledge been absorbed?
- **Behaviour** – have required behavioural changes taken place?
- **Results** – what benefits have resulted from the training (eg better quality, reduced costs)?

Evaluating training usually requires **measurement before and after training**. It is difficult, however, to establish with any certainty what changes are directly attributable to the training alone.

Exam alert

Exam questions may test your understanding of the effectiveness of a staff training event.

CASE STUDY

Whitbread pubs reported improved performance as a result of a change in the company's training scheme. Previously the company's training scheme had aimed to improve the service standards of individuals, and there were also discussions with staff on business developments. It was felt, however, that other companies in the same sector had overtaken Whitbread in these respects.

Whitbread therefore introduced an integrated approach to assessment of the performance of pubs. Assessment is by four criteria: training (a certain percentage of staff have to have achieved a training award), standards (suggested by working parties of staff), team meetings and customer satisfaction. Managers are trained in training skills and they in turn train staff, using a set of structured notes to ensure a consistent training process.

Pubs that fulfil all the criteria win a team hospitality award consisting of a plaque, a visit from a senior executive, and a party or points for goods scheme. To retain the award and achieve further points, pubs then have to pass further assessments which take place every six months.

The scheme seemed to improve standards. Staff turnover was significantly down and a survey suggested morale had improved, with a greater sense of belonging particularly by part-time staff. A major cause of these improvements may well be the involvement of staff and management in the design process.

2.14 Career management and development

KEY TERM

CAREER MANAGEMENT is a technique whereby the progress of individuals within an organisation from job to job is planned with organisational needs and individual capacity in mind.

Career management is both an individual and an organisational issue:

(a) It ensures that the organisation has a reserve of managers in waiting. In flat or delayered organisations this is particularly important, as the jump in responsibility from junior to senior positions is much wider than in organisations with extensive hierarchies.

(b) It ensures people get the right training to enable them to develop the right abilities for the job.

For the organisation, career management also determines whether, as a matter of policy, the organisation will promote from **within when possible**, as opposed to hiring **outsiders**.

KEY TERM

CAREER DEVELOPMENT is based on an individual's education, training and development and is an important factor in any appraisal system.

Education is the person's formal qualifications and may have been achieved before the employment starts (although some education such as obtaining the CIMA qualification may take place at work).

Training relates to the person's immediate work needs. For example, they may need to be trained in order to use the organisation's IT system.

Development considers the person's future needs given their career aspirations. For example, those looking to obtain management positions in the future may need their management skills developing.

2.14.1 Succession planning

Large organisations are able to plan a **logical progression** for individuals through its hierarchy over time. The objective is to ensure that suitable replacements (in terms of experience and ability) are available to take over positions above them as they become available.

Advantages of succession planning	Disadvantages of succession planning
Can be **cheaper** than advertising or using agencies	Large 'talent pools' make it **hard to decide** who to promote
Develops **career structures**	**Reduces 'fresh blood'** at higher levels in the organisation
Motivates employees as rewards are visible (ie promotions are seen by all)	Vacancies may occur **before** suitable replacements are ready for promotion
Maintains the organisation's **culture** as long-serving employees are promoted	**Better candidates** may be available **outside** the business
It is **logical** and **rational**	**Planning requires** resources to manage it
	Job for life is increasingly becoming an **outdated concept** and the best staff may leave before vacancies become available

2.14.2 Barriers to career planning/succession planning

Flatter organisation structures, the growth of **cross-functional teams** and generally **shorter periods of employment** with a particular organisation have led to reduced potential for succession planning. Individuals now tend to take increased responsibility for their own career progression, and are more likely to accept that this may involve working for a number of organisations (and/or for themselves) throughout their career.

2.15 Management development

Management development includes **general education**, **specific learning** and **wider experience**. It is essential if managers are to make the leap from functional to general management.

KEY TERM

MANAGEMENT DEVELOPMENT is the process of improving the effectiveness of an individual manager by developing the necessary skills and understanding of organisational goals.

Pedlar *et al* considered that the **development of management** should be down to the individual concerned and that the organisation should provide a system that increases managers' capacity and willingness to take control and responsibility for their own learning.

2.15.1 Self-development

KEY POINT

Self-development is now emphasised by many professional organisations such as **CIMA**. The modern view is that membership of an organisation does not ensure competence in the future. New knowledge must be learned and skills must be maintained and developed.

Pedlar *et al* found several possibilities for learning. It can be **planned** (conscious), **accidental** (unconscious) and can take place **at or away from work**. Although management development is in some respects a natural process, the term is generally used to refer to a **conscious policy** within an organisation to provide a programme of individual development. A variety of techniques could be used, either on or off the job.

- Formal education and training
- On the job training
- Group learning sessions
- Job rotation
- Career planning
- Counselling

Accidental learning is unplanned. For example, situations at work or socially may develop personal attributes of a manager.

The principle behind management development is that by giving an **individual** time to study the techniques of being a **good manager**, and by **counselling** them about their **achievements** in these respects, the individual will **realise their full potential**. The time required to bring a manager to this potential is possibly fairly short.

2.16 The transition from functional to general management

There is one particular aspect of management development and training that organisations should look at closely – **the transition from functional to general management**. To help with this transition, an organisation should have a **planned management development programme** consisting of several aspects.

(a)   Individuals should be encouraged to acquire suitable **educational qualifications** for senior management. 'High fliers' for example might be encouraged to study for an MBA early on in their career. Senior finance managers ought to have an accountancy qualification.

(b)   **In-house training programmes** might be provided for individuals who are being groomed for senior management. Formal training in general management skills can be very helpful.

(c)   **Careful promotion procedures** should aim to ensure that only managers with the potential to do well are promoted into senior management positions.

(d)   There should be a system of **regular performance appraisal** in which individuals are counselled by their managers on what they have done well and not so well, how to improve their performance in their current job and how to develop their skills for a more senior job.

(e)   **Opportunities to gain suitable experience** should be provided to managers who are candidates for more senior positions. There are several possibilities:

   (i)   Allowing subordinates to stand in for their boss whenever the boss is away

   (ii)   Using staff officer positions to groom future high fliers

   (iii)   Using a divisionalised organisation structure to delegate general management responsibilities further down the management hierarchy

Question 13.2	Human resource development

Learning outcome F1(vi)

Which of the following are aspects of human resource development (HRD)?

(i)   Providing formal training courses
(ii)   On the job training
(iii)   Succession and career planning
(iv)   Job redesign

A   (i) only
B   (i) and (ii) only
C   (i), (ii) and (iii) only
D   (i), (ii), (iii) and (iv)   **(2 marks)**

Section summary

Human resource development has **benefits** for both the **employee** and **employer**.

Training and development should be **carefully planned** if it is to achieve its aims.

The **method of training** or **development** chosen should **meet the needs** of the **employee** and **employer**.

However the training or development is delivered, it should be **evaluated** in order to ascertain its success.

Career and management training provides the employee with **motivation** and the employer with a **source of future managers**.

3 Appraisal

Introduction

Appraisals **review** and **reward performance** and **potential**. They are part of **performance management** and can be used to establish areas for improvement and training needs.

KEY TERM

APPRAISAL: the systematic review and assessment of an employee's performance, potential and training needs.

3.1 Why are appraisals needed?

KEY POINT

Employee appraisal can be viewed as a **control tool** as it aims to influence employee behaviour and **maximise utilisation** of the organisation's **human resource**. The process of appraisal is designed to review performance over the past period and improve it in the future.

Appraisals are needed for a number of reasons:

(a)   Managers and supervisors may obtain **random impressions** of employees' performance (perhaps from their more noticeable successes and failures), but **rarely form a coherent, complete and objective picture**.

(b)   They may have a fair idea of their employees' **shortcomings** – but may not have devoted time and attention to the matter of **improvement and development**.

(c)   **Judgements are easy to make, but less easy to justify** in detail, in writing, or to the subject's face.

(d)   **Different assessors may be applying a different set of criteria, and varying standards of objectivity and judgement**. This undermines the value of appraisal for comparison, as well as its credibility in the eyes of the appraisee.

(e)   Unless stimulated to do so, **managers rarely give their staff adequate feedback on their performance**.

3.2 The purpose of appraisal

KEY POINT

The **general purpose** of any appraisal system is to **improve efficiency**. Personnel appraisal aims to ensure individuals are performing to the best of their ability and developing their potential and that the organisation is best utilising their abilities.

Appraisals **may include**:

(a) **Reward review**, measuring the extent to which an employee is deserving of a bonus or pay increase as compared with their peers

(b) **Performance review**, for planning and following up training and development programmes, ie identifying training needs, validating training methods and so on

(c) **Potential review**, as an aid to planning career development and succession, by attempting to predict the level and type of work the individual will be capable of in the future

The **objectives of appraisals** include the following:

(a) Establishing the **key deliverables** an individual has to produce to enable the organisation to achieve its objectives

(b) Comparing the individual's **level of performance against a standard**, as a means of quality control

(c) Identifying the individual's **training and development needs** in the light of actual performance

(d) Identifying areas that **require improvement**

(e) Monitoring the organisation's **initial selection procedures** against subsequent performance

(f) **Improving communication** between different levels in the hierarchy

3.3 An appraisal system

A **typical appraisal system** is outlined below.

 Identification of criteria for assessment, perhaps based on job analysis, performance standards, person specifications and so on.

 The **preparation by the subordinate's manager of an appraisal report**. In some systems both the appraisee and appraiser prepare a report. These reports are then compared.

 An **appraisal interview**, for an exchange of views about the appraisal report, targets for improvement, solutions to problems and so on.

 Review of the assessment by the assessor's own superior, so that the appraisee does not feel subject to one person's prejudices. Formal appeals may be allowed if necessary to establish the fairness of the procedure.

 The **preparation and implementation of action plans** to achieve improvements and changes agreed.

 Follow-up monitoring the progress of the action plan.

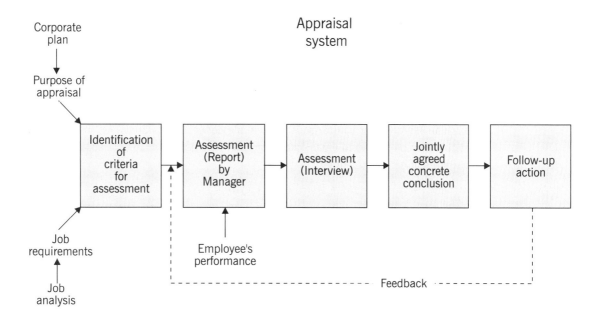

3.4 Problems of appraisal systems

Effective appraisals can be difficult to implement. Three particular difficulties are:

(a)   The **formulation of desired traits and standards** against which individuals can be consistently and objectively assessed.

(b)   **Recording assessments**. Managers should be encouraged to utilise a standard and understood framework, but still be allowed to express what they consider to be important, and without too much form-filling.

(c)   **Getting the appraiser and appraisee together**, so that both contribute to the assessment and plans for improvement and/or development.

3.5 Appraisal techniques

The following **techniques** are often used in an appraisal system.

(a)   **Overall assessment**. Managers write in narrative form their judgements about the appraisees. There will be no guaranteed consistency of the criteria and areas of assessment, however, and managers may not be able to convey clear, effective judgements in writing.

(b)   **Guided assessment**. Assessors are required to comment on a number of specified characteristics and performance elements, with guidelines as to how terms such as 'application', 'integrity' and 'adaptability' are to be interpreted in the work context. This is more precise, but still rather vague.

(c)   **Grading**. Grading adds a comparative frame of reference to the general guidelines, whereby managers are asked to select one of a number of levels or degrees to which the individual in question displays the given characteristic. These are also known as **rating scales**. Numerical values may be added to ratings to give rating scores. Alternatively, a less precise **graphic scale** may be used to indicate general position on a plus/minus scale.

Factor: job knowledge

High ___✓___ Average _____ Low ____

(d)   **Behavioural incident methods**. These concentrate on **employee behaviour**, which is measured against typical behaviour in each job as defined by common **critical incidents** of successful and unsuccessful job behaviour reported by managers.

(e)   **Objectives and results-orientated schemes**. This reviews performance against specific targets and standards of performance agreed in advance. The manager becomes a counsellor. Learning and motivation theories suggest that clear and known targets are important in modifying and determining behaviour. The objectives set as part of an appraisal process should be agreed – and (again) these should be **SMART** (**S**pecific, **M**easurable, **A**chievable, **R**ealistic and **T**ime-bound).

(f)   **Common appraisal standards**. Assessments must be related to a **common standard** (the appraisal standard) in order for comparisons to be made between individuals. On the other hand, they should also be related to meaningful performance criteria, which take account of the critical variables in each different job.

3.6 Self-appraisal

Individuals may carry out their own **self-evaluation** as a major input into the appraisal process. This has the advantage that the system is aimed at the needs of the individual. Other advantages are:

(a)   It **saves the manager time** as the employee identifies the areas of competence which are relevant to the job and their relative strengths in these competences.

(b)   It offers **increased responsibility** to the individual, which may improve motivation.

(c)   This may be a way of **reconciling the goals** of both the individual and the organisation.

(d)   It may overcome the problem of needing skilled appraisers, therefore **cutting training costs** and **reducing the managerial role in appraisal**.

(e)   In giving the responsibility to an individual, the scheme may offer more **flexibility** in terms of timing, with individuals undertaking ongoing self-evaluation.

However, people are often not the best judges of their own performance. Many schemes combine the two – the manager and subordinate fill out a report and compare notes.

3.7 Upward appraisal

A notable modern trend adopted by some major UK companies is **upward appraisal**, whereby employees are not rated by their superiors but by their subordinates. The followers appraise the leader.

Advantages of upward appraisal include the following:

(a)   Subordinates tend to know their superior better than superiors know their subordinates.

(b)   As all subordinates rate their managers statistically, these ratings tend to be more reliable – the more subordinates, the better. Instead of the biases of individual managers' ratings, the various ratings of the employees can be converted into a representative view.

(c)   Subordinates' ratings have more impact because it is unusual to receive ratings from them. It is also surprising to bosses because, despite protestations to the contrary, information often flows down organisations more smoothly and comfortably than it flows up. When it flows up it is qualitatively and quantitatively different. It is this difference that makes it valuable.

Problems with the method include fear of reprisals, vindictiveness and extra form processing. Some bosses in strong positions might refuse to act, even if a consensus of staff suggested that they should change their ways.

3.8 Customer appraisal

In some companies, part of the employee's appraisal process must take the form of **feedback from 'customers' (whether internal or external)**. This may be taken further into an influence on remuneration (at Rank Xerox, 30% of a manager's annual bonus is conditional upon satisfactory levels of 'customer'

feedback). This is a valuable development in that customers are the best judges of customer service, which the appraisee's boss may not see.

3.9 180/360 degree appraisal

180 degree appraisal involves the manager obtaining feedback from the appraisee's colleagues and peers. It may be used as an alternative to, or in addition to, feedback received from the appraisee's supervisor. The feedback may be named or anonymous. The use of 180 degree appraisal gives a wider picture than simply relying on the individual's supervisor. It may also prevent the supervisor from providing unfair feedback on the appraisee, because they know the manager will also obtain feedback from others.

360 degree appraisal involves taking downwards, upwards and customer appraisals together – so it involves the collection of feedback on an individual's performance from a range of sources. Sources may include:

(a)   The person's immediate manager.

(b)   People who report to the appraisee, perhaps divided into groups.

(c)   Peers and co-workers. Most people interact with others within an organisation, either as members of a team or as the receivers or providers of services. They can offer useful feedback.

(d)   Customers. If salespeople know what customers thought of them, they might be able to improve their technique.

(e)   The manager personally. All forms of 360 degree appraisal require people to rate themselves. Those 'who see themselves as others see them will get fewer surprises'.

Sometimes the appraisal results in a **counselling session**, especially when the results of the appraisals are conflicting. For example, an appraisee's manager may have a quite different view of the appraisee's skills than subordinates.

3.10 The appraisal report

Most appraisal systems provide for appraisals to be **recorded**. The form of the appraisal report will vary between organisations and the role involved – report forms of various lengths and complexity may be designed. The layout of the report and factors to be included in the report should be established before the interview. The report is likely to focus on key performance issues that relate to the **job description**. The report is likely to cover key competences. A **competence** is an observable skill or ability to complete a particular task successfully. It can include the ability to transfer skills and knowledge to new situations.

3.11 Interviews and counselling

The extent to which any **discussion** or **counselling interview** is based on the written appraisal report varies in practice.

Maier (*The Appraisal Interview*) identifies **three types of approach to appraisal interviews**:

(a)   **The tell and sell method**. The manager tells the subordinate how they have been assessed, and then tries to sell (gain acceptance of) the evaluation and the improvement plan. This requires unusual human relations skills in order to convey constructive criticism in an acceptable manner, and to motivate the appraisee.

(b)   **The tell and listen method**. The manager tells the subordinate how they have been assessed, and then invites the subordinate to respond. Moreover, this method does not assume that a change in the employee will be the sole key to improvement – the manager may receive helpful feedback about how job design, methods, environment or supervision might be improved.

(c) **The problem-solving approach**. The manager abandons the role of critic altogether, and becomes a counsellor and helper. The discussion is centred not on the assessment, but on the employee's work problems. The employee is encouraged to think solutions through, and to make a commitment to personal improvement.

3.12 Follow-up

After the appraisal interview, the manager may complete the report with an **overall assessment** of potential and/or the jointly reached conclusion of the interview, and with recommendations for follow-up action.

Follow-up procedures typically include the following:

(a) **Informing the employee** of the results of the appraisal, if this has not been central to the review interview

(b) **Carrying out agreed actions** on training, promotion and so on

(c) **Monitoring the appraisee's progress** and checking that they have carried out agreed actions or improvements

(d) **Taking necessary steps** to help the appraisee to attain improvement objectives, by guidance, providing feedback, upgrading equipment, altering work methods and so on

If appraisal systems operate **successfully** as feedback control systems (in other words, if they do alter employees' performance) and identify behaviours to be encouraged, then, assuming organisational success is to some measure based on individual performance, they will influence the success of strategy.

3.13 Improving the appraisal system

In theory, such appraisal schemes may seem very fair to the individual and very worthwhile for the organisation, but **in practice the appraisal system often goes wrong**.

3.13.1 Barriers to effective appraisal

Lockett (in *Effective Performance Management*) suggests that **appraisal barriers** can be identified as follows.

Appraisal barriers	Comment
Appraisal as confrontation	Many people dread appraisals, or use them 'as a sort of showdown, a good sorting out or a clearing of the air'. • There is a lack of agreement on performance levels. • The feedback is subjective – in other words, the manager is biased, allows personality differences to get in the way of actual performance etc. • The feedback is badly delivered. • Appraisals are 'based on yesterday's performance, not on the whole year'. • There is disagreement on long-term prospects.
Appraisal as judgement	The appraisal 'is seen as a one-sided process in which the manager acts as judge, jury and counsel for the prosecution'. However, the process of performance management 'needs to be jointly operated in order to retain the commitment and develop the self-awareness of the individual'.

Appraisal barriers	Comment
Appraisal as chat	The other extreme is that the appraisal is a friendly chat 'without … purpose or outcome … Many managers, embarrassed by the need to give feedback and set stretching targets, reduce the appraisal to a few mumbled "well dones!" and leave the interview with a briefcase of unresolved issues'.
Appraisal as bureaucracy	Appraisal is a form-filling exercise, to satisfy the personnel department. Its underlying purpose, improving individual and organisational performance, is forgotten.
Appraisal as unfinished business	Appraisal should be part of a continuing process of performance management.
Appraisal as annual event	Many targets set at annual appraisal meetings become irrelevant or out of date.

A problem with many appraisal schemes in practice is that they **reinforce hierarchy**, and are perhaps unsuitable to organisations where the relationship between management and workers is **fluid** or participatory. Upward, customer and 360 degree appraisals address this, but they are not widely adopted.

Appraisal systems, because they target the individual's performance, concentrate on the **lowest level of performance feedback**. They ignore the organisational and systems context of that performance. For example, if any army is badly led, no matter how brave the troops, it will be defeated. Appraisal schemes seem to regard most **organisation problems** as a function of the **personal characteristics** of its members.

3.14 Appraisal and reward

Another issue is the extent to which the appraisal system is related to the reward system.

Many employees consider that the **appraisal system** should be **linked** with the **reward system**, on the grounds that extra effort or excellent performance should be rewarded.

Although this appears to be a fair view, there are **drawbacks** to it.

(a) **Funds available** for pay rises rarely depend on one individual's performance alone – the whole company has to do well.

(b) **Continuous improvement** is always necessary – many businesses have 'to run to stand still'. Continuous improvement should perhaps be expected of employees as part of their work, not rewarded as extra.

(c) In low-inflation environments, **cash pay rises are fairly small**.

(d) **Comparisons between individuals** are hard to make, as many smaller organisations cannot afford the rigour of a job evaluation scheme.

(e) Performance management is about a lot more than pay for **past** performance – it is often **forward looking** with regard to future performance.

3.14.1 Performance-related pay

Performance-related pay (PRP) is often introduced when other organisational or HR changes are made, such as:

- The **introduction** of an **appraisal scheme**
- The **development** of **flexible working arrangements**
- The **decentralisation** of **HR** or the **responsibility** of **pay determination**
- The **harmonisation** of **working arrangements** through the organisation

Payment systems are often **modified** as a result of the introduction of PRP.

- PRP may form the **basis** of all **general pay increases**.

- PRP may **replace pay increases for length of service** or **qualifications**.

- PRP may be used as **additional payments above the maximum** for the grade where performance is very high.

All organisations can introduce PRP but it is often best **implemented gradually**.

By **initially introducing** it to **senior management**, they will **experience it firsthand** before they apply it to their staff.

The use of PRP could be **restricted** to **specific groups** of workers to allow **adequate testing** and to **ensure sufficient safeguards are in place** before it is introduced to other workers.

3.15 Management expertise and employee empowerment

There can be **problems conducting appraisals** in organisations where **empowerment** is practised and employees are given more responsibility.

(a) Many managers **may not know enough** about the performance of individual workers to make a fair judgement.

(b) In some jobs, managers do not have the **technical expertise** to judge an employee's output.

(c) **Employees depend on other people** in the workplace/organisation to be effective – in other words, **an individual's results may not be entirely under their control**.

A person's performance is often indirectly or directly influenced by the **management style** of their line manager, who will also usually be the person conducting the appraisal.

However, given the seniority of the manager over the appraisee, the appraisee may be **reluctant** to raise issues related to their manager's management style.

Even the best objective and systematic appraisal scheme is subject to **personal** and **interpersonal problems**.

(a) Appraisal is often **defensive on the part of the appraisee**, who believes that criticism may mean a low bonus or pay rise, or a lost promotion opportunity.

(b) Appraisal is often **defensive on the part of the superior**, who cannot reconcile the role of judge and critic with the human relations aspect of interviewing and management. Managers may in any case feel uncomfortable about 'playing God' with employees' futures.

(c) The superior might show **conscious or unconscious bias** in the appraisal or may be influenced by rapport (or lack of it) with the interviewee. Systems without clearly defined standard criteria will be particularly prone to the subjectivity of the assessor's judgement.

(d) The manager and subordinate may both **be reluctant to devote time and attention to appraisal**. Their experience in the organisation may indicate that the exercise is a waste of time (especially if there is a lot of form-filling) with no relevance to the job, and no reliable follow-up action.

(e) The organisational culture may **simply not take appraisal seriously**. Interviewers are not trained or given time to prepare, appraisees are not encouraged to contribute, or the exercise is perceived as a 'nod' to human relations with no practical results.

3.16 Making improvements

The **appraisal scheme** should itself be **assessed** (and regularly reassessed) according to the following general criteria for evaluating appraisal schemes.

Criteria	Comment
Relevance	• Does the system have a useful purpose, relevant to the needs of the organisation and the individual? • Is the purpose clearly expressed and widely understood by all concerned, both appraisers and appraisees? • Are the appraisal criteria relevant to the purposes of the system?
Fairness	• Is there reasonable standardisation of criteria and objectivity throughout the organisation? • Is it reasonably objective?
Serious intent	• Are the managers committed to the system – or is it just something the personnel department thrusts upon them? • Who does the interviewing, and are they properly trained in interviewing and assessment techniques? • Is reasonable time and attention given to the interviews – or is it a question of 'getting them over with'? • Is there a genuine demonstrable link between performance and reward or opportunity for development?
Co-operation	• Is the appraisal a participative, problem-solving activity – or a tool of management control? • Is the appraisee given time and encouragement to prepare for the appraisal, so that they can make a constructive contribution? • Does a jointly agreed, concrete conclusion emerge from the process? • Are appraisals held regularly?
Efficiency	• Does the system seem overly time consuming compared to the value of its outcome? • Is it difficult and costly to administer?

Question 13.3   Performance appraisal

Learning outcome F2(vi)

Most large organisations have a performance appraisal process.

Required

Briefly describe the most common objectives of a performance appraisal system.   **(5 marks)**

Section summary

Appraisal is an important part of human resource management because it enables **employee performance** to be **measured** and **corrective action** to be taken if necessary. It also forms part of the **reward process**.

There are many **types of appraisal** including: **appraisal by a manager**, **self-appraisal**, **upward appraisal**, **customer appraisal** and **360 degree appraisal**.

Whichever type of appraisal is used it must be **carefully conducted** and **correctly followed up**.

Chapter Summary

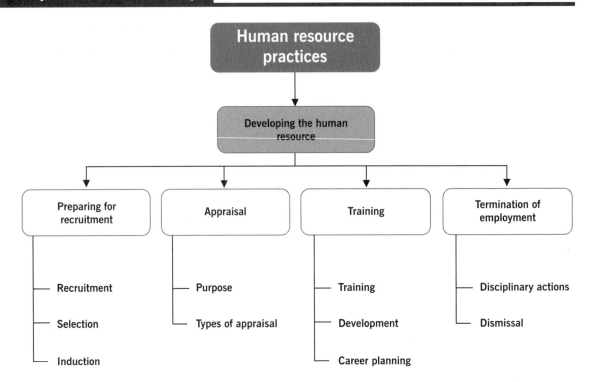

Quick Quiz

1   Why should an organisation take an interest in an individual's personal development?

2   Which of the following is the final stage of recruitment before selection commences?

    A   Producing a job description
    B   Advertising the vacancy
    C   Screening candidates' CVs and selecting some for interview
    D   Interviewing candidates

3   A typing test is an example of which type of test used in the selection process?

    A   Psychological test
    B   Aptitude test
    C   Intelligence test
    D   Personality test

4   In Kolb's learning cycle, which process occurs after reflection?

    A   Theorising
    B   Actively experimenting
    C   Concrete experience
    D   Learning

5   Which of the following appraisal techniques requires the assessor to rate the assessee's characteristics on a scale?

    A   Guided assessment
    B   Overall assessment
    C   Behavioural incident method
    D   Grading

Answers to Quick Quiz

1 Poor personal development can cause high staff turnover, absenteeism or preoccupation with financial rewards and poor performance – self-defeating for the organisation and unhealthy for the individual.

2 C Recruitment ends when a shortlist of candidates for interview has been chosen. Interviews are part of the selection process.

3 B A typing test is an example of an aptitude test as it provides information about a candidate's abilities.

4 A Theorising follows reflection in Kolb's learning cycle.

5 D Grading requires the assessor to rate the employee's characteristics on a rating scale.

Answers to Questions

13.1 Interviews

If interview techniques are taught, it might imply that success at interview will have more to do with a candidate's ability to present themselves in an interview situation rather than their ability to do the job.

On the other hand, an interview is a test of how well a person performs under pressure, in an unfamiliar environment and with strangers. The interview might therefore reflect some of the interpersonal skills required for the job.

13.2 Human resource development

D HRD covers all aspects of personal and management development, including formal training and on the job training, planning the succession into senior management positions, and career planning for individuals (particularly management recruits). Job redesign is also related to development, because the content of a job can be altered to provide better or different learning experiences.

13.3 Performance appraisal

The general purpose of an appraisal is to improve the efficiency of the organisation by ensuring individual employees are performing their role to acceptable standards and to the best of their ability. The process also considers the employees' potential to improve and to develop. Objectives of a formal performance appraisal system include the following:

- To enable a picture to be drawn up of overall staff levels and skills, strengths and weaknesses. This enables more effective HR planning.

- To monitor the undertaking's initial selection procedures against the subsequent performance of recruits.

- To establish what the individual has to do in a job in order that the objectives for the section or department are realised.

- To assess an individual's performance including strengths and any weaknesses. This helps identify training needs.

- To assess appropriate rewards (pay, bonuses etc).

- To assess potential. At the organisational level this permits career and succession planning. At the individual level it facilitates an individual development plan.

Now try these questions from the Practice Question Bank

Number

61, 62, 63, 64, 65

PRACTICE
QUESTION AND ANSWER BANK

Each of the following questions has only ONE correct answer. Each question is worth **2 marks**.

1   Which one of the following is a not-for-profit organisation?

   A   Sole traders
   B   Partnerships
   C   Mutual organisations
   D   Public limited companies

2   What is the main financial objective of public sector organisations?

   A   Profitability
   B   Efficient use of resources
   C   Avoidance of loss
   D   Maximisation of charitable donations

3   Which ONE of the following is NOT a feature normally associated with a non-governmental organisation (NGO)?

   A   Government funded
   B   Independent
   C   Non profit making
   D   Explicit social mission

4   A published statement of an entity's fundamental objectives is known as:

   A   A values statement
   B   A strategy statement
   C   A mission statement
   D   An objectives statement

5   Which form of organisational structure involves grouping together people who do similar tasks?

   A   Divisional structure
   B   Functional structure
   C   Matrix structure
   D   Geographical structure

6   According to monetarist theory, the primary effect of increasing the money supply is to:

   A   Increase prices
   B   Increase reserve requirements
   C   Increase the volume of exports
   D   Increase demand for imports

7   Which international institution was formed to help rebuild economies after the Second World War?

   A   WTO
   B   IMF
   C   G8
   D   World Bank

8   Efficient regulation of companies is said to exist if:

   A   The total benefit to the nation is greater than the total cost
   B   There is greater integration of the world's economies
   C   Greater innovation takes place by all businesses
   D   The effect on businesses is neutral

9   Which of the following would be a connected stakeholder of an organisation?

A   Customer
B   Employee
C   Local community
D   Pressure groups

10   Which of CIMA's Ethical Principles states that individuals must not be party to anything which is deceptive or misleading?

A   Objectivity
B   Professional behaviour
C   Integrity
D   Confidentiality

11   Joseph has just started his first job in an accountancy department. A qualified senior member of staff explains to him what the main aim of accounting is. Which of the following options is the correct overall aim of accounting?

A   To maintain ledger accounts for every asset and liability
B   To provide financial information to users of such information
C   To produce a trial balance
D   To record every financial transaction individually

12   In a typical finance function, preparation of budgets and budgetary control would usually be the responsibility of which of the following roles?

A   The Internal Auditor
B   The Management Accountant
C   The Treasurer
D   The Finance Director

13   Which of the following is a method that a company treasurer can use to manage foreign exchange risk?

A   Exchange agreement contract
B   Forward exchange contract
C   Foreign exchange agreement
D   Corporate money contract

14   Which of the following does company law require a statement of financial position to give?

A   A true and fair view of the profit or loss of the company for the financial year

B   An unqualified (or 'clean') report on the statement of affairs of the company as at the end of the financial year

C   A true and fair view of the assets and liabilities of the company as at the end of the financial year

D   A qualified report, setting out matters on which independent auditors disagree with management

15   To whom should the internal audit department of an organisation report?

A   The Finance Director
B   The Management Accountant
C   The audit committee of the board of directors
D   The shareholders

16   Many large organisations have established a computer intranet for the purpose of:

    A   Providing quick, effective and improved communication amongst staff using chat rooms

    B   Providing quick, effective and improved communication to staff

    C   Providing quick, effective and improved communication to customers

    D   Providing quick, effective and improved ordering procedures in real time

17   An expert system describes:

    A   A database built upon past knowledge and experience

    B   A powerful off the shelf software solution

    C   An online library of operating advice and handy hints

    D   An electronic version of working papers assembled by the Research and Development department

18   Laney suggests that 'Big Data' can be defined by considering the three Vs.

    Which of the following is NOT one of the three Vs?

    A   Volume

    B   Variety

    C   Velocity

    D   Verifiable

19   Electronic Executive Information Systems (EIS) is an example of:

    A   Customer relationship management software

    B   Database management systems

    C   Computer networking

    D   Decision based software

20   Technology which encourages user contributions and interactivity is known as:

    A   Web 2.0

    B   Business to consumer (B2C)

    C   E-commerce

    D   Teleworking

21   'Corrective' refers to a type of systems maintenance performed to:

    A   Remedy software defects

    B   Allow executive level unstructured decision making

    C   Adjust applications to user preferences

    D   Prevent future operation delays

22   Which approach to system changeover has the highest risk?

    A   Parallel

    B   Direct

    C   Pilot

    D   Phased

23   Dial-back security protects an information system by:

    A   Disabling part of the telecoms technology to prevent unauthorised intrusions

    B   Scrambling and unscrambling data transmissions

    C   Requiring users to identify themselves before a connection to the system is provided

    D   Providing the user with a private key

24 Which type of security risk involves overloading an internet site with traffic?

    A   Worms

    B   Trojan horses

    C   Denial of service attacks

    D   Hacking

25 Which type of information system outsourcing involves third parties managing and distributing services and solutions to clients over a wide area network?

    A   Multiple sourcing

    B   Incremental outsourcing

    C   Joint venture sourcing

    D   Application service provision

26 Which sourcing strategy is most likely to create a competitive advantage for the purchasing organisation?

    A   Single sourcing

    B   Multiple sourcing

    C   Delegated sourcing

    D   Parallel sourcing

27 Sustainability in operations management is primarily concerned with:

    A   Making charitable donations to environmental protection groups

    B   Sourcing raw materials from developing nations

    C   Improving the productivity of employees

    D   Efficient use of resources

28 Which of the following is the main characteristic of a demand network?

    A   Products are pushed onto the market by the manufacturer

    B   Products are developed in response to market signals

    C   Businesses in the network operate relatively independently

    D   Interdependence of channel members is reduced

29 According to Porter's value chain, the final primary activity is referred to as:

    A   Marketing and sales

    B   Outbound logistics

    C   Procurement

    D   Service

30 In purchasing, the 'Reck and Long' positioning tool is by nature:

    A   Strategic

    B   Independent

    C   Supportive

    D   Passive

31 Which one of the following is the best indicator of 'quality'?

    A   Cost

    B   Price

    C   Fitness for purpose

    D   Number of complaints

32   Which of the following measures customer, internal operations, innovation and learning, and financial aspects of quality?

A   SERVQUAL
B   Balanced scorecards
C   Value for money audits
D   Total quality management

33   Gaining International Standards (ISO) in quality is mainly dependent upon:

A   Effective processes for documentation and control
B   A shared quality philosophy
C   Commitment from middle managers
D   Benchmarking customer-related performance against competitors

34   The 5Ss are often associated with lean production. Which one of the following is not one of the 5Ss?

A   Self-discipline
B   Sanitise
C   Systemise
D   Specify

35   Kaizen is a quality improvement technique that involves:

A   Continuous improvement by small incremental steps
B   A complete revision of all organisational processes and structures
C   Immediate, often radical 'right first time' changes to practice
D   A problem-solving fishbone technique to identify cause and effect

36   Optimised production technologies (OPT) is an operations management system which aims to:

A   Improve distribution networks
B   Improve supply sourcing alternatives
C   Integrate operations and quality assurance
D   Reduce production bottlenecks

37   An ABC system refers to:

A   A Japanese-style problem-solving device that is particularly helpful in inventory management

B   An inventory management method that concentrates effort on the most important items

C   Accuracy, brevity and clarity in the quality of system reporting

D   A manual solution to managing inventory

38   An approach of producing goods or purchasing inventory only when required is known as:

A   Just-in-time
B   Ad hoc
C   Level capacity strategy
D   Plan-do-check-act (PDCA) quality

39   EOQ represents a form of:

A   Inventory system based on economic order quantities
B   European observance quality certification
C   Equal opportunity quantification index used in HRM
D   Japanese-inspired technique aimed at continuous improvement

40   In which type of layout does the product being created remain in a fixed location and people, materials and other resources travel to it?

   A   Product
   B   Cell
   C   Fixed
   D   Process

41   Which one of the following statements best represents 'a marketing orientation'?

   A   Support for the marketing department from top management
   B   A large marketing budget
   C   High-profile advertising campaigns
   D   A focus on customer needs

42   PESTEL analysis can be used to analyse an organisation's environment. What does the 'P' stand for?

   A   Political
   B   Prices
   C   People
   D   Products

43   Industria is a manufacturing company which makes three types of cleaning product.

   'Budget' uses low grade ingredients and is aimed at the cheaper end of the household market.

   'Premium' uses state of the art ingredients and is aimed at the premium end of the household market.

   'Professional' is a high-strength version which is aimed at professional cleaners.

   Which marketing strategy is Industria following?

   A   Mass marketing
   B   Differentiated marketing
   C   Undifferentiated marketing
   D   Concentrated marketing

44   Which method of market research would be most appropriate to use where the objective is to explore customers' attitudes and motives for behaviour?

   A   Focus groups
   B   Depth interviews
   C   Questionnaires
   D   Observation

45   To be of use for marketing research purposes a segmentation variable must define a market segment that has three characteristics. What are they?

   A   Measurability, stability, accessibility
   B   Stability, substantiality, measurability
   C   Substantiality, measurability, accessibility
   D   Stability, accessibility, substantiality

46   The use of 'skim pricing' as a marketing technique will result in:

   A   Non-recovery of promotional costs
   B   Enticing new customers to buy a product or service
   C   High prices, normally at an early stage of the product life cycle
   D   Low prices so denying competitors opportunities to gain market share

47   Marketing activities which occur in unexpected places and take people by surprise are known as:

    A   Direct marketing

    B   Viral marketing

    C   Guerrilla marketing

    D   Interactive marketing

48   'Market shakeout' involves the weakest producers exiting a particular market and occurs in a period between:

    A   Growth through creativity and growth through direction

    B   Introduction and market growth

    C   Market growth and market maturity

    D   Market maturity and decline

49   Why is the characteristic of a service known as 'perishability' significant in a marketing context?

    A   Because perishability makes it likely that refrigerated facilities will be required

    B   Because perishability increases ethical concerns

    C   Because perishability makes anticipating and responding to levels of demand crucial

    D   Because perishability means demand fluctuates wildly

50   Direct mailing, branding activities and public relations campaigns are all examples of:

    A   Market process

    B   Product placement

    C   Promotion

    D   Market research

51   In social marketing, goods that society discourages because of their negative social effects are known as which ONE of the following?

    A   Demerit goods

    B   Durable goods

    C   International embargoes

    D   Imports

52   According to Bruce (2005), which of the following can be considered to be customers of a charity?

    (i)   Beneficiaries

    (ii)   Trustees

    (iii)   Regulators

    (iv)   The Government

    A   (i), (ii) and (iii) only

    B   (i) and (iii) only

    C   (ii) and (iii) only

    D   All of the above

53   What is the most important difference between consumer and organisational buying behaviour?

    A   Organisational purchase decisions are rarely made by a single individual.

    B   Organisations have more money to spend.

    C   Consumers make up their minds more quickly.

    D   Organisations rely heavily upon trade exhibitions.

54 Jobber suggests splitting employees into groups for the purposes of internal marketing.

Which of the following groups consists of those who are likely to gain from the change or plan, or are already committed to it?

A Supporter
B Neutral
C Opposer
D Beneficiary

55 Kaplan's Four I's of Social Media provide advice to businesses on how to communicate with customers.

Which of the Four I's states that conversations should be used to engage the customer in the interaction?

A Individualise
B Involve
C Integrate
D Initiate

56 Which theorist pioneered the scientific management movement?

A Taylor
B Weber
C Schein
D Herzberg

57 The so-called 'psychological contract' is a notion that is based on:

A Segmenting then accessing a market
B The buyer/supplier relationship
C A distinctive style of testing used in selection procedures
D The expectations the organisation and employee have of one another

58 The main weakness of performance-related pay is:

A There is no attempt to link profits with the pay structure of individuals
B If targets are not met then employees may become demotivated
C Employees rarely work harder for additional remuneration
D It is almost impossible to set appropriate performance targets for manual workers

59 Herzberg's contribution to understanding people in the workforce included:

A Personality testing
B Explaining factors associated with job satisfaction as 'motivators'
C Problem-solving processes that encourage team spirit and co-operation
D An integrated framework involving appraisal, training and motivation

60 Employers wishing to attract and retain talented employees by bringing together pay and non-pay elements and emphasising a positive organisational culture are said to operate a:

A Benefit scoping strategy
B Total reward package
C Talent strategy package
D Consolidated remuneration package

61 Integrating new recruits into the culture, beliefs and mission of an organisation is known, according to Harrison, as:

A Recruitment
B Indoctrination
C Dialogic learning
D Training

62 Which of the following describes an assessment centre and activities that occur there?

A It is any location where job candidates are assessed using comprehensive and interrelated series of techniques.

B It is the organisation's training headquarters where job interviews take place.

C It is any location where a desk-based process of reviewing job application forms for suitability takes place.

D It is the head office of a third party where psychological testing of candidates takes place.

63 An effective appraisal system involves:

A Assessing the personality of the appraisee
B A process initiated by the manager who needs an update from the appraisee
C Advising on the faults of the appraisee
D A participative, problem-solving process between the manager and appraisee

64 Aptitude testing is most commonly used in:

A Staff appraisal processes
B Exit interviews
C Staff selection
D Market research and testing

65 Activities aimed at attracting a number of suitable candidates interested in joining an organisation are called:

A Human relationship marketing
B Recruitment
C Selection
D Human capital harvesting

1 C Mutuals are primarily in business to provide services to their customers. They are not owned by shareholders whom they have to pay a share of their profit to.

2 B Public sector organisations aim to use their resources efficiently.

3 A Non-governmental organisations are independent, non profit making organisations with social objectives.

4 C A published statement of an entity's fundamental objectives is known as a mission statement.

5 B A functional structure involves grouping together people who do similar tasks.

6 A According to monetarist theory, increasing the money supply will increase prices.

7 B The IMF was formed after the Second World War to help rebuild economies.

8 A Efficient regulation of companies exists if the total benefit (of regulation) to the nation exceeds the total cost.

9 A A customer is a connected stakeholder. An employee is an internal stakeholder. The local community and the Government are external stakeholders.

10 C The principle of integrity states that individuals must not be party to anything which is deceptive or misleading.

11 B To provide financial information to users of such information is the main or overall aim of accounting.

12 B The Management Accountant provides information for management: cost accounting, budgets and budgetary control and financial management of projects. The Financial Controller is responsible for routine accounting, accounting reports, cashiers' duties and cash control. A Treasurer would be responsible for treasury management: raising and investing funds and cash flow control. The Finance Director approves the budget.

13 B A forward exchange contract involves a company treasurer fixing the purchase or sale of foreign currency at the current rate. The other options are fictitious.

14 C Option A refers to the statement of profit or loss, not the statement of financial position. Options B and D are distractors, referring to audit reports.

15 C The audit committee of the board of directors. In order to control the risks of fraud and error, the internal audit department should be separate from the finance department.

16 B An intranet provides a storage and distribution point for information accessible to staff.

17 A An expert system could be described as a database built on knowledge and experience.

18 D The three Vs are volume, variety and velocity.

19 D Decision based software provides managers with the information and analysis tools to enable them to make decisions.

20 A Web 2.0 applications include blogs and social networking sites.

21 A Corrective maintenance is carried out to correct residual faults. Options B and C are enhancements (perfective maintenance). D takes account of anticipated changes in the processing environment (adaptive).

22 B As the direct approach involves the old system ceasing operation completely at a given time, this approach is the most risky.

23 C Dial-back security requires users to identify themselves before the system dials them back on their authorised number before allowing access.

24 C Denial of service attacks attempt to disable an internet site by overloading it with traffic.

25	D	Application Service Providers are third parties which manage and distribute services and solutions to clients over a wide area network.
26	A	Single sourcing is most likely to result in a competitive advantage because it strengthens the supplier/purchaser relationship, secures confidential information, aids quality control and creates economies of scale. Under the other methods the reverse is more likely to be true.
27	D	Sustainability in operations management is primarily concerned with efficient use of resources.
28	B	In a demand network, products are developed in response to market signals (demand).
29	D	Primary activities are those across the base of the value chain – the supporting or secondary activities being shown above these. The last primary activity is supporting products sold; that is, service, so D is correct.
30	A	Reck and Long's positioning tool is strategic (the strategic positioning tool).
31	C	Quality refers to fitness for purpose, which means how suitable a product or service is for its intended use.
32	B	The balanced scorecard approach to quality measurement focuses on customer, internal operations, innovation and learning and financial perspectives.
33	A	To gain ISO accreditation an organisation is required to submit documentation to show that its processes meet ISO requirements. The other options are not necessarily required.
34	D	Specify is not one of the 5Ss. The others are Structurise and Standardise.
35	A	Kaizen seeks to improve quality by small, incremental steps. It does not seek radical changes (options B and C) and is not a problem-solving technique (option D).
36	D	Optimised production technologies focus on the removal of production bottlenecks.
37	B	In this paper, you have studied ABC as an inventory management method that concentrates effort on the most important items. It is not the same as Activity Based Costing.
38	A	Producing or purchasing items as they are needed is referred to as just-in-time (JIT).
39	A	EOQ stands for Economic Order Quantity.
40	C	In a fixed layout the product being created remains in a fixed location and people, materials and other resources travel to it.
41	D	A marketing orientation involves structuring an organisation's activities around the needs of the customer.
42	A	In terms of a PESTEL analysis, 'P' stands for political.
43	B	Differentiated marketing involves selling different product versions, each aimed at different market segments.
44	B	The aim of depth interviews is to explore customers' unconscious attitudes and motives for behaviour.
45	C	Stability might seem like a desirable feature in its own right, but it is covered by substantiality.
46	C	Skim pricing, otherwise known as market skimming, involves setting an initially high price for a product to take advantage of buyers who are prepared to pay it.
47	C	Guerrilla marketing events occur in unexpected places and usually involve taking people by surprise.
48	C	A shakeout would occur between market growth and market maturity (shaking some of the weaker 'players' out of the market).

49	C	Perishability refers to the fact that services cannot be stored – for example an appointment at a hair salon. This makes anticipating and responding to levels of demand crucial.
50	C	Promotion includes all marketing communications which let the public know about an organisation's products and services.
51	A	Demerit goods are goods considered to be unhealthy or damaging to society.
52	A	The Government is not considered to be a customer of a charity. Beneficiaries, supporters, regulators and stakeholders (including trustees) are.
53	A	While the other answers are also valid differences, the most important difference is the number of people involved in the decision-making process.
54	A	Supporters are those who are likely to gain from the change or plan, or are already committed to it.
55	B	Involve states that engaging conversations should be used to involve the customer in the interaction.
56	A	Taylor pioneered the scientific management movement.
57	D	The so-called 'psychological contract' is a notion based on the expectations the organisation and employee have of one another.
58	B	The main risk of performance-related pay is demotivation. The other problems can either be overcome or are simply not relevant to PRP.
59	B	Herzberg developed the two-factor content theory of motivation. One factor in the theory is motivators – these produce satisfaction in an individual when present.
60	B	A total reward package brings together pay and non-pay elements and emphasises a positive organisational culture.
61	C	Harrison named the element of the induction process, where new recruits are integrated into the culture, beliefs and mission of an organisation, as dialogic learning.
62	A	Job candidates are assessed at an assessment centre.
63	D	Appraisal should be a participative, problem-solving process.
64	C	Aptitude testing is used during the selection process.
65	B	The process of attracting suitable candidates is referred to as 'recruitment'.

APPENDIX
MATHEMATICAL TABLES

PRESENT VALUE TABLE

Present value of 1.00 unit of currency, that is $(1 + r)^{-n}$ where r = interest rate; n = number of periods until payment or receipt.

Periods (n)	Interest rates (r)									
	1%	2%	3%	4%	5%	6%	7%	8%	9%	10%
1	0.990	0.980	0.971	0.962	0.952	0.943	0.935	0.926	0.917	0.909
2	0.980	0.961	0.943	0.925	0.907	0.890	0.873	0.857	0.842	0.826
3	0.971	0.942	0.915	0.889	0.864	0.840	0.816	0.794	0.772	0.751
4	0.961	0.924	0.888	0.855	0.823	0.792	0.763	0.735	0.708	0.683
5	0.951	0.906	0.863	0.822	0.784	0.747	0.713	0.681	0.650	0.621
6	0.942	0.888	0.837	0.790	0.746	0.705	0.666	0.630	0.596	0.564
7	0.933	0.871	0.813	0.760	0.711	0.665	0.623	0.583	0.547	0.513
8	0.923	0.853	0.789	0.731	0.677	0.627	0.582	0.540	0.502	0.467
9	0.914	0.837	0.766	0.703	0.645	0.592	0.544	0.500	0.460	0.424
10	0.905	0.820	0.744	0.676	0.614	0.558	0.508	0.463	0.422	0.386
11	0.896	0.804	0.733	0.650	0.585	0.527	0.475	0.429	0.388	0.350
12	0.887	0.788	0.701	0.625	0.557	0.497	0.444	0.397	0.356	0.319
13	0.879	0.773	0.681	0.601	0.530	0.469	0.415	0.368	0.326	0.290
14	0.870	0.758	0.661	0.577	0.505	0.442	0.388	0.340	0.299	0.263
15	0.861	0.743	0.642	0.555	0.481	0.417	0.362	0.315	0.275	0.239
16	0.853	0.728	0.623	0.534	0.458	0.394	0.339	0.292	0.252	0.218
17	0.844	0.714	0.605	0.513	0.436	0.371	0.317	0.270	0.231	0.198
18	0.836	0.700	0.587	0.494	0.416	0.350	0.296	0.250	0.212	0.180
19	0.828	0.686	0.570	0.475	0.396	0.331	0.277	0.232	0.194	0.164
20	0.820	0.673	0.554	0.456	0.377	0.312	0.258	0.215	0.178	0.149

Periods (n)	Interest rates (r)									
	11%	12%	13%	14%	15%	16%	17%	18%	19%	20%
1	0.901	0.893	0.885	0.877	0.870	0.862	0.855	0.847	0.840	0.833
2	0.812	0.797	0.783	0.769	0.756	0.743	0.731	0.718	0.718	0.694
3	0.731	0.712	0.693	0.675	0.658	0.641	0.624	0.609	0.609	0.579
4	0.659	0.636	0.613	0.592	0.572	0.552	0.534	0.516	0.516	0.482
5	0.593	0.567	0.543	0.519	0.497	0.476	0.456	0.437	0.437	0.402
6	0.535	0.507	0.480	0.456	0.432	0.410	0.390	0.370	0.370	0.335
7	0.482	0.452	0.425	0.400	0.376	0.354	0.333	0.314	0.314	0.279
8	0.434	0.404	0.376	0.351	0.327	0.305	0.285	0.266	0.266	0.233
9	0.391	0.361	0.333	0.308	0.284	0.263	0.243	0.225	0.225	0.194
10	0.352	0.322	0.295	0.270	0.247	0.227	0.208	0.191	0.191	0.162
11	0.317	0.287	0.261	0.237	0.215	0.195	0.178	0.162	0.162	0.135
12	0.286	0.257	0.231	0.208	0.187	0.168	0.152	0.137	0.137	0.112
13	0.258	0.229	0.204	0.182	0.163	0.145	0.130	0.116	0.116	0.093
14	0.232	0.205	0.181	0.160	0.141	0.125	0.111	0.099	0.099	0.078
15	0.209	0.183	0.160	0.140	0.123	0.108	0.095	0.084	0.084	0.065
16	0.188	0.163	0.141	0.123	0.107	0.093	0.081	0.071	0.071	0.054
17	0.170	0.146	0.125	0.108	0.093	0.080	0.069	0.060	0.060	0.045
18	0.153	0.130	0.111	0.095	0.081	0.069	0.059	0.051	0.051	0.038
19	0.138	0.116	0.098	0.083	0.070	0.060	0.051	0.043	0.043	0.031
20	0.124	0.104	0.087	0.073	0.061	0.051	0.043	0.037	0.037	0.026

Cumulative present value of 1.00 of currency per annum, Receivable or Payable at the end of each year

for n years $\dfrac{1-(1+r)^{-n}}{r}$

Periods (n)	Interest rates (r)									
	1%	2%	3%	4%	5%	6%	7%	8%	9%	10%
1	0.990	0.980	0.971	0.962	0.952	0.943	0.935	0.926	0.917	0.909
2	1.970	1.942	1.913	1.886	1.859	1.833	1.808	1.783	1.759	1.736
3	2.941	2.884	2.829	2.775	2.723	2.673	2.624	2.577	2.531	2.487
4	3.902	3.808	3.717	3.630	3.546	3.465	3.387	3.312	3.240	3.170
5	4.853	4.713	4.580	4.452	4.329	4.212	4.100	3.993	3.890	3.791
6	5.795	5.601	5.417	5.242	5.076	4.917	4.767	4.623	4.486	4.355
7	6.728	6.742	6.230	6.002	5.786	5.582	5.389	5.206	5.033	4.868
8	7.652	7.325	7.020	6.733	6.463	6.210	5.971	5.747	5.535	5.335
9	8.866	8.162	7.786	7.435	7.108	6.802	6.515	6.247	5.995	5.759
10	9.471	8.983	8.530	8.111	7.722	7.360	7.024	6.710	6.418	6.145
11	10.368	9.787	9.253	8.760	8.306	7.887	7.499	7.139	6.805	6.495
12	11.255	10.575	9.954	9.358	8.863	8.384	7.943	7.536	7.161	6.814
13	12.134	11.348	10.635	9.986	9.394	8.853	8.358	7.904	7.487	7.103
14	13.004	12.106	11.296	10.563	9.899	9.295	8.745	8.244	7.786	7.367
15	13.865	12.849	11.938	11.118	10.380	9.712	9.108	8.559	8.061	7.606
16	14.718	13.578	12.561	11.652	10.838	10.106	9.447	8.851	8.313	7.824
17	15.562	14.292	13.166	12.166	11.274	10.477	9.763	9.122	8.544	8.022
18	16.398	14.992	13.754	12.659	11.690	10.828	10.059	9.372	8.756	8.201
19	17.226	15.679	14.324	13.134	12.085	11.158	10.336	9.604	8.950	8.365
20	18.046	16.351	14.878	13.590	12.462	11.470	10.594	9.818	9.129	8.514

Periods (n)	Interest rates (r)									
	11%	12%	13%	14%	15%	16%	17%	18%	19%	20%
1	0.901	0.893	0.885	0.877	0.870	0.862	0.855	0.847	0.840	0.833
2	1.713	1.690	1.668	1.647	1.626	1.605	1.585	1.566	1.574	1.528
3	2.444	2.402	2.361	2.322	2.283	2.246	2.210	2.174	2.140	2.106
4	3.102	3.037	2.974	2.914	2.855	2.798	2.743	2.690	2.639	2.589
5	3.696	3.605	3.517	3.433	3.352	3.274	3.199	3.127	3.058	2.991
6	4.231	4.111	3.998	3.889	3.784	3.685	3.589	3.498	3.410	3.326
7	4.712	4.564	4.423	4.288	4.160	4.039	3.922	3.812	3.706	3.605
8	5.146	4.968	4.799	4.639	4.487	4.344	4.207	4.078	3.954	3.837
9	5.537	5.328	5.132	4.946	4.772	4.607	4.451	4.303	4.163	4.031
10	5.889	5.650	5.426	5.216	5.019	4.833	4.659	4.494	4.339	4.192
11	6.207	5.938	5.687	5.543	5.234	5.029	4.836	4.656	4.486	4.327
12	6.942	6.194	5.918	5.660	5.421	5.197	4.988	4.793	4.611	4.439
13	6.750	6.424	6.122	5.842	5.583	5.342	5.118	4.910	4.715	4.533
14	6.982	6.628	6.302	6.002	5.724	5.468	5.229	5.008	4.802	4.611
15	7.191	6.811	6.462	6.142	5.847	5.575	5.324	5.092	4.846	4.675
16	7.379	6.974	6.604	6.265	5.954	5.668	5.405	5.162	4.938	4.730
17	7.549	7.120	6.729	6.373	6.047	5.749	5.475	5.222	4.990	4.775
18	7.702	7.250	6.840	6.467	6.128	5.818	5.534	5.273	5.033	4.812
19	7.839	7.366	6.938	6.550	6.198	5.877	5.584	5.316	5.070	4.843
20	7.963	7.469	7.025	6.623	6.259	5.929	5.628	5.353	5.101	4.870

INDEX

Notes

Notes